THE
WORK
AND THE
GLORY
*Like a Fire
is Burning*

Building the Kirtland Temple

VOLUME 2

THE

WORK

AND THE

GLORY

Like a Fire is Burning

A HISTORICAL NOVEL

Gerald N. Lund

BOOKCRAFT
Salt Lake City, Utah

THE WORK AND THE GLORY

Volume 1: Pillar of Light
Volume 2: Like a Fire Is Burning
Volume 3: Truth Will Prevail
Volume 4: Thy Gold to Refine
Volume 5: A Season of Joy
Volume 6: Praise to the Man
Volume 7: No Unhallowed Hand
Volume 8: So Great a Cause
Volume 9: All Is Well

First printing in hardbound 1990
First printing in trade paperbound 2001
First printing in paperbound 2005

Visit us at deseretbook.com

Library of Congress Catalog Card Number: 90-83215

ISBN 0-88494-801-3 (hardbound)
ISBN 1-57345-871-6 (trade paperbound)
ISBN 1-59038-497-0 (paperbound)

Printed in the United States of America
Delta Printing Solutions, Valencia, CA

10   9   8   7   6   5   4   3   2   1

Preface

The Bible records that on more than one occasion holy prophets were privileged to see God in heavenly vision. Jacob, Moses, Isaiah, Stephen, John—they and others testified they had seen the Lord. *What if God were to appear to men in this day and age? How would they respond? What would they say? What would they do?*

There are numerous accounts of angels appearing to men and women in New Testament times. Gabriel came to Zacharias in the temple and to Mary in Nazareth. Heavenly messengers appeared at the empty tomb after the Savior's resurrection. There are at least six different appearances of angels recorded in the book of Acts alone, including the account of an angel freeing Simon Peter from prison. And in the book of Revelation we read that an angel appeared to John while he was held prisoner on the island of Patmos. *What if a modern man claimed angels had come in our day? Would we believe or would we scoff?*

The prophet Amos said, "Surely the Lord God will do nothing, but he revealeth his secret unto his servants the prophets" (Amos 3:7). We still honor men such as Abraham, Moses, Daniel, Jeremiah, and call them prophets of the living God. *Should one come today claiming to be a true prophet, a spokesman for the Lord, would we accept him? Would we honor him and seek his counsel?*

Twenty years into the nineteenth century a fourteen-year-old boy named Joseph Smith, living on the frontier of America, said he had seen a vision of God the Father and his Son, Jesus Christ. Later he said he had been visited by angels from the presence of God. He said he was called to be God's prophet.

Not surprisingly, these claims lit a fire storm of controversy. There were those who said Joseph was mad; others credited the devil for what had happened to him. He was mocked, insulted, vilified, threatened. But some listened and believed. When the Book of Mormon was published they eagerly read it. When, under divine direction, Joseph organized the Church of Jesus Christ on the earth again they immediately joined it. When the Prophet called for missionaries to spread the gospel to all who would listen, many responded and fanned out across the face of the land, bringing thousands into the kingdom.

What made the difference? Why did some become so infuriated that they were willing to murder? Why were others so deeply converted that they were willing to die for their faith? What was it about Joseph Smith and the Restoration that generated such passionate and diverse emotions?

The Work and the Glory seeks to answer some of these fundamental questions. It is a multivolume, multigenerational saga which tells the story of The Church of Jesus Christ of Latter-day Saints (commonly called the Mormon church) from its earliest beginnings. But the purpose of the series goes beyond simply retelling Church history. These books explore the reactions generated by a man who claimed divine revelation. They examine the feelings that were triggered by the claims of prophetic office. They probe the motivations of those who believed Joseph, and of those who formed one violent confederation after another to try and eliminate him.

This is all done through the eyes of the Benjamin Steed family, a fictional but typical frontier family in early nineteenth-century America. In *Pillar of Light*, the first volume in the series, we are introduced to the Steed family at the time they arrive in the Palmyra area of upstate New York and meet Joseph Smith. The association proves to be divisive for the entire Steed family. The spiritual outlooks of Benjamin Steed and his wife, Mary Ann, are significantly dissimilar. Joshua, the eldest son, and his brother Nathan also react in dramatically different ways to Joseph's claims. That and the two brothers' competition for the beautiful Lydia McBride eventually fracture the family in profound ways. *Pillar of Light* follows the Steeds through the events surrounding the coming forth of the Book of Mormon, the restoration of the priesthood, and the organization of the Church of Jesus Christ (covering the years 1827 to 1830).

In *Like a Fire Is Burning*, the second volume in the series, the story of the Steed family continues (covering the years 1830 to 1836). As the infant Church expands and spreads westward into Ohio and Missouri, new revelations are given, Church organization expands, the location of Zion is designated, the construction of a temple is begun. Once again the Steeds are swept up in the unfolding drama, and their lives are molded and shaped by the events in which they find themselves involved. There is joy and there is tragedy. There is failure and there is triumph.

To weave a fictional family into real history and have them associate with real historical people obviously requires some literary license. But each of the novels in the series reflects, as much as possible, an accurate portrayal of the historical events associated with the coming forth of The Church of Jesus Christ of Latter-day Saints.

In the first volume no attempt was made to provide notes that would help the reader distinguish between historical and fictional events. A novel is not a history text. Footnotes or endnotes, however unobtrusive, can still break the flow of the narrative and thus may interfere with the purposes of a novel. However, many readers have inquired about the historicity of specific events that were included in volume 1. "Was this event or that event in the novel 'really true'?" they ask.

It became obvious to me that these questions are both sincere and legitimate. Readers want to know which events are truly historical and not the figment of the writer's imagination. Volume 2, therefore, incorporates a feature not found in the first volume. Though there are no notes embedded in the text, I have placed brief chapter notes at the end of the novel that indicate historical events and my handling of them. For those who wish to read more about a specific event, a few primary source citations are also included in these notes.

One other item of explanation may be helpful to the non-Latter-day-Saint reader. Throughout the novel, characters who are members of the Church refer to themselves and other members as "Saints." This may seem a little presumptuous to one used to the more limited use of the term, such as that in the tradition of the Roman Catholic church. In New Testament times the followers of Christ commonly referred to all believers as Saints (see, for example, Acts 9:32; Romans 1:7; Ephesians 1:1; 2:19). The word *saint* comes from the Latin root *sacer*, which means "holy." Since the early disciples consecrated themselves to be holy, it seemed only natural to call themselves Saints. From the very beginning of their history, and for the same reasons, the Mormons followed the practice of the New Testament Church and referred to all members as Saints. Indeed, it is found in the very title of the Church— The Church of Jesus Christ of Latter-day Saints.

Extensive thanks for those who have made this project possible were given in the preface to volume 1. Without repeating all that was said there, I extend my gratitude to those who have contributed so much to this volume. First, to my wife, Lynn—as always she is my first reader and most-valued reviewer. She is my "help meet" in the fullest sense of the word, and because of her I better understand why the Lord said, "It is not good that the man should be alone."

Next, thanks to all the staff at Bookcraft, who have become not only my publishers but my good friends as well; editing, design, marketing, printing, shipping—all become part of what makes a finished book possible. Thanks to Deena Nay for hours of inputting and indexing and cross-referencing and copying. Rick Huchel, as before, provided impeccable research at a moment's notice and thus made available numerous historical details. Cal Stephens read the final draft and made numerous suggestions that improved the accuracy and the readability of the book. A special thanks and an apology to Robert Barrett and Lester Lee. These two fine artists prepared the artwork that has been part of both this volume and the previous one. In volume 1, I neglected to acknowledge their significant contributions. Robert Barrett drew all the internal illustrations, and Lester Lee did the jacket illustrations and the map end sheets.

And, of course, there is Kenneth Ingalls Moe ("Kim") and his wife, Jane. As I said before—and it is only the more true with volume 2—if it weren't for Kim and Jane there would be no series called *The Work and the Glory*. The only way I have of repaying such a debt is to try to write a story that in some small way fulfills Kim's vision of the project.

If the reader becomes swept up in the grandeur of the work of the Restoration, let it be remembered that it is God's work and his glory that is described in this story. If there be any praise or thanks to be given, let it be given to the Father and the Son. It was they who sent forth the Spirit that burned like a fire in the hearts of the men and women who heard and believed and lived in such a way as to generate the fruitful milieu for this novel.

GERALD N. LUND

Bountiful, Utah
August 1991

Characters of Note in This Book

The Steed Family

Benjamin, the father.
Mary Ann Morgan, the mother.
Joshua, the oldest son; twenty-three as this book begins.
Jessica Roundy, Joshua's wife.
Nathan, the second son; two years younger than Joshua.
Lydia McBride, Nathan's wife.
Melissa, the oldest daughter; nineteen.
Rebecca ("Becca"), age twelve.
Matthew, youngest son; nine as the story begins.

The Smiths

*Joseph, Sr., the father.
*Lucy Mack, the mother.
*Hyrum, Joseph's elder brother; age thirty as the book begins.
*Joseph, Jr., twenty-four.
*Emma Hale, Joseph's wife; a year and a half older than
    Joseph.
*Other Smith children are mentioned but play no major role
    in this book.

Others

*Oliver Cowdery, an associate of Joseph Smith's.
*Martin Harris, gentleman farmer from Palmyra.
*Heber C. Kimball, an early convert from Mendon, New
    York, area.

*Designates actual people from Church history.

*Joseph Knight, Sr., and family, a prosperous family from Colesville, New York, area.
*Newel Knight, son of Joseph Knight, Sr.
Josiah McBride, Lydia's father.
Hannah Lovina Hurlburt McBride, Lydia's mother.
*Parley P. Pratt, a farmer from Ohio.
*Sidney Rigdon, a preacher from Mentor, Ohio, area.
Carlton Rogers, a livery stable operator in Kirtland.
Clinton Roundy, Jessica's father; a saloon owner in Independence, Missouri.
*Peter Whitmer, Sr., and family, a family from Fayette, New York.
*Newel K. Whitney, store owner in Kirtland, Ohio.
*Brigham Young, an early convert from Mendon, New York, area.

Though too numerous to list, there are many other characters drawn from the pages of history who are mentioned by name in this book. Thus, actual names used by Joseph Smith or other contemporary sources in their historical accounts will be found here. For example, the Joshua Lewis family in Kaw Township, Edward Partridge, Sidney Gilbert, Sylvester Smith, W. W. Phelps, and dozens of others mentioned in the book, including many of the Missourians, were actual people who lived and participated in the events depicted in this work.

*Designates actual people from Church history.

The Benjamin Steed Family

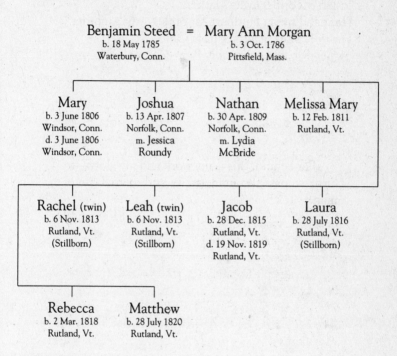

Benjamin Steed = Mary Ann Morgan
b. 18 May 1785
Waterbury, Conn.
b. 3 Oct. 1786
Pittsfield, Mass.

Mary
b. 3 June 1806
Windsor, Conn.
d. 3 June 1806
Windsor, Conn.

Joshua
b. 13 Apr. 1807
Norfolk, Conn.
m. Jessica
Roundy

Nathan
b. 30 Apr. 1809
Norfolk, Conn.
m. Lydia
McBride

Melissa Mary
b. 12 Feb. 1811
Rutland, Vt.

Rachel (twin)
b. 6 Nov. 1813
Rutland, Vt.
(Stillborn)

Leah (twin)
b. 6 Nov. 1813
Rutland, Vt.
(Stillborn)

Jacob
b. 28 Dec. 1815
Rutland, Vt.
d. 19 Nov. 1819
Rutland, Vt.

Laura
b. 28 July 1816
Rutland, Vt.
(Stillborn)

Rebecca
b. 2 Mar. 1818
Rutland, Vt.

Matthew
b. 28 July 1820
Rutland, Vt.

For behold, this is my work and my glory—to bring to pass the immortality and eternal life of man.

—Moses 1:39

Like a Fire
is Burning

The Spirit of God like a fire is burning!
The latter-day glory begins to come forth;
The visions and blessings of old are returning,
The angels are coming to visit the earth.

We'll sing and we'll shout with the armies of heaven—
Hosanna, hosanna to God and the Lamb!
Let glory to them in the highest be given,
Henceforth and forever: amen and amen!

—William W. Phelps

Oh, Lydia, you look so beautiful!"

"Do you really think so?" Lydia McBride turned slowly in front of the long mirror, examining herself with a critical eye.

Melissa Steed didn't hesitate a moment. "Nathan is going to be thunderstruck." She laughed merrily. "I bet he'll just stand there and stare and stare."

Lydia smiled. "I would like that."

She wore the carriage dress her mother had bought special for her when her parents had gone to New York City earlier in the spring. It was the latest design, and more important, this was the first time she had worn it. It had a high collar fastened at the throat with a bow. The bodice was tightly fitted and slightly lengthened, which emphasized even more the slimness of her waist. The sleeves were leg-o'-mutton sleeves, full to the elbow, then fitted to the wrist. The skirt was full but without the elaborate decorations that had been popular a few years earlier. Two large bows matching the smaller one at the neck were attached about mid-thigh and were the only embellishment. The dress was a light powder blue, the belt and the bows a light pink. The effect was simple but elegant, and it complemented Lydia's fair skin and long black hair to perfection.

Finally satisfied, Lydia turned, and threw her arms around the girl who, before the afternoon was out, would be her sister-in-law. "Thank you, Melissa."

Mary Ann Steed, Melissa's mother, came hurrying back into the room, twelve-year-old Rebecca right behind her. Mary Ann carried a needle and thread, Becca an armful of tulips, daffodils, and hyacinth from her mother's garden. A wet cloth had been carefully wrapped around the stems to keep the flowers fresh until the wedding.

"Oh, Becca, those are lovely!"

Becca blushed with pleasure, the dimples in her cheeks deepening instantly as she smiled.

"Those are perfect," Melissa agreed.

Becca looked up, the blue eyes dancing with excitement. "So where do I stand, Mama?"

Mary Ann moved around behind Lydia, found the spot where a small part of the hem of the skirt had pulled out, then began to stitch it back up. "You'll follow right behind Lydia. When Joseph is ready to start the actual marriage ceremony, you step forward and take the flowers from Lydia's arms."

There was a soft knock at the door. "Lydia?" It was Nathan's voice.

"Just a minute," Mary Ann whispered. "I'm almost done."

Melissa grabbed the hairbrush from the chest of drawers and handed it to Lydia.

"Don't come in. Just a minute." Lydia felt a little nervous flutter in her stomach as she began to brush her hair in long strokes. Today was her wedding day, and this was the man she loved more fiercely than she ever dreamed possible.

Mary Ann finished and stood up. She fussed at the back of the skirt for a moment, then stepped back. "All right."

Lydia handed her the brush as Melissa moved to the door and with a flourish opened it wide.

"Lydia, your—" He stopped, his mouth dropping open.

Melissa clapped her hands in delight. "I told you, Lydia," she cried. "I told you."

Nathan moved forward slowly, his eyes wide and filled with wonder. He took her hands. "You're beautiful, Lydia."

She did a little curtsy. "Why, thank you, Mr. Steed." She leaned forward and kissed him on the cheek. "I'm so happy, Nathan," she whispered.

With that, his face fell.

"What? What's the matter?"

"Your father is here."

Lydia nodded, then stopped. "Not Mama?"

Nathan shook his head. "No, just your father." He took a quick breath, holding her hands more firmly. His mouth was tight, his eyes grim. "He's got a magistrate with him. He says he's going to stop the wedding."

One hand jerked free and flew to her mouth. "*What?*"

"You'd better come downstairs."

◆

Josiah McBride was a short man, no more than about five foot seven or eight, and he was slight of build. Now, as he stood face-to-face with Joseph Smith, who was over six feet tall, he looked like a bantam rooster sidling up to confront an opponent twice his size.

The room was nearly filled with people. Joseph's wife, Emma, stood with Martin Harris and Hyrum Smith and his wife, Jerusha. Several of Lydia's friends from town were sitting around the table. Lydia's aunt and uncle, who lived a mile or so south of Palmyra Village, were also there. Benjamin Steed, Nathan's father, stood behind Joseph and McBride, his nine-year-old son, Matthew, at his side. A tall man, obviously the magistrate, stood just behind McBride, looking awkward and very uncomfortable.

As Lydia and Nathan came down the stairs—Melissa, Mary Ann, and Rebecca right behind them—Lydia's father whirled around. "There you are. I was beginning to think these people were hiding you."

"Papa!" Lydia came across quickly to him, but he stepped back, as though she were unclean. She stopped. "Where's Mama? Mama said she was coming."

"Your mother stayed home. There's not going to be any wedding today."

"Mr. McBride—," the officer began, but Lydia's Aunt Bea cut him off.

"Josiah McBride," she said, her eyes spitting fire, "you ought to be ashamed of yourself, ruining this girl's wedding day like this."

He swung around, his face livid. "Bea, you keep out of this. This is none of your affair."

Lydia's Aunt Bea was an older sister to Lydia's mother, and was Lydia's favorite aunt. Unlike Hannah McBride she was gentle in nature, down to earth, caring little for the fancier things that the McBrides were amassing. She and her husband had only boys, and she and Lydia had developed a strong bond from the time Lydia was a tiny girl. She raised up now to her full height, which was still considerably shorter than her brother-in-law's, and looked him in the eyes, lower jaw jutted out. "This *is* my affair. I seem to be the only family Lydia has at the moment, and I'll not have you—"

"Please!" the magistrate bellowed. It shocked both Aunt Bea and Lydia's father into silence. "All right," he went on in a more subdued tone. "Mr. McBride, if you'll let me handle things, I'll see if we can get to the bottom of this."

He turned to Joseph, who stood quietly, his face composed, his demeanor mild and affable. "Are you Mr. Joseph Smith?"

"I am, sir."

"And is it you who plans to perform this marriage today?"

"It is, sir."

He turned his head slightly. "Mr. McBride here says you have no legal standing as a minister and therefore are in violation of the law if you try to unite this couple."

"That's right," McBride started, "this man is a fraud and a—"

The constable gave him such a look that he instantly stopped. Turning back to Joseph, the officer asked, "Mr. Smith, how do you answer these charges?"

"I deny them," Joseph said affably. "Our church was organized a week ago, on the sixth of this month. We met all the legal requirements for the state of New York. We have filed the papers in Fayette, Seneca County."

"That's a lie!"

The magistrate swung around, really angry now. "Mr. McBride, if you say another word I shall eject you from this room until I have completed my investigation."

Lydia's father's eyes bulged in surprise. He opened his mouth; then, spluttering, turned and stomped across the room.

Joseph managed to restrain a smile. "Our church is a legal entity now, officer, and I am an ordained minister in that church. Does that not give me legal right to perform a marriage?"

"Yes, if what you say is true. Do you have any evidence to support your claims?"

Mary Ann stepped forward. "I was present in Fayette on the day the Church was organized. I can attest to you that all was done in order as Mr. Smith has said."

Nathan moved forward to stand by Lydia. "I too was there. What my mother says is true. And Mr. Smith is the leader of that church, which makes him a legal minister."

The officer considered that for a moment, then nodded. He turned toward Lydia's father, who was fuming silently near the window. "Mr. McBride, I am afraid you have brought me out here on false pretenses."

"This is all poppycock. This man is a charlatan. His so-called church is a fraud of the greatest magnitude."

"The truthfulness of one religion versus another does not come under my jurisdiction," the magistrate said dryly. "That is a matter for another court."

"She's my daughter!" McBride screamed, leaping forward to jab a finger in Nathan's direction. "I forbid her marriage to this . . . this . . ." No word in his vocabulary seemed adequate.

Lydia was staring at the floor, her fists clenched, her lower lip trembling. Aunt Bea stepped forward and took her hand. "This girl is of age, officer. I'm her aunt. I can testify to that."

The magistrate looked at Lydia, his eyes kind. "How old are you, child?"

8

"Twenty."

He turned to McBride, his voice suddenly cold. "I don't appreciate the way you have misled me, Mr. McBride." He turned to Joseph Smith. "My apologies, sir. You may proceed."

To Nathan's surprise, his father moved from his place to face the officer. Benjamin Steed didn't like the idea of Nathan marrying Lydia McBride either. He had made his feelings clear on more than one occasion in the last few days since Lydia had shown up on Nathan's doorstep, thrust out by her father for believing in the Book of Mormon and deciding to become a follower of Joseph Smith. Lydia was the pampered, only daughter of one of Palmyra's leading citizens; Nathan, the son of a rough-cut frontier family. "It ain't smart," he had grumbled, "to put a thoroughbred and a mule in the same harness." So what he said next came as a great shock to his whole family.

"Sir," he said to the officer.

"Yes?"

"Is trespassing a punishable offense?"

"Of course."

"Well, I am the owner of this house and the land on which it sits. I consider Mr. McBride to be trespassing on my property. If he does not leave immediately I would like to press charges against him."

The officer was startled for a moment, then smiled. "I think that is a reasonable request, Mr. Steed."

"What?" spluttered McBride. "How dare you!"

Taking a step toward him, the magistrate lowered his voice and spoke determinedly. "I have a fair and reasonable request from this gentleman, Mr. McBride. Are you going to comply, or must I remove you by force?"

McBride stood there for another moment, jaw working, his face mottled with rage. Then he spun on his heel and went out, slamming the door hard enough to make the windows rattle. The constable tipped his hat, and followed after him.

For a moment the room was silent; then softly, Lydia began to sob. Nathan stood there for a moment, awkwardly, not sure what to do, but Lydia's Aunt Bea just gathered her up in her arms. "There, now," she soothed, "don't let him be spoilin' the finest day of your life, Lydia. Don't give him the satisfaction."

———•———

Joseph stood with his back to the big stone fireplace, Nathan and Lydia facing him. Melissa, as maid of honor, stood next to Lydia, whose arms were filled with flowers from Mary Ann's garden. Nathan had his father standing next to him. Becca stood just behind Melissa and Lydia, watching Joseph carefully. She was appointed as flower girl and would take the flowers from Lydia when the signal was given.

Joseph cleared his throat. "There is ample evidence in the Bible that marriage is ordained of God," he began. "After Adam was created, God said that it was not good for man to be alone. He created Eve as an help meet for Adam. Hence the scriptures declare that for this cause should a man—" He stopped for a moment, realizing that what he was about to say applied to Lydia in a special manner. His eyes softened as he looked at her. "For this cause should a man and a woman leave their fathers and their mothers and cleave unto each other."

Lydia's eyes were shining, but she turned to Nathan and gave him a radiant smile.

"Elsewhere in scripture the Lord has also said that marriage is pleasing to him. The Savior taught that what God has put together, let not man put asunder. And in Paul's Epistle to the Hebrews he said that marriage is honorable in all. From this, and from the whisperings of the Spirit, we can know with a surety that what you two are about to do this day is pleasing in the sight of God."

Mary Ann dabbed at the corner of her eyes with a handkerchief, and that was enough to set Melissa off as well. Smiling through the tears, Melissa shifted her weight just enough that her arm touched Lydia's.

"As you stand here together, Nathan and Lydia, you stand united in your love for each other, and also in your faith in God. Therefore, as a minister of Christ's gospel I now act in my office to unite your lives in the bonds of holy marriage."

He turned his head and smiled briefly at the upturned faces

that watched him. "This is a new experience for me, so I may not do this in the traditional fashion."

"Nothing you do is traditional," Emma said. There were some chuckles from those gathered, but she had not meant it facetiously. It was said with love and tenderness and admiration, and it pleased Joseph.

He turned back to Nathan and Lydia. "Nathan, please take Lydia's hand."

Mary Ann nodded at Becca. Smiling demurely, Becca stepped around and took the flowers from Lydia's arms. The room hushed.

"Do you, Nathan Steed, take this woman, Lydia McBride, to be your wife; to love her and cherish her as though she were your own flesh; to care for her in whatever circumstances you may find yourselves; to stand by her in health and sickness, youth and old age, times of prosperity or times of poverty?"

Nathan took a breath, turning to look into her eyes. "Yes."

"And do you, Lydia McBride, give yourself to this man and take him to be your husband; to love and cherish him above all others; to stand by him in whatever circumstances life chooses to place you in, whether those circumstances be good or bad, pleasant or ill?"

All thoughts of her father were now gone. She had eyes for only Nathan as she looked up into his face. "Yes," she answered softly.

"Then I pronounce you, Nathan, and you, Lydia, married, husband and wife, for the rest of your natural lives. Remember that the covenant you make with each other this day is done in the sight of God. As long as you both honor that covenant, he shall smile down upon you."

He took a breath, as though relieved that he had completed the ceremony without major mishap. Then, blue eyes twinkling, he looked at the both of them. "You may now kiss each other as husband and wife."

———•———

For the next six weeks Lydia McBride Steed set about to win the heart of Benjamin Steed, her hardheaded, New-England-born and New-England-stubborn father-in-law.

From the rest of the Steed family there was immediate and total acceptance. Melissa became like a twin sister, the best friend she could imagine. Often Melissa would come over to their little cabin and they would laugh and giggle like two schoolgirls playing house. Becca and Matthew simply adored her, and Lydia adored them back. They became the younger siblings she had never had. Mary Ann—dear, sweet, warm, totally genuine Mary Ann—had become like the mother Lydia lost. And in fact Lydia felt some shame when she realized that, as much as she had loved her mother, in some ways she had stronger feelings for Nathan's mother than she had ever had for her own. Each night Mary Ann had scripture reading and prayer with her family, and often Lydia and Nathan would slip across the fields in the evening to join them. It was amazing how such a simple act had bound the family together, Lydia included.

But Benjamin? Now, he was something else. Though nothing was said openly, she knew of his opposition to her marriage to Nathan and of his fear that Nathan had been saddled with a coddled, spoiled female who could, or would, never adjust to frontier farm life. It had deeply touched her that he had stepped forward to support her, in his own unique way, at that horrible moment on their marriage day when her father tried to destroy everything she wanted. From that day, she determined she would win not only his love but, more important, his respect.

At first she detected in him some small measure of grudging admiration for her courage in taking a stand against her parents for her beliefs, even if Benjamin did not agree with her beliefs. But she wanted more than that. She knew that feminine wiles were not the way, and so while she treated him with respect and cordiality, she never pushed herself on him.

Gradually she began to charm him with her quiet determination to make the transition from only-child comfort to the harsh realities of frontier life. The one-room cabin Nathan had built—not much bigger than her bedroom had been previously—quickly sprouted curtains at the windows and flowers around the front door. She took to cooking, tutored by Mary Ann, with childish enthusiasm. She worked the fields alongside

Nathan, carried water from the creek, pounded out the wash in an iron tub, and even learned how to lead the mule as Nathan fought to keep the plow in soil that had never before felt the thrust of the blade. It thrilled her to catch Benjamin watching her from time to time, approval written in his eyes. She knew that eventually she would win, and it surprised her how much it had come to mean to her that she did win. Benjamin Steed was quiet, taciturn, often blunt to the point of harshness, but she was coming to understand why Mary Ann loved him so, and was starting to have some of the same feelings herself.

But on this morning in late May of 1830, Lydia Steed was not thinking about how to impress her father-in-law. The only thing on Lydia's mind was the struggle to fight the churning in her stomach that was threatening to erupt at any moment. Nathan had warned her that it might be rough and had offered to call for his father to help instead. He had even blushed a little, hinting around that if she was with child the smells might be more than she could take. She had assured him she wasn't and had stubbornly refused to back away. So killing a pig was unpleasant—she was learning how to cope with unpleasant things. Now she wished she had not been quite so adamant.

"Can you hold it steady, Lydia?"

The first shock had come when Nathan killed the pig. He gave the animal some corn; then while its head was down he hit it a massive blow between the eyes with a sledgehammer. It dropped as if it had been shot, kicking violently in its death struggle. Then they had strung it up by its hind legs with a block and tackle, and Nathan had cut its throat. Lydia, simultaneously fascinated and horrified, leaned too close, and the spray of blood had caught the bottom of her dress before she could leap back. Now Nathan had a long-bladed knife, honed on the grinding wheel until it was as sharp as a straight razor, and was scraping the steel-like hair from the coarse hide. The smell of the animal's warm body, not yet dead ten minutes, made her sick to her stomach, but she was holding the carcass steady for Nathan and could not do anything but avert her face.

He peeked around the body and looked at her. "Honey, I'm sorry, but you've got to really brace it now. I'm going to open it up and clean it out. If you don't want to touch where I've skinned it, just hang on to its ears."

She moved around opposite of Nathan, trying not to look into the massive ears as she grasped them tightly. The tiny pig-eyes were now closed, and the ugly snout was still soiled with the slop from the animal's last breakfast. She knelt down, then closed her eyes, wanting it to be over.

"Hang on, here goes." She saw Nathan's arm flash, the blade of the knife glinting red.

Suddenly there was a deep plopping sound, a whoosh of air; then in a rush the hogs entrails came spilling out at Nathan's feet, steaming in the cool morning air. The breeze was blowing from behind Nathan directly into her face. She gagged, not wanting to look, fighting the acrid taste that leaped instantly into her throat. There was a soft sucking noise as the last of what had kept the pig alive pulled free of the stomach cavity.

Lydia doubled over, hand over her mouth. Her stomach heaved, then heaved again. She flung herself away, teeth clamped together, hugging her stomach in a desperate attempt to stop the inevitable. She didn't even make it to the corner of the barn before the retching began. Again and again and again it came.

When she finally straightened and turned back around, weak and pale, Nathan was beside her. He had come behind her without her even being aware of it. He gathered her into his arms, keeping his hands, which were bloody and soiled, away from her. "I'm sorry, Lydia," he said. "I shouldn't have made you be here for this."

She shook her head, trying to swallow down the awful taste in her mouth. She felt as though she had just had a baby.

He dabbed at her forehead with his sleeve, pushing back a wisp of hair. "Why don't you go in the house and wash up. I can finish here."

"No!" It came out fiercely, surprising both him and her.

"Honey, I can—"

"No, Nathan," she said, this time more quietly but with no less determination. "I will see this through."

He started to protest; then, seeing the look in her eyes, finally shrugged. As they turned, Lydia stopped short. Standing near the rail fence that led from the barn down the lane to the Palmyra road was Benjamin Steed. He had a grub hoe in his hand, and Lydia remembered that he had borrowed it from Nathan a day or two earlier. His eyes were grave as he watched the two of them, and Lydia realized with a sudden lurch of disappointment that he had just witnessed the whole thing.

He leaned down, crawled between the rails, and then came over to join them.

"Hello, Pa."

"Nathan." He looked at Lydia, his eyes still inscrutable. "Mornin', Lydia."

"Good morning, Father Steed." She fought the temptation to wipe at the corner of her mouth with the back of her hand.

"How's it coming?" he said, turning to look at the pig.

Nathan glanced quickly at Lydia, then away. "Good. I'm just about to tie it down so I can finish cleaning it out."

Lydia shook her head and walked back to the hog. She embraced it with both arms, averting her eyes from the steaming mass on the ground, holding her mouth open so she wouldn't have to breathe through her nose.

"Lydia—," Nathan started, but she shook her head fiercely, cutting him off. He looked at his father, then with a sigh came back and picked up the knife.

Benjamin set down the grub hoe and came over to Lydia. Gently he took her by both shoulders and pulled her away from the hog. "No, Father Steed, I—"

He put a finger to her lips, cutting her off. Then he looked deep into her eyes. His were filled with respect and affection. "You know those little cinnamon cakes you make that I like so much?"

"Yes." It came out almost as a whisper.

"You go make me a batch of those, and I'll help Nathan finish up here."

She started to shake her head, but he swung around quickly so that he stood by her side. Wordlessly, he put his arm around her, and walked her toward the porch of the cabin. She tried for a moment to resist, but his grip was firm and his pace steady. He shook his head at her, pulling her tight against his shoulder for a moment. When they reached the porch, he set her free, gave her a gentle shove toward the cabin door, and turned and walked back to Nathan without a word.

It was the first day of June when Joseph Knight, Sr., walked up the narrow lane that led to the Nathan Steed cabin. He had come directly from the Benjamin Steed farm, where he had gotten directions to Nathan's house.

When Nathan opened the door and saw who it was standing there, his mouth dropped open. "Mr. Knight?"

"Hello, Nathan."

"But . . . I can't believe my eyes. What are you doing in Palmyra?"

"You remember Josiah Stowell?"

"Of course."

"Josiah come up this way to buy some grain. I decided I'd come with him."

Joseph Knight and Josiah Stowell lived down in the Colesville-South Bainbridge area of the state, just a few miles north of the Pennsylvania state line. It was while working for Josiah Stowell that Joseph Smith had met and courted Emma Hale from Harmony, Pennsylvania. Joseph had eventually told both Knight and Stowell of his experience with the angel Moroni and the gold plates. They had believed him. In September of 1827 they had come to Palmyra to be there when Joseph finally received the plates. That was the night when Nathan had first met the two men. Later Nathan went to Colesville to work for Joseph Knight in order to earn money to pay off the mortgage on the small farm he had bought. He had grown very close to

Joseph Knight and his family, but it had been several weeks since he had last seen them.

He pulled out of his thoughts, realizing that the older man was looking at him with a bit of a strange look. "What?" Nathan said.

"I also came because I'm looking for a dependable, hard-working young man who might be interested in earning some more good cash wages."

Later, long after Joseph Knight had gone back to the village, Nathan held Lydia close and felt her tears against his cheek. "Lydia, I won't go. I need to stay and take care of our farm. Pa can't handle his and mine both."

She sniffed, shaking her head. "He said he could. And I'll be here to care for the animals."

"I know, but—"

Reaching up, she laid a hand on his cheek. "No, Nathan, what Mr. Knight is offering is too generous. We can pay off the rest of our mortgage on the land by the end of the summer."

"I know, but—"

She came up on one elbow and kissed him. "No more buts," she said, smiling at him in the darkness. "You know and I know that this is too good an opportunity to let go. Now, just be quiet and let me have a good cry."

He laughed softly and pulled her close. She couldn't help it. The thought of three months without him was like a piercing pain in her chest. The tears started again as she buried her head against his shoulder.

For a long time Nathan didn't speak, just held her close and stroked her hair over and over. He only let her go finally when she dropped off into a troubled sleep. Then he lay back and stared at the ceiling until after midnight.

In western Missouri the sky was overcast and gray, and there was a stiff southerly breeze blowing. To the west it was much blacker, and there would be rain—if not hail—by afternoon. This was not untypical weather for Jackson County in mid-June, but Jessica Roundy Steed did not mind it at all. After several days of heat and humidity the cool felt good, and she had always enjoyed having the wind blow in her face and tousle her hair.

She looked up. Two young children were approaching on the boardwalk. They smiled at her. "Good mornin', Mrs. Steed."

Jessica nodded and smiled. "Good mornin', Miss Lou. Mornin', Walter." The girl was about sixteen, her brother three or four years younger. They were the children of the new Baptist preacher and his wife, come to Independence just a few months before. The girl curtsied slightly as she spoke.

"Right blustery, ain't it?" Walter said.

Jessie glanced upward. "More rain comin' for sure."

The two nodded solemnly, then moved on.

Jessie watched them for a moment, marveling. How swiftly things changed! Just a year ago when she walked down the street, respectable folk—of which there weren't a lot in Independence—either passed her by without a flicker of recognition or, worse, averted their eyes. Jessica was the daughter of Clinton Roundy, who owned two of western Missouri's more raucous saloons, one in partnership with his son-in-law, Jessica's husband. She would see their shocked glares or hear the whispered comments: "Ain't that the barmaid?" "Imagine a father keeping a girl in a saloon. Shameless!"

That had been then. Now she was the wife of Joshua Steed, largest hauler of freight in Independence and fast on his way to becoming one of the leading men of Jackson County. They lived in a large cabin down near the far end of town, south of the courthouse. By Eastern standards it wasn't much; but compared to the sod huts, tiny cabins, or, in some cases, lean-tos and tents that many lived in, it was palatial.

Her status had changed overnight, though it made little outward difference to Jessie, who was still shy to the point of pain, especially around other women. It was one thing to take the girl out of the saloon, but . . . Her mind slipped back to that day a few months ago when Joshua had stunned her at breakfast one morning. "No wife of mine is going to tend bar for a bunch of Missouri wildcats," he abruptly announced. "I don't want you working in your father's saloons no more." She still marveled at it, but had gladly complied with his wishes, touched that it mattered to him. She had not stepped foot inside a tavern or saloon since that day.

Unfortunately it wasn't nearly that easy to change her nature. For almost twenty years she had lived in a setting almost totally devoid of women, at least women of any repute. To sit in a parlor with a circle of ladies, chatting, sipping tea, and sharing the local gossip over their knitting, was as foreign to Jessie as standing behind the bar serving beer or whiskey to an unending stream of unshaven and foulmouthed ruffians would have been to them.

But Jessica didn't really mind being alone. In a way, she always had been, even in the midst of a tavern full of bawdy men. She tried knitting, crochet, needlepoint, and all the other things women supposedly did, but her hands were hands that drew beer or polished glasses or mopped up tobacco juice from around the spittoons. She had no patience for tedious work. Mostly she read—a skill acquired just a year or so earlier—or took long walks into the countryside. She also thought a great deal about getting pregnant for the second time, and tried to push back the dread she felt whenever she thought about that. She had already lost one child. Would she be able to carry another?

"Mrs. Steed! Mrs. Steed!"

Jessica turned around. Running toward her was nine-year-old Thomas Jefferson Thompson. Thomas was the son of the Negro slave who belonged to Joshua's yard foreman. He had brought the family with him when they came from Georgia. Thomas often helped his father and Mr. Cornwell around the stables and barns, and Jessica had spoken with him often. He was a bright boy, always grinning and with skin like polished ebony.

He pulled to a stop and dipped slightly, executing something between a bow and a curtsy. "Afternoon, Mrs. Steed." He grabbed his hat off his head and started twisting it round and round as he looked up at her.

"What is it, Thomas?" She smiled down at him.

That banished any vestiges of his natural shyness. "The wagons, they're comin', ma'am."

Jessie's head jerked sharply and she stared down the street. "Are you sure?"

"Yes'm. My pa rode out two days ago to see if he could find them. He just got back. Mr. Steed's in the lead Conestoga. They should be here by late afternoon tomorrow, my pa says."

She reached in her pocket and took out a coin purse. The boy's eyes widened with expectation. She took out a silver half dime. "Thank you, Thomas. Thank you for bringin' me the news."

"Yes, ma'am," he crowed as his fist clamped over the coin. "Yes, ma'am."

Lydia McBride Steed closed the Book of Mormon and leaned back, arching her back to lessen the stiffness. She glanced out of the window. It was nearly full dark now, which meant she had been leaning over the table for more than an hour.

She sighed. Dark meant bedtime, and she knew what was waiting for her there. Nothing! Just the emptiness of the mattress beside her and the loneliness pressing in upon her until she thought she would suffocate. There might even be a tear or two, and she hated that. She would lecture herself sternly about being a blubbery wife. During the day, when she was busy and occupied, it worked. At night, she was not so successful.

There was a sound of footsteps on the porch, then a soft knock. Surprised, Lydia looked up. "Come in."

The wooden latch, attached to the leather thong outside, lifted and the door pushed open. Melissa Steed, Lydia's sister-in-law, stepped inside. She was carrying a small basket with a cloth laid over the top. Instantly the smell of warm bread touched Lydia's nose.

"Hello."

Lydia stood quickly, a sudden gladness dispelling the gloom that had started to settle in on her. Melissa always seemed to sense when Lydia was in need of some company. Her visits had averaged three or four times a week in the two weeks since Nathan had left for Colesville. "Come in, Melissa."

"Mama baked some rolls. She thought you might like some."

"They smell wonderful." She felt a quick burst of gratitude for the whole family. They all rallied around her now, and she never failed to be touched by it. She took the basket, breathed deeply of the aroma, then set it on the table. "Sit down, Melissa. I have a crock of butter out in the smokehouse. Let me fetch it."

"There's some in the basket, with a little jar of blackberry preserves too."

Lydia shook her head as she sat down beside Melissa. "Your mother . . ."

"Come on," Melissa said, putting on her little-girl face. "Let's eat some before they get cold."

For the next ten minutes they sat that way, shoulder-to-shoulder, eating hot rolls smothered with butter and jam and giggling like two girls playing kissing games with the boys.

Finally, Lydia pushed the basket away. "I've got to stop," she moaned. "Nathan will have to use the hay winch to get me into the wagon when he comes home."

Melissa looked down, rubbing her stomach. "Don't you just love it, though?" she laughed. "I hope there's eatin' in heaven. If not, maybe I'll choose to stay in that other place."

Lydia looked shocked. "Melissa Mary Steed!"

Melissa started to giggle again, pointing her finger at Lydia. "When you say that, you sound just like my father."

That set them off again, and Lydia had to hold her stomach. When their laughter finally subsided, she rubbed at the tears which had squeezed out of the corner of her eye. "This is your way of punishing me, isn't it? First you feed me, then you make me laugh so hard it hurts."

Melissa sobered. "It's good to hear you laugh, Lydia."

Instantly Lydia felt the pain again. "I know." She took Melissa's hand. "Oh, Melissa, I miss him so much."

Melissa's head bobbed momentarily, then she looked away, deciding this was exactly what she had not come over to do. Her eyes fell on the Book of Mormon. "Don't you just love that book?" she said, forcing her voice back to a lighter tone.

"Yes, I do. I'm nearly finished with it for the second time now." She reached out and picked it up, caressing the cover. "I thought I had a testimony of it the first time I read it. But this time I feel even more strongly about it."

"I know. That's how Mama and I are." Melissa took the book from her, looking more closely at the cover. One part of the light brown leather had a dark, ugly stain. "What's this, Lydia? Did you spill something on it?"

"Don't you know that story?"

22

Melissa set the book down. The stain bothered her in a strange way. She had strong feelings for the Book of Mormon, and this was like a blot of profanity on it. "What story?"

"This is the book you brought to the store."

"The one I gave your father?"

"Yes."

Melissa wrinkled her nose, the impish smile returning now. "I guess I was pretty rude that day when I told you what I thought of you for not responding to Nathan after he went to so much trouble to send the book to you."

"Oh, Melissa," Lydia said softly, "when I think what might have happened if you had not come that day . . ."

She sighed, the memories now bringing their own kind of pain with them. It was partly her father's cavalier attitude that had led to her conversion. When she found out that he had thrown away her package without telling her, it had made her angry enough that she read the Book of Mormon just for spite. And that had led to her conversion, which had led to her estrangement from her family.

She shook off the somber mood, not wanting to think about the separation from her family right now. "My father threw it in the bottom of a trash barrel. By the time I discovered it, a lot of other trash had been thrown in on it too." She reached out and rubbed the dark stain with one finger. "Including some coffee grounds."

"So that's it."

"Yes." She picked the book up and held it to her body. "When he saw it, Nathan wanted to buy me a new one. I wouldn't let him."

Melissa looked surprised. "Why not?"

"Because this is the book that saved me," she answered quietly. "I don't want another one."

———◆———

"Good mornin', Sister Steed."

Mary Ann looked up in surprise, then smiled immediately.

She hadn't seen Martin Harris coming towards her across the fields from his house, which lay just south of the Steed farm. "Good morning, Martin."

"Goin' after that mornin' glory, are you?"

Mary Ann leaned on her hoe and looked down the rows of her vegetable garden. She had neglected it lately and it showed. The tendrils of the morning glory, with its dark green leaves and white flowers shaped like small bells, were snaking everywhere.

"I think morning glory is what the good Lord meant when he told Adam about the ground being cursed for his sake."

She laughed. "I think you're right. 'Morning curse' would be a more fittin' title, I reckon."

He chuckled at that, then swept off his hat and wiped at his brow. "Benjamin around?"

"No. He went down to Waterloo to buy a new plow. He'll be back tomorrow."

"He gonna get one of them that's all iron?"

"Yes." She tossed the hoe over to the edge of the garden, then walked over to join her neighbor. "You know Benjamin," she said. "He don't put much stock in old wives' tales."

"That's what makes him a successful farmer."

Mary Ann nodded. That was true. Just before the turn of the century, a man in New England had invented a plow made entirely of iron. It was a great improvement over the wooden plows in that it could be operated by one man using only one yoke of oxen. Newbold had patented the invention, then found to his disappointment that he could sell only a few of them. Mary Ann could clearly remember that when she was a girl someone had tried to sell one of the newfangled plows to her father. He absolutely refused to consider it. "Iron poisons the soil," he said flatly. "A wooden plow is the product of the earth. It comes from trees which grow from the soil, so when you put it back into the soil, it has returned to its mother." The poison-plow delusion was finally dying out now, but there were still a few of the old-timers around who steadfastly refused to believe it wasn't true. Mary

Ann was grateful that Benjamin was not one of them. For all his conservatism in personal and spiritual values, he was quite forward thinking when it came to running his farm.

"Got a letter from Brother Joseph on Saturday," Martin said.

Mary Ann's head came up. "Oh? Has he seen Nathan yet?"

"No. He said he and Emma were going up to Colesville towards the end of this month. The Knight family are going to be baptized."

"Wonderful! Mr. Knight and his wife are the salt of the earth."

"Yes, they've been a wonderful support to Joseph from the very beginning."

"They have indeed." She brushed back a wisp of hair. "I'll have to tell Lydia. That will please her to know that Nathan and Joseph will be together again."

Martin pulled at his suspenders, watching her out of the corner of his eye. "Mind if I ask you a question, Sister Steed?"

She looked up. "Of course not. What is it?"

"How's Benjamin feeling about the Church by now?"

A frown instantly furrowed her brow.

"If it's none of my affair—," he started quickly.

She gave a little shake of her head to cut off his apology. "No, it's not that, Martin. You know that. You have been a good friend to Ben. If he has made any progress at all, it's because of you."

He let out a rueful laugh. "I'm not so sure of that."

"I am." She stopped again, searching for the right words. "It's hard to say, actually. He doesn't fight me anymore. He never says anything when I read the Book of Mormon to Matthew and Becca. It's almost like we've called a truce for now."

"Yes. That's kind of how it is between us too."

"He's such a good man. If only he could see . . ." She left it unfinished. She knew that Benjamin could have made things a lot worse than they were. Though she continued to hope for better circumstances, she needed to be grateful for what she did have. There were a couple of sisters in the growing little group of Saints who weren't nearly that fortunate.

"I'd like to talk to him about it. Think he'd mind?"

She shook her head immediately. "Ben has a great deal of respect for you, Martin. And you know that if he don't like it, he'll let you know."

Martin laughed heartily. "That's for sure. There's never any question about where you stand with Benjamin Steed." His eyes grew more serious. "All right," he went on. "I'll wait until the time is right, but then I think I'm going to be a little pushy with him. I think it might do him some good to be challenged."

Jessica Steed watched her husband through the window of the freight office as he unhitched the last of the teams and turned them over to the stable hands to lead away. It was nearly dark now, but it was like Joshua to stay and see to the work himself. He was the sole owner of the most prosperous freight hauling company along the western border of the United States, and yet he worked right alongside his teamsters, hitching and unhitching teams, lashing down the loads, hammering steel bands around the wagon wheels in the blacksmith shop. He was not even above grabbing a pitchfork from time to time and showing a new stable boy how to clean out a stall and get it fixed up with new straw. Doing all this not only kept him in touch with every aspect of the business but also created a strong loyalty on the part of his help.

He knew she was here. He had seen her in the office when he drove in the yard. There had been a quick nod on his part, a fleeting smile and small wave on hers. Anything more than that would have been an embarrassment to him. Not that it was Jessica's nature to be showing her emotions openly either. One part of her ached to fling herself into his arms, but it had been a long while since she had given in to such girlish fantasies.

Joshua paused for a moment, the last of the teams gone now, and took a long drink from one of the jugs of beer Thomas Jefferson Thompson had brought from the tavern. A few months earlier the sight of Joshua drinking would have sent chills up and down Jessica's soul. But happily those dark days seemed to be gone now. The desperate plunges into the bottle as an attempt to find escape seemed to have passed. But she would never forget those times, especially the night Joshua learned that his beloved Lydia, somewhere back in New York, had become engaged to be married to his brother. It was late that night that Joshua had come to her home, a bewildered and frightened preacher in tow, and had asked if Jessica wanted to marry him. Though it had hurt abominably to know he had come more in an attempt to escape the pain he felt over Lydia than out of love for Jessica, Jessica had loved Joshua quietly for a long time. She had accepted immediately.

Then had come the other even more horrible night. In her sixth month of pregnancy the awful cramping and the bleeding began. She could never forget the haunted look in Joshua's eyes when she woke up, having passed out and lost the baby.

Jessica's head came up. The final team was on its way to the barn; the last wagonload of freight was gone now. Joshua stood next to Thomas Jefferson Thompson, who was hovering around Joshua like an anxious butler waiting lest his master drop some article of clothing on the floor. Joshua reached in his jacket and pulled out something. Coins, judging from the grin on Thomas's face as he handed them to him. Joshua slapped him affectionately across the buttocks, sending him off to the small cabin behind the barn where his family lived. Only then did Joshua turn and start toward the freight office.

Jessica moved away from the desk, her hands suddenly fluttering nervously at the buttons on her new dress. With an effort, she forced herself to let them drop to her side. *You're his wife, for heaven's sake, not some maiden waiting for her first glimpse of a suitor.* But if that was meant to calm her, it did little. It took a conscious act of will to make herself stand motionless and wait for the door to open.

———◆———

"Joshua, tell me. Please!"

They were moving steadily up the main street of Independence, Joshua's long strides making Jessica have to walk very quickly to keep up.

He shook his head firmly. "I told you it was a surprise."

"From St. Louis?"

"From St. Louis," he answered, using a tone that clearly indicated he was not going to give her any more information. Which was almost as shocking as the whole idea of a surprise. This just was not Joshua. Not the Joshua she knew. He was generous in the allowance he gave her, and never asked for an accounting from her. But in all his trips out he had never once brought her back a gift.

Her perplexity only deepened as Joshua led her past the courthouse and then past the only dress shop in the town; he didn't so much as glance at it as they passed. Then to her further surprise, he finally slowed as they approached the Santa Fe Trail Hotel. It was not much to look at, not by Eastern standards, but it was the best there was in Independence. When Joshua turned in, Jessie broke loose from his grasp. "The hotel?"

He looked at her, grinning like a boy bringing his mother a special present. "I told you it was a surprise."

The desk clerk looked up and smiled. He was a balding man. Jessie remembered him from the saloon, before she had stopped going. "Evenin', Mr. Steed." He looked up at the clock on the wall. It was almost eight o'clock. "Looks like you're right on time."

On time? On time for what? She shot a questioning glance at her husband; but he paid it no mind, just grinned even more foolishly at her. This was so unlike Joshua. She was reeling, feeling a little giddy with the strangeness of it all.

"Which room?" Joshua asked.

"Room eight. Upstairs on the right."

"Thanks."

As they started up the stairs, Jessica tugged at Joshua's coat. "Joshua, what is this?" she whispered. "What are we doing here?"

He shook his head. "You just hold on."

The wooden floors creaked under their weight as they moved down the hall. They stopped in front of the door with a number eight hand-painted on it. Joshua knocked firmly, without hesitation.

There was a short pause, then heavy footsteps. The door opened. To Jessie's total surprise, the man who stood there was as elegantly dressed as any man she had seen since she and her father first came to the frontier in 1826. He was a youngish man, probably no more than thirty, but obviously from the upper classes of society. He was fully dressed, as if for the street, and Jessie realized with a start that he had been waiting for them.

The man stepped forward, his hand outstretched. "Mr. Steed. Welcome." He spoke with a pronounced New England accent.

"Thank you." Joshua looked around the room quickly. "Everything here is all right?"

"Yes, in perfect order, thank you." He stepped back, glancing quickly at Jessica but not speaking to her until Joshua chose to make formal introductions. He motioned them in. "Come, sit down. I have some tea from the boardinghouse next door."

He wore a jacket with long tails. Beneath that was a ruffled shirt with a high collar that came right up to his chin. A double-breasted vest was complete with gold watch fob and chain. The trouser legs were tightly fitted and went clear to the floor at the back of the heel. Held down by loops under the boots, they made his legs seem longer and more slender than they really were. A black top hat and walking cane, now sitting on the small chest in the corner of the room, rounded out the attire.

Jessie had to fight herself to keep from gawking. She was accustomed to men in simple homespun pants, long woolen shirts, and boots that were for working, not mincing across the street. *Mincing.* She had once found that word in a book and looked it up in the dictionary. She loved it. It fit a few of the women in town. But she had never thought of it in connection with a man before. *No wonder they're called Eastern dandies.*

He poured two cups of tea and brought them to where they sat. Only when he had gotten one for himself and taken the chair facing them did Joshua finally speak. "Jessica, this is Doctor Jonathan Hathaway, from Boston."

He smiled. "By way of St. Louis."

Joshua acknowledged that with a nod and went on. "Doctor

Hathaway, this is my wife, Jessica—Jessie, I call her."

Jessie fought to keep her face impassive, but the bewilderment was starting to show in her eyes. *Doctor?*

"It's my pleasure to meet you, Mrs. Steed." His voice was pleasant, cultured. So different from the rough-talking men she was accustomed to.

She felt herself nodding and forced a quick smile. "My pleasure, I'm sure."

Joshua laughed. "Didn't I tell you you'd be surprised?"

She just looked at him. Bewilderment was rapidly turning into total confusion.

Joshua turned back to Hathaway. "We'll have to go a little slow at first. Doc Jones is a good man. Does his best. Wouldn't want him to think we didn't trust him."

Jessica's head came up slowly and she peered at Joshua. Doctor Jones, not much more than a horse doctor with a few herbal remedies and a lot of good common sense, had treated Jessie when she had first miscarried. She turned her eyes on Joshua, silently willing him to look at her. *No, Joshua. Not this. Not here. Not with him.*

"There's a couple of good midwives in town too. But their specialty's helping the baby get out, not keeping 'em in until the time's right." He reached across and patted Jessie's hand. "Doctor Hathaway here, he studied medicine at Harvard. He's learned all the latest stuff there is to know. We're gonna get this fixed, Jess. Once and for all."

She dropped her eyes and stared into the dark liquid, her face feeling as hot as the cup in her hands.

"Now, like we agreed," Joshua went on, looking again at the man in the ruffled shirt, not noticing Jessica at all, "you'll be free to start your practice here. There'll be lots of folks glad that we got us a real doctor this far west. But Jessica gets first crack at your time. Anytime, day or night. She's your first priority. I'll see that you're staked out well until you get established. I'll show you the office we have for you over the barbershop. It's got two large rooms, plus the living quarters."

The man sipped his tea, nodding pleasantly. "It's more than a fair deal you've offered me, Mr. Steed. I've got no complaints. No complaints at all." He took another sip of his tea. "It will take me a while to get all my things unpacked." He glanced quickly at Jessie, then away. "Then I'd like to start with a thorough examination. We'll see if all the parts are working right." He laughed—too quickly—but it instantly died when he saw the look on Jessie's face. He turned back to Joshua quickly. "I guess I can reach you at the stables?"

"Anytime. I won't be leaving again until we see what's going on."

Neither man seemed to take note that Jessica sat motionless in her chair, her head down, her face scarlet, her hands gripping her cup as if it were rope dangling over some bottomless chasm. They went on, sipping their tea, Joshua explaining about the previous miscarriage, the doctor speculating on what might be wrong "with the missus." Numbed, dazed, shamed beyond measure, Jessica stared into the cup, feeling it slowly turn cold in her hands.

It was Friday, the twenty-fifth of June, in the year eighteen hundred and thirty. In the southernmost part of New York State the sun had just set behind the hills to the west. The heat was already leaving the fields, and the first hint of the coolness of the evening could be felt on the breeze that had begun its first stirrings. The sky was still brightly blue, but the light that lay across the land was now muted and soft. The dozen or more shades of green—forested hillsides, new stands of sweet corn, meadow hay, the cottonwoods along the Susquehanna—were beginning to blend almost imperceptibly one into the other.

Like a farmer at the end of a long day's labor, all of nature seemed to sense that the workday was over and that this was a moment to sit quietly and enjoy the evening before it was time to retire. Out beyond the barn, five or six milk cows dozed contentedly, their tails barely switching. A mare and her colt moved slowly along the line of a rail fence, heads down, grazing in the richer grass that grew there. Two swallows skimmed up, down, and around over the meadow, hunting mosquitoes, sometimes swooping low enough that their wings brushed the tops of the grass.

Nathan Steed watched it all from the swing that stood on the back porch of the Joseph Knight home in Colesville, Broome County, New York. He watched it all, part of him at peace and enjoying the scene before him, part of him hurting with the ache of missing Lydia.

Behind him, the door to the house opened. He turned. Polly Knight, wife of Joseph Knight, was standing there, smiling happily. Nathan smiled back. Mother Knight, as everyone called her, was a kindly woman, born before the revolutionary war, weathered more than a little by the years of labor alongside her husband. But along with the wrinkles and the leathered, calloused hands came eyes that warmed everyone they fell on, and a heart as open and wide as the Great Lakes.

"Hello, Mother Knight."

Her eyes softened. "Thinking of Lydia again?" she asked.

A little chagrined that she could read him so easily, Nathan nodded.

"Well, I have a surprise to cheer you up."

"What?"

She stepped out onto the porch, holding the door open wide. For a moment there was nothing; then a tall, lithe figure stepped out beside her. There was a brief pause while Nathan just stared, then he leaped to his feet. "Joseph!" he cried.

Joseph Smith grinned, a sight as welcome as anything Nathan had seen in the last three weeks. "Hello, Nathan."

In two strides Nathan was across the porch and grasping Joseph's hand. "When did you—?" He turned. Two more figures appeared in the doorway. Emma Smith was smiling at him, with Oliver Cowdery right behind her.

"Emma," Nathan said, "what a wonderful surprise!"

She reached out both hands and he took them. "How good to see you again, Nathan," she said. "How's Lydia?"

"Lonesome," he responded immediately. "But no more than her husband." He turned to Oliver and grasped his hand. "Hello, old friend."

"Indeed it is good to see you, Nathan," Oliver said, pounding him on the shoulder.

"John and David Whitmer are also with us," Joseph said. "They're out front talking with Father Knight."

For a moment no one spoke, then Nathan stepped back. He couldn't believe his eyes. Joseph and Emma were still living in Harmony, Pennsylvania, which was about thirty miles south of Colesville. With the press of labor, Nathan had not had an opportunity to go down there as yet. He had not seen Joseph and Emma since the day of his wedding over two months earlier.

"What brings you here, Joseph?"

Joseph turned to Sister Knight. "This good lady and her husband have been pestering me to get up here and get them baptized."

"Really?" Nathan knew the Knight family was on the verge of joining the Church. They had been holding meetings two or three times a week with their married children and some of Polly's brothers and sisters. There was no question they were ready. "So, are we going to do it tomorrow?"

Joseph shook his head. "Tomorrow's Saturday. We thought we'd build a dam in the stream down by the barn. That should give us a good-sized pond by Sunday morning." He laid an arm on Sister Knight's shoulder. "I think the Sabbath should be a good day for baptizing."

Nathan came out from the carding shed where he had a small room in the loft. He stopped, tucking his shirt into his trousers and then pulling up the suspenders over his shoulders. He blinked at the brightness of the sunlight. It was a glorious Sabbath morning. A beautiful day for a baptism. If only Lydia were here. After worship services they could go for a walk along the river and . . .

Angry at himself for letting the gloom start in again, he shook it off and started for the house. On impulse he changed direction and headed for the barn. They had spent most of the previous afternoon building a dam in the stream that meandered through the Knight property before emptying into the Susquehanna. They had picked a low spot, and by dark the pond had begun to form. It would not be very deep, but it would be sufficient.

As he came around the side of the barn, Nathan stopped dead. For a moment his mind refused to register what his eyes were seeing. There was no pond. There was no dam. Logs and sticks and wet canvas were strewn about like a toy house kicked to pieces by a petulant child. The ground was wet and dark in a large circle, showing the extent to which the water level had risen, but the pond was gone now. The stream gurgled softly as the water ran on down toward the river, fully contained again within its original banks.

With a cry of dismay, Nathan turned and broke into a run toward the house.

———◆———

The worship service held in the yard of the Knight home later that afternoon carried an air of tension. When the Saints discovered that some of their enemies had come during the night and torn out the dam, Joseph had not been discouraged. "Dams can be rebuilt," he said. "Next time we'll pick the time and place and not give them warning. In the meantime we'll hold regular worship services this afternoon."

But when the people started to gather at the Knight home, it wasn't just the Saints and the would-be Saints who came. Newel Knight—the oldest of the Knights' children—who lived just a short distance away, nudged Nathan as three men came in and sat down. "Pa says those three are openly bragging that they were part of the group who came last night."

Nathan turned and stared at them, not trying to disguise his anger. They met his gaze with a hardness of their own, and Newel finally laid a hand on Nathan's knee to break off the exchange of cold looks.

It was a good worship service, and though the three men and others who were obviously with them looked disgusted from time to time, they said nothing. Oliver Cowdery preached a sermon about the Restoration and bore testimony that Christ's church was once again organized upon the earth. Joseph invited others to bear their testimonies when Oliver finished.

The moment the benediction was over, the mood amongst the gathered crowd instantly changed. One of the three men that Newel had pointed out stepped forward, thrusting his face into that of William Stringham, husband of one of the Knights' daughters. "William," the man blurted, "I thought you were of a sound mind. How can you believe this insanity?" He said it loud enough for all to hear, and a hush instantly swept across those assembled.

William Stringham was a big man, a rough-hewn farmer who usually spoke little but when he did, he spoke emphatically, using his ham-like hands to make his point. Now he jammed his finger at the man's nose, causing him to fall back a step. "Richard," he said evenly, "don't be putting names on things you don't understand."

"It's of the devil!" a woman cried out from behind Nathan. "Can't you see that?"

Joseph turned and smiled at her pleasantly. "Beggin' your pardon, ma'am, but where might you have seen the devil?"

She sputtered for a moment, her face going livid. "I . . . I've seen you!" she finally cried.

Joseph laughed and turned to Emma. "Then, what say you, Emma? Don't you think the devil is a handsome fellow?"

Emma was not amused. She looked at the woman, her dark eyes troubled. "You don't know," she said. "You don't know my husband. You don't know what he has done, what he's trying to do."

Newel's wife jumped in. "What's worse, Molly Sue Gardner, is that you don't want to know. You've completely shut your mind to the truth."

The woman gasped, shocked by the audacity of it all. Her mouth started to work, but before any words came out, Emma went on quickly, her voice tart. "Why don't you read the Book of Mormon? Then you can decide for yourself."

Joseph laid a hand on Emma's arm, touched by her defense of him but trying to calm her at the same time.

Another man snorted in derision. "We don't have to read that book to know it's of the devil. Besides, we've got the Bible."

Joseph turned to the man. "The Lord told an ancient prophet in the Book of Mormon about our day and men like you. He said that men would cry, 'A Bible, a Bible. We have a Bible. We need no more Bible.' "

From somewhere behind Joseph another man broke in. His wife was trying to shush him up, but his face was flushed with anger. "Well, we don't need no gold Bible from you, Joe Smith, that's for sure."

Joseph turned. His eyes had become that piercing blue that sometimes sent shivers up Nathan's back. " 'Thou fool,' " he said, his voice rising with power, " 'know ye not that there are more nations than one? Why murmur ye because ye receive more of my word?' "

Suddenly Nathan realized that Joseph was still quoting from the Book of Mormon.

" 'Because ye have a Bible, ye need not suppose it contains all my words, neither need ye suppose that I have not caused more to be written.' "

"He reviles against God's word!" the first man shouted. "He says that the Bible is not true."

Joseph whirled, his eyes blazing. "I do not revile against God's word," he thundered. "I love and honor the Bible. It is the word of God. But God has the right and the power to give us more of his word if he so chooses. It is you who revile against God's word by saying that the Book of Mormon is evil."

Surprisingly, that cowed the man and the others as well. For another minute they continued muttering amongst themselves, but soon they tired of it, and one by one they left; and the little worship group at the Joseph Knight home was left alone and at peace.

It was full dark on that Sabbath night when the men moved out of the barn, shovels and axes over their shoulders. There was Joseph Knight, Sr., and his young son, Joseph, Jr. Newel Knight was there with his two brothers-in-law, William Stringham and Freeborn De Mill. Nathan stood beside David Whitmer and Oliver Cowdery. John Whitmer was up at the barn, posted as a guard.

No one spoke. The moon had come up before the sun was fully down, and there was plenty of light by which to see. As they reached the stream, they paused for a moment. Then Joseph finally broke the silence. "All right, brethren, let's work as quietly as we can. I'm not particularly feeling the need for company right now. How about you?"

There were several quiet chuckles, and then they fell to work. It took them about a half hour to put the dam back in place. When they were finished they stood for a moment, gazing silently at the waters that were already starting to deepen.

Then Joseph stirred. "Pass the word to your families, brethren. We'll start the baptism half an hour after sunrise. No one else is to know."

He turned to Nathan. "Nathan, would you mind bringing your bedroll outside and sleeping under the stars tonight?"

Nathan grinned back at him. "I already planned on doing just that, Joseph."

It surprised Nathan a little that Emma Smith was the first to be baptized. He had just assumed it had been done earlier. But Emma had been in delicate health since the loss of her first baby, and the ordinance had not been performed previously. Oliver Cowdery stood waist-deep in the now ample pond formed by their dam, and stretched out his hand for her. Joseph held her other hand and steadied her as she stepped into the water. Oliver smiled at her, then raised his right arm to the square. All present bowed their heads.

"Emma Hale Smith," Oliver intoned, "having been commis-

38

sioned of Jesus Christ, I baptize you in the name of the Father, and of the Son, and of the Holy Ghost. Amen."

Nathan and the others looked up in time to watch as Oliver placed one hand on Emma's back and grasped her arm with the other, then lowered her into the water. He glanced quickly up and down to make sure she was totally submerged, then lifted her up again. As she came up, the water streamed off her hair, flashing in the rays of the early morning sunshine. She wiped the water from her eyes, then broke into a radiant smile. Joseph grabbed a blanket and waded knee-deep out to help her.

"Oh, Joseph," she whispered, "at last I have seen it happen. I have come into the kingdom."

"You could not be happier than I," Joseph said, wrapping the blanket around her shoulders and helping her out of the pond.

"Who's next?" Oliver asked.

As Hezekiah Peck, a brother to Polly Knight, stepped into the water, Nathan heard a gasp behind him, followed by an urgent whisper. "Someone's coming."

Every head jerked around. Down the road, from the direction of the village of Colesville, a whole group of men were coming toward them, some on horseback, most on foot. Even as they watched, the lead man turned into the lane that led to the Knight home.

"Oliver," Joseph said calmly, "we'd best keep it moving."

Hezekiah Peck was baptized, followed quickly by his wife.

Joseph Knight, Sr., was next, but by the time he had waded into the water, the little group of believers was joined by fifteen or twenty men. It was amazing and infuriating to Nathan. These men seemed to have a sixth sense about the Mormons. And obviously the word had been spread. More people, all men, were coming now too, walking swiftly or cantering on horseback. Nathan felt a great sense of dismay. Couldn't they leave them alone? What did it matter to these men? Many had not set foot in a church for more years than Nathan had been living. And yet it was almost as if this was some kind of religious mission for them.

A little angry, and fearful at the same time, Nathan slowly sidled over to where a shovel was leaning against a tree. He was not one for violence, but some of these men looked like they were hankering for trouble.

One of the newly arrived men—Nathan recognized him as one of those who had shouted at Joseph the previous day— strode right up to Joseph. "What are you doin' here?" he demanded.

Joseph met the glare with a smile. "Seems to me that a man with any kind of spiritual bent would recognize this as a baptism."

The man's eyebrows narrowed. "You'd better not be smart with me, Joe Smith. We'll put a stop to this right here and now."

Joseph Knight called out from where he stood in the pond. "Amos Lundwall, this is my property. What we're doing here is perfectly legal. Now, I'll be asking you to step back and let us proceed."

That seemed to cow Amos a little. Joseph Knight was a very respected man in these parts. When nothing more was said, Joseph nodded to Oliver.

"Joseph Knight, Senior," Oliver began again, "having been commissioned. . . ."

The men stood silently as they watched Father Knight come out of the water. That seemed to break the spell. "Hey, old man Knight," someone catcalled from the rear of the group, "whatcha doin'? Washin' sheep?"

There were guffaws and chortles. Mother Knight didn't wait for her husband to completely exit the water. She waded in toward Oliver.

"Look," someone else cried, jabbing a twisted finger. "Mother Knight is gonna go get all her sins washed away. Now, ain't that nice?"

Mother Knight could not have helped but hear the gibe, but she paid no mind. She walked deeper into the water, her head high, as though she were a queen entering her bath in the total privacy of her chambers.

"Hey, old woman," a voice cried, "why don't you let holy Joe Smith do it for you? Or maybe he can get an angel to come down and do it."

And so it went as they proceeded, the jeers and taunts mounting with each new person completing the ordinance. Gradually the mood began to turn more hostile, and Nathan felt his pulse starting to race and his mouth going dry. It wouldn't take much to set this group off.

When Joseph Knight, Jr., stepped forward to follow the example of his parents, two men blocked his way. He was the youngest one there, and this seemed to embolden them. The younger Knight was obviously frightened a little, but he moved forward, starting around them.

The bigger of the two grabbed his shirt. "You want a whippin'?" he muttered. "Just go ahead and step into that water."

The other man turned on Oliver. "You touch this man, and we'll tar and feather you and run you out of town on a fence rail."

Nathan gripped the shovel handle more tightly, and shifted his weight onto the balls of his feet. This could get bad in one quick hurry. But at that point William Stringham intervened. Still dripping wet from his own baptism, the Knights' son-in-law moved forward to face the two men. His bulk towered over them, making them look like two small boys. Not a word was spoken, but the men looked up into that face, set as hard as stone, and finally, dropping their eyes, stepped back. Joseph, Jr., walked into the water, and in a moment had joined the rest of his family.

As the last newly baptized member came out of the water, Joseph leaned over to David Whitmer and Oliver Cowdery and whispered something. They nodded, and began moving from person to person, speaking quietly into each ear.

"We'll postpone the confirming of the new members until later this evening," David whispered in Nathan's ear. "Let's just go to the house for now and see if these men won't go away."

By Monday evening, as the little group of Saints in Colesville gathered for the confirmation—the granting of the gift of the Holy Ghost to those who had been baptized—it looked as though it was going to remain quiet. So far only family members and those known to be sympathetic to them had arrived. Nathan was sitting on the large overstuffed sofa next to Emma. She looked tired and discouraged. He leaned over. "Well, it looks as though we might have some peace tonight."

Emma sighed. "I surely hope so. I don't think I could bear another situation like this morning."

"Me neither," Nathan said fervently.

Even after Joseph had postponed further action, the crowd had not dispersed. The Saints moved first into Joseph Knight's home, then down the road to Newel's, trying to escape them, but the crowd had followed, jeering, hurling insults, making vile threats. But eventually they had seen it was getting them nowhere and had broken up and left. So the group of Saints proceeded with their plans to hold the confirmation service that evening.

At the moment, Joseph was moving slowly around the room, greeting each of the new converts and talking briefly with them in turn. They were still waiting for one more couple, and Joseph seemed content not to rush things.

Just as he finished his rounds and started back toward Emma, there was a sharp knock at the door. Instantly all sound in the room ceased and every eye swung around to the door. Clearly alarmed, Polly Knight glanced at Joseph, then stood and walked to the door. Nathan felt Emma tense beside him.

Polly opened the door slowly. "Mrs. Knight?" It was a gruff male voice.

"Yes?"

"I am the constable from Chenango County. I have a writ here for the person of one Joseph Smith, Junior. Is he here?"

There was an audible intake of breath from the group present, and Nathan felt Emma's hand shoot out and grab his arm. Joseph had stopped in midstride. He gave Emma a despairing look, then sighed and turned to face the man. "I'm Joseph Smith. What can I do for you?"

Mother Knight stepped back, holding the door open. The man entered, looked around at the group, then boldly turned to Joseph. "Mr. Smith, I'm to take you immediately to South Bainbridge, where you'll be standing trial tomorrow to answer the charges brought against you."

Emma's fingernails dug into Nathan's arm. Even Joseph seemed shocked by that pronouncement. "And what charges may those be, sir?" he finally asked.

"You are charged with being a disorderly person and setting the country in an uproar by preaching about angels and claimin' you dug a gold Bible out of a hill somewhere upstate from here."

Emma leaped up. "Don't go, Joseph. Please don't leave me." She clung to her husband. He had his back to her, facing the constable, and her arms encircled his chest. Her eyes were dark with fright and fatigue. The strain of the events surrounding the baptism had left her nerves strung as taut as a bowstring. This only tightened the corkscrew another notch.

He turned around and took her gently in his arms. "Emma." He stroked her cheek. "It'll be all right. I'm going to be just fine." She buried her head against his chest and began to cry softly.

Joseph Knight stepped forward. "Brother Joseph, I have two neighbors. Fine men. Men of integrity. They're not trained lawyers, but they are well versed in the laws of our country. I shall leave immediately to retain them in your behalf."

Joseph looked at him over the top of Emma's head. "Thank you, Father Knight."

"We'll come, Joseph. We'll be there tomorrow," David Whitmer spoke up.

"Yes," Oliver agreed. He turned to the constable. "I suppose that is permissible."

The constable seemed a little cowed by the outburst of grief and affection his coming had triggered. "It will be an open trial, sir. The place will be determined in the morning."

"At what time?" Nathan asked.

"Ten o'clock." He turned to Joseph and touched him on the shoulder. "I'm sorry, Mr. Smith, we must be leaving now."

"No," Emma whispered. "Please."

Newel Knight's wife, Sally, came forward and gently pulled her back. "Come, Emma. It will be all right."

Joseph leaned down and kissed his wife quickly, then straightened. "Let me get my hat, Mr. . . . ?"

"Wilson. Constable John Wilson."

Polly Knight had turned to the hat rack near the door and fetched Joseph's hat. She handed it to him, then as he placed it on his head she suddenly went up on tiptoes and hugged him. She was about four inches shorter than Emma and barely reached his chest. "We'll be praying for you, Brother Joseph."

"Thank you, Mother Knight."

The group followed Joseph out and watched him climb up into the buckboard the constable had brought. He looked once more at his friends, his face composed and serene. Then he turned to the constable. "All right, Mr. Wilson, let us be off. I am anxious to face my accusers, as I have nothing to hide and nothing to fear."

The constable gave him a strange look, then took the reins and clucked at the horse.

As the wagon left the yard of the Knight home and started up the lane that led to the main road that ran between Colesville and South Bainbridge, Joseph leaned back and breathed deeply. "A beautiful night, Mr. Wilson, wouldn't you say?"

Again Joseph seemed to catch the man off guard. He turned and gave Joseph a long look.

"Is something the matter, Mr. Wilson?"

For several moments there was no sound but the soft clop-clop of the horses hooves and the rattle of the wagon wheels on the gravel. Joseph seemed amused by the constable's obvious perplexity. "I perceive that something is troubling you, Constable."

The man reined up and the wagon rolled to a stop. Constable Wilson turned and faced Joseph squarely. "Yes, Mr. Smith. You are correct. Something is troubling me."

Joseph smiled. "Well then, say on. I'm not sure I am the one you would normally seek out for help, but I'm willin'."

The constable did not return his smile. "I must admit, Mr. Smith," he said soberly, "you are a very different man than I was led to believe."

Joseph's head tipped back and he laughed merrily. "That doesn't come as a great surprise, Mr. Wilson. What were you led to expect?"

Wilson thought for a moment, then shook his head. "I'm not sure. A wild man, I suppose. A fanatic."

"Well, thank you for changing your mind."

The constable turned back and lifted the reins, but his hand stopped, poised but motionless. His mouth twisted, and it was obvious that he was fighting some kind of inner battle within himself.

"What is it, Mr. Wilson?"

The reins lowered again. So did his voice. "I have something to confess to you, Mr. Smith." He looked around furtively.

Joseph was puzzled now. "Confess, Mr. Wilson?"

"Yes." He glanced around once more; then, convinced they were alone, went on in a rush. "Did you not find it strange that none of the men who were at your baptismal service this morning showed up for your meeting this evening?"

"I . . ." Joseph was caught off guard by that. "We didn't tell anyone except those who are supporters. I just thought our enemies didn't know."

"Oh, they know, all right. That's why I was sent with a writ to fetch you."

Joseph's eyes narrowed. "So the timing was not just coincidental?"

"Not on your life, sir." His chest lifted and fell as he sighed deeply. "There's more."

"More?"

"Yes. Those men are waiting for us now. I am to bring you to them. They lie in wait, in ambush, less than a mile from where we now stand."

Joseph paled. "So that's it."

The constable's jaw clenched shut, and his eyes took on a determined look. "But now that I have met you, sir, I am of a very different mind. I am duty bound to deliver you for trial tomorrow, but I shall do all within my power to see that you are not harmed in the meantime."

For several moments Joseph was silent, considering the implications of what he had just learned. Finally he looked up. "You are an honorable man, Constable Wilson. I am fortunate to have fallen into your hands."

The man smiled grimly. "Shall we proceed, then?"

Joseph reached down with one hand and gripped the side of the buckboard. "I am ready when you are."

The ambush was laid less than half a mile from the Knight homestead, and it had been carefully chosen. A thick stand of natural woodland ran right to the road on both sides. The sun was down, and the evening light was fading quickly. There was no sign of anyone as they approached.

"Are you sure this is where they were to meet you?" Joseph whispered.

"Shhhh!"

The men would have been impossible to detect if they hadn't moved, but as the wagon approached the heaviest growth of forest, dark figures straightened one by one, on both sides of the road. Joseph felt a sudden lurch of fear. The nearest man had an ax handle and was tapping it softly against his leg. The one next to him carried a stout length of tree limb.

"Steady," the constable murmured.

Three men stepped out into the road, blocking their way. The constable pulled the horse up and the wagon stopped. For an instant Joseph nearly panicked and bolted. What if this was just the constable's way of making sure he did not resist? But he braced his feet and lowered his head slightly. Wilson had said there was to be a signal from him, then the men would set upon Joseph. Clearly that was what they were waiting for now. They moved within a few feet of the wagon, looking up at the constable with expectant eyes.

"Hee yaw!" The constable snapped the reins sharply, flipping the horse hard across his rump. The horse had expected it no more than the men. It lunged forward, the traces cracking like whips as the buckboard was jerked forward. Joseph nearly bowled head over heels into the back of the wagon.

"Hold on!" Wilson yelled. Then to his animal. "Go, horse! Go!"

The three men in the road didn't have time to even shout. They jumped frantically, barely escaping the slashing hooves. Joseph was dimly aware of the uproar behind him, but only dimly. He was hanging on with all his strength as the wagon bucked and shuddered violently, the horse in full gallop now.

"I don't think they have horses," the constable yelled into his ear. "At least not close."

Joseph started to nod, then his eyes caught a dark shadow in the road ahead of them. "Watch out!" he screamed.

But it was too late. They were just coming around a slight bend in the road. The front wheels missed the rock clean, but the back end slewed around wildly, sliding on the packed earth. There was a shattering crack, then instantly the world went crazy.

For a moment Joseph didn't know what had happened, only that he was half upside down, hanging on for dear life, and that the horse was neighing wildly. Then he realized that the buckboard had stopped and was tipped upward at a sharp angle.

"We've thrown a wheel!" the constable shouted. Then in cold fear, "Oh no! Now they've got us."

Joseph leaped to his feet and whirled around. They could hear the sound of angry shouts, men cursing, feet pounding. Frantic, Joseph scanned the road they had just traversed. There it was. "Wilson, get the wheel!"

He leaped to the rear of the buckboard, then turning his back to it dropped into a crouch. He reached down with both hands, grabbed the edge of the wagon, and with a grunt, hefted it up to waist level. "Hurry!" he gasped.

The sound of their pursuers was like a clap of thunder rolling down a mountainside toward them, growing louder with every instant.

Panting like a madman, Wilson wrestled the wagon wheel to where Joseph stood. "Higher!" he commanded.

Blood vessels stood out on Joseph's forehead as he raised his arms another inch.

"It's on!"

As the two men leaped back into the wagon, Joseph heard a cry of triumph behind them. "There they are!"

But it was a moment too late. The constable grabbed the reins. "Hee yaw!" The wagon leaped forward again. Joseph jerked around to see three or four men come pounding up, then slow to a halt in the middle of the road. They shouted something, shaking their fists.

Joseph turned back around to the front, aware of the sudden trembling that was moving down his arms and to his hands. He looked over at his companion. The constable stared back at him. Then suddenly they both began to laugh. "We did it," Constable John Wilson crowed. "We did it!"

Emma's Baptism at Colesville

Chapter Four

Would you give your name and place of residence please?"

"Mr. Josiah Stowell of South Bainbridge."

"And your occupation, sir?"

"Farmer and owner of a lumber mill. I also trade in wheat and other farm goods in the upper part of the state."

"And how long have you known the prisoner?"

Josiah Stowell leaned back in his chair and pulled at his lip thoughtfully. "I think I first hired Joseph Smith in the summer of '25. So about five years now, maybe six."

The prosecutor, who had to that time had his back to the witness, addressing the court, suddenly whirled and jabbed a finger at Stowell. "Did not the prisoner, Joseph Smith, have a horse of you?"

"Yes."

"Did he not go to you and tell you that an angel had appeared unto him and authorized him to get the horse from you?"

Stowell smiled patiently. "No, he told me no such story."

"Well, how, then, did he have the horse of you?"

"He bought it of me as any other man would."

"Have you had your pay?"

Stowell straightened, his face tightening. "That is not your affair."

Justice Joseph Chamberlain frowned. "Please answer the question, Mr. Stowell."

The prosecutor openly sneered in triumph. "I ask you again, Mr. Stowell. Have you had your pay from the prisoner?"

"I have his note for the price of the horse," Stowell retorted tartly. "I consider that as good as cash, for I am well acquainted with Joseph Smith, Junior. I know him to be an honest man." He turned and surveyed the hostile faces that filled the room. "And if Mr. Smith wishes, I will give him another horse this very day on the same terms."

That did not please the prosecutor. "You may step down, Mr. Stowell." He turned and looked at the crowd. "Mr. Jonathan Thompson, please."

A man near the back rose and walked slowly forward to the chair that sat to the side of where Justice Chamberlain was seated. Clearly he was not excited about being part of the proceedings. He sat down, looking at the prosecutor warily.

"Mr. Jonathan Thompson?"

"Yes."

"Occupation and place of residence please?"

"Farmer. My place is a short distance east of here."

"Did not the prisoner, Mr. Joseph Smith, have a yoke of oxen of you?"

"He did, sir."

"Did he not obtain them of you by telling you that he had a revelation to the effect that he was to have them?"

A momentary look of disgust crossed the farmer's face. "He did not. He did not mention a word of the kind you have stated concerning the oxen. He bought them of me as any other man would."

Frustrated, the prosecutor immediately dismissed Thompson and called on several others. The results were the same, and for the first time, Nathan felt his hopes begin to lift.

About noon the court was detained while someone was sent off to fetch the two daughters of Josiah Stowell. When they appeared, the lawyer lit into them with unabashed directness. Nathan couldn't believe some of the questions that were put to them. The innuendos were unmistakable, and several men in the room leered at the two young women when they were asked most specifically about Joseph's behavior toward them, both in public and private. But again the prosecutor was denied whatever it was he had hoped to achieve. Firmly and without the slightest hesitation, both of the girls testified that Joseph's behavior had been circumspect and appropriate in every situation and setting.

And so the day dragged on, the heat in the room becoming oppressive as the afternoon reached its peak. There were innumerable delays while additional witnesses were sent for. It soon became clear that the prosecutor and those who had hired him were scouring the countryside near and far to try and find someone whose testimony would convict Joseph. But it was to no avail. Some swore to things which were so patently absurd that even the prosecutor seemed embarrassed. Others contradicted each other on every hand.

Amazingly Joseph seemed unmarred by it all. He sat quietly in his place next to his two defenders, watching with interest, sometimes smiling in amusement at the absurdity of the testimony, but always calm and unruffled.

Evening came, and finally the two men Joseph Knight had secured for Joseph's defense were allowed to present their case. This time the witnesses were in agreement and spoke with great conviction. James Davidson and John Reid were obviously well known, even in South Bainbridge, and Justice of the Peace Chamberlain listened carefully as they brought forth those who testified of Joseph's integrity.

Finally, at about eleven o'clock, John Reid stood and faced

Justice Chamberlain. "Your Honor," he said, not trying to hide his disgust at the day's proceedings. "It is obvious that the defendant in this case is not guilty of the charges brought against him. We have seen the esteemed prosecutor bring forth the wildest collection of witnesses this county has ever seen. And what have they proven? Absolutely nothing!" He turned and shot the prosecuting attorney a withering look of contempt. "They could not even agree with each other on what Mr. Smith is supposed to be guilty of.

"On the other hand, we have brought witness after witness—honorable men and women of our community—who have testified that the defendant is an honest man, a man of integrity and industry who has done nothing to warrant these ridiculous charges. Therefore, Mr. Davidson and I move that all charges be dropped immediately and that Mr. Smith be released to go home."

"Hear, hear!" James Davidson said clearly.

The prosecutor was on his feet instantly and began a lengthy and rambling rebuttal. As he went on and on, it became clear that he was stalling for some reason. Justice Chamberlain asked more than once if they were ready for a ruling, but the prosecutor begged for "just a little more patience" so the matter could be resolved once and for all.

It was shortly after midnight when a large, burly man slipped into the back of the room. Nathan's concerns shot up instantly. Was this the man the prosecutor had been waiting for? He looked as hard as slate, like he had sipped more than his share of John Barleycorn in his day. But to Nathan's relief, he merely glanced around, then stepped to the back wall and leaned against it, looking bored and disinterested. The moment the man was in place, the prosecutor turned to the justice of the peace and surprised everyone. "We are ready for a ruling, sir."

It only took a few moments before Justice Chamberlain and the others returned. The low buzz of voices instantly ceased when the door opened. Joseph stood, straightening to his full height, and turned to face the justice. Constable Wilson had told Joseph that morning that they were fortunate to have gotten Chamberlain as the judge, for while he was a somber man, he was a fair and impartial one as well.

The judge cleared his throat, then spoke with gravity. He didn't feel the need for any preamble. "Mr. Smith," he said firmly, "the court finds you not guilty. The charges are dismissed."

The courtroom exploded. There were angry cries, a burst of applause from the small group sitting behind Joseph, and Joseph's own great sigh of relief. Joseph turned to the small group of his supporters, smiling wanly. In an instant they were gathered around him, shaking his hand or clapping him on the back in congratulations.

Oliver slipped an arm through Joseph's. "Let's go home, Joseph. Emma will be most anxious to learn of the results."

But at that moment Nathan felt himself shoved aside roughly. "Mr. Smith."

It was the large man who had entered the courtroom a few minutes previously. He clutched a paper in one hand and thrust it under Joseph's nose, the hostility on his face as hard as a slap across the cheek. In that instant Nathan realized why the prosecutor had made that final delay. They needed time to get this man here before the verdict was given.

Joseph seemed to sense it too. "Yes," he said quietly.

"I am Constable Boyd from Broome County. I have a writ here for your arrest on charges of disturbing the peace in Colesville Township. You'll be comin' with me, sir."

"Mr. Boyd."

The constable turned with a sneer, wiping the beer foam from his mouth.

"Do you mean to put me up here for the night?"

"What's it to you?"

The other men in the tavern quieted, turning to watch. The tension in the air was almost as heavy as the cigar and pipe smoke.

"Now that we are back in Colesville," Joseph said quietly,

"we are very near to where my wife is lodged at her sister's house. I would be easily accessible in the morning."

Boyd looked at his prisoner in amazement. "Are you daft, Smith? You'll not be escaping quite so easy from our clutches." He turned and raised his beer. "Right, men?"

There was a raucous cry of assent, and once again the jeering started. It was nearly two in the morning, but the tavern owner seemed to have no reservations about serving liquor all night if need be. And the men were having great sport.

Suddenly, Boyd reached out and grabbed Joseph's shoulder. "Sit down!" he bawled. He shoved Joseph hard toward an empty chair. Joseph stumbled, tried to catch himself, but went down hard on his knees.

He looked up at the constable. "I have not had anything to eat since yesterday. If you won't let me go to my wife, then at least may I have something to eat?"

"The prophet's hungry!" a man near the bar shouted. "Get the prophet some bread and water."

The tavern owner tipped his head back and laughed uproariously. "Yes, bread and water. Food for the holy man."

As Joseph sat down, another man leaned forward, thrusting his face right up next to Joseph's. His breath was foul, his beard stained with tobacco juice. The front of his shirt had stains from the stew he had eaten earlier. "How about some entertainment, holy man?"

Joseph did not answer. The man stared at him for a moment, his lips compressing into a tight line. Then he reared back. Joseph didn't have time to react. The man's hand was a blur. The open palm caught Joseph flat on the cheek, rocking his head backward.

There was a roar of approval.

A man with a bad limp got up from his table and sidled up to Joseph from behind. Joseph seemed to sense his presence, for he started to turn around. The man's hands flashed out and he clapped them over Joseph's eyes. Joseph tried to pull away, but the man was surprisingly strong.

"He says he's a prophet," the man cried to his companions. "Let's see if he can prophesy."

"Yes, let him prophesy." This time it was an old man, nearing sixty or so. Grinning wickedly, he walked in front of Joseph, stopping within a foot of him. Unable to see but aware that someone had approached him, Joseph tensed, expecting another blow. The room fell silent. The man leaned forward. There was a sudden hawking sound, then the man spit directly into Joseph's face. He jumped back and joined the others, and the small man lifted his hands from Joseph's eyes.

Boyd laughed, watching the spittle trickle down Joseph's face. As Joseph reached up to wipe it away with his sleeve, Boyd grabbed his arm. "No, no!" he said. "Before you do that, prophesy. Tell us who spit on you."

The cry was instantly on every lip. "Yes, prophesy! Prophesy! Prophesy!"

———•———

The trial in Colesville lasted eighteen hours. When the prosecutors were unable to find a credible witness that could corroborate their case against Joseph, they sent runners out into the countryside and scoured every ditch and cranny and grog shop within ten miles. But time after time the witnesses contradicted one another so plainly that even the justices, who were clearly in sympathy with the mob, had to dismiss their testimony. Either that or, under cross examination by the men Joseph Knight had secured to defend Joseph, they admitted they were only repeating what they had heard from others and did not know anything from their own experiences.

The most notable thing happened just after midnight. Nathan Steed, Oliver Cowdery, David Whitmer, and Newel Knight were sitting behind Joseph and his representatives. Emma and the others had been sent home to bed hours earlier. Nathan was in half a stupor by then, his eyes feeling like blacksmith's anvils. Then suddenly he jerked wide awake as Oliver reached out and gripped his arm.

Constable Boyd, who had been sitting across the room staring at Joseph for several hours now, suddenly stood and began to make his way toward them.

"What does this mean?" Newel whispered anxiously.

"I don't know," Oliver replied. "Be ready for anything."

But they were not ready for what happened next. The man grabbed an empty chair as he passed it and set it down next to Joseph, winning himself a sharp glance of warning from the three justices of the peace who sat in judgment. Joseph eyed him warily as well, but didn't flinch when the man sat shoulder to shoulder with him.

Boyd waited for a moment, until the eyes of those who had turned to watch him finally lost interest and turned back to follow the proceedings. Then he turned slightly and began to whisper in Joseph's ear. Nathan and the others leaned forward so they could hear.

"Mr. Smith?" Even in a whisper the man's voice sounded like a wood rasp being drawn across a pine board.

"Yes?"

"I have come to apologize and to ask your forgiveness."

Joseph, who had remained completely unflappable through two days of abuse and calumny, was thunderstruck. He gaped at the man, dazed, as though he hadn't understood the words. Nathan, Oliver, David, Newel—they were all staring at the man as well.

The man's face, the one that Nathan had thought looked like a piece of slate, was truly contrite. He shook his head back and forth. "I was told some awful things about you, Mr. Smith, and I guess I was bound and determined to see justice done."

There was a quick explosion of air, registering his complete disgust. He jerked his head in the direction of the riffraff that the lawyers for the prosecution had dragged in—what John Reid, one of Joseph's defenders, had called "a company that looked as if they had come from hell and had been whipped by the soot boy thereof."

"What's happenin' here ain't justice," the constable rumbled. "You'd have to be a blind man not to see that."

Joseph was still staring at the man in wonder. "No," he finally said. "This surely ain't justice."

The man leaned over closer. "About last night . . ." His eyes dropped to the floor. "I'm sorry."

What was last night? Nathan wondered. He turned to Oliver, who just lifted his shoulders, his own face showing puzzlement.

Joseph was touched. He reached out and placed a hand on the man's knee. "It's all right, Mr. Boyd. Thank you."

The constable's voice dropped to a conspiratorial whisper. Nathan strained to hear his words. "I've got to warn you, Mr. Smith. Even if the court acquits you, these men are determined to have you. They've laid plans to catch you afterwards. They mean to tar and feather you, then rail ride you out of town."

Oliver gasped, audibly enough that the constable turned around. "That's right," he said. "Make no doubt about it. They mean to have their way."

"Well, they're not going to!" Newel said fiercely.

That brought several heads around, and Joseph shook his head quickly in warning. The constable ignored them. His head came up, his mouth now set and determined. "I'll see to it that no one hurts you," he said.

Joseph was visibly touched. He laid a hand on the man's shoulder. "Thank you, good friend."

It was full light when they finally stopped outside the gate in front of the home of Emma's sister. The sun had not yet come over the eastern hills but was only minutes away from doing so. There were five of them—Nathan, Joseph, Oliver, David Whitmer, and Newel Knight.

Mr. Seymour's "witnesses" had taken until two o'clock in the morning to finish their testimony. That was followed by two hours of closing arguments by both the prosecuting and defending lawyers. All charges had finally been dismissed. As John Reid summed it up to the judges in his final argument, "Joseph Smith is like the three Hebrews of the Old Testament cast into the fiery furnace. He has come through these proceedings without so much as the smell of smoke on his clothes." But in spite of the acquittal, the three justices of the peace had then launched into a bitter, half-hour diatribe of insult and invective against Joseph. They severely reprimanded him for his behavior—behavior that he had just been acquitted of!

Then had come the wild flight in the night, with Constable Boyd running flank and Joseph's four companions spiriting him through the dark, past the men waiting to catch him, through the air heavy with the smell of hot tar.

Nathan couldn't remember a time in his life when he had ever been so totally exhausted as he was now—physically, emotionally, spiritually. He felt as if someone had nailed his feet to a couple of tree stumps, then tossed a shovelful of sand into his eyes. In the last forty-eight hours he had barely slept during four of them. And the last four days seemed like one long ride on a stagecoach where every few hours the team would bolt and the coach would career wildly down the road before someone brought it to a halt again.

Joseph looked at the lot of them and laughed softly.

Oliver's hands hung down at his side. His eyes were bloodshot and bleary. David's chin was covered with the dark stubble of his beard. Newel's shirt was rumpled and soiled. Nathan looked as if he had been hit over the head with a hayrack.

Oliver looked at his companion in surprise. "What do you find to laugh about, Joseph?"

Gesturing first at himself, then at the others, Joseph chuckled even more loudly. "We look more like candidates for an embalming room than living human beings."

"Even a coffin sounds good right now," Newel agreed, smiling a little in spite of himself.

Nathan did not smile. He turned away quickly. He was in no mood for laughter.

Joseph sensed something was wrong. "Nathan? Are you all right?"

He spoke without turning. "I'm fine, Joseph. Just very, very tired."

"It has been a long and black night," Joseph agreed. "We're all tired." Then he put a hand on Nathan's shoulder and turned him gently around. He peered into Nathan's eyes in that way he had of looking into your very soul. "Is that really all, Nathan?"

Nathan looked down, not able to meet his gaze.

"What is it, Nathan?" Oliver said. "What's wrong?"

Suddenly the dam inside Nathan burst and it all came out in a bitter torrent. "Yes, Joseph, it was a long and black night. And the night before in South Bainbridge was a long and black night. And a couple days before that was the Sabbath, a day that should have been peaceful and holy, a day when we hoped to perform the holy ordinance of baptism. But was it peaceful and holy? No. Instead the servants of hell are allowed to come in with their taunts and gibes and ridicule and break it up.

"Where is the Lord, Joseph? We're doing his work. The Knights only wanted to do his will and be baptized. Or take you as another example. You're his prophet, Joseph. You've been obedient. So why all this? Twice you have been taken through the mockery of a trial. Twice you have stood before a mob and been humiliated with lies of the blackest hue. Why? Why, Joseph? Why doesn't God intervene in your behalf?" He broke free from Joseph's grasp and turned away. "I'm sorry, Joseph, but I guess I find precious little to laugh about right now."

For several moments there was no sound but the first sounds of the morning. Behind the house a rooster crowed, then crowed again. In the distance a horse whinnied its response.

Finally, Nathan felt an arm go round his shoulder. Joseph sighed, then sighed again. When he spoke it was with some sadness and yet with firmness too. "I don't have all the answers, Nathan. And believe me, I've asked myself those questions many times."

"But?"

"But whenever I get to feeling real down about these kinds of things, I remember the Savior's counsel to his Apostles the night before his death."

He turned away and looked out across the open fields, now

touched by the first rays of the sun. "He warned them of coming trouble. He spoke not only of his own death, but of the future when they would face similar trials."

He swung back around, his eyes now soft and filled with wonder. " 'If the world hates you,' the Savior told them, 'don't be surprised, for it hated me before it hated you. If you were of the world, the world would love you. But you are not of the world. You have been chosen out of the world, and so the world hates you too.' "

He stopped. Nathan felt a sudden shame shoot through him. He had not thought about the Savior in this. He was so caught up in his own weariness, his own spiritual exhaustion, that he had not once thought of the Savior.

Joseph's eyes got a faraway look in them. "Then he finished by saying, 'In the world you shall have tribulation: but be of good cheer; I have overcome the world.' "

It was somehow as if someone had taken a lamp down into the dark recesses of Nathan's soul, and held it up high, so that the light penetrated into every corner. "That is the answer, isn't it?" he said, half in wonder.

Joseph nodded. "Tribulation will continue to come, but let us always strive to be of good cheer."

Chapter Five

One of the great ironies of American history was that
the land of the free and the home of the brave was also, for the
first two centuries after its colonization, a land of religious intol-
erance and persecution. It was one thing to make an amendment
to the Constitution which read, "Congress shall make no law re-
specting an establishment of religion, or prohibiting the free exercise thereof"; it was quite another to write that law on the
fleshy tablets of people's hearts.

In retrospect, it was not surprising that troubles arose. The
colonists brought with them from Europe several deeply in-
grained assumptions about religion. Each state or community
had only one legal religion that was protected by the government and supported by taxes from the citizens. To attempt to es-
tablish another church or foster differing religious beliefs was
therefore viewed not only as heresy but also as a civil crime.

In areas where civilization's veneer was still thin and law en-
forcement scattered, religious persecution often thrived. Those

viewed as a threat to orthodox society were socially ostracized, defamed, mobbed, or expelled. The Society of Friends—the Quakers—experienced cruel opposition when they first sent missionaries into the colonies in the midseventeenth century. Roman Catholics commonly faced ugly, violent confrontations. Preachers and missionaries from various religions out of the main line of the American tradition were hounded and ridiculed, pelted with rotten eggs, tarred and feathered, drowned out by shouting or the banging of drums, or sometimes beaten mercilessly.

While the Mormons were not unique in being persecuted, they took more than their share of abuse because, in addition to going against the established religious traditions of the time, they also taught religious exclusivity. In their minds, the original Church founded by the Master had been broken up and gone into apostasy after his death. That meant all other religions, Catholic and Protestant, were without authority and did not represent the Church of Jesus Christ. That did little to endear them in the hearts of their neighbors, and least of all in the hearts of the ministers and religious leaders of established churches.

But if this was a time of religious opposition, it was also a time of religious revivalism. All across the face of the country, but more particularly along the frontier, men and women began to reconsider religion as an option in their lives. Church membership rose sharply. Newspapers proclaimed the imminence of the Second Coming. Tens of thousands of good, decent people began to turn their hearts to God.

One such person was a young man, Parley P. Pratt by name, living with his wife, Thankful, in the northern part of Ohio. They read the Bible earnestly and felt a great longing for a church that had the characteristics of the Church in New Testament times. One day a preacher by the name of Sidney Rigdon came into the area. He led a group of Reformed Baptists who called themselves *seekers*. They too were looking for a return to a more biblical church, and the Pratts quickly joined with them.

But still that did not satisfy the inner longing that seemed to drive Parley. He went to the scriptures like a thirsting man to a cool mountain spring. He began to write passages on slips of paper. He called them his "promissory notes" from the Lord— things like "All things are possible to him that believeth," or "Whosoever shall forsake father or mother, brethren or sisters, houses or lands, wife or children, for my sake and the gospel's, shall receive an hundred fold in this life, and in the world to come life everlasting."

In the spring of 1830, the promissory notes came due. "I feel called upon by the Holy Ghost," he told his brother William, "to forsake my house and home for the gospel's sake; and I will do it, placing both feet firm on these promises with nothing else to rely upon."

The farm was sold—at a substantial loss—and their affairs settled. By late summer they set out, with ten dollars in cash in hand and limitless faith in their hearts. They determined first to visit their families back in New York State, then to follow the promptings of the Holy Spirit wherever they might lead them.

But the young man didn't reach home. As they moved eastward along the Erie Canal, the Spirit prompted him to disembark at Newark and send his wife on to their families. Newark was a small canal town about eight miles east of Palmyra.

It was near the close of a summer's day late in August. Hyrum Smith moved slowly along Stafford Road, about a mile south of Palmyra Village, just across the line of Manchester Township. Ahead of him several milk cows moved briskly along, anxious now to reach the barn so they could be relieved of the weight in their bulging udders.

"Excuse me, sir."

Hyrum turned around to see where the voice had come from. About fifty yards away a young man was hurrying to catch him. Hyrum slowed his step. The man was plainly dressed, but his clothes were well cared for. He was clean shaven but with long sideburns that came down below his ears. His face was round and full, his mouth generous and quickly given to a smile. Dark eyes, alert and intent, peered out from beneath bushy brows.

"Yes?" Hyrum said as the man came up to him, a little out of breath.

"Excuse me, but could you tell me of the whereabouts of Joseph Smith, the translator of the Book of Mormon?"

Hyrum's eyes narrowed slightly. "Why do you ask?"

"I was told in the village that his family lived in this neighborhood."

"But why do you seek him?"

The face was devoid of any guile; the answer came out as simple and as straightforward as if from a child. "A day or so ago, as I was traveling through the countryside preaching, a man gave me the Book of Mormon. I have read a goodly portion of it and know that it is true. I must find the man who is responsible for it."

Hyrum was still a little reticent. "He's gone to Pennsylvania, more than a hundred miles' distance from here."

The young man's face fell. There was no mistaking his disappointment. He sighed, considering what next to do. "Then can you direct me to his father, or any other member of the family?" he finally said. "I must know more about this book."

Satisfied, Hyrum stuck out his hand. "My name is Hyrum Smith. I am Joseph's older brother."

"For true?" the man cried in delight. He pumped Hyrum's hand vigorously. "I am Parley P. Pratt, and most delighted to make your acquaintance, sir."

On September first—having traveled with Hyrum Smith to Fayette to meet the Whitmers and others—Parley P. Pratt was baptized into the Church of Jesus Christ by the hand of Oliver Cowdery, who had by then returned to Fayette.

"Are you ready, Lydia?"

"Almost. Give me just a moment."

Lydia stood in front of a small mirror which hung from the

wall of one of the upper bedrooms in the Peter Whitmer, Sr., home. It was now the third week in October, and the nights were frosting hard. Some heat from the great fireplace in the kitchen below them came up the stairs, but not much. Little puffs of frosty breath filled the air between Lydia and the mirror as she worked to fasten a locket around her neck. She was having trouble because her long hair kept falling across her hands.

Nathan, who never tired of watching his wife, moved across the room. "Here, let me do it."

She lifted her hair and bowed her neck. In a moment he had the clasp fastened, but he held it away from her so she wouldn't know he was finished. Then he bent his head and let his lips brush her skin right at the nape of the neck.

She gave a little shudder, then giggled a little. "Mr. Steed, what are you doing?"

He laughed and kissed the same spot again, then put his arms around her waist and pulled her close to him. "I was just smelling your cologne."

She turned, slipping around in his arms until she faced him. Her head tipped back so that her hair fell in a cascade of black across her shoulders. "It felt like you were doing more than just sniffing my neck."

"Well, you smelled so good, I thought I'd nibble a little while I was there." He kissed her on the lips, then leaned back a little, running his tongue across his lips. "Yeah, you do taste good."

She threw her arms around him, laid her head against his chest, and hugged him tight. For a moment he stood there, stroking her hair, loving the feel of her.

"Don't ever leave me again, Nathan," she whispered, her voice suddenly husky with emotion.

Surprised, he pulled free and lifted her chin. "Why do you say that? I'm not going anywhere."

"I know, but I missed you so much." It came out in a fierce whisper, and there were sudden tears in her eyes. "I'm not good at being alone."

A smile tugged at the corners of his mouth as he looked

down at her, and his eyes were amused. "Lydia, I've been home for almost two months now. How can you say you've missed me?"

Her mouth drew down into a pout. "You're laughing at me."

"Sorry." With an elaborate gesture, he passed the back of his hand across his mouth. When his hand came away, the grin had given way to a doleful grimace.

She fought it. He could see her struggling to hold on to her composure, but she couldn't do it. The laugh came bursting out like a young colt out of a corral.

"Lydia," he reprimanded her with mock gravity, "please! This is serious."

She slapped his chest and tried to pull away from him. "You always do this to me. I can't stay mad at you for even one minute."

He started another retort, but at that moment they heard Mother Whitmer's voice from down below them. "Breakfast is ready."

He turned, craning his head. "Be there in a minute," he called. He took Lydia's hand. "We'd better say our prayers."

As he led her to the side of the small bed with its straw-filled mattress, Lydia thought of the first time they had knelt together as man and wife and how strange it had seemed to her. Being pillars in the Presbyterian church, her family had prayed daily for as long as Lydia could remember. But it wasn't anything like this. They would gather in the parlor right after supper, sit on the couch with their hands properly clasped together, and then Josiah McBride would pray. It was typically a set prayer of some kind, spoken reverently but with formality and some stiffness.

Lydia said her own personal prayers every day as well, but as a child she had been frightened of kneeling in the dark; so she would always sit up in bed with the covers pulled up around her, bow her head, and let the words run through her heart. She never spoke the words aloud. Somewhere as a child she had heard that if you didn't speak out loud, the devil couldn't know what you were praying for.

So on that first night after they were married, when Nathan knelt down at the side of their bed she was caught completely off guard. Seeing the look on her face, he patted the spot next to him. As she knelt to join him, he spoke with great solemnity. "Lydia, I think we need to decide right here and now that we will say our prayers every night and every morning and ask God to bless our marriage and help us to live the gospel better." She had responded instantly with enthusiasm, and she would ever love him the more for suggesting it. But the form Nathan suggested took some getting used to. Each time, one prayed aloud vocally for the two of them. Then they continued kneeling while each said a silent prayer.

It had felt strange to Lydia at first, to speak them aloud, but now their twice-daily ritual was something she treasured. It had been a major factor in her own spiritual development. And she marvelled at that. She had come so far in six months. She knew now what Paul meant when he spoke of the "fruits of the Spirit"—love, joy, peace, gentleness, goodness, faith. She knew why the influence of the Holy Ghost was sometimes called a "prompting," and knew the joy of following those promptings. She also understood why the Holy Ghost was called the Comforter. More than once during Nathan's absence, when the ache of being alone, or some noise outside her room, left her frightened or in turmoil, she had prayed and felt that calm, sweet, gentle peace that only the Spirit could bring.

"It's your turn, Lydia."

She nodded, then dropped her head, squeezing his hand tightly as she closed her eyes and began to pray.

When they were finished, Nathan stood quickly and pulled her up. As she straightened he laid a hand on her stomach, cocking his head slightly as though to listen.

"Silly," she laughed. "It's too soon to feel anything. It's not even two months yet."

He grinned, a little sheepishly. "Remember, you promised you'd tell me as soon as you feel life."

"I will," she said. "Come on, let's go downstairs."

Joseph and Emma had moved back to Fayette from Harmony the latter part of August when Emma's father began to believe all the falsehoods being circulated about Joseph and life became unbearable for them. Nathan and Lydia had gone to Fayette along with the rest of Nathan's family (minus Benjamin, of course) for the second general conference of the Church held near the end of September.

It had been Lydia's first chance, since becoming a member of the Church, to watch Joseph in action close at hand, and she came away deeply impressed. There had been problems to deal with. Hiram Page, a son-in-law to the Whitmers, had found a round stone and claimed he was getting revelation. The Saints were fascinated with the idea that the city of Zion would be built on the American continent as prophesied in the Book of Mormon. Hiram's "revelations" revealed its future location, and the Whitmers and Oliver Cowdery accepted them as from God, even though Joseph strongly disagreed and pointed out that these revelations were in contradiction to the revelations he had already received from God, which said that the location of Zion had not yet been revealed.

Benjamin, who heard about the controversy from his family before they left for the conference, was amused by it all and flatly predicted that Joseph would have to expel Oliver Cowdery and Hiram Page from the Church or surrender control to them. But it had not been anything like that, and Lydia began to understand why Nathan so loved and admired Joseph. Realizing the conference was coming, Joseph decided not to do any more than talk to the brethren about the situation. He also turned to the Lord in prayer and received a revelation directed to Oliver. The revelation clearly stated that Hiram Page was getting his revelations from a false source and directed Oliver to correct the situation. As the conference began, there was no animosity, no bitter recriminations. All present, including Oliver and Hiram, renounced the stone and the revelations received through it as false.

That had opened the way for an outpouring of the Spirit like that witnessed in days of old. It had been a glorious experience for Lydia. They partook of the sacrament, confirmed and ordained many of those who had been previously baptized, and conducted numerous items of Church business. As Joseph put it near the end of the conference, "We have had much of the power of God manifested amongst us; the Holy Ghost has come upon us, and filled us with joy unspeakable; and peace, and faith, and hope, and charity have abounded in our midst."

"Amen," Lydia had breathed.

More important, Joseph had received three different revelations either just before, during, or right after the conference. And that was why she and Nathan had returned to Fayette now, less than a month later. In the revelation given to correct the Hiram Page problem there was an item of much interest to the Saints. Oliver Cowdery was told, "You shall go unto the Lamanites and preach my gospel unto them, and cause my church to be established among them." He was also told that the city of Zion would be somewhere near the "borders by the Lamanites." The Saints understood that to mean Indian Territory.

Just four months previously, President Andrew Jackson had signed into law the Indian Removal Act. For decades the white settlers had clamored for the removal of the native tribes from the Eastern States to permanent Indian settlements. Now it was law, and thousands of Indians were on their way west. Pawnee, Choctaw, Cherokee, Osage, Seminole—more than a dozen tribes were destined for resettlement along the western borders of Missouri, Iowa, and Arkansas, which constituted the western border of the United States.

But the call to Oliver raised some difficult questions. Indian Territory lay over a thousand miles to the west. The journey would take him through largely unsettled and uncivilized territory. Was he to undertake this arduous and dangerous trip alone? Joseph submitted the problem to the Lord, and to the joy of at least one person there, the answer came back: Oliver was to be accompanied by three others—Peter Whitmer, Jr., Ziba Peterson, and Parley P. Pratt. Parley had literally leaped into the air. His promissory notes had been fulfilled.

Preparations for their departure had begun immediately and were now coming to fruition. The sisters around Palmyra and Fayette had undertaken to make the clothing and other items the men would need as they turned their faces west and plunged into the wilderness. Lydia, Melissa, and Mary Ann had been furiously knitting scarves and mittens, stockings and sweaters. Others were making woolen coats, shirts, and trousers. Men were cutting the leather for boots and knapsacks. Now they had all come to Fayette to complete the preparations.

———•———

There were more than a dozen people in the kitchen when Lydia and Nathan came down the stairs. Peter Whitmer and his boys—David, John, Jacob, Christian, Peter, Jr.—were seated at the table, already eating. Next to David was Hiram Page. Joseph and Oliver had already finished and had pulled their chairs back. They were huddled together talking softly. Elizabeth Ann, the youngest of the Whitmer children, watched Oliver from the corner with unabashed admiration. Though she was not yet sixteen, there was no mistaking her interest in the handsome schoolteacher from Palmyra. Mary Whitmer—Mother Whitmer, as her family and the Saints called her—was at the large stone fireplace which took up half of the south wall, stirring a large pot of oatmeal porridge. Her oldest daughter, Catherine, wife to Hiram Page, was at the small oak table, cutting off slices of bread and handing them to Thankful Pratt, Parley's young wife. On the other side of the fireplace, Parley stood warming his hands. He had obviously been outside helping with the chores. He still had on a coat and hat, and his cheeks were touched with pink. Emma, looking pale and drawn, sat in a chair on the opposite side of the fire, watching Joseph and Oliver talking. As Nathan and Lydia entered the room there was a chorus of good mornings and hellos.

Lydia walked directly over to Emma and crouched down in front of her. "Good morning, Sister Emma."

"Good morning, Lydia."

"Are you feeling any better?"

She managed a smile. "Yes, I'm doing fine this morning."

Lydia nodded but didn't believe it for a moment. Emma's eyes, usually lustrous and among her most striking features, were dull and listless. Dark circles beneath them made them seem more sunken than they were. Emma had not been well for almost a month. She was pregnant again, and judging from how large she already was at three months, Mary Whitmer was predicting twins for her. She had lost her first baby, and there was much concern among the women, especially with her condition now.

Joseph's head came up as he watched Lydia talking to his wife. He stood and came over to join them. He took Emma's hand and began to rub the back of it. "Emma, you do still look very tired. Won't you please just go back upstairs and rest for a time?"

She smiled up at him. "We have to finish those last two overcoats and the undershirts. The missionaries have got to have warm clothing."

She was right, of course. It was already past the season for safe travel, and these four men were preparing to launch out on foot on a trip that would take them more than two thousand miles by the time they returned. Unfortunately, the Lord had said nothing about waiting until the weather was more hospitable, so October or not, they would leave the day after tomorrow.

"We can do it, Emma," Lydia said. "Nathan and I don't have to be back for anything. I can help. You go rest."

She shook her head. "It will take every pair of hands to get things ready by then."

Joseph straightened and looked at Lydia. "She pushes herself so hard. She just won't let up."

"Just like you do," Emma chided him.

"But I'm not sick."

"I'm not that sick either. Just a little tired. I'll be fine, Joseph." She reached out and took his hand. "You and the men go collect the firewood, and we sisters will get breakfast over with and start to work."

———•———

"Is it true, Emma, that Joseph received a revelation just for you?"

Elizabeth Ann Whitmer, the youngest of the Whitmer children, was stitching up the hem on a heavy woolen coat. Even at fifteen she was an excellent seamstress, and her eyes did not leave Emma's face as her fingers fairly flew in and out with the needle.

Emma smiled at her. "Yes."

Her older sister, Catherine, looked up from where she was helping her mother cut out pieces of cotton cloth from a pattern traced on newspaper. "Really? Just for you?"

"Yes. Joseph received it in July just after he came back from one of his trips to Colesville."

Lydia looked at Emma more closely. The two of them were working on sewing the pieces of cloth together. Each had a sleeve and sewed it into one side of what would be a heavy undershirt. Lydia was doing the left side, Emma the right. When they finished they handed it to Thankful Pratt, who then sewed the whole shirt together.

Emma colored slightly under Lydia's gaze. "What a wonderful thing that must be," Lydia said.

"Yes," Thankful echoed. "Imagine, a personal revelation, direct from the Lord. Just for you."

"What did it say?" Elizabeth Ann said, her eyes eager.

"Elizabeth," Mother Whitmer chided. "It's not polite to pry."

"Oh, I don't mind, Mother Whitmer. It was a wonderful experience." Emma dropped the piece of material into her lap and sat back. "The Lord called me his daughter. He told me that my sins were forgiven me, and then he said I was an elect lady."

"An elect lady," Catherine breathed. "What a wonderful title!"

"You are an elect lady, Emma," Lydia said quickly. "We all think you are the perfect match for Joseph."

The color deepened along Emma's cheekbones. "Why, thank you, Lydia. What a kind thing to say."

"We all agree," Thankful said fervently. The Whitmer ladies all nodded vigorous agreement.

Emma went on. "Let's see . . . oh, yes, he told me that my calling was to be a comfort to Joseph, that I was to console him in times of affliction."

"Heaven knows you've had enough of those," Mother Whitmer broke in.

"The Lord also said that I was to serve as a scribe for Joseph. I've done that before, so that wasn't a great surprise."

"What else?" Elizabeth Ann pressed.

"I am to make a collection of hymns for the Church."

That brought all of their heads up. "Really?"

"Yes. I love how he said it too. The Lord said that he delights in the song of the heart, that the song of the righteous is like a prayer unto him."

"Hmm," Lydia murmured. "Isn't that interesting? There are some churches that say that music is evil and refuse to sing any hymns. But music can always touch my heart about as fast as anything."

"Mine too," Catherine said.

Emma dropped her eyes now and stared at her hands. The others fell silent, sensing there was more she wanted to say. Finally she took a breath and looked up, letting her eyes run from one to the other. "The Lord also told me that I was not to murmur about the things which I had not been allowed to see. They had been withheld from me for a wise purpose."

"What is that supposed to mean?" Lydia wondered.

"The gold plates."

"Oh."

Emma went on now, her voice very quiet. "Back in Harmony, right at the first, I sometimes served as scribe for Joseph. I knew the plates were there, because I had seen the outline of them covered by a linen tablecloth. But as Joseph translated he always arranged things so that I didn't see the plates themselves. I wanted to see them, but Joseph said that he could show them to no one unless the Lord told him to."

She looked over at Mother Whitmer, her eyes large and sorrowful. "I didn't mind that too much, I guess. Martin Harris had not been allowed to see them. Neither was Oliver when he came. So I felt a little better. Then . . ." She let it die with a little shake of her head and picked up her sewing again.

Elizabeth Ann and Thankful blurted it out at exactly the same moment. "What?"

Mother Whitmer was nodding in understanding. "Then I had my experience."

Emma looked up, the pain evident on her face now. "Yes," she whispered. "When you came back into the house that night and told us what had happened, I couldn't believe it. I was really upset."

"What, Mother?" Elizabeth Ann said, totally caught up now in Emma's account. "What experience?"

Catherine was looking intently at her mother. "You mean with Moroni?"

"Yes."

Both Lydia and Thankful jerked around sharply. "You saw Moroni?" Thankful blurted.

Mother Whitmer laid the scissors down. "Yes."

"Go ahead, Mother Whitmer," Emma said, smiling her encouragement. "I have come to grips with this now. I don't mind at all. Tell them what happened."

Mary Whitmer's face was illumined with a happy glow as she half closed her eyes in remembrance. "It was shortly after Joseph and Emma moved here from Harmony with Oliver. This would have been a year ago last May or June. Well, as you know, Father Whitmer and I don't have a small family, and our cabin is not large and spacious. We were already crowded. Then in one day we added three more adults to our family."

"The burden fell directly on her shoulders," Emma explained

to Lydia. "Father Whitmer and the boys were busy with the farming. Oliver and Joseph spent all day translating. I was still not in good health and not of much help."

"You were of great help," Mary said firmly. "But it was still a great deal of work. I began to wonder why this had come upon me, why I was asked to make such a sacrifice." She sighed. "Then one night, after finishing my many duties, I started out to milk the cows. To my surprise, as I came around the barn there was a stranger standing there. He was dressed in plain clothing and had a knapsack on his back."

"And it was Moroni?" Elizabeth Ann burst out. She obviously had not heard this story from her mother before.

Sister Pratt was troubled. "But I thought Joseph said Moroni was glorious and wonderful to behold."

Mary Whitmer nodded thoughtfully. "I suspect he appeared as a normal man to me so I would not be frightened. I wasn't; I was just surprised to see this stranger standing there in our yard. It was only later that Joseph told me it must have been Moroni."

"What happened?" Lydia was like Elizabeth Ann. She was eager to hear this story told and wanted Mother Whitmer to get on with it.

"He came up to me and said, 'You have been very faithful and diligent in your labors, but you are tired because of the increase of your toil. It is proper therefore that you should receive a witness, that your faith may be strengthened.'

"With that, he untied the knapsack on his back and removed from it the gold plates. He held them right in front of me," she said, her voice tinged with awe. "He turned over each leaf one by one and pointed out the engravings."

"So you actually saw them?" Thankful breathed. "You saw the gold plates?"

"Yes. As clear as I see you now. Then Moroni told me that I was to be patient in bearing the increased burdens. If I did so and endured in faith to the end, my reward would be sure."

For several moments the Whitmer kitchen was silent as the women contemplated what they had just heard. Then something occurred to Lydia. She turned to Emma. "Did Joseph's mother ever get to see the plates?"

Emma shook her head. "No."

She turned back to Mother Whitmer. "So you're the only woman who got to see the plates?"

She nodded, not returning Lydia's gaze but watching Emma closely.

"Do you know how that made me feel?" Emma asked softly. "It was not as if *I* hadn't been asked to sacrifice. It was not as if *I* hadn't been carrying a burden." Her voice suddenly broke. "I lost the baby. . . ."

She couldn't finish, and Lydia got up quickly and went to her. But Emma gave a little shake of her head and waved her back.

"I'm all right," she said. "For a long time I was really hurt by it all. What had I done wrong that the Lord would not give me that privilege? I suppose that's why the Lord told me not to murmur."

"But why wouldn't he allow you to see them?" Elizabeth Ann demanded with all the subtlety of youth.

For a long moment Emma stared back at her, then she finally shook her head very slowly. "I don't know. But . . ." Her head came up, and this time the smile was genuine and deep and touched her eyes as well as her mouth. "But for now, I am trying very hard not to murmur."

It was a cold and drizzly December day in western Missouri. The wife of Joshua Steed sat rigidly in her sitting room, not meeting Doctor Jonathan Hathaway's saddened eyes. To say that she hated this man would be to overstate the case, but Jessica Steed certainly found everything about him distasteful—his perfectly fashionable clothing, his clipped New England accent, the way he minced when he walked, his habit of speaking to Joshua about her as though she were not in the room. Many of the other women in town thought it wonderful to have a real doctor from back East, but she could barely tolerate him.

He laid a hand on her shoulder and she cringed, fighting the temptation to jerk away. "I'm really sorry, Mrs. Steed." The words were right, but there was no sorrow in his voice—only that clinical detachment that so characterized Doctor Hathaway. "You don't seem to have any problems conceiving a child, but your body just can't carry them full term."

Jessie nodded woodenly. It had started again yesterday, the

cramping, the pain, the bleeding. And the anguish in Joshua's eyes. "I understand, Doctor. Thank you."

He was shaking his head, not looking at her, faintly irritated because she had presented him with a problem beyond his medical abilities. He didn't like to think that anything was beyond his abilities.

"Am I all right now? May I go out?"

"Yes. You're still a little weak, but I think you'll be fine if you take things a bit easy."

She stood up. "Have you told my husband this?"

"What?"

"About your opinion that I'm not able to carry children."

His eyes dropped and his fingers fumbled at his watch fob. Of course he had.

"And what did he say?" she asked quietly.

Again he would not meet her eyes.

"Where is he now?" He didn't answer. She already knew. "Which saloon?"

"Now, Mrs. Steed," he began, a little indignantly, "you've got to realize, when a man's got his heart set on having children, he's bound—"

She cut him off curtly. "I'll not be needin' your services any longer."

His head snapped around, and for a moment his mouth went on working, though no sound came out.

"Thank you for your efforts. My husband will see that you are paid adequately."

"But, Mrs. Steed . . . ," he spluttered.

"You already said it, Doctor. I can't carry children. So I'll not be needin' your services any longer."

"But Mr. Steed and I have an agreement. I can't just—"

"Yes, Doctor," Jessie said bitterly, "you can. And don't be worrying about telling him. I'm on my way to find him now. I'll explain that it was my decision." She turned her back on him. "Good-bye, Doctor Hathaway."

She stood motionless, listening to his muttering as he got his hat and walking stick and left, slamming the door behind him. Inwardly, she was trembling, but at the same time she felt a thrill of exhilaration. She had done it. The little barmaid had spoken her mind. The daughter of Clinton Roundy, the timid girl who had once found it difficult to raise her head and look anyone in the eye, had stood her ground, had made her will be known. That, at least, was one thing she could thank Joshua for.

She took a deep breath, then walked to where her shawl was draped over a chair. This next confrontation would be much more difficult, but the anger burning way down deep inside her was still there. Maybe it would be enough to see this one through as well.

She found him in one of her father's taverns, bottle of whiskey in front of him, playing poker with his foreman and some of the other men of the town. Her father was behind the long bar that filled one end of the room.

She paused at the door for several moments, peering inside. She had not been inside either of her father's saloons for over a year, but the moment she smelled the stale smell of beer, the tobacco, sawdust, and unwashed bodies, the memories all came flooding back. In that instant she knew she hated it, hated it all, hated the idea that men needed some kind of place where they could be with other men, where they could talk "men talk," where they could turn to the bottle or the jug to find whatever courage or solace they thought they needed.

Good, she thought. The anger was still there. It would be enough. She pushed through the swinging doors and walked into the room.

Joshua looked up in surprise, then almost instantly his brows lowered and his face darkened. "I thought I told you that I didn't like you comin' in these places anymore."

She stopped directly in front of him. The men at the table had frozen in position and were staring at her. The other men at the bar and around the tables were also gawking. They knew who she was, but they also knew that Joshua Steed had said his wife wouldn't be found in no saloon anymore.

"I would like to talk with you, Joshua."

His jaw tightened. "Not here."

"Then come outside with me."

"I'm busy," he growled.

There was a snicker from the man across the table from Joshua. Jessie turned and looked at him, and the sneer on his face instantly faded. He began to study his cards carefully. She turned back to her husband. "It makes no difference to me," she said evenly. "We can go outside or stay in here. But I need to talk with you."

He laid his cards down, very slowly, tipping his chair back on its two legs. "Jessie, I'm warnin' you." He wasn't stone drunk, but she could tell from the heaviness of his speech that he had been drinking steadily. It always made him sullen, mean, ugly. She hated it.

Her father was coming around from behind the bar, wiping his hands on his apron and calling even as he came. "Jessie, honey, what brings you here?"

She didn't turn, just looked down into the eyes of her husband. "I told Doctor Hathaway I would not be needin' his services any longer."

The chair came back down with a crash. "What?"

She was aware that every eye was fixed on her, but she no longer cared. "I can't carry a child. There's nothing he can do about it. I told him not to come back."

She spun on her heel and walked swiftly out of the tavern, her head high, her face calm.

———————

Matthew Steed was now ten and a half years old. He was still short for his age, but had hit into a growth spurt which left his feet poking too far out of his trousers and his hands too far out of his coat sleeves. It endeared him all the more to his mother, who felt a touch of sadness when she realized that the last of her children was soon to be a child no more.

"Did you get all the eggs gathered, Matthew?"

"Yes, Mama."

Becca looked up from where she was practicing writing on a piece of slate with a piece of soapstone. "Did you check behind the manger where the old white biddy loves to hide hers?"

"Yes." This time it was said with a touch of exasperation. He didn't like having to report to his sister, who was only two years older than he was anyway.

"Good," Mary Ann said. "Where's your pa?"

"He's still over to Mr. Harris's house."

Mary Ann nodded, pleased. Perhaps Martin was making good on his promise to talk some more to her husband about Joseph and the Restoration.

Matthew started to shuck off his coat, but at that moment there was the sound of steps on the front porch. The door flew open and Melissa came bursting in. Flakes of snow speckled her coat, and her cheeks and nose were bright patches of red. She was breathing hard, her breath frosting in the cold air that she brought with her into the house.

"Melissa," her mother said in surprise. "I thought you were going to stay over at Carma Lynn's house tonight."

"I was," she gasped. She pushed the door shut, leaning over to better catch her breath.

"My word, Melissa, what's the matter?"

"I ran. Most of the way."

"You what?" Her mother moved to her in alarm.

"I'm all right." She turned to Matthew, still panting heavily. "Get Nathan and Lydia. Tell them to come. Quick!"

Now Mary Ann was really alarmed. "Melissa, what is it? What's wrong?"

"Nothing bad. I saw Hyrum. In the village." She stopped, noting that Matthew hadn't moved. "Go, Matthew!" Then to her mother, "There's important news from Joseph."

———◆———

Melissa had her hands wrapped around a bowl of hot soup, savoring the warmth. She sensed that she had the undivided attention of her family, and seemed to enjoy holding them in suspense for a moment.

Nathan knew exactly what she was doing and couldn't wait any longer. "All right, Melissa, what is it? You had Matthew running like a scared rabbit."

"And Matthew almost threw us into a panic," Lydia said. "We thought the house had caught on fire or something."

"Yes, Melissa," her mother said, "tell us about this news from Hyrum."

She pushed back a strand of her dark hair from her face, her eyes shining with excitement. "Well, you know about the two men who came from Ohio to see Joseph two weeks ago?"

"Yes," Nathan said. "Sidney Rigdon and Edward Partridge."

"And you know all about their report of what is happening there?"

"Yes."

The arrival of the two men from the West had come as an exciting surprise for the Saints in New York. Sidney Rigdon and Edward Partridge were two of the converts Oliver Cowdery, Parley Pratt, and the other two missionaries to the Lamanites had made in Ohio, though Partridge was not actually baptized until after they met Joseph. When the four missionaries continued their journey westward, Sidney and Edward had determined to come east, meet the Prophet, and tell him what had happened in Ohio.

It was a startling report. After preaching the gospel at an encampment of Indians of the Cattaraugus tribe near Buffalo, New York, Oliver Cowdery and the other missionaries to the Lamanites had continued westward. Parley Pratt convinced his companions that there might be merit in setting their path through the Western Reserve in Ohio. He had not forgotten the "seekers" and the preacher who led them.

Nearly two years earlier the Lord had given a revelation to Joseph Smith, Sr. "The field is white already to harvest," he promised. "He that thrusteth in his sickle with his might, the same layeth up in store that he perish not."

How true that proved to be in Ohio! Parley and his companions went directly to the house of Sidney Rigdon, Parley's friend and former spiritual leader, who lived in Mentor, Ohio. Sidney was skeptical at first but agreed to listen. And more important, he agreed to "seek." He convinced most of his congregation to do the same. Five miles from Mentor was the village of Kirtland, where many of Sidney's congregation lived. The missionaries went from house to house, bearing the news of a restoration.

The people thronged the missionaries night and day, so much so that they had little time for rest or retirement. Many came out of curiosity; others to mock and dispute and disrupt. But Sidney Rigdon had prepared the soil well. He had planted the seeds, and now it was time to reap the harvest. Within three weeks of the arrival of the missionaries, they had baptized one hundred twenty-seven people! Among those baptized were Sidney Rigdon and a goodly share of his congregation.

The report of this incredible success in Ohio shocked the New York Saints. As 1830 drew to a close, Joseph estimated that stretching from Palmyra to Canandaigua, from Fayette to Colesville, there were about seventy members of the Church. That report was received with gratitude and amazement. Seventy members, in less than nine months! Then Sidney and Edward had come with the report that there was now twice that number in Ohio. In one stroke the four missionaries sent to the Lamanites had nearly trebled the membership of the Church!

"Yes, yes," Mary Ann was saying, "we know all about that. So what is this news from Hyrum?"

"Yes, Melissa," Lydia said, "don't make us wait a moment longer."

Melissa smiled secretively, then reached in the pocket of her dress and pulled out a half piece of foolscap. There was writing on it. She waved it triumphantly in front of them. "Joseph received a revelation yesterday. Hyrum let me copy it."

Nathan reached for it, but Melissa laughed and snatched it away.

"Melissa!"

"Say please."

"What does it say? What does it say?" Matthew was getting

as impatient with her games as the rest of them.

She laid the paper down on the table and smoothed it out carefully. She looked up, the excitement fairly dancing in her eyes. "It's a short one, but what it says is very significant."

"Just tell us, for heaven's sake," Mary Ann burst out.

Laughing lightly, Melissa bent her head and began to read. " 'Behold I say unto you, that it is not expedient in me that ye should translate any more until ye shall go to the Ohio.' "

She stopped, pleased to see the sudden shock on Nathan's face. It was not the word *translate* that threw Nathan. He knew that Joseph and Sidney had been working on a translation of the Bible during the past two weeks, a project begun by Joseph back in June. This was not a translation in the normal sense of working from the original languages and putting them into English; rather, it was using the power of the Spirit to restore what had been lost or to correct what had been changed over the centuries. Several significant things, including the lost Prophecy of Enoch, had been given to Joseph during this period. What had caught Nathan's attention was another word. "Joseph is going to Ohio?" he said slowly.

Melissa nodded, as wisely as though she were a sage. "But that's not all. Listen to this." Again her head dipped as she looked down at the paper. " 'And again a commandment I give unto the church, that it is expedient in me that they should assemble together at the Ohio, against the time that my servant Oliver shall return unto them.' "

She sat back, folding the paper. The game was over and she was suddenly completely sober. "There it is," she said softly. "The Lord has called the Church to move to Ohio."

Joshua came home about midnight. He opened the door with great care, then shut it softly. He would sleep on the sofa, not go upstairs at all. There was no sense disturbing Jessie tonight. Morning would be soon enough. Right now he felt like a sheep hide stretched out on a rack and left in the sun to cure. His eyes felt puffy and inflamed.

He took off his coat and tossed it on a wall peg near the door. He tiptoed to the table, found the candle in its holder, then moved to where a few coals still glowed in the fireplace. He knelt down and touched the wick to the hot spot, blowing softly until it burst into flame. He straightened, waiting a moment for the flickering light to fill the room, before turning. When he did so, he jumped, nearly dropping the candle. Jessie was sitting in the large overstuffed chair, watching him, her eyes large and dark in the flickering shadows of the dimly lit room. He recovered his composure quickly. "I thought you were asleep."

"No."

He moved to a chair and sat down, setting the candle on a small table close by. "Look, Jessie, I . . ." He undid the top button on his shirt and leaned back. He had once thought of her eyes as being like those of a fawn—eyes that told him she was shy, frightened, ready to bolt at the first sign of danger. Not tonight. Now her eyes were steady, filled with determination. "Look, I know this last thing has upset you, but—"

"It's not a thing, Joshua. It's called a miscarriage. It's called losing the baby."

He shook his head. This was going to be even worse than he feared. "I know that," he said. "I also know you're upset."

"Do you?"

"Of course," he snapped. "I'm upset too. You think I wanted you to lose it?"

She looked away. "No," she whispered, "I don't think that."

"Then why are you takin' on like this?"

Her head came back around. "Like what, Joshua?"

"I brought Doc Hathaway out here for one reason and one reason only. It cost me a lot of money, you know."

"I know."

"Then why did you send him away?"

"Did you ask me, Joshua?"

"Did I ask you what?"

"Did you even think to ask me how I might feel about that?"

"Feel about what?" he shot back. "Do you want a baby or not?"

It was as if he had struck her. She looked away and her eyes were filled with tears. Instantly he was contrite. He got up and walked over to her. "Jessie, I'm sorry. I know how badly you wanted to carry each of these babies."

He laid a hand over hers, which were locked together and lying rigid in her lap. "I just wanted to help. Doctor Hathaway is the best there is. I thought it would help."

"Doctor Hathaway is an insufferable prig."

For a moment he just stared at her, then he grinned. "You know, all this book learnin' you're doing lately is sure making you talk fancy all of a sudden."

For a moment she stared at him in disbelief, then she quickly withdrew her hands from his and turned away. He sighed. He'd done it again. He hadn't meant to make fun of her. She just sounded so unlike the Jessica Roundy he had married. "I'm sorry, Jess. I didn't mean that."

"I won't see him again," she said coldly.

He straightened, feeling the throbbing in his head. He felt as though somebody had pumped it full of Missouri River mud. He was too tired to negotiate his way through the subtleties of feminine emotions tonight. "Whatever you say. We'll talk about it in the morning."

He started to move toward the stairs, unbuttoning the rest of his shirt.

"Losing the baby's only part of it, isn't it?"

He stopped, not turning. "What's that supposed to mean?"

"This thing that's drivin' you to the bottle. I know you're sorry that we can't have children, but that's not the only thing eatin' at you, is it?"

He swung around. "Leave it alone, Jess," he warned.

She leaped up. "No! I won't leave it alone. Because you won't leave it alone. She still keeps eatin' at you."

He dropped his hands from his shirt. "Lydia McBride has nothing to do with this issue."

"Doesn't she?" Jessie cried. Her voice had gone shrill now. "You and your precious Lydia. Ever since you learned that she's up and married your brother, that's all you can think of anymore."

He let out his breath slowly, trying to keep his temper in check. Then he thought about the baby and the anguished look on her face when it had all started again. He stepped to her and reached for her hands. "Jess," he said softly, "this has been a hard two days for you. You're upset. Let's talk about it in the morning."

She jerked away, flinging his hand aside. "Don't you patronize me!"

He stepped back, stung. "Patronize?" he sneered. "Is that what I'm doing, your highness of the big words? Patronizing you?"

"That's right. You can't stand it that I'm learning things, can you? That I don't have to depend on the mighty Joshua Steed for my every need anymore?"

He shook his head wearily. "I'm not gonna talk to you when you're like this. When you're ready, then I'll talk. Until then, good night." He turned, but hesitated, almost daring her to contradict this final edict.

"I'll tell you what you're looking for in the bottom of that bottle." She flung it at his back, desperate now to wound him. "You're looking for some way to blot out the picture of your dear, sweet Lydia married to your brother. Well, she's probably carrying his baby by now."

Joshua spun around and slapped her, hard—hard enough that it snapped her head back. For a moment shock and hurt filled her eyes, then they narrowed. Her chin came up and she squared her shoulders. The imprint of his hand was already showing bright red on her cheek, visible even in the dim light. "That won't make it go away either," she whispered.

His hand came back up, and for several seconds he stood there, chest heaving, eyes blazing like the infernos of hell itself. Then he let his hand drop to his side again. "At least," he breathed, "Lydia *can* have children."

He turned, grabbed his coat, and stalked out of the front door, slamming it hard enough that it rattled the windows.

As the sound echoed through the room, Jessie dropped her head into her hands. There was no sound, but in a moment, her shoulders began to shake convulsively and her fingers dug into the flesh of her face.

On the second day of January in the year 1831, a conference of the Church was held at the Peter Whitmer, Sr., cabin in Fayette. The revelation received a week or so earlier had caused no small stir among the Saints. Following Joseph's opening remarks several people asked him about the call to gather to Ohio. In the presence of the congregation, Joseph inquired of the Lord and immediately received a revelation.

As Lydia McBride Steed listened to Joseph give them the Lord's answer, part of the words struck her with great force.

" 'And that ye might escape the power of the enemy, and be gathered unto me a righteous people, without spot and blameless: wherefore, for this cause I gave unto you the commandment, that ye should go to the Ohio: and there I will give unto you my law, and there you shall be endowed with power from on high.' "

Lydia felt a great cry well up inside her. *But what about our farm? What about the cabin Nathan built for me with his own hands? What about my flower garden and my vegetables?*

Over the past months Lydia had developed some surprising feelings about the plot of land that she and Nathan lived upon. She was a village girl, born and raised above the store that her father owned. She had never had the pleasure of seeing land plowed and sown, the sweeping green carpet of spring wheat replacing the rich black of the soil and then eventually becoming a waving sea of gold as harvest time approached. She had loved their little plot of land. She loved working at Nathan's side as he tamed it and made it submit to his will. Were they simply to walk away from all that now?

And then, as though the Lord had heard her inward cry, a few moments later came this: " 'And they that have farms, that can not be sold, let them be left or rented as seemeth them good.' "

She turned to Nathan. She could see the sorrow in his eyes too. But there was also something resolute on his face. "Are we going to go?" she mouthed silently to him.

For several moments he just looked at her; then finally, slowly, but with no doubt in his eyes, he nodded, then nodded again.

As the wagon loaded with bags of wheat swung around and headed down the lane, Melissa raised her hand and waved. "Good-bye, Papa."

Benjamin turned and lifted a hand.

"Good luck with those men from New York City."

He waved again, then turned his attention back to the mules pulling the wagon.

She watched him until the wagon turned onto the road that led south into Palmyra Village. A moment later he and the wagon disappeared behind the trees that lined the creek between their farm and the Martin Harris property. He had high hopes for the day's wheat auction. The buyers from Baltimore and Philadelphia and New York City were moving through western New York buying everything they could get their hands on. The market was good, and it looked like Benjamin Steed would continue to prosper.

Melissa stood on the porch for another minute, then the cold began to penetrate beneath her coat. Shivering, she turned and hurried into the house.

As she came into the warmth of the main living room of their cabin, her mother gave her a strange look. Melissa knew why. Her father went into Palmyra several times a month for one reason or another. Normally Melissa gave him a quick kiss on the cheek and said good-bye from the comfort of the house. Today she had bundled up and gone outside to watch him load the last of the wheat, then stayed on the porch long enough to see him gone.

Well, there was a purpose in that, and Melissa decided there was no profit in delaying it further. She took off her coat and scarf and hung them up, then slipped the heavy woolen mittens in the top drawer of the chest that stood by the door. When she was finished she went to the table and sat down. "Mama, can we talk?"

Mary Ann was in the portion of the room that served as their kitchen. She was pounding some coarse cornmeal into a finer flour, using a wooden pestle and a large wooden bowl. She stopped. For a moment she debated. The cake needed to be started soon or it would not be done by the time Benjamin returned.

"Please, Mama."

She set the bowl aside, dusted off her hands on her apron, and came over to sit beside her daughter. "What is it, Melissa? You look troubled."

"I am troubled," she cried. She had been stewing and fretting about this for almost a month, and now the emotions came out in a rush. "Mama, I want to go to Kirtland."

Mary Ann's face softened. "I know, Melissa. I know."

"No, Mama, I *really* want to go!" Instantly she was sorry, and reached out and placed her hand over her mother's. "I know you do too, Mama. But I also know that Papa will never agree. You've heard what he says."

Mary Ann sighed, and it was a sound of deep sorrow. "As you know, your father has always had strong feelings against Joseph Smith. Then when Joshua and he . . ." The pain was too much and she looked away. "Your father has always held Joseph somewhat responsible for that."

"I know, Mama, but—"

Her mother went on quickly and Melissa stopped. "Now, Nathan and Lydia are going too. After all your father did to help Nathan run his farm last summer while he was in Colesville, he feels a little betrayed. And this time there is no question that Joseph is directly responsible for it."

Melissa's breath exploded in a burst of frustration. "I know that, Mama, but it *is* Nathan's farm. He and Lydia are married now. Papa can't be telling them what to do for the rest of their lives."

Mary Ann nodded sadly. "That's part of what's hurtin' him inside."

Melissa felt a sense of hopelessness sweep over her. "Mama, these last few weeks . . . I . . ." She shook her head, fighting back the tears.

"What, Melissa?"

"Mama, I've got to go," she whispered. "I've felt it so strongly lately. The Spirit is whispering to me that there's something waiting for me in Ohio."

For a long moment Mary Ann looked at her oldest daughter, and her eyes filled with affection and love. Melissa was not the Steed's first daughter. There had been Mary, born before Joshua and dead within an hour of her birth. When Melissa was born the cord had been wrapped twice around her neck. She was black from head to toe. Even now the feeling of terror came back to her. Was she to lose her second daughter as well?

Moving with the swiftness of experience, the midwife slashed the cord, unwound it from around Melissa's neck, then grabbed her by the heels and held her upside down. She slapped her across the buttocks, then again, the crack of her palm sharp and hard. "Breathe, baby, breathe!" Mary Ann cried from her bed. Then there was a soft gasp, followed instantly by a howling cry. It was just as though someone were pouring life into Melissa's body. A healthy red glow started from her chest; then, moving rapidly, spread upwards and downwards through her body, banishing the blackness.

For as long as she had life, Mary Ann would never forget the feelings she had as she then took the squalling baby in her arms. She could still picture Melissa's face, as clearly as though all this had happened just yesterday. She was furious at being so badly treated. The tiny fists were clenched; her face was screwed up in protest as she howled and howled and howled. Never had anything sounded so absolutely wonderful. Now her face carried a different kind of pain, and it cut deeply into Mary Ann's heart.

"I could go with Nathan and Lydia—," Melissa started, but Mary Ann shook her head. "Why, Mama?"

"You know Papa will never agree to that. They have no idea how they are going to get there or where they will be living once they arrive. They could be living in a tent. You're still single and—"

"Don't you think I know that!" It was flung out in desperation. "Mama, I'm almost twenty years old now. I'm old enough to do this."

"I know you are," Mary Ann said wearily, "and you know you are."

"But Papa won't accept it," Melissa finished for her.

"Melissa, Melissa." How could she make her understand? "Joshua is gone. Now Nathan and Lydia are leaving. If you go too, it will break his heart."

"Papa doesn't have a heart."

"Melissa Mary!"

She was instantly contrite. "I'm sorry, Mama. I love Papa. You know I do. But I'm so tired of being treated like a child. He treats me like he does Rebecca."

Mary Ann started to deny that, then just shook her head. "Melissa, can you be patient in this? I know you're anxious, but this is not the time to fight for it. It will be another month or so before everyone starts to leave. Maybe something will—"

"Joseph and Emma have already gone," Melissa said curtly. "They left two days ago with Brother Rigdon and Brother Partridge."

"I know, I know. But they had a sleigh and a horse. Everyone else is going to have to wait for the canal to open again. There's time."

Melissa stared at her mother for several seconds, then stood up slowly. "Is there, Mama?"

"Yes, there is. Be patient. Don't give up hope."

"All right, Mama," she said woodenly.

"Joshua?"

He looked up from the books, quill pen poised.

"Do you believe in angels?"

He grunted in disgust. "Of course not."

"Hmm." The book that had lowered slightly came up again, and in a moment Jessie was engrossed once more. For several minutes the only sound was the howling of the wind and the chatter of snow pellets against the window. It was the last day of January, and it was obvious that the winter of 1830-31—which had been a long, hard one—was still not ready to relinquish its hold on the Great Plains.

Joshua picked up another sheaf of freight bills and began to enter the figures in the ledger. After a moment he stopped and gave his wife a strange look. "What makes you ask a fool question like that?"

She didn't look up. "What?" she murmured.

He just glared at her.

Her eyes finally raised and looked at him over the top of the book. "What?" she repeated, this time paying attention.

"Why'd you ask that?"

"Why'd I ask what?"

"About the angels."

"Oh." She shrugged. "I heard some missionaries in town

talking about it. They were saying God still speaks to men today and that sometimes he does it through angels."

He humphed again, making his feelings clearly known, and went back to his figuring. Immediately Jessica went back to her reading.

Five minutes later Joshua finished. He wiped off the tip of the quill, capped the bottle of ink, and closed the book. He sat there for a moment, watching Jessie. It irritated him that she could get so totally caught up in her reading that she blocked things out around her. "What missionaries?" he said abruptly.

"Hmm?"

"Jessie!" It came out sharply.

It startled her, and the book clapped shut. "What?"

"What missionaries? I don't know about no missionaries in town."

"Oh, there was some who came in from back East just after the first of the year." She nodded, remembering. "In fact, it was after you left to take that shipment of salt pork to St. Louis. Supposedly they're going out to teach the Indians, but they've been preaching some to the whites too."

"What are you doin' listenin' to missionaries?"

She looked away quickly. "I was just passin' in the street. I only stopped for a minute. I was curious."

"And do you believe in angels?"

She overlooked his sarcastic sneer. "Hadn't really thought much about it till today."

"Well?"

"I don't know. I suppose I do. But I don't think they go around appearin' to people."

"That's good. Neither do I." Abruptly he stood up, the subject closed in his mind. "It's time for bed."

She glanced down at her book. "I'll be right there."

"Jessie, I said it's time for bed."

She sighed and put the book aside, not meeting his eyes.

As she moved to the lamp and picked it up, he watched her. The light caught her profile and showed the flatness of her stomach. He hesitated, not wanting to bring it up but not able to leave it alone. "You sure you won't consider seeing Doctor Hathaway again?"

She stiffened. "That subject is closed, Joshua. I told you that."

"Jessie, you can't give up. Not yet."

"I said that subject is closed." She strode away from him into the bedroom, not waiting for him to follow. By the time Joshua had gone around to pull the shutters tight and secure the front door and finally came in the bedroom, she had already slipped into her night dress and was sitting on the chair waiting for him. He sat down on the bed in front of her and put up one foot. She grabbed the boot and began to pull. It came off, and she dropped it with a clunk. He raised his other leg and put it in front of her.

"They claim this angel came back to bring a special book."

Now it was Joshua who was preoccupied. He was thinking about furs. The mountain men would be coming in from the West in the next month as spring began to break. Maybe this time he ought to take the furs all the way to New York City himself instead of selling them off in Cincinnati to the buyer there. A day or two before, he had seen a paper from Boston. In it were advertisements for women's coats, men's beaverskin hats. The prices had shocked him. It was clear someone was making a great deal of money on the furs, and it wasn't Joshua Steed. But maybe that could be corrected.

He looked up absently. "What?"

"The missionaries. They said they have a special book. They said an angel came and told some man about some gold plates buried in a hill." Jessie let his other boot drop to the floor. "Sounds pretty farfetched to me."

Joshua had been about to lower his other leg. It stopped in midair. "What did you say?" he said sharply.

Jessica was suddenly stammering. "I . . . I was just talking on, Joshua. I'm sorry."

He grabbed her hand. "What did you say? About gold plates?"

"It was nothin', Joshua. I didn't mean nothin' by it."

"Tell me!" he cried. "What about gold plates?"

She cowered back, not sure what she had done to trigger this. "The missionaries, they were talking about them. They had a book. I saw it. One of them held it up. They said it was trans-lated from these gold plates by some man in New York. An angel supposedly gave them to him."

She paused, glancing quickly at Joshua's face. There was a strange look of excitement mingled with anger, maybe even dis-gust. "I didn't believe it, Joshua," she added quickly. "Not any of it."

"Joseph Smith."

It startled Jessie. "What?"

"Was the man's name Joseph Smith? The one who got the plates?"

"I . . . I think so." She felt a rush of relief that this sudden in-tensity was not directed at her. "Yes, I think you're right. I think they did call him Smith."

"Where were these men from?"

"I don't remember if I heard."

His grip on her hand tightened like a vise. "Think, Jessie! Were they from New York?"

Her eyes narrowed as she thought back on what she had heard. "Yes, I think so. At least they talked about things that happened in New York. And they sounded like they was from back East."

"Where are these men?"

She hesitated. "Well, they were down by the courthouse."

"No, I mean where can I find them?"

"I don't know. I heard a lady say afterwards that they're stay-ing out in Kaw Township, but two of them have opened a tailor shop here in town so's they can support themselves."

Joshua grabbed his boots. "That must be that new shop down by the mercantile store." He stuffed one foot into a boot and began to pull hard.

"You're goin' there now?" Jessica asked in surprise. "It's after nine o'clock."

"Joseph Smith used to work for my family in Palmyra. If these men know Joseph, they may also know my family. I'm goin' now."

He pulled his other boot on, strode out of the bedroom, and grabbed his coat. In a moment he was gone, the door slamming shut behind him.

Jessica didn't move. The flickering light of the lamp reflected in her eyes, now wide and filled with hurt. After several moments, she stood slowly, blew out the lamp, and crawled into bed. But for a long time she lay there, staring into the darkness.

"Yes," she finally said, speaking to the ceiling, "and if they know about your family, they may also know about your precious Lydia."

It was only fifteen minutes later that Joshua returned. He slipped into the bedroom without lighting a lamp and undressed quietly.

"Did you find them?"

"No. The storekeeper next door thought they were out in Kaw Township. Either that or back across the line in Indian Territory. They don't stay in town every night."

"Oh." She tried to keep the relief out of her voice.

"I'll try again in a day or two."

Of course! But she did not answer him, and in a minute he slipped into bed beside her, turning his back to her. Five minutes later he was snoring softly.

———————•———————

In the northeastern corner of what would eventually become the state of Ohio lay an area known as the Western Reserve, so called because when the various colonies relinquished claims on their western lands, Connecticut compromised. They gave up all but a parcel in what would become Ohio, holding that reserve, which they then sold to a group of investors. One of them, General Moses Cleaveland, was sent to survey the land. Seven years later, the same year that Ohio was made the seventeenth state of the Union, Thomas Jefferson negotiated another of history's great land acquisitions, the Louisiana Purchase. Now the Mississippi River belonged to the United States, and suddenly Ohio had water access to the Gulf of Mexico and the Atlantic Ocean. By 1825, the year the Erie Canal was finished, work on the Ohio Canal was begun. When completed to the Ohio River, it opened up an extensive system of internal waterways. One could ship goods or travel by water from New York City to New Orleans or from the East Coast to Independence, Missouri, halfway across the continent. Ohio lay at the center of that vast network.

When first purchased, Ohio was one massive forest of trees—oak, maple, black walnut, locust, wild cherry, sycamores, and many more—with a thousand varieties of bushes and undergrowth that went with them. Settlers quickly learned to "head for the tall timber" as they discovered that the highest trees, the nut-bearing trees such as oak or beech, marked the best soil. Two years after that initial survey by Cleaveland, Judge Turhand Kirtland, one of the land agents for the Connecticut Land Company, came to Geauga County, Ohio, and surveyed two of the townships. The first family moved in and built a log cabin in 1811. Others quickly followed. By 1818 Judge Kirtland was selling some of his land for two and three dollars per acre, a handsome profit on land that had been purchased from Connecticut for about twenty-five or thirty cents an acre.

At first, agriculture was the primary occupation of Kirtland's residents. But the village was situated on the east branch of the Chagrin River, a meandering stream with several smaller tributaries. In an area near the river, known as Kirtland Flats, various mills and small factories began to develop. A sawmill was constructed in 1819. A year later a gristmill was added. There was a tannery, and an ashery which took wood ashes and turned them into the potash used in making soap. Grandison Newell started a factory to manufacture chairs, stands, beds, tables, candle boxes, and other wooden items.

In 1823 Sidney Gilbert and his partner, Newel K. Whitney, built a store near the riverbank and near the junction of the Chardon and Painesville roads. A brick kiln was begun nearby. In 1827 Peter French, who owned most of the land in the flats, built the first brick building, a two-story hotel across the street from the Whitney store. Kirtland had become a full-fledged village and was rapidly becoming an important location in northern Ohio.

It was to the Gilbert and Whitney store that Carlton Rogers came on the afternoon of February first, 1831. Carl, as all but his mother called him, was the oldest son of Hezekiah Rogers, owner and manager of Kirtland's largest and most prosperous livery stable. At twenty-two, he looked younger than his years. That was largely due to his red hair and the generous sprinkling of freckles that came with it. His skin was fair and prone to sunburn whether it was midwinter or the dead of summer. But he had a ready smile and a pleasant disposition, and Newel K. Whitney, the store's proprietor, was always pleased to see him come in the store.

"Good afternoon, Carl."

"Afternoon, Mr. Whitney."

"What can we do for you today?"

Carl removed his gloves and pulled a long paper from his trousers pocket. "I've got a whole list here."

The storekeeper took the paper, reached behind the counter, and pulled out a set of reading glasses. He perched them on the end of his nose and scanned the list. "Hmm. Looks like your pa is going to start that new carriage shed he's been talking about."

"Yep. Spring's coming. He'd like to get started on it."

"All right. Make yourself comfortable there by the stove. This will take a few minutes."

Five minutes later Carl looked up as Whitney brought a large coil of hemp rope and dropped it on the growing pile he was making in the center of the store's main room. "Hope you brought something to carry all this stuff in."

"I've got the wagon."

Whitney started to turn, then turned back. He lifted the glasses from off his nose and peered out of the window that was behind Carl.

Carl turned to see what had caught his attention. A horse-drawn sleigh had pulled up. There were four people in it, bundled up heavily in blankets and robes. The two men in front had scarves covering the lower part of their faces, and so it was difficult to tell who they were. The man in the back, the one closest to them, jumped down lightly, then turned to the person who had been sitting next to him. Carl could see now that it was a woman. Her face was red and she looked very cold.

"That someone you know?" Whitney asked.

Carl shook his head. "Ain't never seen him before."

"Hmm. Must be strangers in town."

The man outside turned, looked up at the sign on the storefront above the porch, then bounded up the steps. The bell on the door tinkled as he opened it, then shut it again firmly. He was a tall man, a good six feet. As he unwound the scarf from around his neck and face, he looked at the two people watching him. Carl noted that his hair was light, his complexion fair, and that his eyes were a startling blue.

The man nodded and smiled briefly at Carl, but then his gaze fixed on Newel Whitney. In three steps he strode across the room, extending his hand. "Newel K. Whitney, thou art the man."

It was as if he had hit Whitney with a stone. Newel stared at the newcomer; then, bewildered, took the proffered hand. "Sir, you have the advantage of me. I could not call you by name as you have me."

The man smiled, enjoying Whitney's perplexity. "I am Joseph the Prophet. You've prayed me here. Now what do you want of me?"

If Whitney was surprised before, now he was stunned. His mouth dropped open and he gaped at his visitor. "You're Joseph Smith?"

"Yes. We have just arrived from New York, a cold and arduous journey." He smiled even more broadly. "Did you not pray for me to come?"

"I . . . well, yes, my wife and I have been praying that . . ." His voice trailed off. "But how did you know?"

Joseph grew more serious now. "While yet in New York, I

had a vision in the which I saw you praying. The moment I saw you just now, I recognized you instantly."

Carl Rogers, who had been watching the stranger and Mr. Whitney intently, was startled. The whole interchange was most peculiar, but with the talk of visions and prayer his eyes really widened. He had heard that both Mr. Whitney and Mr. Gilbert, partners in the store, had become Mormons some months previously when a group of ministers had come through preaching. He wasn't sure what that implied, or even what the term *Mormon* meant, but now his curiosity was piqued.

"Have you a place to stay?" Mr. Whitney asked.

The man who called himself the Prophet Joseph shook his head. "No. I see the hotel across the street, perhaps we can find a room there."

"Nonsense. My wife and I have a commodious house." He pointed out of the west window. "Just right across the street. You shall stay with us."

"That's very kind of you, but—"

"I insist." Whitney peered out of the window to where the sleigh still sat waiting. "Are there four of you?"

"No," Joseph answered. "My two traveling companions are from this area, one from Mentor, one from Painesville. They will be returning to their homes. It is just my wife and I." A look of concern crossed his face. "My wife is seven months pregnant and not in good health. This is most kind of you, Mr. Whitney."

Newel Whitney suddenly realized that Carl Rogers was still standing nearby, looking awkward but watching the proceedings with interest. "I'm sorry, Carl," Whitney apologized. "I got carried away. Mr. Smith here surprised me so."

"That's no problem, Mr. Whitney. In fact, I'm in no hurry. Why don't you go get your guests settled. I'll wait here."

Joseph's face split into a wide smile. "Well, how thoughtful of you, young man!" He extended his hand. "Joseph Smith is my name. What's yours?"

Carl took the hand, surprised by the firmness of the grip. "Carl Rogers."

"Carl's father owns the livery stable here in town," Whitney explained.

"Then I'm sure we'll be seeing more of you," Joseph said.

The directness of his gaze was disconcerting, and Carl looked away, a little embarrassed. "I hope so, sir."

It took Joshua over a week before he finally found the missionaries alone in the small apartment over the tailor shop. Twice he had seen them on the street preaching, but he had no desire to talk to them in the presence of any of the local Missourians. He had also found the one called Frederick G. Williams alone in the tailor shop one day, but Williams was from Ohio and had only joined the other four men when they came through Kirtland. Joshua immediately left. It was the ones from New York that he wanted.

Finally, on a Sunday evening, much later than callers usually came, Joshua climbed the stairs and banged on the door. There were three of them there—an Oliver Cowdery, a Peter Whitmer, Jr., and one called Parley Pratt. Though they had obviously been in the process of preparing for bed when Joshua knocked, they seemed eager to talk with him and quickly invited him in. He ignored their invitation to remove his coat, but he did sit down.

"How may we help you, sir?" the one named Cowdery asked when he was settled. Oliver Cowdery was a small man, no more than five feet five or six, but he was clearly viewed by the other two as the natural leader, and so Joshua turned his full attention to him.

"It is my understanding that you men might know Joseph Smith."

The blunt directness of his statement shocked them all a little. "That is correct," Cowdery said. "Do you know Joseph?"

Joshua ignored the question. "Do you know any of the families around Palmyra Township?"

"Of course," Cowdery said, smiling broadly. "I myself taught school in the village. That's how I came to meet the Smith family."

"Do you know of the Benjamin Steed family?"

Both Cowdery and Whitmer lit up. "But of course," Whitmer said. "I have not personally met the father, but Mrs. Steed and the children have been in my father's home on numerous occasions. We live down in Fayette Township."

"I know Nathan, the oldest son, very well," Cowdery broke in eagerly. "In fact, I baptized him with my own hand. I was also there the evening he baptized his mother and sister Melissa."

"Baptized them?"

"Yes." Cowdery was elated, and the words came out in a torrent. "The authority to baptize was restored to the earth through angelic ministration. Joseph has organized a church—Christ's church—on the earth again. The Steeds were one of the first families to join."

"My—" Joshua caught himself. "The father? Did he join this church too?"

"No."

Joshua grunted inwardly. Well, at least that was something.

Whitmer spoke up again. "Sadly, Mr. Steed has not as yet seen fit to believe. But he has permitted his family to join. The two younger children were baptized a few weeks after the rest of the family."

Joshua felt a sudden pain shoot through him. "The youngest. Tell me about him."

Cowdery gave him a sharp look, reading more in Joshua's face than Joshua wanted to show. "Matthew is going on eleven now. He's sharp as an ax blade fresh off the grinding wheel. A delightful young man."

"And Melissa? Tell me about her."

"A wonderful girl," Whitmer said warmly. "Very lovely. A strong spiritual testimony of the work."

Parley Pratt had been watching Joshua closely, though to this point he had not spoken. Now he stirred. "You obviously know the Steeds well, sir."

Joshua only nodded.

Pratt was not about to be put off so easily. "May I ask how you know them? Are you from New York State?"

Joshua looked at him steadily for several moments, then turned back to Cowdery. "You said Nathan is the oldest son. That is not true."

"He isn't?" Whitmer asked.

"No."

"No, that's right," Cowdery said. "I said oldest son, but I do remember that Nathan had an older brother, name of Joshua, as I remember. He left home some years back."

"Of course," Whitmer agreed. "Now I remember. Sister Steed prays for him in every prayer she offers."

Joshua's eyes came up to meet Cowdery's. "Still?" he asked in a strained whisper.

Cowdery nodded, looking perplexed by Joshua's sudden show of emotion. "Yes. They've not heard from him since he left. He was supposed to have come—" He stopped, his eyes suddenly widening. "West."

Joshua nodded slowly.

Cowdery was staring at him in wonder. "You're Joshua," he said in amazement. "You're Joshua Steed."

"Yes."

Cowdery jumped up and came over and pumped Joshua's

hand vigorously. "Of course. I should have noticed. I've only met your father once or twice, but the resemblance between you is strong."

For the next ten minutes they talked, Joshua eagerly probing for every detail he could draw from Cowdery and Whitmer. Pratt indicated that even though he was originally from New York, he had most recently been living in Ohio. He had met the Steeds but did not know them well, and therefore said little.

Finally, Oliver Cowdery held up his hands, warding off further questions with a laugh. "I'm sorry we can't be more helpful, Joshua, but remember, we've been gone almost four months now. We've been told that most of the Saints are gathering to Ohio, but we haven't specifically heard which families. Perhaps your family—"

"My father will never leave that farm."

"That's what Nathan said too," Whitmer volunteered. "But I'll wager four bits that Nathan and Lydia will go."

Joshua looked down at his hands quickly. This was the question he had specifically avoided asking. "So they did marry?" he asked slowly.

"You knew Lydia too?" Cowdery asked.

"Yes." He kept his voice flat and dispassionate.

"She's a wonderful woman. It almost didn't happen, you know. Lydia was dead set against Joseph Smith, and when Nathan wouldn't turn his back on what he believed, she broke off their engagement."

That startled Joshua considerably. "When was that?" he demanded, quickly calculating. It had been last summer—no, summer a year ago, summer of '29—that he had been making plans to start east early the following spring and see if Lydia might still have him. Then had come the news from a man passing through Independence that Lydia and Nathan were promised to each other.

Cowdery seemed puzzled by the sudden interest in details.

But Joshua couldn't help it. He had to know. "Do you remember when it was that Nathan and Lydia broke the engagement?" Joshua asked again. "Think."

The dark eyes were half hooded as Cowdery tried to remember. "Well, I baptized Nathan in late May or early June."

"Of '29?"

"Yes. Joseph and I were well along with the translation of the Book of Mormon by then, so yes, it would have been '29. Nathan wrote Lydia about being baptized." He looked up. "She had gone to Boston."

"Yes, I heard that."

"It was the letter about his baptism that really upset her. She came right home. So by the time Nathan's letter got to Boston and she made it back home it would have been July, maybe early August. They broke off the engagement a short time after that when it became clear that their differences over Joseph Smith were too deep."

Joshua felt a great emptiness inside him. "So that would have been July or August of '29?" he asked in a low voice.

"Yes."

It hit him like a blow. He had planned to return to New York in the early spring of '30. By then, he told himself, he could be a successful freight operator and return in triumph to make reconciliation with his family. He was also filled with thoughts of Lydia and hopes that they could pick up again where they had left off when he had fled. "So when did they get back together?" He didn't want to hear it, but he couldn't bear not knowing.

"That one I do know, because Nathan and your mother had come to Fayette for the organization of the Church. That was April sixth, not quite a year ago now. When Nathan returned from there, Lydia had had a complete change of heart. She was baptized the next day, and they were married a few days after that."

Joshua stood and walked to the window, his fists clenching and unclenching, trying to calm the sickness spreading through him. He should have gone. He should have followed his instincts and gone back East. He would have left in late February or early March and been in Palmyra before April when Lydia had finally decided to marry Nathan. Instead, when he heard that Lydia was getting married, and to Nathan, something had snapped in him. That had been the night he drank himself into a stupor, then dragged a minister out of bed and took him to the house of Clinton Roundy, where he asked the saloon keeper for the hand of his daughter, Jessica, in marriage.

"Is everything all right, Mr. Steed?"

Joshua felt the eyes of the three men boring into his back. He took a quick breath and turned around. "Yes, everything's fine."

"They're expecting a baby, you know."

Joshua swung around to Peter Whitmer, the pain knifing through him. "No, I didn't know that."

"Well, she was last October when we left," Pratt volunteered. "In fact, it was due sometime this spring. Maybe they're already parents."

"No," Cowdery said, "I think it's not due until May." He watched Joshua's face for a moment, then leaned forward. "May I ask you a question, Mr. Steed?"

"About Nathan and Lydia?" *Absolutely not.* But he kept his face inscrutable.

"No, about your family. I know it is not my affair, but why have you never written your parents?"

Joshua felt a quick rush of relief. This was not pleasant ground, but it was safer. "I did. I wrote several letters."

"You did? They never got them, at least they hadn't by the time we left."

"I never mailed them." It came out quietly, completely belying the churning storm going on inside him. He looked at Cowdery. "Did Nathan ever tell you why I left?"

"No."

Good! He took a deep breath. "Well, it doesn't matter now. I planned to go back. I still do. Maybe this summer."

Pratt stirred in his chair, still obviously intrigued by what was going on in Joshua's mind. "We've decided that one of our number needs to return and make a report to Joseph. It's been determined that I shall go. I shall be leaving at the first of next week. Would you like me to take a letter back with me? I'll see that your family gets it."

"No!" It came out short and hard. A letter now was not the answer.

Pratt seemed not to be surprised. "All right," he said, his voice still mild. "Do you object if when I see your family I tell them I have seen you?"

Joshua considered that. It might be the easiest way. "No," he said.

"Good. I'm sure your mother will be thrilled."

Noting the play of emotions on Joshua's face, Oliver decided to change the subject. "What do you do here in Independence?"

"I own and run a freight company." He was going to let it go at that, then he remembered that one of these men might be seeing his family shortly. "I've got fourteen wagons and the teams to pull them," he added.

From the look on their faces it was clear that they were suitably impressed. *Well, let them be.* Let the word go back that Joshua Steed had made his own way in life.

"So you knew Joseph, then?" Cowdery asked.

"Yes. He and Hyrum worked for my father when we first came to Palmyra."

"Then you know about the angel Moroni and the Book of Mormon?"

"Yes," Joshua answered, his voice suddenly curt, "but I'm not interested in that." He stood up. "I never believed any of it then, and I'm not about to now."

Oliver and the others also stood. Oliver smiled, not taking offense. "We're sorry to hear that, but we believe every man has a right to choose his own faith."

"Is that what you're out here doing? Preaching Joseph Smith?"

"No," Whitmer said quietly, "we're preaching the gospel of Jesus Christ, which Joseph restored to the earth."

"Your kind is always quick with the good answer," Joshua retorted angrily. "Sounds like the same thing to me." He felt a quick pang of regret as he saw the surprise in the men's eyes. What had brought about this sudden anger? *Well, let them won-*

der, he thought. He *was* angry—angry at himself, angry at the fate that had cheated him when he was so close to winning what he most longed for. And Joseph Smith was part of all that too. If it hadn't been for his tales of the gold plates . . .

He brushed that thought aside angrily. What was done was done. And that had nothing to do with these men. They seemed decent enough, in spite of their foolishness. And they had kindly told him of his family. He forced himself to speak with more control. "I don't want to discourage you, but you won't have much luck here. People out here are too busy dealing with real-life things."

"Oh, to the contrary," Oliver said amiably, "we're having good success. Many are listening to us, and we have already baptized enough to start a branch of the Church here in Independence."

Joshua just shook his head and moved to the door.

"When Parley returns we hope he can convince Joseph to come see for himself how the work is going."

The anger was back instantly. Joshua's voice went very cold as he turned to Pratt. "You tell Joseph for me that if he comes to Jackson County he might not find things to his liking out here."

Oliver's voice took on a firmness of its own. "Joseph goes where the Lord calls him, Mr. Steed."

Joshua straightened to his full height, his eyes turning ominous. "This is the frontier, Mr. Cowdery. Law and order out here ain't what you're used to back East. This ain't no place for the weak."

Oliver's eyes glittered with anger. He obviously did not like being threatened. "I came over a thousand miles to get here, a good part of that on foot. Being religious doesn't make us weak, Mr. Steed."

Joshua snorted in derision. "You got no idea what hard is, mister. So you tell him. You tell Joseph for me that if he tries to bring his angels and his gold Bible out here, these Missouri wildcats just might jam them right down his throat."

With that he spun on his heel and went out, slamming the door behind him.

———◆———

Carlton Rogers hung back, looking at the displays behind the glass counters in the Gilbert and Whitney Store. Newel Whitney gave him a curious look once or twice, but seemed to sense that Carl was hanging back because he wanted to talk to him in private.

In about five minutes, the store was empty of customers. Newel wiped his hands on his apron and sauntered over to where Carl stood by the stove.

"Mornin', Carl."

"Mornin', Mr. Whitney."

"How's your family?"

"Right fine. Thank you for asking."

They both fell silent, and Carl started to squirm a little. He began to trace the line of the floorboards with his toe.

"Something we can help you with today, Carl?"

He looked up, glanced quickly out of the front window to make sure no one else was headed for the store, then finally turned to the storekeeper. "Would you mind if I asked you some questions? Not about the store," he added quickly. "More personal-like?"

A little surprised, Mr. Whitney nodded. "Sure. Let's sit down."

Before doing so, he grabbed the poker and used it to open the door on the cast-iron stove. He leaned down, got two pieces of wood and shoved them into the belly of the fire, then shut the door again. Satisfied, he sat down across from Carl. "All right, son. What is it?"

Carl felt his face flame and knew it approached the color of his hair. He always blushed so easily. But this had been bothering him for some time, and so he was determined to seize the opportunity while he had it. "About two weeks ago I was in the store. Remember?"

"Of course, I remember. That was the day Brother Joseph arrived."

"Right. Umm . . . that's kind of what I wanted to talk to you about."

"I see. What in particular?"

He blushed even more deeply. "I'd appreciate it if you didn't say anything about this to my pa."

Whitney gave him an understanding smile. "Of course not."

"It's not that I'm trying to hide anything, you understand." It came out more quickly than he had planned, and he forced himself to pace his next words. "It's just that Pa has some feelings about the Mormons and . . ."

"I understand," Whitney reassured him. "I won't mention this to him."

"Thank you."

Whitney waited and Carl began to fidget again. He had rehearsed this over and over in his mind, but now to actually say it sounded foolish.

Newel Whitney was a perceptive man. Not yet forty, he was already a partner in a successful mercantile establishment. He had a reputation for honesty and integrity and a wise head. It didn't take much to guess what was on Carl's mind. "Is this about some of the things Joseph said that day?"

Carl felt immense relief. "Yes."

"About the vision?"

He looked down, but nodded.

Whitney sat back, pulling up one knee as he talked. "To understand what that was all about, I need to start a little earlier. Do you have time?"

"Yes."

"All right." He paused for a moment to collect his thoughts. "I think you know about the four missionaries who came here last fall from New York."

"Yes. I never met them, but everyone was talking about them."

"Yes, they were. Well, actually my wife and I had been followers of Mr. Sidney Rigdon, the Campbellite preacher."

"I know Mr. Rigdon."

"The Campbellites—or 'Disciples,' as we called ourselves—believed in baptism for the remission of sins, but they did not give the gift of the Holy Ghost. The book of Acts specifically says that Peter and the other Apostles had the power to give the gift of the Holy Ghost. That was the one thing about the Disciples that troubled my wife and me greatly. It was something we greatly longed to have.

"Well, one night my wife and I were praying to the Father, asking him to show us the way. This was before the missionaries ever came. It was about midnight. We were in our house, just right over there." He pointed across the street toward the west. "We prayed most earnestly."

Carl had gone very quiet now and was watching Newel Whitney intently.

"Suddenly, the Spirit rested upon us. A cloud seemed to overshadow the house. And then it was like we were out of doors. The house passed away from our vision. We were not conscious of anything but the Spirit. A solemn awe came upon the both of us. We saw the cloud and felt the Spirit of the Lord with great power.

"I can't tell you how that felt, Carl." He shook his head. "There are not words that can adequately describe it. But it was wonderful!" His voice dropped in pitch, tinged now with wonder. "Then a voice spoke out of the cloud. It said, 'Prepare to receive the word of the Lord, for it is coming.' "

Carl felt a little shiver go up his spine. He must have looked as if he were going to speak, for Mr. Whitney paused and looked at him expectantly. He gave a little wave of his hand to indicate that Whitney should go on.

"At the time we didn't know what it meant, only that somehow the word of the Lord was coming to Kirtland."

"And then the missionaries came?"

His question seemed to please the storekeeper. "Yes, it was just a short time later that the four men from New York arrived with the news of the restoration of the gospel and with copies of the Book of Mormon." He let his foot back down to the floor and leaned forward. "And they claimed that the priesthood of God had been restored to the earth. That priesthood included the authority to bestow the gift of the Holy Ghost."

"So your prayers were answered." Carl had not made it a question, but a conclusion.

"That they were. However, that was not the end of it. I am of a much more practical mind than my wife. I tend to undertake every endeavor with some caution." He smiled, as though chiding himself a little. "I suppose that partly accounts for my success in the mercantile business. Elizabeth was baptized right away. I took a few more days before I was convinced. Then I too was baptized."

"And did you receive the gift of the Holy Ghost?"

"Indeed. It was a most marvelous experience. At the baptismal service, the gifts of the Spirit were clearly manifest. Some prophesied; others, like myself, felt a great joy infuse our souls, purging our sins as though by fire."

Carl felt quick envy. "That must have been wonderful."

"It was," Whitney said in a faraway voice. "I still bask in the light of that experience."

A movement out of the corner of his eye caught Carl's attention. He turned and saw a woman and her two children coming down the hill from town. She had a large bag on one arm and was obviously headed for the store. He turned back to Mr. Whitney and spoke quickly. "But Joseph—Mr. Smith—said you had prayed him here. You didn't actually pray for him to come, then?"

"No, not specifically. The voice we heard only said that we were to prepare for the word of the Lord, because it was coming."

"But Joseph actually saw you praying?"

He lifted his hands, palms upward, as though the evidence spoke for itself. "You heard what he said. And you saw that he knew me the moment he saw me, though we had never before laid eyes on one another."

Carl sighed. His face was puzzled. "I don't understand how that is possible, Mr. Whitney."

The older man chuckled. "If you understand one thing, then understanding the other becomes very simple."

"What is that?"

"You have to understand that Joseph Smith is a prophet. Like Moses and Abraham and Peter and Paul. Once you believe that, then visions and the ability to give the gifts of the Spirit are much easier to comprehend."

The bell tinkled softly as the door opened and the lady and her two children came in the store. Carl stood quickly and stuck out his hand. "Thank you, Mr. Whitney. Thank you for your time."

Whitney gripped his hand and held it for a moment, even when Carl started to pull it back. "Think about it, Carl. Just think about it."

"I will, Mr. Whitney. I promise."

As Carl Rogers walked back up the hill from Kirtland Flats, he moved slowly, barely aware of his surroundings. He was at that moment a very thoughtful and, in many ways, a very troubled young man.

It was quiet in the Steed home on this March midmorning. It was still too wet to work the fields, and Benjamin had gone into town to have some metalwork done at the blacksmith shop. Melissa had gone with him. Matthew and Rebecca were attending the school just about a mile down the road. That was another sign of their growing prosperity. Both children were now attending the primary school in Palmyra Village. The bread was mixed and rising; the breakfast dishes were done; the laundry and ironing weren't due to be done until Thursday. That meant Mary Ann Steed had an hour or more before she had to start lunch for Benjamin. It was one of those times that were starting to come to her more frequently now that her family was growing up.

She went to the chest in the corner of the parlor and opened the top drawer. Inside there were two books, both treasured by her. A large family Bible with black leather cover took up most of the room. Next to it was the Book of Mormon. She reached down and caressed its cover. This was the book Nathan had bought for her, one of the first ones off the Grandin press. But it was the Bible she took out.

Moving to her favorite rocking chair, she sat down. It was located next to the south-facing window in the kitchen. It was her favorite chair because not only did it catch the sun, but from here she could see Ben when he brought the team back to the barn or the children when they came from school.

She settled in, letting the warmth of the sunshine soak in for several moments. Finally she took her reading spectacles from the small lamp table and put them on. Mary Ann treasured the Book of Mormon. She had read it now four times and was going through it for the fifth. But she had grown up with the Bible, and if anything, the Book of Mormon had only served to deepen her love for it. She made it a point each week to spend time with both books. Today, she decided, she would read something in the four Gospels.

But this didn't seem to be the day for reading. She started, then in a few moments she let the book slip to her lap again and gazed out of the window. Her thoughts were on Ohio. Nathan and Lydia were now busily engaged in their preparations for departure. Melissa was still unmovable in her decision to go as well; she didn't know when or how, but going she was. And Mary Ann would lose yet another of her children.

Unbidden, the ache inside her rose to the surface again. The groups were forming. Hyrum had gone on ahead. Newel Knight would be taking the Colesville Branch. Mother Smith, Joseph's mother, would take a group from around Fayette. Martin Harris was gathering the ones from Palmyra and Manchester. Soon there would be no one left. No one left to talk to about the Book of Mormon, or Joseph. No one with whom to gather for worship services. No more conferences in the warmth of the Whitmer cabin, where the Spirit had so often touched her and others. It was as though she were watching the world move slowly away from her while she stood rooted to the spot, unable to move.

Finally she got stern with herself. She had come in here to read, not daydream or wallow in self-pity. She looked down. She was in the seventeenth chapter of Matthew. She started again, picking up where she could last remember reading with any comprehension. She decided she would read aloud to keep her focused on what she was doing.

" 'And when they were come to the multitude, there came to him a certain man, kneeling down to him, and saying, Lord, have mercy on my son: for he is lunatick, and sore vexed: for oft-times he falleth into the fire, and oft into the water.' "

She stopped. This was a story that always touched her. In Vermont, a family named Chandler had lived two farms down the road from them. They had a fourteen-year-old boy, Thomas by name. One day when the Chandlers were at the Steeds' for a cornhusking, Thomas suddenly stopped in the midst of what he was doing. His body stiffened, then his eyes rolled back. Mary Ann could still hear the anguished "Oh no!" of his mother. She lunged for him, but she was an instant too late. Thomas hurled backwards, hitting the ground with a sickening thud. He began to shake violently. White foam bubbled out of his mouth as he jerked and shook, while all looked on in horror.

It was the Steed children's first experience with someone afflicted by epilepsy, and it had terrified them. That night Mary Ann sat them down and read this very account to them. Then she talked about the Savior's love for people, regardless of whether they were like other people or not. "Others will shun Thomas because they think he is strange," she told them, "but if you are to be like the Savior you cannot do that. You must always remember, Thomas may be different, but he still needs to be loved."

She continued on, now caught up in the story and no longer needing to read aloud. "I brought him to thy disciples," the anguished father told the Master, "and they could not cure him."

Mary Ann looked up thoughtfully. How it must have shamed the disciples—to stand and hear this sorrowing parent declare their inadequacies for all to hear. The Savior rebuked them for their lack of faith, then stepped forward. The result was clearly stated. The boy was healed "from that very hour."

It was one of the great miracle stories of the Gospels. For a moment, Mary Ann sat there in silence, thinking about Thomas and that day at the cornhusking. Finally, with a small sigh, she dropped her eyes and continued to read. Suddenly something leaped out at her.

Afterwards, when the disciples were alone with Jesus, they asked him why they couldn't cast out the evil spirit. Jesus told them it was due to their unbelief, then talked about having faith like unto a mustard seed. Then came the words that caught her eye. The account closed with these words of the Savior to his disciples: "Howbeit this kind goeth not out but by prayer and fasting."

Why had she never seen that verse before? She went back three or four verses and started again, reading slowly, concentrating. The disciples were troubled because they had not been able to effect the miracle. Jesus taught them about faith. But then, then . . . "Howbeit this kind goeth not out but by prayer *and* fasting."

She closed the book slowly, keeping a finger in the place. Were there some things so difficult, some challenges of such monumental proportions, that prayer alone was not sufficient? She opened the book and read the words one more time, feeling a quickening of her spirit. "This kind goeth not out but by prayer *and fasting.*"

She closed the book again and set it aside, her mind racing. If fasting and prayer could work a miracle as wondrous as casting out an evil spirit, could it soften Benjamin's heart as well? Could it help him to see and feel the power of the Book of Mormon? Could it cast out the bitterness he felt about Joseph?

She paused, trying to calm her soaring hopes. Could it get them to Ohio?

———————

An hour and a half later Benjamin returned from town. Mary Ann served him a lunch of bread and soup. As he finished, and prepared to go out again, he stopped to kiss her on the cheek. "Thank you."

"You're welcome."

"I'll be out in the barn."

"All right." She watched him move to the door, then spoke. "Ben?"

He stopped and turned around.

"I . . ." She took a quick breath. "I'll not be eating with you from time to time over the next few days."

His brows furrowed. "What?"

"I'll be fixing all the meals, of course, but sometimes I just won't be eatin' with you."

"Why not?" He peered at her more closely. "You feelin' all right?"

"Yes, yes. I'm fine. It's just . . ." She let it trail off, not sure that she could explain.

"Just what?" he demanded.

"I've . . . I would like to fast for a time."

"Fast?"

"Yes. Go without food and water."

He gave her a long appraising look. Then finally he nodded slowly. "Is this about the kids? Lydia and Nathan?"

She smiled a little, feeling a quick rush of relief. "In a way."

He shrugged, not pleased but not really angry either. "Whatever you think is best."

He opened the door and was gone.

She watched him stride across the yard and disappear around the barn. "Thank you, Ben," she finally murmured.

The Benjamin Steed cabin had been started the day after the family arrived in Palmyra Township in mid-September in the year eighteen hundred twenty-six. They moved in three days before the first snowfall.

The main floor—all one room—served as kitchen, living area, and sleeping quarters for the parents. Upstairs there were two long and narrow bedrooms—one for the boys, one for the girls. On the coldest days, thin sheets of ice formed on the sloping ceilings of each bedroom. Above his brothers and sisters, Matthew, six years old when they first moved in, slept in a narrow loft stuffed with heavy comforters.

But the amenities were added one by one—planking for the floor, glass panes for the windows, a big oak chest for Mary Ann's linens. Two years after they moved in, an extension off the south wall became a separate kitchen with a large slate sink and a sluice to bring water directly into the house from the nearby creek. Last fall, after another bumper crop of wheat, Benjamin had added a second wing to the east. Now it was no longer a cabin but a spacious and comfortable home. The walls had all been plastered and painted. Oak trim had been added in the main sitting room. Each bedroom had a small wood-burning stove to heat it during the winter. There was even a painting of mountain scenery in the parlor.

Nathan Steed stood in the yard in front of the house, letting his eyes run across the original part of the home as his mind recalled those days of huddling around the fireplace, or racing down the stairs on winter mornings to stand on the great hearthstone that held the heat through the night.

The door opened and Lydia was there. He looked up, a little embarrassed to be caught reminiscing. "Nathan, Mother Steed has supper on."

"Comin'." The mood of reverie gone now, he strode quickly across the yard and onto the porch.

Lydia pushed open the door for him and stood back so he could enter past her. There was enough room for the two of them, but he pushed against the roundness of her belly and stopped as though he had become stuck. "Uh-oh, Mrs. Steed," he said. "I can't seem to get past you and this baby."

She slugged him and then gave him a push. "I don't think it's the baby; I think I'm feeding you too good."

He laughed and put his arm around her. "I think you're right. How did the only daughter of a rich storekeeper ever learn to cook like that?"

Lydia smiled, pleased at his comment. "Mostly from your mother."

As they entered the main part of the house, Lydia stopped and looked up at him. "What were you doing out there?"

He looked down at her, deciding once again that the pregnancy had only deepened her loveliness—that and her conversion to the Church. He had always loved her eyes, but now they had grown even darker and were like two great windows through which Nathan could peek into the innermost recesses of her soul.

She cocked her head to one side. "Well?" she said.

"Well what?" He had forgotten what she asked.

"You were just standing out there. What were you doing?"

The smile on his lips slowly faded. "Saying good-bye, I guess."

She sobered too, knowing instantly what he meant. "I know," she said softly. "I've been trying not to think about it." Then she shrugged it off and slipped her arm through his. "Come on. Your mother is waiting."

As they entered the main room, Matthew spied them and jumped to Lydia's side, taking her hand. "Nathan, I get to sit next to Lydia. You can sit on the other side."

"Ah. And who said you could sit by my wife?"

Lydia put an arm around her young brother-in-law's shoulder. "I did. I like to sit between two handsome men."

Thirteen-year-old Becca, laying the last of her mother's best silver on the table, hooted, but Matthew fairly beamed. In July he would turn eleven. He was quickly turning into a scaled-down replica of Nathan. Even the tuft of hair on the back of his head that had escaped taming for years was finally starting to lay down of its own accord.

"Matthew, you help your mother get the bread on now." Benjamin Steed was at the low table near the rear window. There was a slab of butcher's block laid across the top and he was carving what had been, up until that morning, their biggest—and meanest—red rooster.

"Yes, Pa."

Lydia went into the pantry and came out a moment later carrying a jar of peach preserves. She walked to the table, pried off the lid, and began to spoon them onto a saucer. Nathan watched her heavy awkwardness with warm affection. Her time was somewhere near the end of May. That was four weeks yet, but she looked to Nathan as though she might deliver at any moment. He felt a quick spasm of concern. Maybe they *should* wait. Starting a strenuous journey in the last month of pregnancy was not the wisest course of action.

On impulse he walked over to her, took her in his arms, and pressed his lips to her forehead. "Are you going to be okay?" he asked.

She looked up at him in surprise, then seemed to understand. "Of course. I'm fine."

"All right, you two," Melissa said, untying her apron. "That kind of behavior already got you in trouble."

Mary Ann spun around from where she stood over the stove. "Melissa Mary!" She was blushing even as she gave her daughter a stern look.

Lydia laughed, pulling away from Nathan and patting her belly. "Melissa's right, Mother Steed. Look what your son has gone and done to me."

Nathan laughed aloud as his mother's face instantly colored even more. He was also pleased to note that his father's mouth was twitching a little at the corners, though he did not look up to follow the playful bantering. Nathan knew that his father didn't find Melissa's daring quite as shocking as did his mother. In fact, secretly, it seemed to please him a little. But then, of the older children, Melissa had always been her father's clear favorite.

Walking casually, Nathan went over to his sister. Then suddenly his arms darted out and grabbed her. He swept her up in his arms, swinging her off her feet. "You think 'cause you're twenty now, you can say anything and get away with it?" he cried.

"Nathan, put me down," she squealed, pummeling his chest with her fists. But she was laughing too hard to do much more than flail the air.

"You don't learn to mind your tongue, young lady, I'm gonna have to go down to the gristmill and tell that Keller boy just what kind of wild woman you are."

Now it was Melissa who blushed, and more furiously than her mother had. "Nathan!" She was mortified that he would mention James right out like that, in front of everybody.

He set her down. "Did I say something wrong?" he asked innocently, then ducked quickly to avoid her sweeping blow.

Their mother, watching with warm affection, decided to intervene and spare her daughter further embarrassment. "The dumplin's are ready, and it looks like your father has the chicken carved. Let's eat."

"Yeah!" Matthew exclaimed. "I'm hungry."

When they were seated, Benjamin turned to his wife. "Mother, would you say grace please?"

Every head bowed and Mary Ann folded her arms. For a long moment there was silence, and Nathan knew this wasn't going to make things easier.

Finally his mother spoke, her voice low and strained. "Our Father who art in heaven, hallowed be thy name." She cleared her throat quickly. "We thank thee, Father, for the bounties of the earth, and for thy goodness to us. We thank thee for this food which thou hast given us. May we always remember that it comes from thy gracious hand, O Lord."

The silence settled in again. It grew heavy in a very short time.

"O Father," she finally continued, obviously struggling now, "we are most thankful for the life that Lydia carries within her. As she and Nathan leave tomorrow in obedience to thy command to gather to Ohio, wilt thou bless her? Bless her with strength as they commence their journey. Bless her that this new child may not come before its time. Bless them both that they may find a place to live in their new abode before the baby comes."

In the silence that followed, Nathan could hear both Melissa and Lydia sniffling. There was a quick sigh, and though he did not open his eyes, Nathan sensed his mother's shoulders straightening. It was her natural gesture whenever she was dealing with some burden that could not be thrust aside.

"Father," she went on, her voice stronger now, "we thank thee for the restoration of the gospel to the earth again in our day, and for thy church. We thank thee for having the gift of the Holy Ghost on earth once again.

"Bless Joshua, dear Lord, wherever he may be. It would

please us deeply to learn of his whereabouts, but as in all things, Father, we ask that thy will be done. But wherever he is, and whatever he is doing, we ask thee to watch over him and keep him safe. In the name of Jesus, amen."

There were soft amens around the table. His mother reached immediately for the dumplings, blinking quickly so the tears would not well over and give her away any more than her voice had already. Lydia reached across the table and touched her hand.

Benjamin took the platter filled with chicken and pushed off two large pieces onto his plate. He glanced quickly at his wife, then at Nathan. "I was in town yesterday." He handed the platter to Nathan.

Nathan took some meat. As he handed it to Matthew, he finally looked back at his father. "Yes?"

"There was a canawler at Phelps's tavern." A "canawler" was one of the captains that plied their barges up and down the length of the Erie Canal. Nathan's father took the dumplings from his wife, who was warning him with her eyes. She didn't know what was coming, but it was clear she guessed she might not like it.

Benjamin ignored her and went on as he spooned out the dumplings and the gravy in which they swam. "He said the ice on Lake Erie is just now breaking up. The steamers won't be running along the Great Lakes until it's all clear. He said everything is waitin' at Buffalo to get out."

Nathan frowned. That was not good news. With Lydia's condition, they couldn't stand any delay.

"It ain't gonna hurt nothin' if you stay here another month," his father said without looking up. "Give the weather a chance to warm up a little. Martin Harris will be leaving about the end of May. Let the baby come. Then you can go chasing after Joe Smith if you want."

Nathan felt a quick flash of irritation. "We want to travel now with Mother Smith's group, get there before the baby's born."

"Humph!" It was an open expression of disgust. "You think old Mother Smith is really going to get you there?"

Mary Ann's head came up sharply. "Ben!"

"Well," he said, meeting her gaze defiantly. "What is she? Sixty, if she's a day."

Nathan felt a weariness come over him. Why did it always have to be this way with his father? "Joseph's mother will be fifty-six in July," he said quietly.

His father shrugged that aside. "It ain't right that an old lady is left by herself to take a group of people three hundred miles into the wilderness. If goin' to Ohio is really a call from the Lord, like Joseph says, why don't some of the Smiths' menfolk stick around and help you get there?"

Melissa jumped into the fray. "Pa, that's not fair. Father Smith went with one group. Hyrum was going to take the Colesville Branch, but Joseph asked him to come as soon as possible."

"Yeah, and where's Joseph? Off in Ohio already."

Matthew and Becca had stopped eating now, their eyes swinging back and forth between the principal players. Nathan was fighting to keep the anger out of his voice. "You know that Joseph went ahead to get everything in readiness for the rest of us."

Mary Ann put her fork down. "Mother Smith is a small woman, but she is full of faith, and she's got more spunk than a roomful of bantam roosters. She'll do better than some men I could name."

"Probably better'n a man like Joseph," Benjamin retorted. "Him draggin' Emma off on a three-hundred-mile journey by sleigh, and her six months with child. That's not a wonderful husband."

Mary Ann bridled a little at that. "The Lord told Joseph in a revelation to go ahead and prepare the way."

"Drag your expectant wife across the country in a sleigh? What kind of revelation is that?"

Nathan had picked up his cup to take a drink. Now he slammed it back down, sloshing milk across the tablecloth.

But before he could say a word, Lydia broke in. She smiled at her father-in-law, her eyes soft as they searched his face. "Thank you, Father Steed."

Benjamin, gearing up for battle with Nathan, was completely disarmed. He turned to her in surprise. "For what?"

"I know you're concerned about me traveling, with the baby being this close." Tears welled up as she reached out and squeezed his hand. "You're a good man to be worried about me like that. But this isn't just Nathan's doin', you know. I want to go. The Lord has asked it of us. I want my baby to be born in Kirtland because that's where we're supposed to be."

The exchange said something about what had happened between these two in the last year. Nathan's father just looked at Lydia for a long moment, their eyes locked; then finally he nodded. He was satisfied. That didn't mean he agreed with her, but he was satisfied. He picked up his fork and began to eat again. In a moment the others followed suit, relieved that the tension had been shunted aside.

Nathan reached under the table and put his hand on Lydia's knee. In a moment her hand came down and took his, squeezing it for a moment. And for the hundredth time, Nathan marvelled at the woman sitting next to him.

———————

"Pa?"

Nathan's father was at the head of the horse and small wagon Nathan had rented from the livery stable in town, holding the horse steady. He was gazing out across the black wetness of the fields dotted here and there in the low spots with an occasional patch of snow. He turned.

"Until the farm sells, you feel free to work my land. There's no sense letting it lie fallow."

"It'll sell."

Nathan wasn't so sure. In the revelation given during the January conference, the Lord had not seemed too concerned about whether all the land was sold or not as the Saints left their homes to gather to Ohio. They were not to be overly concerned about the riches of the earth. It was the riches of eternity that mattered.

Some were successful, of course, selling their property at fair market value. But selling farms and houses and other property took time. With only a few months, many were either forced to sell at a substantial loss or leave things in the hands of neighbors or friends.

It had not been a simple choice for Nathan either. This was his first land. He had cleared it. He had built the cabin and barn. He had worked two different times for Joseph Knight in Colesville to pay off the mortgage.

He pushed his thoughts aside. For all he loved his farm, there was no question about leaving. Not in his mind, not in his wife's. The Lord had called them to Ohio, and to Ohio they were going.

As he glanced at his father out of the corner of his eye, an unexpected rush of emotion swept up inside Nathan, catching him by surprise. He and this taciturn man had their differences, especially when it came to Joseph Smith, but they had also stood shoulder-to-shoulder over the years, clearing land, plowing, harrowing, shoeing the mules, building rail fence, splitting planks.

Nathan stuck out his hand. "Thanks, Pa," he said, his voice suddenly husky. "Thanks for everything."

His father gripped his hand, hard. "You take care of that girl of yours, you hear?" he said gruffly.

Nathan laughed softly. *What about me?* But he understood perfectly all that was included in his father's words. "I will, Pa. I will."

Behind them, all the women were in tears. Matthew was rubbing at his eyes with the back of his hand, trying hard to be brave. Becca made no such effort. She was openly bawling now. Melissa threw her arms around Lydia and they hugged each other hard.

"I'm going to miss you, Melissa," Lydia whispered. "You're the sister I never had."

Melissa answered fiercely, loud enough for her father to hear. "I'll be comin', Lydia. I don't know when, but I'm comin' too."

"You know you'll have a place when you do."

They stepped back from one another, then Lydia took a deep breath. It didn't help. She began to sob as she turned to Nathan's mother. "Good-bye, Mother Steed. Thank you. For everything."

They embraced, holding each other for several moments without speaking. Finally Mary Ann pulled back. "You'll write as soon as the baby comes?"

"Yes."

"It will seem strange to be called Grandma."

Lydia smiled and wiped at the tears. "Will you come and see him?"

"You're so sure it's a him?"

Lydia laughed. "I think so."

"Yes, we'll come see him." Her eyes darted to Benjamin, then back. "I don't know when, but we'll come."

They both turned, and Lydia walked slowly to Benjamin. She stopped, looking up into the weather-hewn face. "Father Steed?"

"What?" He didn't turn, just kept staring out across the fields, but Nathan saw his Adam's apple bob once, then again.

"Will you come with Mother Steed and see your grandson?"

He finally turned and looked down at her. "I've got to get the crops in. Then there'll be the summer's work to do."

It had come out curt, almost abrupt. But Lydia only smiled all the more warmly. She laid her hand on his arm. "By late fall he'll be crawling. There isn't anything much better than seeing your first grandson crawl."

He chuckled in spite of himself. "We'll see."

"Good." Then in one moment her lips were trembling. She threw her arms around him and hugged him fiercely. "I'll miss you, Father Steed. You've been awfully good to me."

He patted her shoulders awkwardly, like a man afraid to touch a skittish colt, but wanting to nevertheless.

And then it was over. Nathan helped Lydia into the wagon. There were last-minute cries of farewell, and promises to write, and fierce attempts to hold back the tears. Then Nathan snapped the reins, and the horse flicked its ears and leaned into the harness. In a few moments they turned out of the lane and onto the main road to Palmyra Village. Nathan reached out and clasped Lydia's hand. She took it, squeezing it hard in return, but neither of them spoke as they made their way south toward town. From there they would be traveling to the home of one of Lydia's friends, where they planned to stay before departing with Mother Smith's group.

As they drove down Main Street and past McBride's dry goods store, Nathan saw Lydia's eyes follow the storefront for as long as they could without her turning her head.

"Do you want to stop and try again?"

She shook her head. She and Nathan had gone in a week ago to tell Lydia's parents they were leaving. Josiah McBride would not even let them cross the threshold of his store. When she had asked if she could come by on this night to say good-bye to her mother, he had shaken his head emphatically, back stiff, mouth tight. Hannah McBride had no wish to say anything to a daughter that had so deeply and fully betrayed her. Later Nathan had tried to tell Lydia that that was her father speaking, not her mother. In either case, Lydia had no recourse but to write a letter and send it in with a friend. Whether they had opened it, she would probably never know.

"I will, Lydia," Nathan said softly. "I'll tell them you only want a minute to say farewell."

"No."

He sighed and drove on past, his eyes smoldering, a deep anger hardening inside him. For the first time in his life, Nathan had an overwhelming desire to walk up to a man and punch him squarely in the nose.

"Do you know what it is?" she suddenly asked.

"What what is?"

"Papa's hurt?"

"He hates Joseph Smith."

"That's part of it, but no. It's having to face the people."

"Face them about what?"

"About me. No one in the village blames him. After all, I've always been"—her voice dropped as she quoted sarcastically—"a 'willful and headstrong girl.' In a way, it would be better if they did criticize him. He could deal with that. But the oozing sympathy every time he and Mama go to church, the sidelong looks of pity, the women clipping off their conversations when he and Mama enter the room—that's more than he can handle."

And that was why what was at first white-hot anger had now solidified into something as rock-hard and unbendable and cold as the depths of a mountain glacier. Over the past year Lydia had finally come to accept that. It still hurt, so much that she had to force herself not to dwell on it, but at least she understood.

She sighed, fighting back the burning beneath her eyelids. "We've got a big day tomorrow, Nathan. Just take me to Caroline's house."

To be a full five feet tall, Lucy Mack Smith, mother to the Prophet Joseph, would have to go up on tiptoes, and stretch at that. She was not only tiny in height, but she was also small in frame, a wisp that would easily blow away in any kind of serious windstorm. But the spirit that lived inside must have been big enough to fill two or three bodies of that size. With a mixture of amusement and amazement, Lydia Steed watched her getting everything and everyone settled on board the canal boat. So did the captain of the boat.

He was a big, dirty man, with a foul-smelling cigar stub jammed between yellowing teeth. Normally berth assignments on a canal boat were done on a first-come, first-served basis, often accompanied with ugly bickering and sometimes open fights for the best positions. With a group as large as this, the latecomers would end up sleeping on the floor, or on the tables that were set up and taken down each day. But immediately upon the arrival of the group of Saints, Mother Smith took things in hand and began assigning places based on need and circumstances. The captain had sneered at her attempts at first. Now he seemed content to let her put things in order.

"How many children?"

"Four."

"Sex and ages?"

"Three girls and one boy. Uh . . . ages? Let's see." The man turned to his wife.

She shook her head as though this was no surprise. "Girls, twelve, nine, and three. A boy, seven."

"All right," Mother Smith said, pointing down towards the opening that led into the covered area of the boat. "There are four berths in the ladies' section. Next to the Shurtliffs. Brother Griffin, you'll have one in the men's section. Your boy will have to sleep on the floor next to you."

"Personal belongin's go in the space near the stern," the captain said. "That's the back of the boat to you."

"But . . ." The man stepped to the doorway and peered into the gloom of the inside cabin area. "Do you have a larger bunk?" he asked. "I'm a big man—"

The captain cut in. "All the berths are the same size. And by the way, you take a bottom one. Don't want you crashin' down on someone if the braces break."

The man jerked around, his face darkening instantly.

Mother Smith stepped between them, ignoring the captain. "It's all right, Brother Griffin," she said cheerfully. "Pay him no mind. Just hope you get to sleep next to someone that don't kick much. The beds are pretty close together."

There were several good-natured chuckles around her, but Lydia saw that Brother Griffin was not mollified. In a huff, he gathered up the two valises and a large burlap bag stuffed to the bursting, and followed his wife and children into the inside cabin.

About eighty people had gathered in Kingdon, a small community not far from Fayette, to make the journey west, but one canal boat could never hold a group that size, so they had split the party. Mother Smith took charge of the larger group—twenty adults and about thirty children. They had the larger boat and so could accommodate more. Thomas B. Marsh, a convert who had been baptized in September of the previous year, would lead the second group and follow close behind the first.

It was fascinating to Lydia to watch Mother Smith. She was in her midfifties. She was tiny, and rarely raised her voice in anger. Yet she commanded respect, even from the men.

Mother Smith made the assignments for three more families, including her own children, then turned to Lydia and Nathan. If the task had wearied her, she gave no sign. She smiled kindly. "Now, dears, we have just the place for you two."

"Anywhere is fine for us," Lydia said quickly.

"There're two bunks back by the captain's cabin," Mother Smith went on, as though Lydia hadn't spoken. "They're not in either the men's or women's section. That way, Nathan, you can stay close to your wife."

"Normally, I put the crew there," the captain spoke up. He grinned, the cigar bobbing like a cork in a washtub. "But I wouldn't want no babies bein' born halfway between here and Buffalo."

"Mother Smith, I don't want any special treatment. Nathan and I—"

A finger came up and waggled at her. "Now, you listen to me, young lady. You've got the baby to think about."

"Really, Mother Smith—"

"Shush you, now," she said sternly. Then with a twinkle in her eye she turned to Nathan. "Is she always this sassy?"

Nathan chuckled. "From time to time."

Lydia dug an elbow into his side, but Mother Smith just reached out and patted Lydia's arm. "It's probably a little stuffier back there, but it'll be better that way."

Lydia took her hand. "Thank you, Mother Smith."

Nathan reached out also and shook her hand gratefully. Then he picked up their things and they started for the cabin.

Canal boats were typically about fifty to fifty-five feet in length. They looked a lot like a drawing Lydia had seen once of Noah's ark—only on a much smaller scale, of course. Blunt nosed, low in the water, and with a shallow draft—most places along the canal system carried only four feet of water—they were more scow than boat. They definitely were not things of beauty like the sleek ocean-going schooners she had seen lining the docks of Boston.

Instead of open decks, the major part of the boat was filled with the long, wooden cabin area that ran from stem to stern. No higher than four feet above the deck, it had a flat roof where the passengers could come out in the day and sit or stand as the journey progressed. On this particular boat, the cabin was painted a bright yellow. Others were painted with garish reds, blues, greens, and oranges, or combinations of those colors. Having grown up just a block away from the Erie Canal, Lydia had always wondered why the boats were painted with such bright colors. Perhaps they were painted to match the bawdy reputations of the canawlers that captained them and the women who cooked on them.

Inside, the cabin area was partitioned off into two sections, one for the men, one for the ladies. Each wall was filled with wooden berths that were now folded up and attached to the wall with leather straps. The forward section was for the women. The only toilet facilities consisted of a common hairbrush, a single towel, and a bucket of water—drawn by rope from the canal whenever necessary. That made Lydia frown. Long stretches of the canal were stagnant and filled with refuse and the occasional body of a cat or chicken.

With over four dozen people crowding into the limited space, finding their places and getting settled, the air was close and stifling. As Lydia and Nathan picked their way down the main passageway between the people, the smell almost made Lydia gag. She was now long past the queasy time of her pregnancy, but this was like an open assault on the nostrils. The air reeked of stale tobacco smoke, human perspiration, rancid lard from the big cooking kettles, stale perspiration from stacks of blankets that had seen too many hot and humid summer passages, and the peculiar sharpness of whiskey. Every canal boat had a small bar for its gentlemen passengers, alcohol seeming to be the universal anodyne to help dull the "ecstasies" of canal travel.

The men's section was unbelievably filthy. The floor was fouled with the remnants of the tobacco chewers' spittle, and beneath the tables she could see scraps of bread, fried bacon, and other remains from previous suppers. Come night, there would be roaches and perhaps a rat or two to contend with. She gave a little shudder, and Nathan reached out and took her hand and squeezed it.

Thankfully, the cramped crew quarters were near the rear door, and as Nathan put their things away as best he could in the limited space, Lydia stepped to the door and inhaled deeply. They would leave the door open once everyone settled down. It would be cold tonight, not far above freezing, but she decided she could bear that more than trying to sleep with the door shut and letting the smell from the men's section creep through the walls.

"This is disgraceful," she said after they got their things stowed and she stepped back out into the cabin area. "It's like pigs have been living in here."

Nathan stepped back out and surveyed the cabin area. She was right. It was a disgrace. "I'll be back in a minute."

Up on top, he found Mother Smith watching the captain getting the last of everything situated. "Sister Smith?"

"Yes, Nathan?"

"Have you been downstairs yet and seen what the cabin area looks like?"

She wrinkled her nose, the blue eyes, which were so like Joseph's, suddenly crackling with indignation. "Yes, I have. And I gave the captain a piece of my mind too. He promised me faithfully he'd have it all clean for us. He just got back from taking a group to Syracuse."

"Would you mind if I organized a few of the brethren and sisters and we cleaned it up a little?"

She looked up at him quizzically for a moment.

"What's the matter?"

"Most everybody's mad at me for not putting them in the right bunk or getting their children close enough to them." She shook her head in exasperation. "Can you believe it? Some of these families didn't even think to bring any food. A week or more at least until we're in Ohio. What did they think they were going to eat, manna from heaven?"

Before he could answer, her face softened and the eyes began to twinkle. "To tell the truth, Nathan, I don't think I can handle you comin' to me with a solution to a problem. All I know how to do is handle people without solutions." She patted his arm. "I think that's a wonderful idea. The captain said he's got a mop and some brooms."

He laughed. "You're wonderful, Mother Smith. I know there are a few who grumble, but we all love you for what you're doing."

"Thank you, Nathan. That's very kind."

"I'll go see what we can do."

He walked back to Lydia, told her what he was doing, pushed her gently back down on the bunk when she tried to get up, then went from person to person. Most agreed immediately to help, though some snapped at him that they had more than they could handle just getting settled.

Within an hour they had transformed the place. The men lifted the tables and stowable bunks while the older children swept under them, and the women followed right behind them with mops and buckets of water. Younger children scrubbed at the table tops and wiped off the chairs and benches. Before they were through, even the grumblers had relented and pitched in. By the time they went back up top, the group was in high spirits again.

Nathan brought up a chair for Lydia so she could be on top as the boat cast off. A ragged cheer went up as the captain waved to the mule skinner at the head of a team of three mules. He popped a whip above their heads and the animals started forward. The canal boat gave a small lurch, then began its slow movement forward. The excitement quickly died as they left the village of Waterloo and moved out into the open countryside at a steady four miles an hour.

Waterloo, which was three or four miles north of Fayette, was situated along the Cayuga-Seneca Canal. From here the group would travel east on the canal to the head of Lake Cayuga, then turn north to eventually join the Erie Canal. There they would turn west again and head for Buffalo. As the farmland slipped slowly and silently by them, a deep sense of melancholy settled over Lydia.

To be actually on the boat, moving slowly but inexorably farther and farther away from home, hit her hard. She knew what it was. With the finality of a woman's intuition, Lydia knew she would never be returning to Palmyra. She would never see her parents again. She would write—she had already decided that—but would they answer her letters? She wasn't sure. Would this child (she still felt it was a boy) now in her womb ever know his grandparents? Not likely.

Just as intense were her feelings about the Steeds. There was at least some hope there, but really, when she was honest with herself, how much? Images filled her mind: Matthew, with his blond rooster tail that couldn't be tamed and his ever inquisitive nature; sweet Rebecca, with her dimples and solemn eyes; and Melissa and Mary Ann and Father Steed . . . She felt her eyes start to burn, and she blinked quickly, fighting for control. She didn't want to cry. Not now. Not with Nathan so excited. Not with all the Saints so filled with hope and enthusiasm.

"Low bridge!" the captain bawled from behind them. "Everybody down." As they ducked low they saw a wagon, on which were seated a father and two sons, crossing above them. The children on the boat and the boys on the wagon exchanged excited calls. Lydia smiled briefly, turning her head around to watch them drive on as the boat moved away. As she turned back and her smile faded, Nathan reached across and began to rub her back. He took a deep breath. "Lydia," he started. "It will be all—"

But just then they heard the voice of Mother Smith. She was at the front of the boat again, calling everyone to order. Parents called to their children; people turned their chairs to the front; those who were standing found a place on the top of the cabin area.

"Brothers and sisters," she said again. "As we begin this journey to Ohio, I would remind you that we travel by the commandment of the Lord, just as Father Lehi in the Book of Mormon did, just as Moses and the children of Israel in the wilderness did."

"Amen!" It was one of the teenage boys in the back. Several turned and smiled at him. He went a scarlet red and ducked his head.

"If we are faithful, just as Father Lehi and the prophet Moses were faithful, we have every reason to expect the Lord's blessings to follow with us. It is a solemn thing to leave our homes"—Mother Smith's eyes caught Lydia's for a moment—"and, in some cases, our families, in order to keep the commandments of God. We must therefore lift up our hearts to God continually and ask him to bless us on our journey. Without those blessings, I think we shall not prosper."

Now many of the adults were nodding, their faces sobered and thoughtful. For the moment, even the children seemed subdued. Lydia, who had been looking out across the fields as Mother Smith talked, finally turned to watch her.

"We shall ask Sister Catherine Folger to take the lead as we sing the hymn 'A Mighty Fortress Is Our God.' After that, Brother Porter, could we ask you to offer a prayer for our safekeeping?"

Porter Rockwell, nearly sixteen years of age, was sitting just behind the Steeds. He nodded. "Be pleased too."

Those few who were still standing found a place and sat down cross-legged on the roof of the cabin. Sister Folger, a young mother from Farmington Township, stepped forward, lifted her arm, and briefly hummed a pitch.

At first the hymn sounded a little ragged. They, of course, had no instrument to accompany them. And there were no hymnals. There was also no attempt at harmony. There were just thirty or forty voices, including those of several of the older children, singing in near unison. Without prompting they immediately began again when they had finished.

The first time through, Lydia sang softly, her mind only partly on the song. But the music began to stir in her. She had always loved the majesty of Martin Luther's hymn, and now, as they started again, the words began to sink deep into her soul. She lifted her head and this time sang the hymn in full voice.

> A mighty fortress is our God,
> A tower of strength ne'er failing.

The sound floated across the water and then out across the fields just coming to life with spring's gentle touch.

> A helper mighty is our God,
> O'er ills of life prevailing.

For the past three months, every time she and Nathan had talked of making this journey she had brushed aside his expressions of concern for her and the baby. It would be all right, she would laugh. The baby wasn't going to come before its time. Stop being such an old brood hen, she would tell Nathan. But down deep inside she felt a cold knot of anxiety. What if she were wrong? If this were her second or third child she would better know how to predict, what to expect. Secretly she was terrified.

> He overcometh all.
> He saveth from the Fall.

She felt a little chill start up the back of her neck, and tears sprang to her eyes. In that instant, the knot inside her was loosed. She felt the fear and the sorrow and the loneliness begin to dissipate, as though all of that were a morning mist blown away by a freshening breeze, leaving nothing but a crystal clearness in its place.

> His might and pow'r are great.
> He all things did create.

It was not just a hymn any longer. It became a prayer, a song of supplication. This little band of Saints—perched on the roof of a well-worn canal boat, newly embarked on their journey to Ohio—were part of God's kingdom once again restored to earth. They were leaving their homes in direct obedience to God's command. He would be their fortress and their protection. *No,* she corrected herself. *Not their fortress. My fortress. My strength ne'er failing.*

She leaned back against Nathan, lifting her voice even higher, tears streaming unashamedly down her face now.

And he shall reign forevermore.

It rang out, echoing as though they sang in some great and grand forest glade, hushing everything across the landscape.

Even as the last of the notes carried out across the water, she turned to Nathan, leaning up to whisper in his ear. "Thank you."

His eyes widened a little. "For what?" he mouthed.

She pulled close again. "For not giving up on me. For writing me that letter. For sending me the Book of Mormon." Her voice caught. She smiled through her tears. "For loving me enough."

———•———

It was clear that Martin Harris had not been doing farm work this morning. But then, he rarely did anymore. He mostly supervised the help he hired from the surrounding townships. But even then, he was dressed a little more to the nines than usual. He looked like he had come directly from church. He wore a coat with tails; a vest with gold chain across the front and a watch tucked in the pocket; a linen shirt with ruffles down the front; breeches puffed at the sides and tucked into the knee-high, highly polished brown leather boots—or at least they had been highly polished before he had left his horse and walked across the plowed field to join Benjamin Steed. The earth was still damp, and globs of it clung to his boots. But if he was bothered by it, he gave no sign.

"Guess you've heard nothing from Nathan and Lydia?" he asked.

Benjamin shook his head. "It's only been three days since they left. Don't expect we'll hear much for another two weeks or so."

"Hope all goes well with the baby."

Benjamin looked at him sharply. Martin knew his feelings about his son and daughter-in-law packing up and leaving with her almost ready to deliver. Was he rubbing it in a little, the fact that this new faith of theirs—and Martin's—took priority over family? But Martin was chewing on the stub of a weed, looking out across the fields of their two farms, his eyes far away. Benjamin decided the comment had been one of sincere concern. He relaxed a little. "Thank you. Do you still plan to leave at the end of the month?"

His friend and neighbor finally looked around, coming back to Benjamin. "Yes. As I mentioned to you before, Joseph wrote to me a while back and asked me to close things out here. I'll be taking the rest of the copies of the Book of Mormon, and it looks like we'll have about forty or so people."

Benjamin felt a little flash of irritation. "I still don't understand why Nathan and Lydia couldn't have just waited and gone with you."

There was a long look of appraisal, then Martin finally nodded. "I'd have been happy to have them with me." He smiled, but it was a sad, almost melancholy, expression. "But then, I've learned that some folk have their own mind."

Benjamin looked away, knowing what was meant, embarrassed by the pain on Martin's face. Martin and Lucy Harris had recently separated and were no longer living in the same house. From what little Benjamin could gather, the marriage had never been a wonderful one, but when Martin went off chasing after Joseph Smith, and especially when he mortgaged his farm to finance the publication of the Book of Mormon, it had been like throwing boulders in the bottom of an already sinking boat. Lucy Harris would definitely not be going to Ohio with her husband. And while Martin was turning his back on a lot in Palmyra, in some ways it was probably a relief to him as well.

"We've come a long ways, Ben," Martin finally said.

Benjamin nodded. "You more than me."

"Not really. You've made for yourself a fine place here."

"I know, but you and your pa, you came when this was frontier."

There was a soft sigh, tinged with an air of regret. "Yes, and now, it's just not the same."

Benjamin murmured an assent, watching his friend closely. Just last month Martin had sold a goodly portion of his land at public auction—about a hundred and fifty acres—and paid off the three-thousand-dollar mortgage he had contracted to pay for the printing of the Book of Mormon. All that land. Gone now. *And for what?* Benjamin thought. *To pay a debt that wasn't really his.* Benjamin shook his head. No wonder Martin was in a reflective mood.

Martin was watching him closely, seeming to read his thoughts. "You ever think of leavin', Ben?"

"What?" The question had caught him from the blind side.

"You ever think about selling out and movin' on?"

"Of course not. Why should I? I got a good piece of land here. The price of wheat is good. It'll be another successful season."

Martin took the stub of weed out of his mouth, flipped it away, and turned to face Benjamin directly. "Exactly."

"What's that supposed to mean?"

Martin laid a hand on his shoulder. "You and me, Ben, we need more than success. We need to be succeeding."

One eyebrow came up, and Martin laughed. "Sounds like I'm talking fool's talk, don't it?" He laughed again as Benjamin's eyes answered his question. Then he slowly sobered. "Think back to when you first came, Ben. You and your boys clearing land, building that little cabin, digging a well, putting in fence. It was hard work. A lot of hard work."

"Well, that we can agree on," Benjamin said fervently.

"Now, look at you. You've got one of the finest farms in the township. You've tripled the size of your house. You hire your help now. You've even put some cash in the bank, I hear."

"So? A man's got a right to the fruits of his labor."

"Of course, of course," Martin said, "but that's not my point, Ben. Think of it. Are you happier now than you were then, at the first?"

Benjamin turned and looked at him. "I . . ." He stopped, the question really hitting him. In the summer of '26 he had up and pulled stakes, leaving a beautiful farm in Vermont. Before that it had been a farm in Connecticut. The longest he and Mary Ann had stayed in any one place was five and a half years. They had now been here almost five years.

Martin was right. There really was something exhilarating about the contest between man and wilderness. He had left Vermont because he had beat it—the harsh winters, the rock-strewn countryside, the challenge of conquering the land. And now, in an instant, he realized that he was starting to feel those first feelings of restlessness again. He had pushed them aside, and they weren't compelling. Not yet. But Martin was right.

Searching his face, Martin suddenly smiled triumphantly. "That's what I mean. And that's exactly where I am, Ben. The exciting things have been done. We're a success, you and me. So why aren't we happier?"

"I'm not unhappy," Benjamin retorted, a little defensively now.

"No, of course not. Neither am I. Not in that sense. But it's not the same, is it?"

Their eyes met and locked, but Benjamin didn't answer.

"Is it?" Martin said, gripping his arm.

Benjamin finally let his eyes drop. "No, not really."

"That's what I mean. Success isn't enough for us. What we need is the succeeding. We need to be doing things, and when they're done, we need to move on and start again."

"You're leaving because Joseph Smith left," Benjamin said bluntly.

"Yes," Martin acknowledged honestly. "Yes, I am. But I was ready, Ben. I'm looking forward to starting again, seeing what I can do." He changed the subject with sudden swiftness. "Have you had any luck in selling Nathan's farm yet?"

"No."

"Didn't think so." He looked away, this time to the south, across Benjamin's fields to the line of trees that marked the creek that served as property line between their farms.

"Why do you ask?"

"I'm leaving for Newark this afternoon."

Benjamin turned, realizing that this was what Martin Harris had really come to say.

"I'm meeting with the man who purchased my land. He has others with him. Developers from the East. Boston, Springfield, Providence."

Benjamin still waited, letting Martin take it at his own pace now.

"He says they're looking for prime farmland. Big parcels. Thirty or forty acres at a cut. They're looking to hire men to run them for them."

Gradually it dawned on Benjamin what Martin was saying. "You mean—"

"Yes." His voice rose in excitement. "Suppose I told them about both yours and Nathan's farms being for sale. They say they're paying good money."

Benjamin was stunned. Sell the farm? Just when it was paying off in rich dividends? What would Mary Ann say? What would the children think? Then it hit him, as though someone had jabbed him with an ox goad. He wasn't asking questions about how *he* felt about doing it. "Where would I go?" he asked slowly, his eyes narrowing with quick suspicion.

Martin threw back his head and laughed. When he straightened, his eyes were full of amusement. "Ben, Ben," he said, still chuckling, "you can go anywhere you want. There's a big country out there."

"But you're going to Ohio?"

"That's right."

"And Mary Ann and Melissa, they've got their hearts set on Kirtland too."

"I've heard the reports, Ben. There's worse places than Ohio for a man who's looking for a new start. Besides which, there's a lot to be said for a man being close to his grandchildren."

Surprisingly, Benjamin was not angry. He laughed now too, ruefully. "You and Mary Ann. You never give up, do you?"

"Not on a good man like you."

Benjamin shook his head, sobering. "Leave the farm?" he mused, now half speaking to himself. "For Ohio?"

"It's not Ohio that's troubling you," Martin said with quick shrewdness. "It's the idea of following after Joseph."

Benjamin didn't answer. He and Martin had been over this ground many times before.

"Let me ask you two questions, Ben."

Benjamin nodded.

"That first spring you were here, you hired Joseph and Hyrum as day labor. Since then, you've hired a lot of other men to help you with this or that. Have you ever had better workers, more honest help, than the Smith boys?"

That was easy. Benjamin still felt shame when he thought of his decision to fire Joseph and Hyrum because the townspeople were wagging their tongues about Benjamin Steed hiring Joseph Smith. He shook his head firmly. "No."

"All right. Second question. Since your family decided to follow Joseph and join the Church, aren't they the better for it?"

The silence stretched on for several moments.

"Come on, now, Ben. You're an honest man. Be honest with yourself for a moment."

Benjamin began to kick the dirt, fighting his personal feelings about Joseph, making himself consider Martin's question honestly. It had been about a year now since they had been baptized.

"Well?"

Benjamin slowly nodded. "I've got to admit that things have not turned out to be as bad as I feared."

Martin laughed. "You stubborn old fool. I didn't ask you that. I asked you if things were better since they joined the Church."

Ben tried to take offense at his friend's directness, but they knew each other too well for that. Besides, Martin had him. "Yes, I guess I've got to admit that things have been better."

"How?"

That was a harder question, and his eyes narrowed thoughtfully. "Well, Mary Ann and me, we've always had a good marriage, but . . . I don't know. She seems so much happier now, so much more willing to try and please me. It's just been better."

"What about the kids?"

He sighed, giving up in total surrender now. "All right, all right. At first I thought all this scripture reading and having family prayer every night and going to Sabbath services was pushing too much religion on them."

"But?" Martin prodded.

"But," he finally admitted, "they have been better. There's less fightin' now, and they seem more willing to help without complaining about it."

"So," Martin said triumphantly, "there you go. Look, Ben, no one's going to force you to be baptized if you move to Kirtland. But if Joseph Smith and the Church of Christ have blessed your family, why are you so dead set against them?" Before Benjamin could answer, Martin went very serious. "You think about selling your farm, Ben. You think about making a new start somewhere. And if you decide to do it, maybe Kirtland is as good a place as any."

———————

Well over a thousand miles to the west of where Martin and Benjamin stood talking, Jessica Steed was walking down the streets of Independence. She slowed her step as she saw the three ladies coming down the board sidewalk toward her. Immediately she stopped to look in the window of the small dress shop she was passing. She didn't want to have to face them—with their curious looks; with their whispered asides; with their eyes that stared, then darted away the moment Jessica looked in their direction. The display in the shop was meager and provided little to keep her attention so captured, but she didn't care. Let them think what they wanted.

"Good morning, Mrs. Steed." It came almost as a chorus.

She turned slightly, managing to look a little surprised. "Good morning."

"Nice day, isn't it?"

"Yes." They moved on, and in the reflection of the window she saw them looking back at her over their shoulders.

"Do you think she's expecting again?"

Jessie couldn't tell for sure which one had whispered it, but she was pretty sure it had been done deliberately so she would hear.

"So soon?" came the hushed answer.

A third voice chimed in, and this time the dripping sympathy made Jessie want to gag. "She does look very pale."

Jessica turned and hurried on, away, not wanting to hear any more.

Expecting again? So soon? She laughed bitterly to herself. *From whom, pray tell?* After their bitter confrontation over Doc Hathaway, the tension had become a palpable thing between her and Joshua, exploding into open confrontation at the slightest provocation. For a time, Joshua had taken to sleeping at the freight office. When he finally came back home, they both settled for an unspoken truce. That had lasted for about a week. Then he had come home from his visit with the missionaries from New York.

At first, she tried to keep her questions casual, as if it were of no more than passing interest to her. She asked about his family. Did the men know them? How were they doing? What had he learned? But Joshua had come home cold and sullen. He was in no mood to talk, and if he answered at all, it was with little more than noncommittal grunts or murmurs.

Angered, she began to push. He warned her off with his eyes, but now she sensed that Lydia was behind this. Something had been said about Lydia, something that had hurt him. And that in turn hurt her so deeply that she lashed out at him, demanding to know. He swore at her, cursed her jealousy. And finally, after she had goaded him into a fury, he told her. If he had waited, he could have married Lydia.

That was the last time she had let him into her bed. He was still coming home at nights, but usually late, often drunk, and he slept on a cot in the second bedroom.

Ten days ago he had come home long enough to gather his

things before he left with a mumbled good-bye to take a load of freight to Fort Leavenworth and St. Joseph. *Expecting? Hardly.*

Jessica had had a life of loneliness—all those years waiting on men in her father's saloon—but she had never known hurt like this. Not even her beloved reading had dulled it. Two days after Joshua left with the wagon train she went back to her father and volunteered to help behind the bar. Shocked, frightened of what Joshua would say when he returned, Clinton Roundy had finally agreed only because his daughter adamantly refused to take no for an answer. To his great relief it took Jessica Steed, housewife, less than half a day to realize that Jessica Roundy, barmaid, had died long since.

She shook her head, angry that she kept letting these emotions churn inside her to the point where she could think of nothing else. Too bad she couldn't follow Joshua's example and find her solace in the bottom of some whiskey bottle or a jug of rum. Or maybe poker. That seemed to bring out the same glassy-eyed stupor in most of the men she had known.

Jessica stopped, suddenly realizing what she was doing. She felt a wave of revulsion. Which was the stronger liquor—whiskey, or self-pity? Was this what she had come to? An embittered, mean-spirited woman who sought and imbibed personal hurts like a derelict wino begging for a drink at every bar and saloon he passed? One hand came up and she touched her face. It was burning. With fever? No, with shame.

She shook her head, shocked that she had not seen it sooner. No wonder she slept alone. No wonder Joshua avoided her eyes anymore and would rather sit at a table until his vision blurred. What was there to see at home?

Angry, sick at heart, Jessica turned and started back the way she had come. She had been on her way to take a walk down to the river. It was a long walk, several miles. She had chosen it particularly so it would fill the day. Now, determined to throw off this creature she had made of herself, she started for home. She wanted to take a long look at herself in the mirror.

Captain Patrick McIntosh chewed steadily on the stump of his unlit cigar even though it was starting to come apart in his mouth. The light from a half-moon was enough to show the flecks of tobacco on his lower lip or at the corners of his mouth. Nathan watched him and reflected. Many of the company of Mormons felt uncomfortable around this hard-muscled canawler who smoked tobacco strong enough to fumigate a barn and sang bawdy songs to himself. But Nathan had come up on deck that first night after Lydia had fallen asleep. He wasn't tired and couldn't bear to spend any more time than was absolutely required in the cramped berth. The captain had been up top, smoking his cigar. On impulse, Nathan sauntered over and began to visit with him. It had turned out to be such an enjoyable experience, that it had now become their nightly ritual.

The air was cold, and their breath left little puffs of silver in the moonlight. It would take two or three weeks of good warm weather to bring out the hordes of insects that were common to these parts. Off to the left, about a quarter of a mile away, a lamp-lit window glowed warmly in the darkness. It was the only light to be seen in any direction. Below them a young child began to fuss. There was the creak of someone walking on the wooden deck, then the sound of a mother soothing the child.

The captain began to hum softly, a tune Nathan had not heard before. His voice was deep and had a remarkably good timbre to it. Then he began to sing softly, as though he were alone and singing to himself.

> Buffalo gals, won't ya come out tonight,
> Come out tonight, come out tonight?
> Buffalo gals, won't ya come out tonight,
> And dance by the light of the moon?

He sang it again, then lapsed back into humming it. Finally, Nathan spoke. "Buffalo gals?"

The man stopped and took the cigar from his lips, spitting out a piece of tobacco that had stayed on his tongue. "Yeah, Buffalo gals." He shook his head, his eyes closing. "Now, there's a place for you."

"Buffalo?"

"No, Goose Island. Just this side of Buffalo. It's where all the canawlers stop. The song suggests that the gals from Buffalo come out and join them."

"And do they?" Nathan asked, guessing the answer already.

"Yeah. The ladies"—he gave a short bark of laughter, amused by his own choice of words—"they're always willin'." He flipped the cigar away, and there was a soft plop as it hit the water. "We'll see Goose Island once we pass Lockport."

"Lockport? Those are the big locks that go over the Niagara ridge?"

"Aye, and what a sight to see! A double staircase, five stories high. One for ascending, one for descending boats. Gates big as a barn. In the height of the season, canal boats line up for miles. You gotta fight for your place, or you'll lose two, maybe three, days." He spit out over the deck and into the water. "This early in the season, you'll miss most of that, but that's all right. It ain't always pretty."

"I've noticed that most of the teams are mules. Why not horses?"

"No, thank you."

"Why not?"

"Mules rest less, and they can eat rougher food. Besides, a mule's smarter."

"Smarter than a horse?" The Steeds had a team of mules and a horse. It was much easier to like the horse.

"Yes, sir. A horse'll walk right off a bridge if you're not watchin' him real close. Mule'll never do that."

"Hmm." That surprised Nathan, but he saw the wisdom of it immediately. Whenever the canal came to a ravine or creek or river, aqueducts carried it across the low spots. Narrow plank bridges for the teams ran along both sides of the aqueduct. They had no railings of any kind.

Captain McIntosh fished another cigar from somewhere inside his jacket and jammed it into his mouth. He made no effort to light it. Finally, he gave Nathan a sidelong glance. "You a Mormon too?"

Nathan nodded.

"You know this Joe Smith personally?"

"Yes. Very well."

"Is it true what they say? That he's seen angels?"

For a moment, Nathan considered the question, remembering his own reaction when he had first heard Joseph's account. "Well," he said slowly, "there's those that think he's lyin' straight out. But I know Joseph well. He's an honest man. He says he did, and I believe him."

That seemed to satisfy the captain. He pulled at his lower lip. "The missus, she's got real strong feelings against the Mormons."

"You're married?" It was blurted out, and instantly Nathan felt his cheeks burn. "I'm sorry, I—"

The captain hooted softly. "Don't you never mind, laddie. Catches most people by surprise, I reckon." He suddenly looked a little sheepish. "All that talk about Buffalo gals and Goose Island. Can't say as I blame you."

"No, I . . . I just thought . . . you bein' on the canal all the time . . ." It was lame and Nathan knew it.

McIntosh looked away, suddenly embarrassed, but wanting nevertheless to have it said. "Don't stop at Goose Island no more. Not since the missus and I got hitched up."

Nathan had to look away to hide his surprise. He felt a sudden shame—for his own feelings and for some of the things those in the company had said about this man. Then in a flash he understood something else. "The boy, the one helping as your mate. He's your boy, isn't he?"

"Yep. He's my oldest. Got three more back home. Two girls and another boy." It was said with pride.

"I'd like to meet them." He really meant it.

"That'd be nice. But anyway, as I was saying," the captain went on, feeling awkward about exposing his feelings, "the missus was gonna come on this trip with me. She usually does. But when she heard I was takin' a group of Mormons, she said there was no way she'd be minglin' with them kind of folks. I tried to talk her out of such fool notions, but didn't do no good."

"I know," Nathan said. "We've seen it happen before."

"Darn shame," he answered firmly. "Can't remember ever seein' a people with more religion than you folks. Mornin' and evenin' devotionals, prayers for a safe journey." He suddenly chuckled. "That Mrs. Smith. She's a whip, ain't she?"

"She sure is. She's one fine lady."

He straightened, and pulled his coat around him. "Well, never been much for religion, myself. But I just want you to know, mate, when I be getting back, I'll be tellin' the missus that she was wrong. I'll not be having her say anything bad about the Mormons anymore. Not in front of me anyway."

Nathan was touched. He stuck out his hand. "Thank you, Captain. Thank you very much."

"You're welcome, laddie."

The captain turned and went down the ladder and to his cabin. Nathan watched him go, and made a silent vow with himself. The Bible said, "Judge not, that ye be not judged." He thought of the captain. The soiled shirt and the wet stump of a cigar were not the man. Not by a long shot.

One of the characteristics of the Church of Christ was its mission to spread the news of the Restoration. Within weeks of the organization of the Church, Samuel Smith, one of Joseph's younger brothers, had gone on a mission for the Church. Since then, others had begun to move through the villages and hamlets of New York and Pennsylvania. Then Oliver and Parley and the others had gone west. They had stopped at Kirtland, and look what that had done for the Church.

At that moment, Nathan made another vow. Once they got to Kirtland and the baby came and he'd gotten Lydia settled in a new home, he was going to talk to Joseph about missionary work. And maybe, just maybe, Joseph would let him come back to Waterloo, or wherever the McIntosh family lived. It was something Nathan suddenly wanted to do. Not that he wanted to leave Lydia and the baby. Even the very thought of that left him with a sudden ache. But to share the joy that he felt, the comfort that came from having the restored gospel? That was something he wanted to do very much.

———•———

"You still awake?"

Mary Ann turned over onto her side. "Yes. You too?"

She felt her husband nod in the darkness.

It was silent for several moments. "Why?" she asked.

Again more sensed than seen, he shrugged.

She reached out and laid a hand on his arm. "You've put in long days lately. You should be exhausted."

He didn't answer that, but turned and put his hands beneath his head and stared up at the ceiling. "You still goin' without food?"

That startled Mary Ann. Over the past several weeks she

had fasted four, maybe five, times, but her husband had not commented at all. The last time had been two days ago. She decided to answer him honestly. "I was planning on doing it again maybe tomorrow."

He grunted, but there was no way to read what he meant by it. She lay perfectly still, afraid that there was another question coming, the question she had been dreading since she first told him. Why are you doing this? And what did she say then? How would he respond if he knew she was fasting and praying that his heart would be softened and that he too might be converted?

Another minute passed, and she felt herself begin to relax. When he spoke again it once more took her by surprise.

"I think we need to go over as a family and visit Martin Harris sometime soon."

"Oh?"

"Before you know it there won't be any more opportunites left to get over there and see him."

"Yes, I know." She had been dreading Martin's departure for over a month now. Losing Martin Harris as a neighbor was a blow. He had become good friends with Ben, and Mary Ann had long nurtured hopes that Martin might be the instrument the Lord chose to bring her husband to accept the faith. But more depressing was the fact that Martin was taking the last group of Saints with him. All the others had left now—the Colesville Branch, the Fayette group with Mother Smith. There would still be a few left, but they were scattered across a distance of better than a hundred and twenty-five miles. The association with fellow Saints that she had come to treasure would be sorely missed.

She realized he was waiting for more of an answer than that. "I think it would be nice if we did. He's been a good neighbor."

"That he has."

She turned and peered at him in the darkness. They had shared this bed now for coming up on twenty-six years. She could tell when he had something on his mind, and now she was curious.

He stirred slightly, then settled back in again. Finally, he turned his head to look at her. "You ever forgiven me for makin' you leave Rutland?"

For a moment she just stared at him in the darkness, completely caught off guard by this turn in the conversation. Then she forced herself to consider his question. Finally she spoke. "Of course." She spoke without reservation. She loved Palmyra. She had made good friends. They had a house that was half again better than the one they had owned in Vermont. And most important, the move to Palmyra had brought her to where the Restoration was taking place, brought her into contact with Joseph, given her the answers to prayers about which church she should join.

"Good."

She came up on one elbow. "Why do you ask?"

"You still in a forgivin' mood?"

There was little better than a half-moon out this night, and the sky was cloudless. It provided just enough light through the window curtains that she could see he was smiling. She was dumbfounded. He was teasing her! Teasing was not part of Benjamin Steed's nature. He could laugh and have a good time, but he hadn't played with her like this—tantalizing her, dangling the bait in front of her—for years.

She lay back, deciding to play it straight until she could learn what was prompting this remarkable mood in him. "I suppose," she said lightly. "What have you done that needs forgivin'?"

She sensed the smile slowly fading. He was serious again now. Completely. Finally he took a deep breath. "I sold the farm."

She came up like a pheasant exploding from cover. "You what?" she cried.

"I sold the farm."

She just stared at him, her mouth working but nothing coming out.

He was grinning again. "Well, actually, I haven't agreed to anything yet. I wanted to talk to you first. But I have an offer."

"I . . ." Too stunned for words, she lay back slowly.

"Some men that Martin met through the man who bought his property, they're willing to buy our land *and* Nathan's. They want a package deal. The money's good. Real good."

"But . . ." It was as if she were gasping for breath. "But why, Ben? We've just got this one to where . . ." She shook her head, suddenly wanting to cry.

"I know this is sudden, but—" He stopped, and then it was there again. He was leading her on. Savoring the moment. Enjoying her dismay. Which only bewildered her all the more. "If I was to stay on a week or two longer, get things all squared away, do you think you and the children could be packed up and out of here in three days?"

This time her cry was one of complete alarm. "Three days!"

"Yeah. Like I say, I'd stay on and finish things up."

"This is . . ." She clenched her fists, feeling a tremendous surge of futility. Three times she had watched this man take a piece of wilderness and turn it into productive, coveted farmland. Three times she had watched him tire of it and had to pick up everything they owned and move on. She turned icy cold. "This is crazy, Ben," she started again, fighting to keep her voice under control. "You just lie there and suddenly announce you've sold the—"

"Otherwise," he said quietly, "you'll miss the only canal boat I could find that has passage to Buffalo."

"—farm and that we're to be out of here—" She stopped, blinking in surprise.

He began to chuckle.

"What did you say?"

"I said, I could find only one boat with passage to Buffalo."

"Buffalo?"

"Of course you could wait and go with Martin and his group. But they won't be leaving for another three weeks. You'd miss the birth of the baby."

She was obviously reeling. "The baby?" she repeated dumbly.

He went on musing, as if she had not spoken. "That means

once you get to Buffalo, you'll have to find your own passage to Kirtland. Think you can manage that?"

She sat up again, this time very slowly. "Kirtland?" she whispered.

He sat up too. "Yes," he said innocently, "isn't that what they call that place?"

"Kirtland?" she said again. *Dumbfounded* didn't begin to describe her reaction now. "Are you . . . do you mean . . . ?"

"Martin tells me there's lots of opportunity in Ohio." He put his arm around her, sobering again now. "The question is, are you willing to sell the farm and leave here?"

She threw her arms around him, knocking him backwards onto the bed again. "You *are* serious!" she shouted.

He laughed aloud now, fully enjoying his little coup. "Yes, Mary Ann, I am. Wouldn't hurt us none either to be close to our first grandchild."

She rolled over onto her back, wanting to leap up or pound the mattress or throw open the window and shout the news to the world.

"The sale is set, soon as I give them the word. The first order of business is to decide if you can be ready in time to catch this boat that's leavin' Thursday. I was only suggesting that. You could wait and we could all go together."

She calculated quickly. "Two or three days to Buffalo, maybe that much more to Kirtland—I could make it in time!"

He nodded. "Assumin' Lydia hasn't had it by now, and provided that you aren't delayed too long in Buffalo or somewhere else along the way."

"Would you mind terribly, Ben?" Her mind was racing. "It would leave an awful lot for you to do."

He laughed again, thoroughly enjoying himself now. "I thought this whole thing through carefully," he drawled. "Way I figured it, woman, once you heard the news, you wouldn't be good for much more than three days any way. I say, get you and the kids ready and be on your way Thursday."

She sat up and hugged her knees, the joy racing through her

body and making it tingle. *Three days!* She would have to decide what they could take. Enough clothes for each of them. The essentials for a month. What if Nathan and Lydia hadn't found a home yet?

Suddenly she stopped. A phrase had leaped into her mind. *"This kind goeth not out but by prayer and fasting."* Tears sprang to her eyes. They were going to Kirtland!

She turned to the man lying next to her. Suddenly she felt that her heart was going to burst. She reached out, laying her hand against his cheek. "Ben?"

His hand came up and covered hers. "Yes?"

"You know what this means to me, don't you?"

For a moment he lay still, then she felt him nod.

She swallowed, the lump in her throat almost choking her; then fiercely, as fiercely as she had said anything in a long time, the words came out. "I love you, Benjamin Steed."

He turned his head. "And I love you, Mary Ann Morgan."

Suddenly she leaped out of bed, startling him.

He sat up, alarmed. "What is it? What's the matter?"

"I've got to go tell Melissa."

"Now?"

She twirled around, hugging herself. "Yes, now. She'd never forgive me if I didn't."

———————

Spring temperatures had broken up the ice on the vast inland seas called the Great Lakes, but they had not yet been warm enough to melt it completely away. Then stiff winds out of Canada began to blow, shoving the blocks and chunks of ice, some as long as a ship, against the leeward shorelines, jamming them one against the other with incredible power—shoving and pushing until block mounted on block, fracturing, refreezing, shattering again, mounting up into impenetrable massifs. Located at the northeastern tip of Lake Erie, the harbor at Buffalo, New York, had not been spared this last blow of nature's wintry fist.

This was the scene that awaited the company of fifty Latter-day Saints led by Mother Smith when they arrived in Buffalo in the early part of May, 1831. It had taken five days to make the journey from Waterloo to Buffalo—longer than expected due to a break in the canal bank a few miles east of Lockport, which took a full day to repair. The company was tired, dirty, and irritable. Tempers were near the breaking point. That all changed as they entered the city of Buffalo, passing row after row and street after street of houses. They were here. The first leg of their journey was over. A mood of excitement swept over the group.

Then they entered the harbor. Inside the harbor itself the water was mostly clear, though chunks of ice drifted here and there around and between the hundreds of ships and boats at anchor there. But across the mouth of the harbor stretched a blue-white wall of ice easily twenty feet high. There was no break in it. The harbor was sealed. The vessels might as well have had the Appalachians between them and the open water. There would be nothing coming or going through that mountain of ice.

The excited chatter on the boat suddenly hushed. Even the children were awed into silence. Then, as the canal boat slipped into its berth and they saw the chaos that reigned on the docks, a deep gloom descended over them all. No one spoke as they filed off the boat one by one, carrying their belongings, to join the crush of people that jammed Buffalo harbor.

By the time the group reached the dock and found an empty place to set their belongings down, Lydia Steed was ready to cry. She looked up at Nathan as she placed a hand on her back. "I need to sit for a minute or two," she said.

Nathan leaped to her aid. He grabbed an empty wooden crate and turned it over, brushing it off, then helped her to it. "Are you all right?" he said, peering at her closely.

"I'll be fine."

He looked dubious, but finally nodded. "I want to say goodbye to Captain McIntosh. I'll be right back."

She watched him go, envying him the ability to stride off like that so quickly. As he moved away, Mother Smith disembarked—the last, as usual, to do so. She stood for a moment and looked at the crush of people around them, then stopped a man who was passing by. "Excuse me, sir, might you know where we could find passage to Fairport Harbor in Ohio?"

He looked at her as though she were daft. "Beggin' your pardon, ma'am, but every ship and boat and scow in this harbor is booked solid."

For the first time, Mother Smith looked alarmed. "How long have you been here?"

"Not quite two weeks."

Two weeks! Lydia felt her heart plummet. She turned her face away quickly, not wanting anyone to see that her lower lip had suddenly started to tremble.

Lydia was exhausted. Three days ago she had started to cough. The days were warming, but the nights were still cold, and by morning even the inside of the little room she and Nathan shared was like an icehouse. At first the cough was just a minor irritation; then it had deepened, going down into her chest. Now it even hurt when she breathed deeply. Then the pains had started. She had not said a word to Nathan. She was sure part of it was the coughing, which tore at the weight of the baby even though she would grab her stomach and try to cradle it each time the coughing began. The previous two nights had been awful. The pains started in the late afternoon or early evening and continued intermittently until about midnight. She was fairly certain it was false labor. The pains were very irregular and weren't terribly hard. But how hard was hard enough? And what if this were prelude to the real thing? Between the coughing and the labor pains and the worrying herself sick about both, she was worn to the breaking point.

She lifted her eyes to the blue-white wall of ice that loomed as high as some of the big steamers. Two weeks? And how much longer before that wall opened? July, if they were lucky.

Stop it, Lydia. But she couldn't stop her eyes from staring at that impenetrable wall. Even a week could mean disaster for her.

"Well, just what are we supposed to do now?"

Lydia turned, feeling a quick flash of irritation. Sister Durfee again, from Canandaigua. She was a bride of less than a month and was traveling with her husband and parents. She had barely gotten on board before she started complaining. The quarters below deck were filthy. They smelled awful. Her berth wasn't long enough to get comfortable in. The food was inedible. The mules were not moving fast enough. At that one, the captain had carefully explained that he was not allowed to move faster than four miles an hour because otherwise the wake from the boats washed out the canal banks. It made no difference to Sister Durfee. An extra mile or two an hour wouldn't make that much difference. Her husband hovered around her continually, patting her hand, trying to soothe her, obviously embarrassed by her continual whining.

Lydia felt like jumping up and screaming at her. *Try being pregnant. Try being sick. Then you can complain if you wish.*

"How are you doing?" Nathan had returned to stand by her side.

How am I doing? What do you want me to say? Do you want me to be brave? Do you want me to smile and say this is all for the gospel's sake and it's wonderful? Well, I'm sorry, but right now the gospel seems pretty remote. She fought the bleakness, fought the urge to let it all come pouring out. But she couldn't look up and bat her eyes and tell him everything was wonderful, either. Fortunately, at that moment she was seized by another coughing spell, and she was saved from having to answer. Nathan reached out and took her hand, trying to comfort her but not knowing what to do.

As the coughing gradually subsided, suddenly Don Carlos Smith jumped up and pointed. "Look!" he cried.

They all turned to where he was pointing. About fifty yards further on down the dock there was a group of people.

"It's Newel Knight," Nathan exclaimed.

Mother Smith peered down the wharf. "Bless my soul, so it is."

"It's the Colesville Branch," Don Carlos said.

The group had spotted them at the same moment, and there were cries of surprise and gladness. Newel came rushing towards them, accompanied by his father.

"Mother Smith," the senior Knight said happily as he took her hands, "how good to see you! We wondered how far behind us you were."

"But," Mother Smith said, trying to hide her disappointment, "you left a week before us. And you're still here?"

"Yes," Newel said glumly. "There've been no ships out of here in a fortnight."

The older man turned, his face beaming. "Nathan! I wondered if you would be coming."

They shook hands and embraced. Then Nathan turned to Newel and they clapped each other on the back. Nathan stepped back. "You remember my wife, Lydia?" he asked.

They nodded and stepped forward to shake her hand. Lydia stood with some effort. She must have looked as bad as she felt, for the face of Joseph Knight showed instant concern. He put his arm around her. "Are you all right?" he said softly.

She nodded, managing a wan smile, touched that he would care.

"Where is Mother Knight?" Nathan asked. "Is she with you?"

"Of course, of course," Newel said. He turned to Mother Smith and the rest of the company. "Come, we have a place over here. It's not much, but it provides some shelter from the rain and wind. There's no housing to be found anywhere in town."

Ten minutes later, as the two groups were renewing their associations, they received another surprise. This time it was Lydia that saw them first. Another canal boat was pulling up to the dock. Thomas B. Marsh was standing at the prow of the boat, waving to them. It was the rest of the group from Waterloo. The two companies had departed from Waterloo at the same time, and for the most part had stayed together; but the Marsh company had gotten behind Mother Smith's group as they went through the Lockport locks, and they had not seen them since.

It was a happy reunion with all three groups coming together, and even Lydia felt her spirits lift a little. Martin Harris was still to come with another company, but here on the docks of Buffalo Harbor was virtually the whole body of New York Saints.

When things settled down a little, Mother Smith turned to the Colesville group. "Have you told the people hereabouts that we're Mormon?" she asked.

Several looked startled, then horrified. "No!" one man said, dropping his voice to an urgent whisper. "We have not mentioned a word about our religion. Nor must you. If they know who we are, we shall not get a boat."

"Or housing," someone else added.

"Nonsense," Mother Smith snapped, for the first time showing irritation. "If we are ashamed of Christ, how can we expect God to prosper us on our journey? We have had devotionals every day on the journey here."

Thomas B. Marsh stepped forward. He was a tall, dour man, and he was shaking his head vigorously. "Do that here and we shall be mobbed before morning. Sometimes wisdom is the better part of valor."

Mother Smith rose to the full height of her four-foot-eleven frame, her blue eyes snapping with anger. "Then mob it shall be. We shall attend to our prayers before sunset, mob or no mob. And if you do not do the same, then I shall not wonder if we get to Kirtland before the either of you."

"We shall see," Marsh retorted, quite agitated now. "But we shall not be party to our own demise." He turned to his group. "Come, let us go into the city and see if we can find a place to sleep."

There were hoots of derision from the Colesville Saints: "There is no room." "There's nothing anywhere." "We've been here a week and haven't found anything." But Marsh was determined, and his group moved away. For a moment the remaining two groups stood around, an awkwardness now between them.

Finally, Mother Smith looked up. Clouds were racing across the sky and a stiff breeze was starting to blow. Way off to the west the bottoms of the clouds looked ominously gray. She turned. "Brother Humphrey? Brother Page?"

The old gentleman who had joined them in Waterloo stepped forward along with Hiram Page, brother-in-law to David Whitmer. "Yes, Mother Smith."

"I want you to go along the docks and inquire of the boatmen. Ask them if they know of a Captain Blake. He once captained a boat owned by my brother Stephen Mack. After my brother's decease, Captain Blake purchased the boat from his family."

"Yes, ma'am."

"If you find him, tell him that I ask for his kindness in memory of my brother. Tell him we have fifty people seeking passage to Fairport Harbor in Ohio."

When Brother Humphrey and Brother Page returned from their quest, they brought good news, in a way. But in another way, they brought just one more set of problems. The two men had quickly located the captain, and he did indeed still own the steamship he had purchased from Stephen Mack's family. He also responded with warmth and kindness to the pleas of the sister of his former employer and offered her group passage. Unfortunately, like everything else in Buffalo, his ship was already fully booked, and all he could provide was deck passage. That meant camping out in the open with no shelter.

Mother Smith's group had taken leave of the Colesville group the next morning and moved on board the steamship. Before they were fully settled, the rain began. It was a slow, steady, cold drizzle. Blankets and other makeshift shelters were quickly soaked, and water dripped steadily onto everything on the deck. That had been two days ago. It had rained off and on ever since. Lydia could not remember ever having been so cold and miserable.

Nathan had gone into town and, through some miracle—or, more likely, his sheer stubbornness—had found some wagon canvas and purchased it. It was not fully waterproof, but when he pitched it at an angle it kept all but the worst off her. But the cold dampness—partly from the rain, partly from the sea—penetrated everything. Her cough was now deep and frightening, and she could tell that she had started to run a fever. The previous night, Nathan had got one of the other elders and they had given her a blessing by the laying on of hands. It had helped with the fever, but the cough had not abated.

Nathan had been wonderful. She still hadn't said anything to him about the false labor—if it was false—but she could tell he knew that she was in pain. He rarely left her side now, solicitously trying to meet her every need. But he couldn't get her warm, and he couldn't keep her dry. And he couldn't make that massive wall of ice go away. As long as that was still blocking their way, there would be no end to the misery.

Now he sat next to her, holding her against him to keep her warm. She pulled her shawl more tightly around her and shut her eyes, trying to blot out the world around her.

"And how are you doing, my dear?"

Lydia looked up in surprise. Mother Smith was kneeling in front of her. She held a parasol over her head, but Lydia could see two or three points of light through it, and she noticed that the shoulders of Mother Smith's dress were wet.

She forced a bleak smile. "We're doing all right." If there was one bright spot in all of this it was Mother Smith.

She laid a hand on Lydia's. "Now, this baby knows we don't want a New York baby, doesn't it? We only want an Ohio baby."

Lydia laughed in spite of herself. "I keep saying that every night." The corners of her mouth pulled down again. "If we could just get the ice to cooperate."

"It will. It can't stay forever."

Lydia just shook her head in amazement. Her admiration for Mother Smith soared higher with every passing day. Nothing daunted her. She was indefatigable, and equal to whatever challenge confronted her. At fifty-five, she should have been the one being cared for, but instead she was caretaker, leader, foreman, and midwife to the whole company.

"Mother!"

They all turned. It was William Smith, the twenty-year-old

younger brother of Joseph and Hyrum. He came up to stand in front of his mother.

Mother Smith looked up into his eyes, since he was almost a full foot taller than she was. "Yes, William."

"Do come see the confusion yonder, Mother. You must put a stop to it."

"What is the trouble?"

"Some of the brethren and sisters are arguing in a most heated manner about whether we are wise to stay on the boat."

Lydia's head came up slowly. That was an argument that interested her.

"Some say we should seek overland transportation. Some are even suggesting we catch the next canal boat and return home."

There was a lurch of hope inside Lydia. Home? Never had any word struck such longing in her breast.

"And some of the younger sisters are flirting with the gentlemen passengers—complete strangers—in a most shameful manner. People on the docks are gathering, watching. They're starting to talk."

Lydia saw the emotions play across Mother Smith's leathered face: first the weariness, then the disappointment, followed quickly by a tightening of the lips and a flash of anger in those clear blue eyes. "All right," she said grimly, "I'm coming." She gave Lydia a quick kiss on the cheek, murmured her farewell, then followed after her son.

"Come on, Lydia," Nathan said. "We'd better go too."

Lydia shook her head. "Nathan, it's not our problem. We're not part of it."

"She may need our support."

She spun away from him. "*I* need your support!" she cried. Tears sprang to her eyes, catching her totally by surprise. She forced them back, biting at her lip.

Nathan was stunned. "I . . ." He stepped to her and enfolded her in his arms. "Of course," he whispered. "I'm sorry. Come, lie back down."

That was even worse. She turned around and buried her

head against his shoulder. "I'm sorry, Nathan. I didn't mean that. You've been wonderful. It's just that . . ." The tears welled up again and she had to stop.

He rubbed her shoulders, then her back. "I know," he said. "I know."

They stood that way for several moments, then Lydia lifted her head. "You go. You're right. Mother Smith needs all the support we can give her. I'll just lie down for a while."

He searched her face, then finally nodded. "Are you sure?"

"Yes. I'll be fine now."

He turned his head. She followed his gaze. Back near the stern, beyond the big side paddle wheels, they could see Mother Smith standing in the midst of the company. Many had their heads down, looking guilty. But one or two were talking to her, heads up and defiant.

"Will they never let up?" Lydia whispered. "She must be exhausted. Why can't they let *her* rest?"

Mother Smith had gone the previous day to find temporary housing for some of the mothers and children who had gotten sick in the rain and cold. She had finally found, through sheer perseverance, an elderly woman who had agreed to take them in for a brief time. She had then stayed well into the night, talking to the woman about the restoration of the gospel. She had not returned to the ship until after two o'clock that morning.

"Because we're all human, I guess," Nathan said.

Lydia's head snapped up and she stared at him, her eyes wide and still luminous from the tears.

He seemed startled, and she could see that his thoughts were racing. Then his face fell. "Honey, I didn't mean you."

Because we're all human. And tired and pregnant and hungry and cold. In an instant her mind was made up. She slipped an arm through Nathan's. "Come on."

He hung back, baffled by the sudden switch in her.

"Come on, Nathan. You're right. She needs our support at least."

Mother Smith had already lit into the group by the time

they arrived. Even the defiant ones had dropped their eyes now and stared at the wet deck.

"We call ourselves Saints," she said, "and we profess to have left the world and all that we possessed for the purpose of better serving our God. Will you, at the very onset, subject the cause of Christ to ridicule by your unwise and improper conduct?"

She waited for an answer. No one spoke or moved.

"You profess to put your trust in God. Then how can you feel to complain and murmur as you do?"

Lydia felt guilt touch her heart, and she too found herself not able to meet those piercing blue eyes that were sweeping the group.

The voice raised a notch in pitch. "You are even more unreasonable than the children of Israel. Here are you sisters, pining away for your rocking chairs. And here are you brethren, grumbling that you shall starve to death before journey's end. How can that be? Have I not set food before you every day, and made you, who have not provided for your own, as welcome as my own children at my table?

"Where is your faith? Where is your confidence in God? Do you not realize that all things were made by him and that he rules over the works of his own hands?"

She stopped for breath. It was as though the stillness of a cathedral had settled over the group. Even the crowd on the dock who had been standing by watching "the Mormons" had fallen absolutely quiet.

Mother Smith scanned their faces, one by one. "Suppose," she began again, this time her voice barely above a whisper, "suppose that all of us here, all of us who call ourselves Saints, should lift our hearts in prayer to God that the way might be opened for us. Do you not think that he could cause this wall of ice to part so that we, in no more than a moment, could continue our journey?"

Just then a man from the shore cried out. "Is the Book of Mormon true?"

Mother Smith swung around. "That book was brought forth

by the power of God, and it was translated by the gift of the Holy Ghost. Would that I had the voice that could sound as loud as the trumpet of Michael, the Archangel! I would declare the truth of that book from land to land, and from sea to sea, and the family of Adam would be left without excuse." She smiled briefly, with a little twinkle of humor in her eyes. "Including you, sir."

The crowd chuckled as the man began to squirm. Slowly Mother Smith turned back to the company. "Now, brethren and sisters," she pronounced, "if you will, all of you, raise your desires to heaven, that the ice may be broken up, and we be set at liberty, as sure as the Lord lives, it will be done."

There was a moment of silence, as electric as that moment in a thunderstorm before the blast of lightning splits the night. Lydia knew not what was in the hearts of the others, but she knew what was in hers. *O God.* It was a cry from the uttermost depths. *Forgive me. Forgive my murmuring cries. Forgive my quickness to turn my face from thee.* There was a brief pause, as though her spirit took a deep breath. Then, *I ask not for myself. I ask only for the child, this precious life that you have seen fit to send to us. If it be thy will, may our journey continue, so that this son of thine can be born safely in Ohio with the rest of thy people Israel.*

There was a thunderous crack. She felt the ship shudder beneath her feet, and heard the buildings lining the wharf rattle. She jerked around so hard that the baby lurched within her, jabbing her sharply with pain. For a moment, she could only stare, not comprehending. The sound had come from the harbor's mouth. For a moment there was nothing to see, just the mass of ice blocking their way. Above and behind her she heard the captain shouting. "Every man to his post! To your posts!"

Then to everyone's utter amazement, the ice jam began to crack. A seam of dark water began to open, piercing first the base, then the wall of ice. It was as if hell itself were being pried open to make way for them.

"Full steam ahead!" The captain's voice was a hoarse scream.

The smoke stacks belched black smoke, and the two side paddle wheels groaned and rattled as they started to turn.

"You people down there!" The captain, his face a mottled red, was bellowing at them. "Find a place and hang on. We're going through!"

People on the docks were screaming and pointing. The path of dark water was widening by the second.

"Come on, Lydia," Nathan shouted in her ear.

As they raced back to their place on the deck they passed the starboard paddle wheel. It was picking up speed quickly now, churning the water into a foaming cauldron. The front end of the boat was swinging around, turning into the channel that opened before them, a channel that was still widening even as they watched. The crack in the wall had now split enough that they could see through to open water. The ice was shrieking and groaning like a wounded animal.

The captain shouted again from above them. "It's going to be close."

Nathan made Lydia lie down on their makeshift bed, and he threw a blanket over her shoulders. "Hang on, Lydia!"

She grabbed at the handle of their valise, but her hand froze in midair. She was staring forward at the wall of ice now looming toward them with increasing speed. She screamed, "We're going to hit it, Nathan!" She buried her head, grabbing for Nathan's arm.

Vaguely she was aware of the screams of other passengers, the shouts of the crew. Then there was a tremendous crash just behind her. She whirled around, her eyes flying open. One of the buckets of the starboard paddle wheel had smashed into a jagged shard of ice thicker than an ox's withers. First one bucket, then another shattered into a thousand splinters.

"We're through! We're through!" She wasn't sure who had shouted it. Maybe her. But Nathan was on his feet pointing back toward the rear of the boat. He leaned down and grabbed her arm and pulled her up. The wake of the boat led in a straight line

174

from the gap through which they had just plunged. In awe they stared as that twenty-foot high floating wall began to move again, like two massive gates being closed. Again the air was rent with the deafening sound of great masses being thrust together. Even as they watched, the narrow opening closed again, shutting in the harbor, trapping the other boats, leaving the Colesville and Thomas B. Marsh groups to wait for another day.

Leaving Buffalo Harbor

Isaac Morley, a young emigrant from Massachusetts, had arrived in Kirtland not long after the first cabin had been built in 1811. He cleared enough land for a small cabin of his own and then returned to New England for Lucy Gunn, his childhood sweetheart.

In many ways Isaac Morley and his wife had been a typical frontier family, except for the fact that they had been even more industrious than most. The first one-room cabin had long since given way to a spacious frame house. There were fields of corn, along with barley and wheat. They made their own molasses and vinegar, kept hives of bees and sold the honey, produced peppermint oil, made lye from ashes for soap. Early on, Isaac had planted several dozen maple trees so they could tap their own syrup. Now called "Morley's Grove," the maple trees were in full leaf now in late May, shimmering a brilliant green behind the house.

In addition to bearing nine children and raising seven of

them, Lucy grew a patch of flax and raised sheep. The linen and woolen clothes she made not only outfitted her family but also was sold in the village. Isaac was also a skilled cooper and, besides meeting his own needs, sold the barrels, tubs, buckets, and other items in town. It was not surprising that he had been appointed one of three trustees when local government was first instituted in Kirtland. He was quiet and gentle, kind by disposition, but he commanded respect from everyone who knew him.

When missionaries to the Lamanites had arrived in Kirtland late last fall, Isaac and Lucy Morley, two followers of Sidney Rigdon, were among the first to be baptized into the Church. When Joseph Smith arrived in early February with the news that Ohio was to be the new gathering site for the Saints, Father and Mother Morley, as they were known to most of the residents, offered part of their farm as a place for the newcomers. And so it was to the Morley farm that Lucy Mack Smith and the group from New York came after their arrival in Fairport Harbor. That had been almost a week ago. Now the group faced the tasks of building homes in which the newcomers would live.

On this clear May morning Nathan stood in the midst of about twenty acres of timber felled by the hands of professional slashers two or three years previously. The air was still, and smoke from more than two dozen small fires hung in thick layers, stirred only by the movement of the men who moved back and forth tending the fires. The smoke was thick in places and dug at Nathan's eyes and filled his lungs, making him want to breathe as shallowly as possible.

He and Father Morley and about nine or ten other men were getting the logs ready for use in building cabins, barns, sheds, and rail fencing. They were using a process called "niggering." Instead of using axes and wedges to cut the logs into the needed lengths—an enormous effort, considering the number of houses being built—they would build small fires at each place where the trunks needed to be cut. One man could tend several fires, and after two or three hours of slow burning, one good whack with an ax would finish the job.

Nathan had never cleared ground this way. They had always worked it through in what his father called "the grunt and swing" method, man and ax against the forest. The idea of slashing particularly fascinated him. Father Morley claimed it had taken no more than three days for the two slashers to level the plot they now worked. That was astounding, since normally two men could work for three weeks or more to clear a heavily timbered acre. When Nathan showed interest, Father Morley explained how they worked.

They would come in and study the lay of the land and the prevailing winds carefully. Then, moving in strips thirty or forty feet wide, they would begin notching the trees on the side that faced the center of the strip, making the notches deeper and deeper as they moved windward. Once the strip was finished, the slashers would wait for the winds to come. When they did, they would leap into action. Moving swiftly to the tree previously picked as the "starter," they would deliver a few final ax blows to the trunk, already deeply notched. Then, as the wind rose and began to catch the topmost branches with its power, the tree would begin to sway a little. When the wind got high enough, nature took over. There would be a shattering crack and the starter tree would snap off and crash headlong into its nearest neighbors, sending them in turn hurtling against the next ones. Like some gigantic game of dominoes, in a matter of three or four minutes, twenty or thirty acres could be leveled.

The trees were then trimmed and the branches burned, then the logs left to dry and season for three years. Father Morley's decision to clear an additional twenty acres three years ago had proven to be perfect timing, and the new families had a rich harvest of lumber from which to draw.

Finally the pall of smoke got to Nathan. Making sure all his fires were burning well, he moved over to the edge of a field of new wheat where the air was clear. As he breathed deep gulps of the cool air gratefully, he saw Father Morley leave his fires and come to join him.

"Niggering does have its drawbacks, don't it?" he said easily.

Nathan nodded. "But I've cleared forest the other way too. I can live with a little smoke."

"Agreed." They fell silent and looked out across the fields towards the Morley home and barns.

"You have a beautiful farm here."

That seemed to please him. "Took a while to get it to this point."

"And now we're takin' it away from you."

Morley gave him a sharp look. "Didn't mean that."

"I know, but it's true, just the same. Here we are, all coming in and taking over your land."

"Can't be takin' what is given freely," Morley said evenly.

Nathan nodded, amazed again at the man's attitude.

Not only had the gift been given, but what was more remarkable, there was no begrudging of it. This represented a loss of more than a few acres of prime farmland. But there was no resentment, no lingering regrets for his charity. That was clear in his eyes, on his face, and in his voice. The gift *had* been freely given. No one had taken it from him.

Morley suddenly raised his head, squinting into the morning sun. A woman was coming across the fields from the direction of the house. She was small, and Nathan instantly recognized her. It was Mother Smith.

She waved. "Nathan!" she called.

He felt his heart lurch. "Lydia!"

Father Morley clapped him on the shoulder. "Go. We can handle this."

Nathan broke into a run, skirting the new wheat, then cutting across to meet Mother Smith.

"Has it started?" he called anxiously even before he reached her.

She smiled, taking his hand. "No, no, Lydia is fine. That baby ain't ready to come quite yet. It'll be tomorrow at least, maybe a day or two longer than that."

"Are you sure?"

Her blue eyes sparkled with amusement. "Yes, I'm quite sure."

"Oh." He didn't try to hide his disappointment, though he knew in a way it was best this way. Lydia still had the remnants of the terrible cough she picked up on the trip, and Nathan had been considerably worried about her. The warm weather was helping, but the cough had really drained her strength, and every day she could wait before having the baby would be a blessing.

"It's Joseph."

Nathan looked at her more closely. "Joseph?"

"Yes, he sent a boy from town. Says you're to come to the house immediately. He's on his way out with some news. Says to be waiting for him at the house."

"What is it?"

Her shoulders lifted and dropped. "The boy didn't say. Just said to have you there waiting. Parley's already here."

"Oh?" It had been a pleasant surprise for the group to learn that Parley Pratt had returned from Missouri in mid-March, but they hadn't seen much of him since. He, Sidney Rigdon, and others had been doing missionary work in the surrounding settlements.

"Come on," Mother Smith said, already turning to head back to the house. "Won't do none to keep Joseph waiting with whatever news he's bringing."

———•———

Parley was there with Mother Morley, Lydia, and several of the rest of the sisters. They were laughing merrily as Nathan came into the house.

"Hello, Parley," he said, striding across the room to grip his hand. "How good to see you again!"

"Shhh," Lydia said. "Brother Parley's right in the middle of telling us some of his missionary experiences."

Parley gave him a look of helplessness and pointed to a chair. "Sit down, Nathan. Joseph's not far behind me, but in the meantime these good sisters insist that I tell them the story of me and the constable's dog."

"The constable's dog?"

Lydia smiled. "Start again, Brother Parley, so Nathan can hear."

Parley ran a hand through his hair, obviously enjoying this. "Well, as I was saying, after Oliver and I and the others left Kirtland and continued westward, we passed through the neighborhood where I first lived out here. We stopped and found the people eager to hear more of the news of the Restoration. We stopped at the house of a man by the name of Simeon Carter. He treated us kindly and was responsive to our telling him about the Book of Mormon. But right as we were in the midst of speaking with him, there came a knock at the door."

He'd evidently gotten this far before, because Lydia and several other sisters were nodding their encouragement to him.

"It was an officer from a magistrate who had issued an order for my arrest on some frivolous charge. I left the Book of Mormon with Carter, and Brother Ziba Peterson and I accompanied the man. I remember it well. It was dark and cold and the roads were very muddy and traveling was difficult."

"So what happened?" one of the single young sisters asked.

"It was late in the evening when we arrived at the place of trial, but there was a whole group of men there to bear testimony against us." He frowned. "False testimony, that is. The magistrate had also obtained a judge who bragged openly that it was his intention to thrust us into prison for the purpose of testing our apostleship."

Parley sighed wearily. "We tried to tell him we were not Apostles, only elders, but it soon became obvious the whole thing was a mockery, and so I treated the proceedings with great contempt, making no attempt at defense."

Nathan nodded, remembering the trials in South Bainbridge and Colesville and how far astray Lady Justice could sometimes be shoved.

Now Parley was into new material for the group, and they were listening intently. And as for him, he was really warming to his subject. Nathan had not seen this side of him in the brief time he had been at Fayette.

"Well, it didn't take them long to pass sentence. Guilty I

was. I had two choices: either I could pay them a substantial sum of money, of which I had not in the world, or I could go to prison. When I refused to answer such nonsense, I was tantalized, abused, and urged to settle the matter. Finally, I called upon Brother Peterson, and together we sang a hymn to the court. We sang 'O How Happy Are They.' "

Nathan chuckled. "I'll bet they loved you for that."

"To say that it exasperated them further," Parley agreed with a sly grin, "would be to somewhat understate the matter. They began to press me most earnestly for the money. Fed up with the whole business by then, I stepped forward and made them a proposal."

Lucy Mack Smith leaned forward. "What?"

"Said I, 'If it please the court, I have a proposal for a final settlement. If the witnesses will repent of all their false swearing, and the judge of his wicked judgment and of his persecution, blackguardism, and abuse, we shall all kneel here together, and I will pray to God that he might forgive you in these matters.' "

Lydia clapped her hands in delight. "You didn't."

Parley nodded firmly. "I most certainly did."

"I assume they did not accept your offer?" Mother Morley was smiling broadly.

"No," he drawled. "They seemed less than enthusiastic. After some time, the court adjourned, and I was taken to a public house and locked in until morning, since the prison was some miles away from where we were."

"What about Brother Ziba?" another sister asked.

"They released him and he was allowed to return to the others." He took a breath, the merriment in his eyes now unmistakable. "Well, come morning, the officer, a Mr. Peabody, came to get me. He had with him this huge bulldog—biggest, ugliest dog I ever saw. About that same time, my brethren also arrived to see about my welfare. Speaking in an undertone, I urged them to continue their journey and promised that I would shortly join them. After they left, Mr. Peabody and I sat by the fire for a time, and then I asked if I could step out into the public square. He accompanied me, along with his dog.

"Whilst we were standing there, I turned to the officer. 'Mr. Peabody,' says I, 'are you good at running a footrace?' 'No,' he says; then, pointing to his companion, he says to me, 'but my dog is, and he's been trained for many years to assist me in my office. He will take any man down at my bidding.'

" 'Well,' says I, 'you have compelled me to go with you a mile, and I have gone with you twain. You have given me an opportunity to preach, to sing, and you have given me both lodging and breakfast. I must go on my journey now. If you are good at a race, you may accompany me. If not, good day, sir.' And with that, I took off, determined to start on my journey as quickly as possible."

The whole group was laughing now, the vividness of Parley's imagery making laughter irresistible. "What did he do?" Nathan finally managed to get out.

With great seriousness, Parley went on. "For several moments, the man stood amazed. And even though I stopped, turned to him, and again invited him to a race, he still stood amazed. I then renewed my exertions, and increased my speed to something like that of a deer. Only then did he realize what I was about and started in pursuit. But by that time I had gained close to two hundred yards on him. I leaped over a fence and was heading for a patch of timber, where I hoped to take leave of his sight.

"He was coming after me now, hallooing and shouting at his dog to seize me. I could hear him behind me. 'Stu-boy, stu-boy— take him—get him, boy—down with him.' "

A tiny smile began to play at the corner of his mouth. "Well, I could outrun the constable, but the dog was another matter. I looked over my shoulder and saw him bearing down on me. Just as he was about to leap at me, a thought popped into my mind, quick as lightning. 'Why not assist the officer,' I thought, 'and send the dog on into the forest?' So I clapped my hands, lifted my finger, and pointed in the same direction. 'Stu-boy, stu-boy,' I shouted, imitating the officer. 'Get him, boy—take him down.' "

Nathan was laughing so hard that he could feel tears welling up in the corners of his eyes. Lydia was holding her stomach, trying to stop it from shaking.

"Well, that old dog hastened on past me, being urged forward by both his master and myself, all three of us running in the same direction. Needless to say, I split company with the two of them, and did not stop until I caught up with my companions later that evening."

He sat back now, basking in the enjoyment of his audience. As the laughter still rippled through the room, a voice from behind them spoke. "A scripture comes to mind, Brother Parley."

Surprised, they all turned to see the Prophet Joseph standing in the doorway. He too was chuckling and had obviously been listening for part of the story.

"What scripture, Brother Joseph?" Parley asked.

"It comes from the Sermon on the Mount. It says, 'Give not that which is holy unto the dogs.' "

That started them all over again. "Please," Lydia begged finally. "Stop, or I'll have the baby this very day."

"Well, it's all right if you do"—Joseph paused, looking with pleasure at Lydia and Nathan, then smiled the more broadly and finished—"now."

The group quieted, sensing something was up. Lydia looked puzzled. *Why now?* her eyes asked as she looked up at Joseph.

"If laughing alone can bring the baby, then I fear that a surprise or two might put you into instant labor."

"A surprise?" Nathan asked, as bewildered as Lydia by the direction the conversation was taking.

"What is it?" Lydia leaned forward, watching Joseph intently.

He stepped back and another figure stepped into the doorway.

For a moment Nathan just gaped, then he leaped to his feet. "Ma!"

"Hello, Nathan. Hello, Lydia."

In two strides Nathan was to Mary Ann and embracing her. He stepped back, incredulous. "But how did you . . . ? When did . . . ?"

Mary Ann just smiled and then looked at Lydia, who sat openmouthed. "Joseph said the baby hadn't come yet. We're not too late, then!"

When he saw how befuddled Nathan and Lydia looked, Joseph laughed right out loud. He turned to Lydia. "Well, I can see one surprise was not quite enough to do the trick. How about a few more?"

Without waiting for a response, he waved his hand. A small figure with blond hair came rocketing through the door. "Nathan! Nathan!" He hit Nathan about waist high, nearly bowling him over.

Lydia turned to stare in amazement. "Matthew?" she whispered. Then she looked up to the doorway. Tears sprang to her eyes. "Melissa! Becca!"

"See, Mama," Melissa said, smiling through her own tears, "I told you Lydia would wait for us, didn't I?"

The initial shock and the joyful greetings were over. Mother Smith and the other sisters had left so the family could be alone with Joseph and Parley. Nathan sat back, reeling, looking at his mother. "This is *my* father you're talking about?"

His mother clasped her hands in delight. "Can you believe it?" she said softly.

Mary Ann sat on one side of Lydia on the sofa, Melissa sat on the other. Melissa had slipped one arm through Lydia's and was holding it tightly. "We still haven't come out of the daze yet," she said. She wiped at her eyes with the back of her hand, the joy still brimming over.

Lydia just shook her head, as she had been doing for the past five minutes. "I thought it would be at least a year before we ever saw you again. And here you are in Kirtland. Right here. I can't believe it."

Matthew spoke up. He had been patient long enough. "Lydia, when am I going to be an uncle?"

She became very solemn. "How about tomorrow?"

"Really?" His eyes got wide.

"Really?" Nathan echoed.

She laughed. "Why not? Mother Steed is here now and—"

She stopped. Her voice was suddenly trembling, and she couldn't finish. She waved her hand in front of her face, trying to make the tears stop. "I'm sorry." She looked at her mother-in-law. "I just still can't believe you're here."

Mary Ann put an arm around her shoulder and leaned her head against Lydia's.

Matthew turned back to Nathan. "Papa said to tell you he sold your farm too."

"Good."

Becca broke in. "He should be here in another week or so."

"That is incredible," Joseph said. "I always said your Benjamin was a good man, Sister Steed. This only goes to show how true it is."

"But he doesn't want to be baptized or anything though," Matthew said soberly.

That caught them all by surprise. "How do you know that, Matthew?" Joseph said.

He shrugged matter-of-factly. "I asked him."

"You did?" his mother said.

Nathan laughed aloud. "Good for you. What did you say?"

Embarrassed now, Matthew looked at the floor. "I asked him why he didn't believe the things Joseph has told us."

Joseph's eyes softened and he reached out and put an arm around Matthew's waist. "Only a child," he murmured. "Would that more of us were like them."

Nathan opened his arms. Matthew left Joseph and walked into them. Nathan motioned to Becca too, and in a moment both of them were in his grasp. "Do *you* believe the things Joseph has told us?" he asked them.

Both of them nodded in unison.

"And how do you know they are true?" Parley asked, smiling as proudly as if they were his own children.

"Because Becca and I prayed to Heavenly Father." Matthew turned to his sister. "Didn't we, Becca?"

Becca ducked her head, her cheeks coloring. "Yes."

"And?" Nathan asked gently.

"We felt really good inside," Matthew said firmly. "So we knew it must be true."

Nathan turned to his mother and saw that her eyes were glistening a little. He turned back to Matthew. "And did you tell Pa about that?"

His head went up and down.

"And what did Pa say then?"

"He said it was good that I found out for myself."

"He did?" Melissa blurted.

"Yep."

Now it was Mary Ann who held out her arms, and Matthew went over to her. "I'm proud of you, son," she whispered.

"And I'm proud of you too, Matthew," Joseph said. "What a joy to see the faith of youth!"

Suddenly, Joseph started. He pulled a pocket watch from his vest and glanced at it, then stood. "I was in town when word of your arrival came," he said. "Emma knows nothing of your being here. Let me run over and get her. We live in a cabin just behind the house. She'll be so excited to see you again. She was taking a nap with the twins when I left."

"You had twins?" Mary Ann cried. "Oh, Joseph, that's wonderful. We've been so busy with our arrival, I didn't even think to ask about Emma."

A shadow crossed his face, and he looked away quickly. "Emma did have twins, but they only lived about three hours."

"Oh, no, Joseph."

"Yes." He finally turned back. "It's been a very difficult time for Emma."

Melissa was puzzled. "But you said the twins were taking a nap."

Joseph was still grave. "Out of another's tragedy, we were blessed with a way to help lessen Emma's grief."

"Oh?" Mary Ann said.

Parley, seeming to sense Joseph's pain, spoke for him. "By coincidence, Sister Julia Murdock, wife of John Murdock, gave birth to a set of twins on the day following the day Sister Emma gave birth to hers." He sighed. "But in this case, it was the mother, Julia, who died, leaving her husband with five children to care for, two of them only five or six hours old."

Joseph brightened a little. "With no way to care for them, Brother John offered the twins—a boy and a girl—to Emma in hopes that it might relieve her grief somewhat. And it has. They have been a wonderful blessing to us."

"How marvelous," Mary Ann said. "How old are they?"

"About three weeks now. They were born on the first of May. We named them Joseph and Julia." He moved to the door. "If they're awake, we'll bring them." He turned to Parley, smiled, then looked to Mary Ann. "We still have one more surprise— this time for you, Sister Steed."

Lydia and Nathan glanced quickly at each other, then Lydia said: "Oh yes, Mother Steed, a most wonderful surprise."

"I'll ask Brother Parley to tell you," Joseph said. "It is he who brought the news. I'll go get Emma."

"Yes," Nathan said eagerly, "tell them, Parley."

Parley stepped forward as Joseph went out of the door. "As I'm sure Joseph has told you, Oliver and I and the other missionaries ended up in Independence, Missouri, laboring among both the Lamanites and the white settlers there."

Mary Ann nodded. "Yes."

"While we were there we had a visitor one night. He came to inquire of us if we were from New York. He was particularly interested in a family that lived in Palmyra Township." He paused, then grinned. "The family he was inquiring after was the family of Benjamin Steed."

For several moments Mary Ann looked puzzled. "Our family?" she started, then suddenly her eyes widened and one hand flew to her mouth.

Parley nodded slowly. "Yes."

"Joshua?" Melissa cried. "You found Joshua?"

"Yes, Melissa," Nathan said, "they found Joshua."

It was just past four o'clock in the afternoon of the day following the arrival of the Steed family. Outside the Morley home, Nathan stood with Joseph and several other of the brethren. No one spoke much, but Nathan kept looking at the house, his eyes anxious.

Inside, Lydia was barely aware of the shrill cry that came from her throat as she bore down. Beads of sweat stood out on her forehead, and her knuckles were white where she gripped the bedposts.

"Don't stop!" Mary Ann cried. "Don't stop! It's almost there."

Feeling as if she were pushing everything inside her out with the baby, Lydia came up on her elbows, gasped, and bore down again. Suddenly there was a tremendous sense of relief, and in an instant the pressure was gone. There was a plaintive cry from a tiny throat.

"That's it!" Lucy Morley said in satisfaction. "You've got yourself a baby!"

Lydia fell back on the bed, panting heavily. For a moment she kept her eyes closed, listening to the howl of protest at being brought so rudely into the world. Then suddenly a stab of fear jolted her. Her eyes flew open. Sister Morley had her back to Lydia, holding out the baby while Mother Smith tied off the cord. Lydia's eyes sought those of Mary Ann's. "Is it . . . is it all right?"

Mary Ann moved to her side, picked up a damp towel, and began to sponge her forehead. She was smiling warmly. "Is *he* all right, you mean?"

"A boy?" Lydia would have shouted it had her voice not been so hoarse.

Mary Ann nodded, tears suddenly filling her eyes. "Yes, a fine, healthy boy."

Sister Morley turned. The tiny head was dark, still bloody in spots, but covered with a sheen of wet black hair. "I'd say about eight pounds and sound as a twenty-dollar gold piece." She quickly wrapped a small blanket around the infant, then handed the tiny bundle over to Lydia. "Congratulations, Mother."

———•———

Nathan let his finger gently stroke the hair, marveling at its incredible softness. He watched the tiny eyelids flutter momentarily and wondered if infants dreamed, and if so, how. Was it just visual images? Or perhaps thoughts without words.

The door opened and his mother stepped out of the bedroom. She looked at him and smiled. "Lydia's asleep finally," she whispered.

"Good. She looked exhausted."

Mary Ann came to where he sat in the rocking chair. "All right, Papa, now its Grandma's turn." She had helped Lydia get settled while Lucy Morley had washed the baby, and so she had not held him yet.

Nathan stood, careful not to jostle the baby. When his mother was settled he passed the tiny bundle into her arms.

"Oh," Mary Ann breathed, "he is *so* tiny." She looked up and tears filled her eyes. "I'm so glad we were here, Nathan. My first grandchild."

Nathan knelt beside the chair, laying his hand on her arm. "So are we, Ma. Lydia was frightened." His mouth pulled momentarily. *And her own mother wouldn't come*, he thought.

Mary Ann pulled the blanket up and tucked it under the baby's chin and cuddled him even closer. "And how does it feel to be a papa by now?"

He shook his head. "It hardly seems real. Like it's just someone else's baby." He looked down at his son. "And yet . . ."

When he didn't finish she looked up.

He shrugged, a little embarrassed by his own feelings. "Since we learned that Lydia was with child, and especially during the past few weeks, I kept thinking about having our own child. But just in the last hour, holding him here, I've—" He suddenly had to stop, for his throat had a great lump in it. He tried to swallow it down. "I've had feelings like I never dreamed I could . . ." He looked away quickly. "He's my son," he finally managed. "This is my son."

Mary Ann reached out and touched his cheek. "Yes," she said, her own voice barely audible. "The first of the next generation of Steeds."

The Rogers and Sons livery stable on the southern outskirts of Kirtland was a well-kept company. They had a large barn with room for almost a dozen and a half horses. There were two carriage sheds, a tack shed, and a small blacksmith shop. Corrals out back were large enough to house another dozen head. The man who had recommended the place to Benjamin Steed when he drove into town late in the afternoon of May twenty-ninth had said that Hezekiah Rogers was a shrewd but honest businessman who ran a neat and well-organized operation. Now that he saw it, Benjamin Steed was impressed. It always pleased him to see someone care for his things, be it land, buildings, or other property.

"That's a fine-looking team, Mr. Steed."

"Thank you. I especially appreciate them. I sold two mules and another horse to get them."

Hezekiah Rogers laughed. "Well, they're sure better looking than a team of mules. And how long would you think you'll be boarding them with us?"

He considered that for a moment. When he arrived in Kirtland, first off he had inquired in town and found out about a small place for rent. He and his family would be able to stay there until Benjamin could find a place of their own. After unloading their belongings, he had gone over to the livery stable. "I'm not sure," he finally said to Hezekiah Rogers. "I've just arrived in town this afternoon. I'll start looking for a place of my own tomorrow."

"No problem. It'll be a dollar per week for the team. No extra charge for the wagon."

"Fair enough. By the way, do you know how far the Isaac Morley farm is? My family is staying there. I met Mr. Morley in town, and he said he'd go fetch them and meet me here."

"It's only about two miles out on the Painesville Road."

"Well, they shouldn't be long, then."

Rogers made an entry in a large ledger book, then turned and stepped to the door of the small office. He opened it and stuck his head out. "Carl!"

In a moment a young man in his early twenties came trotting up. He was sunburned and freckle-faced, and had a head of red hair that would have set him off in any crowd. "Yes, Pa?"

"Take Mr. Steed's team and wagon out back. Unhitch the team and give them a good rubdown, then half a bucket of oats for each one."

"Yes, Pa."

Benjamin watched him go. "Fine-looking boy."

"Thank you."

Just at that moment, there was a loud squeal from outside the office. "Papa! Papa!"

Ben smiled. "I think this is my family now."

The door to the livery office burst open and Becca came running in, pigtails flying. He opened his arms and she flew into them, throwing her arms around his neck.

"Hello, pumpkin." He swung her up and around, which took some doing, for at thirteen now, she was quickly growing into a young woman.

Matthew came hard on her heels and just as excitedly threw himself at his father. Ben hugged them both, then turned to the owner of the stable. "Thanks again, Mr. Rogers. I'll be back in touch."

"No hurry. Thanks for using our stables."

"Glad I did." He looked down. "All right, you two, do you have anyone else with you?"

With a whoop they took his hands and dragged him outside to see the rest of the family.

———•———

Carl Rogers had just started to curry the horses when he heard the commotion out front. Curious, he moved over to the barn door, which was partly open, and looked out. This was obviously a family reunion for the Steeds. The man whose horses he was now caring for was surrounded by a very happy group of people. He had an arm around a woman who was obviously his wife. A young couple with a baby in arms were standing next to them. Two children, a boy and a girl, were prancing around like two lambs frolicking in a meadow. An older man, whom Carl recognized as Isaac Morley, sat in the wagon seat smiling down at them. Another woman stood in front of Mr. Steed, but he couldn't tell much about her since her back was to him—only that she was fairly tall and as slender as a willow switch. Her waist was small enough that Carl guessed he could nearly touch fingertips if he put both hands around it.

He started to turn and go back to work just as the slender woman slipped her arm around Mr. Steed's waist. That brought her around full face toward Carl. He stopped. She was young— about twenty, he guessed—and obviously another daughter. She had the dark hair and the straight features of her father. She was laughing up at him, and that was what had made Carl stop. Her eyes were dark, but even at thirty feet away he could see them flashing. Her whole face was alive with a radiance of joy that was arresting.

"Papa," Carl heard her say happily, "isn't this wonderful? Here we all are, in Kirtland. Thank you, Papa, thank you."

Her father laughed ruefully. "Oh, Melissa, Melissa. As if I could have kept you away."

Carl pulled the door shut again, feeling like an intruder, and went back to the horses. But as he began to pull the curry comb through the mane of the one horse, he kept one ear tuned toward the door. He could hear the faint murmur of voices but couldn't distinguish what was being said. Then he distinctly heard her laugh again. Feeling a little foolish, he set the comb down, gave the horse a pat, and moved to the door again. He pushed it open slightly, his eyes going immediately to Melissa's face.

She was now talking to the young married couple. As she spoke she tossed her head, which made the long dark hair bounce lightly on her shoulders. She laughed again. It was a wonderful sound, and Carl found himself enchanted watching her.

To his disappointment, after another moment or two the family began to load into the wagon. Melissa sat in the back, blocked from his view by the driver of the wagon. He watched, hoping for one more glimpse of her, as the wagon turned around and headed back toward the main part of town.

"Hmm," he mused. "Melissa Steed." He decided that the next time he was in town he would see if he could find out any more about the Steed family.

———◆———

Jessica Steed watched her husband pull on his boots. He pushed his feet down firmly into them, stomped on them a couple of times to get them comfortable, then stood up. "We've got a load we need to take down to the river landing. I'll not be coming back in time for dinner."

"All right. But you will be back for supper?"

"Yes. Shouldn't take us much past two or three this afternoon."

"All right."

He turned to the mirror over the dresser and picked up the brush. He began to pull it through the thickness of his dark hair. She watched him. When he was satisfied with his hair, he examined his beard, brushing it into place along the line of his jaw. It wasn't actually preening, but it always amused her that he spent as much time in front of the mirror as she did.

"Are you going to answer your mother's letter?"

He stopped, not turning around. The letter from his mother had been waiting for Joshua when he returned from a short three-day trip. It had touched Jessie to watch him read it. It was the first time she had seen real joy in him. But afterwards he had become withdrawn, reticent to talk about it. Jessica wanted to know. After all, they were her family now too.

He still didn't answer. She decided not to push it, though it irritated her that he felt it was none of her affair. Finally he finished and turned and caught her watching him. "You doin' anything today?"

"I'm gonna bake some bread." She took a quick breath, trying to decide whether to break the news. Suddenly anxious, she clasped her hands together. "Then this afternoon I think I'll go see Doc Jones."

He had started to turn toward the door where his hat hung on a peg. He stopped and turned back slowly.

She felt like a field mouse under the scrutiny of a circling barn owl. She forced a shaky smile. "Yes, Joshua. I think I may be with child again."

She felt a stab of pain. There was no joy in his expression, just dullness and hidden pain.

Finally he turned and took down his hat. He put it on his head, adjusted it carefully, then looked over at her. "No way you'll consider Doctor Hathaway?"

She shook her head.

"He's a real doctor," he said, biting out the words, "not some farmer turned quack physician."

"We've gone over this before, Joshua." She felt the old tensions rising in her. She didn't want to fight him again, but this was not negotiable. Not this time. Not ever. She would rather do without medical help than go back to Hathaway and his icy superiority.

He started to say something, then just shook his head, the frustration evident on his face. "Have it your way," he said flatly. He spun on his heel and went out of the door, not bothering to shut it behind him.

With heavy heart, she moved slowly to it and pushed it shut.

The Gilbert and Whitney store lay just a short distance from the east branch of the Chagrin River. It was a lazy stream, not moving fast enough to stop the water skeeters from skimming clear across its ten-foot breadth. Melissa Steed looked at the water for a moment. It was a hot day, and she was tempted to walk down the grassy bank, remove her shoes, and dangle her feet in the tepid water. Though not terribly long, the walk from the rented house where her family now lived had been hot and dusty, and her feet were sticky inside her shoes. But it was only ten in the morning. The longer she waited to get her things at the store and make her way back, the hotter it was going to be.

Besides, inside the store it would be cool, and Melissa loved the inside of Newel Whitney's store. The smells, the shelves of merchandise, the tools hanging from nails driven into the wall —she loved it all, and if she was going to linger, her first choice would be to do so in there.

"Hello."

She jumped, startled, and whirled around.

He was not particularly tall, no more than three or four inches above her own five foot five. He was smiling at her, red hair catching the sun brightly, the freckles a peppering of red across his nose and cheeks. He was smiling, and his teeth were neat and even. "I'm sorry, I didn't mean to startle you."

"You . . . you didn't."

"I just saw you standing here and . . ." His already ruddy complexion deepened noticeably. "I wondered if you were think-ing about going wading."

She smiled at his perceptiveness. "Actually I was."

He grinned. "It does sound good, doesn't it?"

She nodded, still a little bewildered. Who was he? Where had he come from? Why was he talking to *her*?

"I'm sorry." He stepped forward and stuck out his hand. "My name is Carlton Rogers. My friends all call me Carl."

Without thinking she curtsied slightly, then instantly berated herself for it. It was a girlish thing to do. And Melissa was hardly a girl anymore. "How do you do?" she answered, more demurely now. "My name is—"

"Melissa Steed."

Her eyes widened. "You know my name?"

"You came to my father's livery stable the other day to meet your father."

"Oh." She didn't remember seeing him at all—which was most strange, for she was sure she would have remembered him if she had seen him even once.

He was suddenly a little embarrassed. "I didn't mean to interrupt you, but I saw you coming down the hill and thought you might be coming to the store here." Actually, he had learned that the Steeds had moved into a house on Main Street temporarily while Mr. Steed looked for some property he could buy. Carl had been watching the house on and off for several days, hoping for just such an opportunity as this. "Do you have things to buy?" he finished.

"Yes."

"Me too." He smiled and she saw how it softened the corners around his eyes, which were the same color of green she had once seen in a painting of the sea crashing onto the seashore. He looked to be a little older than she was, maybe twenty-three or so.

"I have a cart," he said. He turned and pointed, and she saw the small four-wheeled cart with its pull handle. "It's a walk back up the hill. You'd be welcome to put your stuff in with mine." He colored again and looked down at her feet. "That is, if you don't mind."

One part of her counseled for demureness. That called for a polite refusal, or at least an appropriate wait and at least a semblance of reluctance before responding. But demureness had never been a strong characteristic Melissa had cultivated. She smiled. "That would be very nice, thank you."

———•——

It was nearly noon when Jessica came around the corner of her house, carefully holding the bowl containing the yeast start she had borrowed from the neighbor. She stopped short. Her father was sitting on the front porch, smoking a cigar. At the sight of her, he immediately stood up.

"Hello, Jessie."

"Hello, Pa."

She went up the steps and joined him on the porch. He dropped the cigar and stomped it out. He knew she didn't like either him or Joshua smoking the foul-smelling things inside the house.

"Joshua's not here, Pa. He had to take a load down to the river."

"I know." He stepped quickly and opened the door for her. She gave him a sharp look, but he ignored it. She went in and he followed her.

"Sit down, Pa," she called over her shoulder. "I need to care for this yeast, then I'll be right with you."

She went into the kitchen, set the bowl on the table, wet a towel in the bucket of water that stood in the sink, then wrung the towel out and placed it over the bowl. She moved the bowl slightly so the yeast start would be in the sun for the next hour or so. That would start it rising, and soon she would have enough for a new start of yeast of her own and would return the bowl to her neighbor.

She wiped her hands and went back out into the sitting room. She sat down, folded her hands in her lap, and looked at Clinton Roundy. There was no mistaking the fact that they were father and daughter, though she realized with a start that he was starting to look old.

He began to squirm a little under her examination and wouldn't meet her gaze. She felt her heart sink. Something was amiss. Her father did not make social calls, not even to his daughter and son-in-law. Something was on his mind, and she could tell he was hurting with the pain of it. *He needs money,* she thought. She shook it off immediately. Unless he had squandered his money something fierce, he was one of western Missouri's more prosperous citizens.

"To what do I owe this?" she finally said, seeing that he wasn't going to go further without some encouragement.

"Uh . . . how have you and Joshua been doin' lately?"

"We're doin'." She wasn't about to say more. Their troubles were between the two of them.

Her father began to squirm again. She suddenly felt sorry for him, and guilty that she was not helping him through it. "What is it, Pa? What's wrong?"

He bit his lip, reached in his pocket for another cigar, remembered her ban, and quickly dropped his hands to his side again.

"Come on, tell me."

He took a deep breath. Took another. Then, finally, he leaned forward. "Has Joshua said anything to you about how he's doing lately—moneywise, I mean?"

She felt a quick thrust of disgust. "How much do you need, Pa?"

He blinked, looking baffled. Then understanding hit him. "It's not me, Jessie. I'm talking about Joshua. I don't need anything. It's Joshua. He's been losing money."

She just stared at him.

"That's right. Lots of it."

"But how could he? The company's doing twice the haulin' of anyone else in town."

Again he looked bewildered for a moment, then realized she was not following him. He looked at his hands, as though shamed for having to say it. "He's not losing it at the freight company, Jess," he said in a low voice. "He's losing it at the poker table."

She came straight out of her chair. "What?"

"That's right. There's a new man in town. Came in about two months ago. He comes out of Pittsburgh. A real sharpie with cards." He shook his head sadly. "Joshua's good, but he's no match for this one."

Feeling herself reeling, Jessie dropped back down in her chair. So that was why he had been coming in so late some nights. Joshua usually went to one of the taverns and spent the evening there, but he had been returning much later than usual for the past while. She had not felt undue concern, because he did not seem to be drinking heavily.

She lifted her head to look at her father. "How much?"

"What?"

"How much has he lost?"

Her father shook his head. "No one knows for sure. I've seen him lose more than a thousand dollars in the last three weeks."

"A *thousand dollars!*" It came out more as a shocked whisper than a shout.

"Maybe more. He's gone through his savings. He's now borrowing from others. Clem Simpson. Ezekiel Mecham." He paused. "Me. Word is he's gone to the bank and got a mortgage on the business."

He looked down at the floor, his face a study in misery. "I'm not asking for the money he owes me. You know that, Jessie. Joshua's been good to me. It ain't that at all. I'm just getting worried. It's like the thought of winnin' has a hold on him and won't let go. He's got to beat this card sharp. No matter what."

She stood and walked slowly to the window.

"But he's not good enough. Not anymore. He's got to be stopped before he loses everything. Will you talk to him, Jessie?"

She nodded, numbly.

"Don't tell him it was me that—"

She turned her back on him. "I'll talk to him." It came out so quietly, he had to strain to hear her.

"Thank you, Jessie. I know he'll listen to you. I just can't seem to—

"I said I'll talk to him!" she barked.

Her anger shocked him. He stood now too, fumbling with his hat. "All right, Jessie. Thank you for listenin'. I'm . . ."

She did not turn and he finally let it trail off and exited quickly. Jessie did not turn around as the door shut behind him.

Four days after the arrival of Benjamin Steed in Kirtland, his son and daughter-in-law were entertaining visitors in the small one-room cabin they had moved into just two days before. This was part of the legacy Father Morley had provided through the giving of his land and timber to the Church. Nathan and Lydia were sitting on a wooden bench with their backs against the rough-hewn wall of logs. Across from them in their only two chairs sat Sidney Rigdon and Parley Pratt. The baby was asleep in a small rocking bassinet that Sister Morley had dug out from her attic and dusted off for them. The men had come at their request. Benjamin Steed had sold their farm back in Palmyra along with his own. Five hundred dollars. He had brought the cash with him, and now they had it in hand.

Since their arrival in Kirtland, Lydia and Nathan had heard much talk about a new economic order, "the law of the Lord," revealed through the Prophet Joseph. There was no question in their minds about whether or not to live this law, only about how to do it. Joseph, off to one of the nearby communities to meet with some of the Saints, had sent Sidney and Parley to respond to their queries.

Now, as Sidney Rigdon spoke, Lydia watched him closely. Though perhaps not as striking as the Prophet Joseph, he was a distinguished looking man and commanded immediate respect. He was not as tall as Joseph and was starting to show a tendency toward stoutness. He had bright, alert eyes beneath narrow eyebrows. His nose was large, but it was straight and well-formed. Like Martin Harris, he wore a Greek-style beard, with the whiskers coming under the chin and throat, leaving the chin itself clean shaven. His voice was clear, and he articulated his words with great precision.

"Has Joseph let you read the revelations on consecration?" he asked.

"Yes," they both said at once.

"We read them together last night," Lydia added.

"So I think we understand the basic principles," Nathan said. "It's the more practical questions that we have."

Parley laughed. "Most of the problems with the law of consecration are practical. That's why Joseph got the revelations in the first place."

"Why do you say that?" Lydia asked.

"Haven't you heard about 'the family' out here at the Morleys'?"

Nathan and Lydia looked at each other. "I guess not," Nathan responded.

Sidney shook his head sadly. "That was a disaster."

Parley explained. "Shortly after Oliver and I and the others left Kirtland for Missouri, some of the new converts decided they wanted to live the same order as that practiced by the disciples in ancient times. Remember, in the book of Acts, it talks about the disciples having all things in common?"

"Yes, we're familiar with that," said Nathan.

"Well, this group, among whom were Father and Sister Morley, decided they would share all things in common, like a large family. A group of them moved out to the Morley farm." Parley pulled a face. "Before you could turn around and shake a stick, there was a group large enough to bring on a famine. But they didn't know what they were doing. There were no guidelines, no rules to govern how things were handled. Members of the 'family' assumed that anything belonging to one person belonged to everyone. They would take one another's items—clothes, personal belongings—and use them without leave."

"Levi Hancock decided he would join the family," Sidney went on. "He was out here one night. He had a beautiful pocket watch. One of the family saw it and walked up and took it from his pocket without asking. Levi was a little taken aback, but thought that the man would bring it back soon." He shook his head. "Instead he went off and sold it."

"He sold it?" Lydia cried. "Just like that?"

"Yes, just like that. Levi was quite peeved and demanded to know why he had done such a thing. The man simply replied, 'Oh, I thought it was all in the family.'"

Parley chuckled, but with a trace of sadness. "Levi said he

didn't much like the doings of the family if that was how they worked."

"I don't blame him," Nathan said.

Sidney went on. "When we finally arrived back from New York with Joseph and Emma and learned what was happening, Joseph persuaded the family to abandon their plan and wait for the Lord to reveal a more perfect law. That's when the revelations about consecration began."

"And *consecration* is the important word," Parley broke in. "The Lord said, through the Psalmist, 'The earth is the Lord's, and the fulness thereof.' In other words, nothing that we have in this life really belongs to us, not in the sense of true ownership. So we consecrate ourselves to give whatever we have been blessed with to the Lord, since it is his anyway."

Sidney nodded vigorously. "That's exactly right. We are only stewards, or caretakers, of his properties. This is why it is sometimes called the law of consecration and stewardship."

"Nathan and I have already discussed this. We have no problems with either of those principles," Lydia said. "That is why we have decided to give the five hundred dollars to the Church."

"That's wonderful," Sidney responded warmly, "but it's not quite that simple. That would be charity. The law of consecration is much more than simple charity."

"That's what we're trying to understand," Nathan said. "Tell us what we should do with our money."

But before Sidney could answer, the baby began to fuss. They waited for a moment, but the soft cries increased, then turned into an angry wail. Lydia smiled and got up and took him out of his bed. He stopped crying almost instantly, which brought a laugh from each of the men.

"Just ten days old, and already he knows his mother," Nathan said, with evident pride.

"Joseph said you will bless him during the conference this week."

"Yes. I think we'll wait until the last day. The Sabbath seems to be an appropriate day for such a thing."

Sidney nodded. "It will be good for the Saints to see a child blessed. Many have not witnessed that before. What shall you call him?"

Lydia looked at Nathan as she answered. "Nathan's mother says he's the spittin' image of Nathan as a baby, so I think we'll have two Nathans in the family now."

Nathan smiled. "Yes, I think we'll call him Nathan Benjamin."

"Wonderful," Parley said.

"So," Nathan said, eager to pursue the main question that was troubling him, "what do we do if we want to accept this law God has revealed to us?"

"First you meet with Edward—Bishop Partridge. He's been called to act as the Church's agent in these matters. Together you and he will determine what stewardship you ought to have. This is done based on your wants, your needs, and your circumstances."

"Stewardship?"

"Yes. This will be how you make your living. A farm, a store, whatever you and he agree on together."

"We just assumed we would continue to farm."

"That's fine. Most do. But the law is designed to accommodate all needs and wants—farmer, merchant, blacksmith. It doesn't matter. What matters is that you two and Bishop Partridge decide together on what your stewardship shall be."

"All right. Let's say we decide Lydia and I shall be farmers."

"Fine. The first thing you do is give your property to the Church—or, in other words, you consecrate it to the Lord."

"So we give him the five hundred dollars?" Lydia asked. Little Nathan had promptly fallen asleep again in her arms, and she was as intent on the conversation as was Nathan.

"Yes. This is done with a legal document. If it were property, you would do it by legal deed. In your case you would convey the five hundred dollars to the Church. At that point, for all intents and purposes, it is no longer yours."

Lydia spoke with quiet solemnity. "But in the eyes of the Lord it never was ours."

"Exactly right," Sidney agreed, pleased. "So you give Bishop Partridge your cash. Let's say that you and he have decided that you need about thirty acres of land to farm. If your family were larger, it could be much more than that. But let's say thirty, as an example. At that point he then gives you thirty acres, again by legal deed."

"But," Nathan cried, "that's where I get confused. Where is he going to get thirty acres of land to just give away?"

"This is the genius of the plan," Parley said. "It comes from what is called surplus property."

"Surplus?"

"Yes. Let's keep on with the example Brother Sidney has used. One way the bishop could give you the land is to take the very money you have given him and purchase it."

"But then he wouldn't have any surplus. It comes out an even trade."

"Unless," Lydia said slowly, beginning to see where Parley was leading, "unless it didn't take the full five hundred dollars."

"Exactly!" Parley cried, eager now for them to see it. "Good farmland in Kirtland is selling for about five dollars an acre. Thirty acres will take a hundred and fifty of the money you have given. Then let's say it takes another hundred and fifty to build you a cabin, get you a horse or two, some tools."

"There's still two hundred dollars left," Nathan finished for him.

"Which," Sidney said, emphasizing his point with a sweep of his hand, "can then be used to buy someone else his stewardship."

"That's what Father Morley's done, isn't it?" Lydia said.

"Yes. He had more acres than he needed—surplus—and has given them to other Saints who are in need."

"So the poor are truly blessed," Lydia said softly. She felt a little thrill to think that they could be part of such a noble endeavor.

"But"— Nathan's mind was working quickly—"if you have more poor than people with surplus, don't you have a problem?"

"Yes," Parley agreed. "But there is another source of help for the poor. This is also called surplus." His eyes twinkled a little. "Let's keep going with this farm we've already given you. You and Lydia are hard workers, good farmers. You plant wheat, corn, maybe some barley. Come next fall you have a good harvest. Let's suppose you sell your crops for five hundred dollars."

"That would be nice!" Lydia exclaimed.

Sidney laughed. "Parley is always the eternal optimist."

Parley accepted the banter in good form. "I like to keep the arithmetic simple," he grinned. "So, you make five hundred dollars. But let's say that you and Lydia and little Nathan only need two hundred dollars of that to live that year. What do you do with the rest?"

"We give it to the Church as surplus," Lydia exclaimed.

"That's right." Sidney sat back, pleased with their afternoon's work. "And you do this because you believe that you are only a steward of the Lord's property. It is the Lord's way, Nathan and Lydia, I tell you. The poor are blessed, not by taking from the rich against their will, but by the rich humbling themselves and giving of their surplus through love."

"You are right," Lydia said, deeply impressed. "It is brilliant. And so simple." She looked at Nathan, who was suddenly smiling mischievously. "What?" she asked.

"I like this plan. We've not even met with Bishop Partridge yet, and already we have a thirty-acre farm and have made five hundred dollars profit in the first year."

Chapter Fourteen

Wh
en the four missionaries to the Lamanites left
Kirtland about three weeks after they had first arrived, they left
nearly a hundred and thirty new members of the Church in
Ohio, with more coming in all the time. One of the most important factors in this remarkable growth was the manifestation of
the gifts of the Spirit found in the new Church. The Bible
clearly taught that those gifts had been present in the New Testament Church, and there was great resurgence of interest in returning to Christianity as it was found in the New Testament.

The Church of Jesus Christ restored to the earth through the
ministry of Joseph Smith was a church filled with revelation,
both general and personal. By the spring of 1831, Joseph had already received and recorded about fifty revelations which counseled individuals on spiritual matters, gave the Prophet direction
on how to run the infant Church, or otherwise showed those
things which were pleasing or displeasing to the Lord.

Nor was revelation confined to the Prophet Joseph. Again

and again, the Holy Ghost was operative in the lives of the new Saints. Samuel Smith, one of the Prophet's younger brothers, came to Harmony shortly after the appearance of John the Baptist to Joseph and Oliver. He was very skeptical about the things Joseph and Oliver told him, but agreed to retire to the woods and make it a matter of earnest prayer. A short time later he returned, convinced of the truthfulness of their report, and was baptized by Oliver. He returned to his parents, as Joseph later reported, "greatly glorifying and praising God, being filled with the Holy Spirit."

The day the Church was organized was, in Joseph's words, "a happy time spent in witnessing and feeling for ourselves the powers and blessings of the Holy Ghost."

In Colesville, during the month of April 1830, Newel Knight became possessed of an evil, dark influence. He suffered in both mind and limb as his face was distorted and his body began to twist and contort in a most terrible manner. Finally he was caught up off the floor and tossed about most fearfully. Neighbors and relatives gathered to witness the frightful scene. The Prophet Joseph arrived and, upon seeing Newel, immediately took his hand and in the name of Jesus Christ commanded the evil spirit to leave him. Instantly, Newel was freed. He testified that he saw the devil leave him and vanish from sight. The Spirit of the Lord then rested upon Newel and the visions of eternity were opened to his view.

During the first conference of the Church, held in June of 1830, much instruction and exhortation was given, and the Spirit of the Lord was poured out upon those present without measure. Many prophesied, while others had the heavens opened to them. Some testified that they were filled with unspeakable love and peace.

In June of 1830, under the direction of the Lord, Joseph began work on a "translation" of the Bible. This was not an attempt to translate from ancient languages, but an inspired translation by the Spirit. Passages which had been changed down through the centuries were corrected, lost passages were restored. Several jewels of scripture—writings of Moses, including the Prophecy of Enoch—were the direct result.

And so it continued, revelation following revelation. The sick were healed, the troubled were comforted, the hearts of men were changed. Prayers were uttered and prayers were answered. Walls of ice were split and walls of unbelief tumbled. Inspiration, prophecy, new scripture, miracles, love, peace, testimony—they were poured out upon the Saints in abundance, and like two of the disciples of old, hundreds were led to exclaim, "Did not our hearts burn within us?"

But the adversary also knew of this power and influence and sought to deceive and confuse and mislead. Shortly after the turn of the century, as the great religious revival swept across America and camp meetings sprouted like weeds in a fertilized garden, so-called "manifestations of the Spirit" became commonplace. Men would scratch themselves and howl like baboons. Women would swoon. Some would jump up on tables, arms and legs twisting grotesquely, faces hideously distorted. For a time, the meetings and "manifestations" became so common that one part of New York became known as the "Burned-Over District," so named from the notion that so many people were "on fire" with the Spirit.

Shortly after they were first married, Mary Ann had prevailed upon Benjamin to attend a camp meeting with her. She could remember it with sharp clarity. It was one of the things which had completely soured Benjamin on organized religion. The meeting was held in a large meadow, near the center of which grew a large oak tree. Warning of the dangers of evil spirits, the preacher called on all present to help "tree the devil." The men formed a large circle around the perimeter of the field. Then, dropping to their hands and knees, they began to move slowly toward the tree, throwing their heads back and howling like wolves or barking like dogs. This, said the preacher, would drive any evil spirits into the tree, where they could no longer interfere with the functioning of the Spirit.

Not surprisingly, along with the true manifestations of the

Spirit being shown in the Church, there also came some that were not so true. False spirits and strange notions began to creep in. Hiram Page and his "revelations" from the stone were only the beginning. Many of the new converts came from denominations in which bizarre and disturbing behavior was part of their worship experience, and they brought these notions with them into the Church of Christ. This was especially true in Kirtland where the influx of new members was so dramatic. And with the departure of the missionaries to the Lamanites, no experienced leadership was left to correct these false notions until Joseph sent John Whitmer to Kirtland in mid-January 1831, then arrived himself in early February.

One man would hit his head against a steel bar so hard that it would knock him unconscious and he would then have "visions." Young people would imitate Indians, dancing around madly; some would run out into the fields, climb up on stumps, and preach to unseen congregations. Another man called Black Pete claimed to be receiving letters from heaven. One day he saw a ball dancing above him in the air. He chased after it, trying to catch it, until it led him off a sharp cliff. Had it not been for a tree that broke his fall, he would not have lived to share his "visionary experience."

Such phenomena were not commonplace, however. They involved only a small minority. Most of the members were astonished and saddened and looked upon such goings on with great suspicion. But even though the members who participated in the bizarre behavior were small in number, they created considerable havoc. When Joseph arrived he immediately set about to stop these excesses, which were, he declared, "calculated to bring disgrace upon the church of God, to cause the Spirit of God to be withdrawn, and to uproot and destroy those glorious principles which had been developed for the salvation of the human family."

It didn't take long after his arrival in Kirtland for Benjamin to start hearing about these aberrations, and Mary Ann had a real challenge on her hands in trying to answer his questions. It brought many of his feelings about church and religion back to the surface, and for a time he became sharply critical of Mary Ann's new faith.

Fortunately, just before Ben had arrived, the Lord had given a revelation to the Saints designed to put down the false spirits and crazy notions that were cropping up. "Behold verily I say unto you," the Lord had said, "that there are many spirits which are false spirits, which have gone forth in the earth, deceiving the world: and also satan hath sought to deceive you, that he might overthrow you. Behold I the Lord have looked upon you, and have seen abominations in the church, which profess my name."

That had pleased Benjamin, to know that Joseph was not encouraging these things, that the Lord called them abominations. More important, the Lord had given the key whereby the Saints could distinguish between what was true and what was not. "Why is it that ye can not understand and know that he that receiveth the word by the spirit of truth, receiveth it as it is preached by the spirit of truth? Wherefore, he that preacheth and he that receiveth, understandeth one another, and both are edified and rejoice together; and that which doth not edify, is not of God, and is darkness." That too had seemed to placate Benjamin's concerns.

Though his questions had subsided in the last few days, Mary Ann was still not too disappointed that Benjamin had declined her invitation to attend the fourth general conference of the Church that convened on Friday, June third, at the schoolhouse near the Morley farm. She so wanted him to feel the Spirit's manifestations for himself, but as it turned out, the conference opened with the same contrast being exhibited—the true and the false, the good and the evil—and she was not sure Benjamin was ready yet to deal with the differences.

Almost from the moment of the opening prayer, a false spirit began to manifest itself. As Joseph stood to speak, a horrid shriek rent the air. A man by the name of Harvey Green was thrown on the ground and went into convulsions. Harvey Whitlock and John Murdock were seized and bound so that they could not utter a word. Leman Copley, who had donated a significant portion of his farm near Thompson, Ohio, for the settlement of the Colesville Branch, was sitting in an open window near the back of the schoolhouse. He was hurled violently backward, turning a complete somersault and landing on a bench.

It was a frightening thing, and Mary Ann had felt cold chills course through her body as the power of evil was unleashed. But Joseph had immediately stepped forward and rebuked the evil influence. He laid his hands on Harvey Green, and instantly the evil spirit left the afflicted man. He then told the assembled group that this was a fulfillment of the passage in Paul's Second Epistle to the Thessalonians, that the man of sin—Satan—would be revealed. He explained that Satan had been cast out and they could now proceed under the direction of the Spirit.

And so it proved to be. What followed was remarkable, as spiritual edification took the place of the earlier disturbing influences. The Spirit of the Lord fell upon Joseph in a most unusual manner, and he prophesied that John the Revelator was then working among the ten tribes scattered by Shalmaneser, king of Assyria, seven centuries before Christ's birth.

Joseph also said it was time for some of the elders to receive the office of high priest, making them the first to be so ordained since the gospel had been taken from the earth. When Lyman Wight, a rough man but one of great dedication, was called forward, as part of the ordination Joseph promised him that he would see the heavens opened.

The moment the ordination was completed, Lyman stood on his feet and began to prophesy. He predicted that the Savior's coming would be like the sun rising in the east and would cover the whole world. The Lord would appear in his brightness and consume the wicked before him. Brother Wight's face had changed at that point and become infused with sorrow. "And some of the brethren," he said, "shall suffer martyrdom for the sake of their religion, and will seal their testimony with their blood."

Then a tremendous thing happened. It seemed that Lyman's

whole countenance was transformed into a brilliant, transparent white. Mary Ann had stared at him in wonder as he clapped his hands with joy. "I see the heavens opened," he cried. "I see the Savior standing on the right hand of God."

That had been the first day of the conference, and Mary Ann would ever consider herself blessed to have been there to witness it. On the rest of that day and on the following, much important business had been transacted. Other high priests were ordained. Additional men were given the priesthood. Some previously baptized were confirmed. Father Morley and a man named John Corrill were called to serve as counselors to Bishop Partridge and help with the work of assigning and managing those things associated with the law of consecration.

But that was all done now. Today was the Sabbath, and the last day of the conference was to be primarily a worship service. Mary Ann looked around and noticed that Martin Harris was in attendance. He and his Palmyra-Manchester group had recently arrived in Kirtland. She turned and looked at Nathan and Lydia, Nathan with his tiny son in his arms. Joseph was giving him some last-minute instructions on how to bless and name his son. That would be something else that would take place on this day.

Mary Ann slipped her arm through her husband's, glad that he had not refused to accompany her to this meeting. In fact her heart was brimming over with joy. They had come to Kirtland. She had arrived in time to help Lydia with the birth. Her husband was here and mingling daily with men of the faith—good, strong priesthood holders that would bless his life, she hoped. It was more than she had ever dreamed could happen.

Ben, sensing her feelings, looked down at her. She smiled and squeezed his arm.

"What?" he asked.

She smiled, her eyes radiant with happiness. "Thank you for letting us be here for this."

Mary Ann and Ben stood in the shade of a large beech tree, for the moment alone. Matthew and Becca had spied Newel Whitney and his family arriving and had gone off to greet the

Whitney children. Melissa and two or three other young women were gathered around Emma, gurgling at the twins. Nathan and Lydia were sitting on a couple of chairs they had brought from the house. The baby was asleep in Nathan's arms. Joseph, still waiting for more of the Saints to arrive, finished giving instructions to Nathan, then stood and walked over to Martin Harris and Bishop Edward Partridge.

The yard of the school was filling up quickly now, and Mary Ann marveled again at the number of Saints flocking in for the final meeting of the conference. Joseph had shocked them all when he told them there were now close to two thousand members of the Church. Two thousand! Many of them were here today. In just over a year's time, from fifty or sixty to two thousand—it left her reeling with wonder.

"Good morning, Sister Steed."

They turned. Mother Smith had come to join them.

"Good morning, Sister Smith."

Benjamin tipped his hat. "Mornin', Mother Smith."

"Mr. Steed." She looked over at Nathan and Lydia. "An exciting day. How good that you could be here."

"Yes, it is."

They stood there for a moment in companionable silence, watching the people. Then Lucy Smith turned. "Oh, look! There's Elsa Johnson."

Mary Ann turned to see where Mother Smith was pointing. A wagon was just arriving with an older couple in it. It was evident that this was a prosperous rig. The wagon looked new, and it was pulled by a matched team of handsome bays. Both the man and the woman were well dressed.

"She's the one I told you about. With the arm."

"Oh yes," Mary Ann said, looking more closely now. Who had not heard the remarkable story of Elsa Johnson?

Mother Smith pursed her lips in wonder. "I talked with her yesterday. She still has no pain and uses it for all her work. It's marvelous."

"What's this about her arm?" Benjamin asked.

Mary Ann looked up at her husband, surprised for a moment, then realized that he had not heard this story. Suddenly a
thought popped into her head. "She had a wonderful experience
with Joseph," she answered. Then to Mother Smith she said,
"I've not heard her tell that personally. Do you think she would
mind if we asked her to tell us her story?"

If there was one thing to be said for Lucy Mack Smith, it was
that she was not slow. For a moment she peered up at Mary Ann,
then glanced at Ben, who was only half following the conversation as he watched the people. Her head began to bob as a sly
smile stole across her face. "Now, there's an idea." She looked
over to where her son was still visiting with a cluster of people.
Obviously they still had some time before things would be getting underway. With sudden determination she grabbed Mary
Ann's hand. "Come on."

Holding her breath, Mary Ann looked up at Ben. "Do you
want to come?"

He looked at her, and she knew he had been following more
of the conversation than she first thought. But his eyes were also
curious, and to her joy he finally nodded.

Mother Smith was not one to spend time in idle chitchat
when she had something on her mind. She led them right up to
the Johnsons, introduced Mary Ann and Ben, then asked Elsa
straight out if she would share her experience with them.

Elsa Johnson nodded immediately. She was a pleasant-look-
ing woman, nearing her midforties, Mary Ann estimated. She
had light brown eyes, and her hair, just starting to gray, was
pulled back away from her face and tied in a bun at the back of
her head. Her face was tanned and lined with wrinkles from the
sun; her hands were rough and calloused.

John Johnson was also a kindly looking man, weathered and
plain but with blue eyes that bespoke wisdom and integrity.
When they were seated he spoke first. He looked at his wife,
then back to Mary Ann. "It was a marvelous thing," he said. "I
was there. Saw the whole thing with my own eyes."

Elsa picked it up from there. "For the last six years I have been hardly able to use my arm at all." She lifted one elbow slightly. "It was almost completely paralyzed. I couldn't use it to do any work at all. In fact I couldn't even raise it to the level of my head."

"Chronic rheumatism," John Johnson said somberly. "It gave her a lot of pain. Doctors couldn't do nothing for her."

"When word came of the restored gospel," Elsa went on, "our son Luke joined immediately. John and I felt good about it too, but hadn't yet made up our minds."

John spoke softly. "In the Bible Jesus said that signs would follow those that believe—blessing people with infirmities, healing the sick, raising the dead, casting out devils. Some friends, including a minister, wanted to go to Kirtland and meet Joseph. So we decided to go too. We found Joseph and Emma living with the Whitneys. I can still remember it very clearly. We were all sitting together there in the Whitney home, visiting with the Prophet."

"We were all impressed," Elsa broke in. "He was so kind, and so dignified."

For the first time in the conversation, Benjamin spoke. "Did you tell Joseph why you had come?"

Her husband's mouth softened into a rueful grin. "I guess we were all thinkin' about it, but no one wanted to say it straight out to Joseph. So we were just kinda visitin' and all that."

"Suddenly," Elsa said, "one of our company just blurted it out. Can't even remember now for sure who it was. But out it came. We'd been talking about the priesthood being restored to earth. And suddenly this person just up and says, 'Here's Mrs. Johnson with her lame arm. Has God given any power to men now on the earth to cure her?' " She laughed quietly, her cheeks coloring a little. "It was so sudden. We were all a little embarrassed by it, I suppose."

Mary Ann leaned forward eagerly. "What did Joseph say?"

John chuckled. "Nothin'."

"Nothing?" Mary Ann echoed in surprise. "He didn't respond at all?"

"Not then," he answered. "The conversation resumed and went on to other things for several moments."

Mary Ann turned as she noticed that Elsa was blinking rapidly. Tears had filled her eyes as she spoke. "Then, without warning, Joseph stood up." She swallowed quickly. "He walked over and stood in front of me. A hush came over the room." She looked away, her lips trembling.

Mary Ann moved slightly so she could see Benjamin more clearly. His brows were furrowed and it almost made him appear to be frowning, but on closer examination she could see he was listening intently.

Tears were making wet streaks down Elsa Johnson's cheeks now. Embarrassed, she wiped at them with the back of her hand. Her husband reached over and laid a hand on her shoulder in silent encouragement.

Finally she sniffed back the tears and spoke once again. "Joseph reached out and took my hand. Then, in the most solemn and impressive manner, he looked into my eyes. 'Woman,' he said, 'in the name of the Lord Jesus Christ, I command thee to be whole.' I . . ." She stopped, too overcome to continue.

Someone a little way off from them laughed and the sound carried softly to them, but none of the five of them even noticed. Mother Smith slid over enough to lay a hand on Sister Johnson's arm and pat it slowly.

John Johnson was staring at his wife, his bottom lip starting to tremble a little now too. Surprisingly, when he looked up, he looked at Benjamin and not at Mary Ann. "Joseph turned and left the room without another word," he began, his voice low now and quavering. "We were all completely astonished and just stared after him." Suddenly his voice steadied. "Sir, do you have any idea how I felt when I turned around and looked at my wife? Even as I looked at her, she started to raise her arm. Her face was aglow with wonder. Up came her arm, without the slightest hesitation. Up, up. It passed the level of her waist, then the level of her shoulder. We all just gaped at her, like kids watching a miracle happen."

He turned to his wife, his eyes filled with love and gratitude. "I shall never forget that picture in my mind—her sitting there, laughing and crying all at once, her arm held high in the air."

Elsa had finally composed herself enough to meet her husband's gaze. She spoke to him as if there were no one else there. "I went home the next day and put out a wash for the first time in six years." She lifted her arm high above her head and rotated it around in a large circle. "That's been at least two months ago now. As you can see, the infirmity has not returned."

Benjamin's eyes were riveted on Elsa Johnson's hand as it came back down again, but he said nothing. Mary Ann finally broke the silence that followed. "Thank you, Sister Johnson," she said, her own eyes now shining too. "Thank you for sharing that wonderful story with us."

Joseph was at the pulpit, which consisted of a short length of log squared and tacked onto a plank base. He stood tall and erect. He had removed his suit coat and stood in breeches and white long-sleeved shirt. The sun was nearly at its zenith now, and in its light his hair gleamed like a field of burnished wheat ready to harvest.

He looked around the congregation, finally letting his eyes stop on where Nathan and Lydia sat with their family gathered around them. His eyes sought out Nathan's, and Nathan felt a little thrill go through him. The moment had arrived.

"As you know," Joseph said, his voice loud and distinct and carrying clearly to the furthermost ear, "even before the Church was organized the Lord revealed his will to us concerning the naming and blessing of children. In that revelation he commanded every member of the Church having children to bring them to the elders before the Church to have them blessed in the name of Christ."

He smiled, his eyes softening. "As many of you know, Brother Nathan Steed and his wife, Lydia McBride Steed, were blessed with a healthy baby boy about two weeks ago. It will now be our pleasure to have Nathan bring that child forth and carry out this ordinance in his behalf."

There were murmurs of approval and soft calls of congratulations as Nathan stood and took little Nathan from Lydia. His mother reached up and squeezed his arm happily as he started past her.

When he joined Joseph he turned and faced the sea of faces. He felt a sudden panic, but then Joseph's arm came up and one hand rested on Nathan's shoulder, and he felt the fear leave him. He remembered Joseph's counsel earlier that morning. "Let the Spirit speak, Nathan. It is the Lord's blessing you are giving, not your own." Relieved, he felt a great calm come over him.

"You may have anyone who holds the higher priesthood stand in with you for the blessing, Brother Nathan," Joseph said. "Are there any particular brethren you would like to have join you?"

"You, of course," Nathan said quickly. "And Hyrum." He looked around. "Martin Harris and Brother Sidney and Brother Parley." For a moment his eyes fell on his father, and he felt a sudden pang of longing. How wonderful it would be if Benjamin were a priesthood holder and could stand with them!

The other brethren were all sitting close enough to hear and immediately stood as Joseph motioned to them. With great solemnity they gathered in a circle with Joseph and Nathan. Nathan looked down. Little Nathan, who had been sleeping, was now awake, his eyes squinting against the brightness of the sun. His little mouth twisted, then opened in a big yawn, and his arms extended into a wonderful stretch. It brought smiles from the men looking down at him.

"Brethren," Joseph said, "normally we hold the baby with both hands, but with this many elders in the circle, would you hold the baby with your right hand and put your left hand on the shoulder of the man next to you." He turned to Nathan. "Nathan will act as voice."

For one moment before he bowed his head, Nathan caught a glimpse of Lydia's face, watching him intently, eyes glowing with happiness. He smiled, then looked down at little Nathan. The men began to bounce the baby lightly up and down, which little Nathan seemed not to mind at all. He closed his eyes and promptly went back to sleep again. Nathan too closed his eyes, letting his heart swell up with the joy of the occasion.

"Our Father in Heaven," Nathan began, "in the name of our Lord and Savior, Jesus Christ, we take this tiny baby in our arms, we who are elders in thy priesthood, and we do so in order to give him his name and also a blessing in the name of Jesus."

He paused, offering a quick, silent prayer that he could let the Spirit speak through him. "We are most pleased, Heavenly Father, that thou hast seen fit to bless our family with this choice infant. We are grateful that he was born healthy and strong and that all went well with his mother in this birth.

"Now, dear Lord, it is time to give this new little person who has come into this life a name, the name that he will be known by throughout his life here on earth. The name that we, his parents, have chosen to give him is—"

A thought leaped into his mind. It took him so much by surprise that he simply stopped, speechless. Taken aback, he shook it off, took a breath, and started again. "The name we have chosen is . . ."

His voice trailed off into silence. Again the thought came, this time with such clarity that it stunned him. Amazed, he focused inward, searching his heart. Was this how the Spirit conveyed the Lord's will? For several seconds all seemed suspended, then it came, that sweet peace of confirmation. The answer was clear.

He took a deep breath, and raising his voice he continued slowly. "The name the Lord has chosen for this boy is—" He stopped, then spoke each word slowly and distinctly. "His name shall be Joshua Benjamin Steed."

He heard a gasp from someone in the congregation and wasn't sure if it was Lydia or his mother or Melissa, or all three together. He sensed Joseph's amazement next to him. Still a little dazed by it all, he continued. "Little Joshua, as your father, and as an elder in the Church of Jesus Christ, I now give you a blessing by the power of the holy priesthood."

The rest of the blessing was somewhat of a blur to Nathan. He spoke of blessings of health and of a sound mind for his son.

He spoke of faith and testimony and service to the Lord. But he was still reeling from what had happened, and it came out without much conscious thought.

As he finished and the chorus of amens rumbled through the congregation, the men in the circle stepped back. Hyrum Smith and Martin Harris were looking at him in open surprise. Joseph was nodding thoughtfully now.

Nathan shook hands around the circle and, amid the smiles of the Saints, returned to his place as Joseph went on with the meeting.

As he approached his family, Nathan met the wide-eyed stares of each of them. His father's eyes registered open disapproval; Melissa's were shocked; his mother's surprised but accepting. Smiling crookedly, he shrugged his shoulders and sat down next to his wife. As he handed her the baby, she looked down at her son. "Joshua?" she said in wonder.

"I'm sorry, Lydia," he whispered. "When I stood up, I—"

She shook her head quickly. "It's all right, Nathan." Her eyes were suddenly glistening. "In that moment that you paused, it was . . ." She groped for words. "It was like suddenly I was inside your mind, and in that moment, I knew. I knew you were going to name him Joshua."

"You did?" he echoed dumbly.

"Yes."

"Then it wasn't just me?" he said, relief washing over him.

"No." She smiled through the tears, then looked down at her baby. She pulled the blanket back from his face and gazed down on him in wonder. "I don't understand it, but if that is the Lord's will, then little Joshua you shall be."

They sat quietly in the grass of the schoolyard. The last of the conference congregation were nearly gone now. Nathan and Lydia were talking with Joseph and Emma, and Mary Ann and Benjamin both seemed content to wait for them to finish. Melissa had taken the children back into town with Martin Harris so that the grandparents could have dinner with Nathan and Lydia.

Mary Ann stole a glance at her husband. Finally, she could bear it no longer. "Well?" she asked.

"Well, what?"

"You know what. Aren't you going to comment about today?"

"What in particular?"

She sighed, knowing he was being deliberately obtuse. "The blessing of Joshua. The conference." She hesitated. "What Sister Johnson told us."

His mouth opened, then shut again. Finally, he simply shrugged. "It was nice."

It was nice. Was that all? Mary Ann couldn't let it go at that. "What about Sister Johnson's story? Do you believe her?"

He didn't answer for almost thirty seconds, his face furrowing in contemplation. "I . . ." He shook his head. "Well, I don't think she's lyin'."

"What's that supposed to mean?" Mary Ann said. "If she's not lying, then she's tellin' the truth."

"Or what she thinks is the truth."

The feeling of frustration was almost palpable enough to touch. "Meanin' you think she was deceived?" she said, fighting not to snap it out.

But Benjamin shook his head. "I don't know what to think," he finally admitted.

Mary Ann felt a quick surge of hope. It *had* touched him. Accepting it meant facing up to several other things as well, and he wasn't ready for that. She knew that, and she was wise enough not to push him on it. But it had touched him.

"What do *you* think?" he asked, turning to her.

She looked up at him, loving him with a fervor that had been increasing almost daily since that night when he announced he was selling the farm and they were moving to Kirtland. "I think," she said, choosing her words carefully, "I think of what Nicodemus said about the Savior. I think it could also be said of Brother Joseph."

"What did he say?"

"Nicodemus said, 'No man can do these miracles that thou doest, except God be with him.' "

He thought about that, then again only gave her that enigmatic look that she wasn't sure how to interpret. Suddenly he stood up, pulling her up with him. Joseph and Emma, Nathan and Lydia were coming over to them.

"Well, Brother Benjamin," Joseph said jovially, "what did you think of your son's blessing for your grandson?"

Ben shot a look at Nathan, "Well, I certainly didn't expect him to name him Joshua."

Joseph laughed, cutting off Nathan's quick defensive gesture. "I think the Spirit"—he emphasized the last two words slightly—"caught us all a little by surprise on that one." He gave Benjamin a long look, his eyes probing. "And what about you, Benjamin Steed?"

"Me? What about me?"

"Do you not wonder about God's purposes for you? You know that it was the Lord who brought you to Kirtland."

Mary Ann gasped a little inwardly. It was so like Joseph to be this direct, but with Benjamin it wouldn't take much to push it too far. She saw Nathan and Lydia stiffen as well.

After what seemed like a full minute, Benjamin's mouth relaxed into a sardonic grin. "I thought I came by wagon," he said. "I didn't particularly notice the Lord in there beside me."

"Benjamin!" Mary Ann blurted it out in shock.

But Joseph threw back his head and laughed. "Ah, Brother Benjamin, you are a rogue, you are."

Benjamin laughed right back at him. "Now, there's a title that I can wear more comfortably than saint."

"That may be so," Joseph said, still chuckling, "but that still doesn't change the fact that the Lord has a purpose for you."

Amazingly, Nathan's father was in a bantering mood. "Are you going to get a revelation telling me I ought to be baptized?" he asked in mock soberness.

"Don't need no revelation to know that," Joseph responded in a similar tone.

Mary Ann was reeling. Was this her Benjamin talking like this? But now she saw the humor leave his eyes, and she felt a sudden clutch of anxiety.

"I never was much for bathing with my clothes on," Benjamin said, more cool now.

Joseph became instantly serious. "You know I wouldn't have you baptized one moment before *you* are ready, though nothing would please me more."

Benjamin nodded slowly, accepting that.

"But . . ."

Instantly the tension shot up again.

"But what?" Benjamin finally asked when Joseph did not finish.

The smile slowly stole back across Joseph's face. "But you know that now that you've come to Kirtland, you're like a mouse in a town full of cats. You're going to have to watch yourself around here, Benjamin Steed."

"I will, Joseph," Ben drawled. "I will."

The whole village is ablaze with excitement," Nathan said glumly as he took off his hat and hung it on its peg. He had spent the morning in Kirtland and had just returned. "There shall not be one missionary that has not departed before the month is over."

Lydia watched her husband closely, sensing his bitter disappointment, and feeling guilty that she should be so relieved that he had not been one of them. "Perhaps there will be more called, Nathan."

He shook his head and went over to the sink to wash.

Lydia watched him with heavy heart. On the Monday following the conference, now a week ago, Joseph had received a revelation that electrified the gathered Saints. Joseph and Sidney were instructed to travel to Missouri, where the next conference of the Church would be held. Thirteen pairs of missionaries were called as well. They too were to make their way to Missouri, preaching the gospel along the way, lifting up their voices in the congregations as they went. The calls had come to many of the people they knew. Father Morley was to go with Ezra Booth, the minister converted through the miracle of Elsa Johnson. Martin Harris and Bishop Partridge were to travel with Joseph and Sidney. Parley Pratt and his brother Orson, whom he had converted after his own baptism, would be companions to each other. David Whitmer, Thomas B. Marsh, Samuel Smith—it seemed like few had been missed.

It was a triple blow to Nathan. Lydia understood that clearly. First, he longed to be called to the ministry—had, in fact, dreamed of little else since their arrival in Kirtland. To have more than two dozen missionaries called and his name not included had devastated him. He was beginning to wonder if the Lord thought him worthy. Lydia tried to talk him out of such doubts, but she didn't dare express her strong feeling that—for now, at least—the Lord recognized her special need to have him with her.

The second frustration was only marginally easier for him to accept. And this one hit Lydia hard as well. In the Book of Mormon, the prophet Ether had foreseen that the city of Zion, the New Jerusalem, was to be built in the Americas somewhere. Hiram Page had started to receive revelation through his so-called "seer stone" about its location. The Lord had rejected that and would say only that it was somewhere "on the borders by the Lamanites." As part of the revelation on the day following the June conference had come this electrifying promise: The land of the Saints' inheritance (which everyone assumed to mean Zion) would be revealed when they arrived there. And so "Zion fever," as Sister Morley called it, was sweeping through Kirtland. Knowing that others had been called to go there and would likely be there when the announcement of the exact location was made was very hard for Nathan.

The third thing that made this so hard for Nathan was the news that Joshua was in Independence. The family had written immediately after they heard the news from Parley Pratt, but again there had been no answer. Nathan saw the call to Zion as an opportunity to go and find Joshua and reunite the family. But no call had come.

Personally Lydia dreaded the reestablishment of contact with Joshua. He was a part of her past that she had put behind her, not without considerable relief. At first her infatuation with his dark handsomeness had been mostly for fun. It also titillated her somewhat to know that her father absolutely opposed the match. But then Joshua had started to change. He had turned hard and mean, given to drink. And Lydia had met Nathan. She shook her head, still marvelling that two brothers could be so vastly different. The news of Joshua's whereabouts had been met with joy in the family. Lydia was not so sure.

As he finished drying his hands on a towel, Nathan now turned around and smiled briefly at her, but his eyes were still filled with frustration. He walked to the window and pulled aside the curtain.

She waited a minute, watching his back, loving the man who stood before her hurting inside. She took a quick breath. "Nathan?"

"What?"

"Perhaps you should talk to Joseph."

He didn't turn, just shook his head once briefly.

"Maybe there are more calls yet to come."

"It's done, Lydia. If the Lord didn't see fit to call me, I'll not be pressing Joseph to change the Lord's mind."

"What does your father think? He seemed excited to think you might be called to go to Missouri too."

"Pa is still feeling guilty about what happened with Joshua," he said shortly. "He was hoping I could find him and make everything all right again."

She stood and walked to him. Again he did not turn, just kept his gaze fixed on the grove of maple trees out behind the Morley house. For a moment she stood there, feeling the agony of indecision. Could she bear to have him gone from her? Little Joshua was not even a month old yet. But on the other hand she couldn't bear to see him ache like this. She put her arms around his waist and laid her head against the broadness of his back. "Then, go to Joseph," she urged. "Tell him how you feel."

"I can't." He straightened and turned around, encircling her in his arms. He managed a smile. "There'll be plenty of time. I can't believe the Lord doesn't want me as a missionary."

"You'll make a wonderful missionary," she said fiercely.

He leaned down and kissed her. "Too bad you're not giving the calls." Hearing a faint cry, he looked toward the far corner of the room, his face brightening. "Is little Joshua ready to get up?"

Lydia laughed, loving this man with a depth that hurt with an exquisite kind of pain. "Sounds like it. He's probably over there waiting for his papa right now."

"Good." He kissed her again. "I'll get him."

"Bring his blanket and we'll take him for a walk."

When Nathan and Lydia returned with their baby to the cabin half an hour later, Hyrum Smith was waiting on the porch. Hyrum waved and they waved back.

"Hyrum," Nathan said, springing up on the porch and gripping his hand. "This is a surprise. What brings you out from town?"

He smiled. "Needed the exercise."

Lydia sensed that there was much more to it than that. Hyrum had come out to talk to Nathan. "If you'll excuse me," she said, "I'll go in and feed Joshua."

Hyrum turned quickly. "If you don't mind, Lydia, I'd like to talk to both of you. May I come in?"

"Please do," said Nathan. His curiosity was piqued, and he barely waited until they were all seated inside. "What is it, Hyrum?"

Joseph's older brother gave them both a long look, then seemed to make up his mind. "Newel Knight came into town today."

"Oh?"

"Leman Copley has broken the agreement."

"What?"

"As you know, the Colesville members were settled as a

group on Copley's farm. He consecrated it to the Church, signed an agreement that the Saints could live on it."

"Yes, I saw Newel at the conference. He told me all about it."

"Well, Copley has lost the faith. He claims Joseph forced him to sign his land over against his will. He's kicked them off his farm."

"Oh no," Lydia cried. "What will they do?"

"For now, they're coming into Kirtland."

"For now?" Nathan said. There was something in Hyrum's eyes that suggested this was why he had come.

"Joseph inquired of the Lord," Hyrum said solemnly. "They've been commanded to go to Missouri."

Nathan's eyes jerked up.

"Yes," Hyrum said, "the whole branch. The preparations have already begun. They hope to leave before the end of the month."

"But . . ." It was overwhelming. Nathan knew these people. The Knights were like a second family to him.

"Joseph asked me to come and see you."

Lydia was watching Hyrum closely, and she felt her heart drop. Like Nathan, she sensed there was specific purpose in Hyrum's coming. Now she thought she understood. "Does Joseph need the money?" she asked.

Nathan turned to her. Of course, that was it. He turned back to Hyrum. "Is that it, Hyrum? Do you need the money from the sale of our farm to help them?" He glanced at Lydia and she nodded. "Tell Joseph it is his."

Hyrum laid a hand on Nathan's arm. "No, my good friend. That is not it, but how generous of you to offer."

"Then, what?" Lydia asked. "What does Joseph need of us?"

Hyrum looked first at her, then at Nathan. Then he smiled slowly. "Nathan, Joseph thinks you ought to accompany the Colesville group."

It hit them both like a well bucket dropped from full height. "What?" Nathan cried.

"They could use some help getting there. That would give you a chance to find Joshua." He smiled, a little envious. "And most likely you'll be there when the Lord reveals the location of Zion."

———— •———

"Hello, Mr. Rogers."

"Good mornin', Melissa." Hezekiah Rogers smiled at her warmly. "Carl's out back in the tack shed fixing a saddle."

"Thanks." She went back out of the office and around to where Carl was working. The door to the tack room was open, but Carl had his back to her, concentrating on driving a rivet into where the stirrup fastened to the main body of the saddle. She tiptoed up to him and put her hands over his eyes. "Guess who."

"Emily Dodd."

"Emily Dodd?" she cried in dismay.

He laughed. "Carleen Brown?"

She slapped him across the shoulder.

He laid down his tools, stood, and gathered her up in his arms. "How about Mrs. Carlton Rogers?"

"Hmm," she said, only partially placated. "I like the sound of that."

"Then, I think I'd better talk to your pa and make it official."

She shook her head quickly. "Let's wait until after Nathan leaves. That's all Pa can think about right now."

"Is that the only reason?" he asked quietly.

Melissa looked away, not able to meet his eyes.

"That's what I thought." He sat back down, picked up the hammer, and went back to work.

She stepped to him and laid a hand on his shoulder, not knowing what to say.

Finally he slammed the hammer down again. "Melissa, I don't have any objection to your religion. You can be a Mormon. You can even teach our kids to be Mormons. But I can't help it if I just don't feel anything for it."

"Are you still reading the Book of Mormon?"

Now it was he that looked away.

"Carl, if you would just read it. Ask God if it's true."

He got up and walked across the room, keeping his back to her. "I did read in it. Like you said."

"Did you pray about it?"

He turned. "Melissa, I don't think that it's not true. I don't have any trouble believing that maybe Joseph Smith is what he claims to be."

"Then, what is it?" she cried. They had gone over this and over it.

"I just . . ." He picked up a piece of bridle leather and began to knead it in his hands. "It's like I don't feel a need for it. I'm happy. I believe in God. Why do I have to join some church in order to be a better person?"

And that was where it always came to, and Melissa didn't have an answer for him. All she knew was that she loved him so much that it left her aching inside whenever she wasn't with him. But she also loved the Church. She didn't want to be her mother, knowing and loving God but always being alone in her faith. She finally just dropped her head and shook it slowly. "I don't know."

He came to her and took her tenderly into his arms. "Melissa, I'll never try to take your religion away from you. I promise."

"I know."

"Then, why can't we marry?"

She looked up, her eyes suddenly moist. "Oh, Carl, I want to. You know that."

"But?"

She sighed. "But," she finally whispered, "I just don't know."

His jaw set and he let her go. "You've got to decide."

She sighed again, this time more deeply. "I know." She forced a smile. "But not this minute. Just hold me for now, all right?"

He did, pulling her to him and stroking her hair gently. Finally, she pulled back a little and looked up. "By the way," she said grumpily, "who is Emily Dodd?"

"When do you actually leave, Joseph?" Lydia asked.

"Day after tomorrow."

Melissa was down near the end of the table beyond Becca and Matthew. She leaned forward so she could see past them. "And how long will it take you?" she asked.

Joseph shrugged. "Parley says it took him three weeks to return from Independence. It's between eight and nine hundred miles."

"How long will it take you, Nathan?" Becca asked.

"About the same. Joseph is going by way of Cincinnati. But Newel has arranged for some wagons for us. We'll take our goods to Wellsville, then catch a steamer down the Ohio."

Matthew's face screwed into a puzzled frown. "Newel?" he said. "Is Brother Whitney going?"

"Not Newel Whitney," his mother smiled, "Newel Knight. He's the president of the Colesville Branch."

"Oh."

Joseph turned to Nathan. "Newel said you'll be no more than ten days behind us."

"Yes," Lydia answered, "if we can get him ready in time." She sighed, not wanting to think about him being gone from her. "It will be so exciting to learn where the land of Zion is to be located."

Emma was nodding. "I wish we could all go and be there when the Lord reveals it."

Mary Ann turned to Joseph's wife. "Where will you be staying while your husband is gone, Emma? We'd be right pleased to have you stay with us, wouldn't we, Benjamin?"

Nathan looked up quickly, fearing his father's reaction. But it had been Mary Ann's idea to have Joseph and Emma over for this farewell dinner before Joseph departed, and evidently she had already discussed this with Benjamin. He nodded without hesitation. "You've been mighty kind to my family, Joseph. We'd consider it a pleasure to have Emma with us."

Emma smiled at the two of them, and Nathan was struck again with what a handsome woman she was. Her dark hair was pulled back away from her face and filled with curls at the back of her head. Her eyes, dark as the water in a deep well, were bright now with warmth and gratitude. "You are both very kind. Thank you, but Joseph has already arranged for me to stay with the Whitneys."

"Yes, thank you, Benjamin." Joseph stopped, touched. "That is very Christian of you."

"Well, if it doesn't work out at the Whitneys'," Ben answered, speaking to Emma, "you just plan to come here. We have the room."

And they did, Nathan thought with just a touch of envy. His father had surprised them all by arranging for the purchase of a house in town rather than buying farmland. It was a comfortable frame house on the road that led south to Hiram and Mantua. With it had come thirty-some acres of cleared land. But his father did not plan to farm it. He had already sent for the surveyors to mark it off into individual residential lots. Members of the Church were flocking to Ohio, and they had to have places to live. His father was going to become a businessman, a developer of real estate. That absolutely floored Nathan. He still found it hard to believe.

Joseph sat back, appraising Nathan's father calmly. "You're not still thinking that I'm filled with the devil, are you, Ben?" It was not so much a question as a simple statement.

There was a moment's pause, then Benjamin slowly shook his head. "No, Joseph, I'll admit to that much. And I'm sorry I ever said such things about you."

The blue eyes fairly danced with pleasure. "Good. That's progress, wouldn't you say?"

Benjamin was not about to be bested. "Maybe," he drawled, "but that's not to say I don't wonder about your common sense. I mean, running off to the ends of the world to find something called Zion—sounds pretty daft to me."

Joseph laughed and picked up a chicken leg. "Daft I can live with," he said. He took a bite. "It was all that devil stuff that was getting to me."

———•———

Jessica Steed came awake with a start the moment Joshua's hand touched her. She jerked up to a sitting position, clutching the sheet to her as she looked around wildly, trying to get her bearings.

"Jess, it's me. It's all right."

It didn't register, only that there was a dark shape looming over her. She shrank back against the coldness of the brass headboard.

"It's me, Jessie. Wake up."

"Joshua?" Her hand brushed across her eyes.

"Yes. Come on, wake up."

He stepped back and let her fight off the torpor. She had been so deep in sleep that in waking up she felt as if she were clawing her way out of a pit with steep, slippery sides.

"What is it, Joshua?" She looked around, trying to see the clock in the darkness. "What time is it?"

"It's not even ten-thirty yet. For heaven's sake, what time did you go to bed anyway?"

"About an hour ago." She didn't add that she went to bed early now almost every night when he didn't come home. When dusk began to settle and the house darkened, she didn't even bother lighting the candles or a lamp. She would just slip into her nightdress and crawl between the sheets, falling asleep almost instantly. That alone was indication she was pregnant again. By supper time she felt as drained as if she had walked fifty miles across the prairie.

"Well, get dressed. I need you."

She gaped at him for a moment.

"Come on, Jess," he commanded sharply. "This can't wait."

She swung her feet over the edge of the bed. "What is it, Joshua?"

"Get going. I'll tell you while you dress."

As he stood up and stepped back, she caught a whiff of the whiskey. It had mixed with the smell of cigar smoke and chewing tobacco and was foul enough that it made her turn her face away. "You've been drinkin' again, haven't you?" she said in disgust.

"Jess, this ain't no time for one of your lectures."

"What is it you want? Where we goin'?"

"You just dress while I talk."

She leaned over to the small night table where she kept a small kerosene lamp, its wick barely glowing. His hand shot out of the darkness and gripped her wrist, startling her. "I'm just going to turn up the lamp, Joshua."

"No light. Just dress."

She stood slowly and went to the wardrobe. She opened it and groped for her dress, not hurrying, trying to ignore the deep sense of foreboding that was surging up inside her.

"All right," he said, his voice lowering, "listen! There's a poker game goin' on, and I—"

She whirled around. "Poker?"

"Yes."

"This is about poker?"

"Shut up and listen!" he snarled. "I've got to get back. If I'm gone too long they're gonna suspect somethin'."

She stood rock still, staring at him in the darkness.

"Here's what I need you to do. Get dressed. Go out the back door and down the alley to the back of your father's saloon."

"Joshua?" A note of pleading had crept into her voice and she hated herself for it, but she had to stop him. She didn't want to hear what he was about to say.

He rode right over her. "Go up the back steps. Your pa will have the door unlocked. Don't make no sounds. The poker game is moving from the main saloon hall up to your pa's living quarters. They think I've gone for more money."

"Is this the man from Pittsburgh?"

"*Will you just listen!*"

She turned around. Her fingers fumbled at the buttons of her nightdress, and finally it fell from off her shoulders.

"There's a tiny nail hole in the door to the bedroom. You'll be able to see from the bedroom into the room where we're playing. I'll see that this Everett fellow is seated with his back partly to you. You should be able to see his cards clearly."

Once more she turned to face him, clutching her dress in

front of her like a shield. "No, Joshua. I won't cheat for you again."

"You will!" he barked. "If I tell you to, you will."

"Please, Joshua, I've never forgiven myself for helping you rob the poor farmer from Virginia. Don't make me do this."

He was across the room to her in one leap and grabbed her shoulders, his fingertips digging hard into the flesh. He shook her roughly. "Don't you say it!" he yelled into her face. "Don't you tell me you won't do it." The stench of the whiskey made her gasp. Abruptly, he let her go, and stepped back, his hands dropping. "You want me to lose everything?"

Her head jerked up. "Is it that bad?" she whispered.

He stepped back farther. She could hear him breathing heavily in the darkness.

"Well, is it?" she demanded, her voice and her anger suddenly rising. After her father had come to see her about this poker thing, she had jumped on him about it. There had been an ugly confrontation, and for three nights he had not come home. But finally he had, and he had sworn there would be no more games with the man from Pittsburgh.

"Yes."

"How bad?"

There was a long moment, then with pain, "Bad. If I can't win big tonight, I'll have to sell almost everything to pay the bank."

She felt her knees go weak. Too shocked and hurt and disgusted to speak, she turned her back on him again and began to dress.

When he spoke again it was strangled, filled with shame, and yet also defiant and challenging. "You know the signals that'll tell you what I've got. Same as before. If he's got the better hand, you just press your thumb up hard against that nail hole. If I'm better than him, leave it clear."

She nodded numbly. "All right, Joshua."

"Jessie, I . . ." She could hear him swallow in the stillness of the room. "I swear to you, if I can come out of this, I'll never—"

She swung around so abruptly that it cut him off in midsentence. She stared him down in the darkness, letting him feel the fulness of her loathing.

He backed up a step, then his shoulders squared, and his face jutted forward. "You just do it right, Jessie," he muttered. "Don't you foul me up on this one." He turned and started for the door and the stairs. "Remember, don't make no noise comin' in. They're probably already there by now."

Wilson Everett was a professional gambler, there was no mistaking that. He had all the signs and made no effort to hide them. That was part of the mystique, in fact. There were always those who thought they were maybe just good enough to knock him off. It was a fool's dream; but then, as Joshua had always said, poker was a fool's game. But this time Joshua was the fool, and he didn't like it. Not one bit.

Jessica watched Everett through the tiny hole in the door, seeing now his bewilderment. His fortunes had suddenly changed, and the gambler's instinct told him something was wrong. But he hadn't yet figured out what. He had called for a new deck, watched Joshua closely. But he still lost steadily.

There were five people in the room, but only four at the table. Clinton Roundy, Jessica's father, was not playing. He kept the liquor handy and watched quietly from one corner. Judge Samuel Lucas, the county judge for Jackson County, and Zebediah Sloan, owner of the largest sawmill in the county, rounded out the circle of players. Lucas had played shrewdly, cautiously, and was down no more than a hundred dollars. Sloan had lost heavily and showed an increasingly frightened demeanor as he continued to do so.

Joshua poured himself another glass of whiskey, winning a sharp look from his father-in-law. He laughed, held it high in salute, then downed it in two gulps. Jessica felt a great sense of despair sweep over her. Liquor and pride—it was a deadly combination, and it was only her being the way she was that made the second element in the combination possible.

"Whose deal?" the judge asked.

"Mine," Everett said. Zeb Sloan gathered up the cards and shoved them across to him. But Everett paid them no mind. He was still watching Joshua, his dark eyes hooded and thoughtful. Without breaking off his gaze, he reached in his pocket and took out a cigar. He took out a small penknife, cut off the end of the cigar, leaned over to the candle, and began puffing until the cigar tip glowed a bright red. Not once did he let his eyes break off their silent appraisal of the man across the table from him.

Joshua sat back, basking in the new respect he saw in the other man's eyes.

Everett took another deep puff, then blew the smoke at the ceiling.

"Come on, Everett," the judge complained. "You gonna deal or what?"

Everett picked up the cards and began to shuffle them slowly. His eyes still did not leave Joshua. "Hear that old Roundy here has a daughter. Understand you married her."

It was to Joshua's credit that his eyes showed nothing of the sudden start he felt inside. "Yes," he said slowly. "Almost two years ago now."

"What's the game, Everett?" Sloan was getting impatient.

"Seven-card stud." He smiled at the mill owner. "What say we make this interesting? Twenty-five dollars to open, no ceiling on the bets."

Jessica shifted slightly so she could see the other two men's faces through the tiny hole. Sloan paled. Judge Lucas's one eyebrow came up. Joshua nodded, too eager. This was what he was hoping. No limits. Get the right hand, then go for the whole thing all at once.

"She a looker?"

Joshua was startled this time. Jessica saw it on his face.

"Who?"

"This wife of yours."

At that moment Jessica hated her husband. She saw the panic in his eyes, could read his thoughts as if they were a page in one of her books.

Joshua slapped one hand on the table. "Look," he snapped, "do you want to talk about my wife or do you want to play cards?"

She turned away, sick, ashamed. She didn't expect flattery from Joshua. She knew what she was. A *looker? Hardly.* It was the duplicity in him that filled her now with loathing. He knew he couldn't afford to hurt her feelings, not with her holding his financial fate in her hands. But he was also shrewd enough not to say something she would know was a lie. That would be worse. So he had said nothing.

Suddenly Jessica felt the revulsion well up in her like bile, only now the disgust was for herself. Once before she had helped Joshua cheat in a card game. It had been almost three years ago now, but she still was haunted by the face of that naive, dolt of a farmer from Virginia when he looked at his poker hand and realized Joshua had just won everything, his teams, his wagons, a small fortune in freight—a life's work and a family's dream. And Jessie had made it happen. She had seen his hand—he being so naive that he didn't even suspect that the barmaid behind him might be helping his opponent—and signalled Joshua.

Since that night, Jessica had had a recurring dream. It always left her hollow and empty inside. There was a woman, a kindly, weary-looking mother with tattered dress. Clinging to her skirts were three small, emaciated children with tear-stained cheeks. The cabin was in shambles—a door swinging on one hinge, broken windows, a well that was choked with weeds. Suddenly the family's faces would light with joy. Their father was coming, their trial was at an end. Always in the dream, Jessica could not see the man's face. He would be half-turned from her view. But as the wife and children ran up to him, shouting aloud with excitement, he would slowly open the broken gate, keeping his back to them until they began to pluck at his clothes, begging him to greet them. Then finally, with infinite slowness, he would begin to turn. It was the farmer. His eyes were but sockets in his face, his mouth pinched and drawn back across his teeth. Then, with that same maddening slowness, he would lift his hands, palms up and fingers outstretched, and hold them out to his children. There was nothing in them, but Jessica would always feel the nothingness running through his fingers, like unseen sand falling to be caught by the wind and drift away.

With sudden resolve, she stepped back away from the door, careful not to make any noise. She retrieved her shawl from the bed, wound it around her shoulders, and quietly slipped out of the door into the night.

———•———

Seven-card stud is not a game for the faint of heart. Two hole cards are dealt facedown, then four faceup, and the final hole card facedown again. The player with the best five cards wins the hand. Bets are placed after each deal of the cards. Joshua had finally gotten the hand he was after. Two queens and two aces. One more of either and he would have a full house. A powerful full house! What was better, Everett thought he had a winning hand too. Lucas and Sloan had dropped out on the second deal. Now Joshua and Everett sat facing each other, faces like carved stone, the only movement coming when they dropped another fifty or hundred dollars into the center of the table.

The moment had arrived. Joshua sensed it. Everett was grim. He showed two nines, an eight, and a jack. Two were clubs, so he might be playing for a flush, but Joshua didn't think so. The man was bluffing; he could see it on his face. Joshua's gambler instincts told him it was so.

He smiled to himself, keeping his eyes veiled and showing nothing. But he didn't have to rely on his instincts, did he now? He looked casually at the door to the bedroom. The nail hole was still clear, no warning sign of pink flesh to tell him there was danger.

Everett was dealing. He flicked Joshua his final hole card. Joshua let it lie until Everett had dealt his as well. Both hesitated for a moment, then by unspoken consent they both picked them up together. *The ace of diamonds!* It took every ounce of willpower Joshua had to keep his face impassive and his eyes hooded. It would be a good time to lie back a little, throw Everett off guard. "Queens still lead, so I'll bet a hundred," he murmured.

For a long moment Everett eyed him, his mouth pulled back slightly, giving him a somewhat feral look. Finally he leaned forward and began to count his remaining money. "Should we make this interesting, Steed?"

Joshua felt his heart leap. It was so much better when the sucker made the offer. "What you got in mind?" His eyes flicked to the door and back. The nail hole was still black and clear. Slowly, as though just flexing his hands, he closed his fingers, all except the small one, which he left extended. It was the prearranged signal. *I got my third ace, Jess. We did it!*

Everett looked up. "I've got almost three hundred left. I'd guess you're a little shy of that?"

Joshua looked down, then back up quickly. "Maybe a little, but I'm good for it."

"I'll see to the difference," Clinton Roundy said quickly. He too was sensing that this was it. The one they had been waiting for.

"Then, what say we toss it all in?" Everett said. "Winner takes everything."

Joshua pulled at his lip, then finally nodded slowly. It was no less than he had hoped for. One last time he let his eyes flick to the nail hole. It was dark and clear. He finally nodded. "Agreed."

A spot on Everett's cheek began to twitch slightly. Joshua had agreed too quickly. He looked at his cards, then at Joshua, then at his cards again. But he couldn't back down now. He had called for the offer. Quickly he shoved the remaining three hundred into the center of the table. "What've you got?" he growled.

Joshua grinned, then reached down and turned over his three hole cards. "Full house, aces and queens."

The breath rushed out of Everett as he stared at Joshua's cards. Then, slowly, like the sun peeping over a hill, he smiled. He flipped his three hole cards over. Two of them were nines. "Sorry, Steed," he said, fighting to control his jubilation. "Four nines."

Jessica walked along the dusty street in a stupor. It was past midnight, and the streets of Independence were deserted. The storefronts were dark and shuttered. There were only one or two windows in the whole town showing any light, and those lights were dim, barely glimmering behind the drapes that shut the world out. It was as though she were walking through the remains of some ancient city where all the inhabitants had long ago either died or fled.

There were no tears—she had passed that point much earlier—but the sorrow clawed at her, stripping off every defense she had tried to erect. And the guilt. That was a burden that made every part of her ache with the carrying of it. She had betrayed Joshua. In the hour of his greatest need she had turned her back on him. And why? She taunted herself with the answer. Were her feelings so easily hurt? Was her ego so easily bruised? She kept trying to push her feelings away, as if they were an obnoxious drunk pressing her for a handout, but they wouldn't be pushed.

There was anger too. Was a wife required to become a thief in order to prove her loyalty to her husband? At what point did a man take responsibility for his own stupidity? She had not asked him to gamble with Wilson Everett. It was not her ego that had brought them to the brink of financial ruin. If you wanted to talk about betrayal, what about what Joshua had done to her?

And all of this was mixed with a third emotion. The enormity of what she had done now lay upon her. She didn't know how long it would be before Joshua or her father realized she was no longer there. She prayed fervently that it would come quickly, before he lost too heavily. Joshua was already drunk. He was still functioning, but she knew him well enough now to know that when he drank that heavily it left him teetering on the brink of losing control. Crossing the line into rage would be as simple as stepping off a porch step. Coming to that realization just before she reached her home, she had felt real fear. She could not go home and simply wait for him to find her. And so she walked—numbed, lost, forlorn, afraid.

"Jessica!"

The shout spun her around. A dark figure was across the street, coming in her direction. In one instant her heart leaped and began to pound, so hard that it hurt inside her chest. Her initial impulse was to bolt, to dart between two of the darkened buildings and hide somewhere, anywhere.

"Jessie? You slut! Is that you?" The voice was heavily slurred, jumbled even as he shouted out at her.

She fell back a step, her eyes wild, her panic almost complete. Then suddenly she stopped. Her chin came up. She would not run from him. She clasped her hands together to stop the trembling and waited for Joshua, determined not to flinch in the face of his anger.

He broke into a stumbling run, almost falling as he jumped off the boardwalk and hit the softer dust of the main street. He was waving something in the air, and Jessica felt a second, even more desperate lurch of panic as she realized it was a pistol. But still she held her ground.

"You . . . it *is* you!" At closer range, even in the darkness, she could see the whites of his eyes, wide and frightening. His chest was heaving up and down, his face jutted out toward her. The smell of whiskey was so strong that she guessed he had spilled some of it on his clothes as well as filling up his insides with it.

"Yes, Joshua," she said quietly, "it's me."

"I knew you were trying to run!" He screamed it at her, his face inches from her own.

"I'm not running, Joshua. I'm right here."

"You witch!" He fell back, half sobbed, and one hand came up to rub at his eyes. "I'm ruined. Ruined!"

It was as if he had stabbed her. "Joshua." She reached out toward him, not daring to touch but beseeching. "We can rebuild, Joshua. I'll help you. We'll work together. We can go somewhere else if you want."

Behind them a window screeched as it was lifted. Joshua jerked up and Jessica turned around. A woman in a nightcap stuck her head out.

At the sight of her, Joshua's face went livid, and he waved the pistol at her. "Get out of here!"

The woman jerked back inside, her eyes wide.

The pistol dropped to his side, and for a moment it was almost as though Jessica weren't there. "I had him. I was so sure. It would have been all right. I could have won everything."

"It still can be," Jessica soothed. She finally touched his arm.

He jerked back as if she had touched him with a hot anvil iron. "You left!" he yelled. "Why did you leave? I could have won!"

"Joshua, I couldn't. You had no right to ask me to cheat for you."

His hand flashed out so swiftly that she barely saw it coming. He struck her across the cheek with the flat of his palm. It cracked in the stillness of the night, like the branch of a tree shattering in a cold frost.

"Had no right?" he shrieked. He struck her again, knocking her backwards. "Whore! Slut! You're my wife. I have every right."

This time she saw his fist double. "No, Joshua, no!" The blow caught her high on the cheekbone. She slammed back against the storefront, then fell to her knees, lights flashing crazily in front of her eyes.

"Do you hear me?" He was screaming at her, his eyes like a wild animal's, the rage unleashed and untamable now. He raised his fist again. "You'll do whatever I say, whore. Daughter of hell! Do you hear me?"

"Don't, Joshua, please." She raised one arm, but it was like putting out a hand to stop a charging bull. He swung again. She spun away, and his fist caught her a glancing blow alongside the head. It knocked her flat, dazing her for a moment.

"Hey!" It was a man's voice from above them.

Joshua swung around. This time a man was leaning out of the window. He was holding a lamp up high, trying to see. "What's going on down there?" he yelled.

Cursing, Joshua stepped over Jessica. "None of your business! Get out of here! Go back to bed."

From behind the man a woman's voice sounded clearly. "There's a woman down there. He's hitting her."

"Get away from her!" the man shouted.

"I said get out of here!" Joshua was past any point of reason. He lurched forward, raising the pistol toward the open window.

"He's got a gun!" the woman screamed. The man jerked backwards.

Jessica stumbled to her feet, staring in horror as Joshua tried to steady the weaving pistol. She jumped as the blast of the pistol shattered the night.

"Get outta here!" Joshua screamed, nearly incoherent now. He fired at the window again.

Blind with terror, shocked beyond thought, Jessica had only one impulse. She turned and began to run. The pistol roared again behind her, then she heard Joshua's cry of dismay. She darted into the narrow passageway between two stores, catching a glimpse of him swinging around toward her as she did so. It was so dark that she could see nothing. Throwing up a hand to ward off any obstacles, she ran blindly. Behind her, Joshua was screaming her name. She didn't stop, only ran all the harder, into the darkness, into the safety of the blackness of the night.

———◆———

Clinton Roundy grabbed the front of Joshua's jacket and shook him out of his stupor. "Joshua! Listen to me! There's no time for this. You've got to get going."

"She ran, Clint. She cheated me, then she ran." His head dropped on his chest. "I hit her."

Clinton Roundy's eyes hardened, but he just shook his head. They were in the small room above the freight office, where Joshua had sometimes slept when he and Jessica were fighting. The door opened and Obadiah Cornwell, Joshua's foreman in the freight company, slipped inside quickly. He peered outside for a moment, then shut the door again. "All right, everything's ready."

Clinton picked up the mug of strong, black coffee and jammed it into Joshua's hand. He then forced it up to his mouth. Joshua drank, then winced as the hot liquid seared his tongue.

"Listen, Joshua," Clinton said urgently. "You've got to get out of here. The man you shot at has gone for the constable. They don't know who it was yet, but as soon as they find Jessica you're going to be in one heap of trouble. And if she tells them about our little deal with that nail hole and Wilson Everett, we're both gonna end up in jail."

"That or with a slug in your gut," Cornwell said. "Everett ain't gonna take kindly to you trying to slicker him."

Joshua nodded dumbly.

"I've got a horse saddled in the yard," Cornwell went on. "There's some clothes and food enough in the saddlebags to hold you till you catch up with that wagon train heading for Santa Fe."

"Santa Fe?"

"Yes," Roundy said. "You remember, it left four days ago."

"But my business . . ."

"You ain't got no business no more!" Clinton had lost any patience he had. He snapped it out sharply.

"That ain't true, Clint," Cornwell said. He turned back to Joshua. "We'll have to sell off a bunch of the stock and wagons, but even at worst they can't take those wagons and teams you've got on the trail. I'll try and hold things together here."

"But don't you be comin' back until you hear from us," Roundy said, softening a little. It galled him that Joshua had struck Jessie, but he still had an anger of his own at his daughter for denying them of their victory. They were so close! "We've got to let this die down first," he said.

Cornwell reached out and took the cup from Joshua's hand. "You've got to get moving. If they find you it's gonna be too late."

Joshua nodded, then staggered to his feet. He clutched at his father-in-law's shirt. "I wish I hadn't hit her, Clint."

"I know."

"I didn't mean to hit her. If only she—"

"Joshua!" Cornwell grabbed his arm. "There ain't no time for this. Go!"

Joshua stared at him for a moment, then straightened his shoulders. "Right," he said.

Roundy opened the door. "You're gonna have to circle around town. Don't be riding down Main Street."

Joshua sighed. The foreman handed him his hat. "We'll write you in Santa Fe," he said.

For a moment, Joshua seemed cold sober. "Right," he said again. He jammed his hat on his head, and stepped out of the door.

As Cornwell shut it behind him, he looked at Clinton Roundy, who just shook his head. "I think we'd better be gettin' to our beds too," Cornwell said. "Wouldn't be good to have someone find us here either."

Roundy nodded. They stood together for a moment in silence. There was the sound of a horse's hooves below them, which quickly faded away. Roundy reached over and blew out the lamp, and they left without saying anything more.

It was shortly after sunrise when Jessica knelt down by a small stream. She took a kerchief from her dress pocket and wet it. She began to sponge the swelling under her eye with one hand, letting the fingers of her other hand gingerly explore the damage. The side of her head ached abominably, and the cheekbone kept shooting pain up into her eyes and temples. She felt below her nose and felt the encrusted blood which had now dried. In her flight, she had not even been aware that her nose had been bleeding. She knew she must be a sight. If the eye was not already black and blue, it would be shortly. The skirt of her dress was torn in several places and muddy from where she had stumbled across a swampy area near a pond sometime during the night.

She stood, careful not to move too fast and send the explosions of pain rocketing through her head again. She looked around, trying to get her bearings. Since first light she had been following a wagon track. The sun was at her back, and she was pretty sure she had been traveling in the same direction for much of the night. That meant she was west of town. Behind her was a line of trees, and she remembered that an hour or so before, she had crossed a small river. That puzzled her for a moment. Some distance west of town the Kansas River joined the Missouri, but the Kansas was a big river in its own right, much bigger than the one she had crossed.

Then she remembered. There were two rivers that drained the water from the central highlands of Jackson County into the Missouri. East of town was the Little Blue River; west of town, the Big Blue. That meant she was not far from Kaw Township. She felt her spirits lift a little. There were settlers starting homesteads out here on the prairie. Perhaps she could find someone who would take her in until Joshua's fury cooled enough that she could reason with him.

She squeezed the last of the water from her handkerchief, dabbed at her cheekbone one more time, then moved back onto the road. She turned her face to the west and began to walk again.

———•———

Kaw Township embraced all of that part of Jackson County that lay west of the Big Blue River and from the Missouri River south to the county line. The western edge of the township also served as the western border of the United States of America. Beyond that was Indian Territory, that vast reserve of land which President Andrew Jackson had set aside for the resettlement of the various native tribes.

Mostly the land was rolling prairie, an undulating sea of grass and wild flowers that always left newcomers from the East a little breathless with the vastness of its scope. Along the creek and river bottoms the timber was heavy and varied—oak, hickory, black walnut, elm, cherry, honey locust, mulberry, cottonwood, and maple. Plum, grapes, crab apple, wild raspberry, blueberry, and a multitude of other smaller trees and shrubs made the lowlands an almost impenetrable tangle. But beyond that, it was as though the land had been carefully cultivated and cared for.

With the limited timber, most of the settlers' houses were low and squat, made either of double-hewn logs or, more commonly, from slabs of sod cut from the incredibly wiry prairie turf, so tough it took two span of oxen to pull a plow through it.

The home in which the missionaries to the Lamanites had chosen to live was a mixture of both. The walls were of logs, but only shoulder high. The roof line was low enough that a grown man had to stoop to enter. Cedar shingles were a luxury beyond the reach of any settlers in Kaw Township. Instead, a tight crosshatch of tree limbs and thick willow sticks formed the base. Over that, slabs of prairie sod were laid. It was a functional, if not an attractive, shelter. The climate in western Missouri was much milder than that in New York and Ohio. The worst problem occurred when it rained hard enough to soak through the sod and begin to drip streams of mud on everything inside the house.

But today Oliver Cowdery was not worried about rain. It was already on its way to becoming a hot day in mid-July and he was in the small garden area behind the cabin, hoeing out the morning glory that was taking over their patch of sweet corn. Ziba Peterson and Peter Whitmer were about a hundred yards behind him, down by the creek, gathering dead sticks and tree limbs to be used for their cooking fire. Frederick G. Williams was in Independence, tending to the small tailor shop they ran to keep them in funds.

"Sir?"

The quiet voice brought Oliver around with a jerk. For a moment he just stared, his mind not registering what his eyes were seeing. Then he dropped the hoe and ran to the battered figure that was standing there, hands open, eyes pleading.

"Can you help me, sir?"

Oliver barely caught her as her knees buckled and she collapsed into his arms.

It was the next morning, about the same time, that Oliver was once again in the garden, trying to complete the task he had started the previous morning.

"Halloo the house." The sound came floating across the fields gently, almost like an echo.

Oliver straightened, squinting into the bright sunshine. Peter Whitmer, near the front door, pounding out some cornmeal, looked up too, then leaped to his feet. Down by the road that ran between Independence and Kaw Village there were five—no, six—men walking briskly toward him. They all had hats on and knapsacks and bedrolls slung over their shoulders. These were traveling men, not some just come out for the day from the village. Oliver peered more intently. They all had traveling gear except for one, the one in the lead. He carried no pack. Now Oliver could clearly recognize that it was Frederick Williams. He was bringing company home.

Oliver started. He raised his hand to shade his eyes, not daring to believe. But there was no mistaking it. The man just behind Williams was tall, broad of shoulder, and striding along like no other man Oliver knew.

"Joseph?" he whispered in awe.

"It's Joseph!" Peter cried.

"And there's Martin Harris," Oliver shouted. He threw the hoe down and leaped across the vegetables. As he broke into a run for the road, Peter Whitmer was hard on his heels, crying, "Joseph! Joseph! Joseph!"

———◆———

"I can't believe it," Oliver said again, for at least the tenth time. "I can't believe you're really here."

The five newcomers were eating elk stew, mopping it up with johnnycake and corn dodger and washing it down with warm milk from the brindle cow the missionaries kept behind the cabin. The new arrivals were seated at the split log table while the four missionaries stood around watching them eat.

Joseph looked up at Oliver and smiled. "After eight hundred miles, the last two hundred or more on foot, neither can we, right, brethren?"

They all groaned.

"And there are others coming too?" Oliver asked after a minute.

"Yes, Oliver. We left Newel Knight and the entire Colesville Branch in St. Louis waiting for a steamboat. Brother Sidney Rigdon is with them."

Martin shook his head ruefully. "They wanted us to wait and come with them, but you know Joseph; he'd rather walk two hundred miles on foot than wait three or four more days doing nothing."

"They shouldn't be many days behind us," Joseph Coe spoke up.

"There's a river steamer due in here next week," Peter Whitmer said. "On the twenty-fifth, I believe. The *Chieftain*."

"That's the one they've got passage on," Martin said.

"Nathan Steed is with them," Joseph said to Oliver.

"Really?" he cried. "That's wonderful. What about Lydia?"

"No. He won't be staying. Nathan is just helping Newel get the Colesville group here. He's also most anxious to find Joshua."

Oliver's face fell. "Now, there's a tragedy, then."

"Why?"

"Joshua's gone."

"No!"

"Yes, and good riddance to him too." He quickly told Joseph of the woman who had shown up on their doorstep the previous day. Joseph's mouth tightened as Oliver described her condition.

"We have taken her to the Lewis family, not far from here. They are a good family who were baptized a few months ago. They will care for her well."

"But Joshua is gone."

"Yes," Ziba spoke up. "We went into town to press charges against him. What he did to her is shameful, just shameful. But he's disappeared. No one knows what's happened to him. They've got the constable out looking for him now."

"That is going to be a hard blow for Nathan." Joseph sighed. "And his family. They were so excited to have finally located him again."

Oliver's face still showed his disgust. "He's a man filled with anger. I met him some time ago, tried to talk to him about you. He boiled over almost instantly."

"I know. I had hopes of talking with him too, putting some of the old feelings behind us."

"Well," Frederick Williams said, "there's no chance for that now." He straightened a little. "So tell us, has the Lord revealed the location of Zion yet?"

Joseph brightened. "No, Brother Williams. But he promised that if we would come here to Missouri, he would reveal the place to us."

"Wonderful," Ziba exclaimed. "That's wonderful."

"It is to be the gathering place for his people," Martin breathed. "The Colesville Branch will only be the first of many."

"Will you then leave Kirtland?" Oliver asked.

"No," Joseph said firmly. "For now, at least, we are to build up both places." He pushed his plate aside and leaned back. "We are trail worn and weary. We would like to rest for today, then tomorrow we shall have you show us around this country. Maybe then the Lord will show us his will concerning Zion."

"Brother Lewis?"

"Yes." The farmer stood in the doorway, framed by the light from within.

"My name is Nathan Steed. I'm with the group of Saints that just arrived from Ohio this morning."

"Oh yes," Lewis said. "Come in, come in."

Nathan didn't move. "I understand you have a woman living with you now, Jessica Steed?"

"Yes, we—" His eyes widened. "Nathan Steed did you say?"

Pain filled Nathan's eyes. "Yes, I'm her brother-in-law. If you don't mind, I wonder if I might speak to her outside."

There was some concern in the man's eyes, but he finally nodded. "I'll ask her to come out."

"I don't blame him anymore," Jessica said softly as they sat on a log out behind the Lewises' sod hut. "I betrayed him in a way. I can see why he got so angry."

It was not yet full dark, and in the soft light, the bruises around her eyes and mouth were muted, softened considerably. But even in the fainter light, and even after close to a week of healing, they still contrasted so starkly with her fair skin that it made one gasp to think of what must have caused them. Nathan's jaw set, and he shook his head angrily. "There is no excuse for what he did to you, Jessica. None!"

She sighed, her eyes filled with a different kind of pain now. "He wasn't always like that. But when he drank . . ." She couldn't finish and looked away.

Nathan changed the subject and began to talk of his family. He told her about his mother and father, about Melissa and her beau. His eyes were soft with loneliness when he began to describe Matthew and Rebecca. She asked questions, hungry to know more. Finally, she looked across to him. "And what of your wife?"

So he began to talk about Lydia, told of her beauty, told of her decision to join the Church even at the cost of losing her family. And then he told her about little Joshua, told of his experience when he blessed him. His eyebrows pulled down into a deep frown. "Now," he said, "I am all the more puzzled as to why I was to call him Joshua." He shook it off. "Anyway, I'd really like you to meet Lydia sometime," he finished.

She gave a short, soundless laugh. "I've always hated her, you know."

That really startled Nathan, and this time she laughed out loud. "Strange, isn't it? I've never met her, and yet I've hated her—or rather, I've hated what she was in Joshua's mind." And it all began to come out. Jessica had never had anyone to talk to about the hurt and the loneliness and the longings she had felt. But somehow the kindness in Nathan's eyes and his burning indignation over what Joshua had done to her opened up a gate inside her and it all came flooding out. She talked quietly but steadily for almost fifteen minutes. She told him of how Joshua had come to her that night, drunk and hurt, and asked her to marry him. She told of his long absences, of his drinking, and of his poker. And eventually she told him of Doctor Hathaway and the curse she bore in her body. It was as though she had been carrying around a burden for so long that now that she had a chance to set part of it down, she wanted to set it all down.

When she finished, they sat silently for a long time, listening to the final night songs of the birds and the whispering of a breeze in the prairie grass. Finally, Nathan stirred. "Jessica?"

"Yes?"

"Once we get the Saints settled here, I'll be going back. Why don't you come with me? Come live with my family."

Now it was her turn to be startled. She had not expected that. After a moment she shook her head.

"Why not? My father has a spacious house. You need a family now, Jessica."

She sighed, not unhappily. "I've only been with the Lewis family about a week now, but they have asked that I stay with them permanently. I could help with the children." She paused, becoming more sure of herself even as she spoke. "Missouri is my home now. And the Lewises are really wonderful."

For a moment Nathan considered pressing the issue, but he could sense that Jessica had spoken from her heart, and so he only nodded.

"I'm reading the Book of Mormon now."

"Really?"

She nodded.

"And?"

"Brother Lewis is going to ask Joseph if I can be baptized."

Spontaneously, Nathan reached out and touched her arm. "That's wonderful. I would like to be there."

Her eyes widened for a moment with a thought. "Could you do it, Nathan?"

"I . . . well, yes, of course. I'm an elder."

"I would like that, I think."

"So would I."

A thought jumped into Nathan's mind. He gave her a sharp look.

"What?"

"Jessica, I . . ." His mind was racing. "In the Church we have the priesthood. The priesthood is the power to act for God on the earth."

"Yes, Brother Lewis has talked about it."

"In the book of James, in the New Testament, it says that when we are sick we should call for the elders of the Church, and they shall pray for the sick and anoint them with oil, and the Lord shall raise them up."

"But . . ." She was totally perplexed. "But I'm not sick, Nathan."

"Not in the normal sense," he said, his voice eager now, the words coming in a rush. "But something's wrong with your body that you can't carry a child."

She looked away. "I know."

"But that's just it," he cried. "Let us give you a blessing. Let us bless you by the power of the priesthood which we hold. I can't promise you anything, but it is worth a try."

For a long, long moment Jessica stared into his eyes. "All right," she finally said. There was little hope in her voice as she spoke.

Though not nearly as large or comfortably furnished as the home Benjamin had built for them in Palmyra, the new Steed home, purchased from one of the early settlers, was still one of Kirtland's finer places to live. It was one story along the front, but the roof was built after the New England, Cape Cod style, sloping upward to the back of the house, then dropping vertically. This allowed for an attic in the back part of the house large enough to provide bedroom space for all three children, though Matthew and Becca shared one of the two rooms so that Melissa could have the other to herself.

Mary Ann was still finding furnishings as best she could, so the parlor was still bare except for three wooden chairs Benjamin had purchased from the Whitney store. The sitting room, where they spent most of their time when not in the kitchen, had a sofa and a high-backed stuffed chair. Against her better judgment—guests should always be received in the parlor—Mary Ann had agreed that they would meet in the sitting room.

There was a knock at the door. Melissa was up in an instant. Mary Ann smiled. "Your father will get it, Melissa."

"I know, I know." She hurried to the kitchen door and looked into the entryway. "Papa?"

"I'm coming, I'm coming." The grumbling voice came from the bedroom where her parents slept. Melissa waited for a moment; then when her father still didn't appear, she swung around. "Mama, maybe you'd better go."

"I'll get it," Matthew cried, getting up from his chair.

"You will not!" Melissa cried. "You and Becca are to stay in the kitchen. Do you hear?"

Becca stuck out her lower lip. "I want to hear," she pouted.

Melissa gave her sister her sternest look. "I'll tell you everything later. You stay here."

The knock sounded again.

"Mama!" Melissa was pleading. But at that moment the bedroom door opened and her father came out. He was smoothing down his hair, which he had wet from the bowl of water on the dresser and brushed hard to make it stay down. Melissa hurried and shut the kitchen door as her father walked past and moved to the front entrance.

"You look lovely, Melissa," Mary Ann whispered. She was suddenly having very tender feelings for this oldest daughter of theirs whom they were about to lose. She had on a long dress of deep pink, which showed off her dark eyes and fair skin wonderfully. A ribbon of matching color pulled her black hair back away from her face.

If Melissa heard, she gave no sign. She was listening intently at the door. There was the murmur of voices, and then the front door shut firmly. Melissa couldn't bear it. She swung around. "Oh, Mama, do you think Papa will be nice?"

Mary Ann finally stood and moved to her daughter's side. "Yes, dear," she soothed. "Believe it or not, your father can really be quite charming when he wants to. Now, what say you and I make our entry and find out if this young man of yours is here for what we think he's here for."

"You're not Mormon, are you?"

Carlton Rogers blinked, but Melissa's jaw dropped a little. She shot a glance at her mother, who was also staring at Benjamin. If he noted the effect his question had on his wife and daughter, he gave no sign of it.

"I beg your pardon?" Carl Rogers blushed deeply, the effect of which was heightened all the more because of his red hair and freckles.

"You're not a member of the Mormon church?"

"No, sir." The oldest son of the owner of Kirtland's largest livery stable had recovered his composure.

"You know that Melissa is?"

"Yes, sir."

"Does that bother you?"

"Papa!"

Benjamin turned to Melissa and waved her off with his eyes. Mustering his courage now, Carl answered. "Bother me, sir? Why should it? Melissa and I have discussed it thoroughly."

"Well, as you know, there are some people in the area who have taken it into their heads that Mormons are a threat to their way of life, or at least to their religion. There's already been articles in the newspapers."

"Yes, sir, I'm aware of that."

"Do your parents know that Melissa is a Mormon?"

"Yes, sir."

"Does that bother them?"

"Not that they've said. They very much like your daughter, sir."

"Hmm." Benjamin sat back, giving the boy a long, careful appraisal. Melissa looked to her mother, her eyes beseeching her to intervene. But her mother was almost in as much shock as Melissa that Benjamin Steed was pursuing this line of questioning.

Carl smiled briefly at Melissa, then turned back to her father. "You're not a Mormon yourself, are you, sir?"

Benjamin's left eyebrow lifted slowly. "No," he finally said.

"But your wife and children are?"

"Yes."

"Does that bother you, sir?"

Benjamin's mouth opened, then shut again. Melissa almost clapped her hands with the joy of seeing her father nonplussed. And she could have hugged Carl for being bold enough to answer back. Then in panic she focused her eyes on her father. If Carl made him angry, it would not be a good thing.

For several moments, the room was in complete silence, the only sound being that of a wagon rattling past outside the window. Then Ben's eyes seemed to soften, and Melissa read begrudging admiration there. "No, not anymore," her father finally said.

Carl took a deep breath, and his face grew red again. "Then, sir, if I may, I would like to ask you and your wife if I may have the hand of your daughter in marriage."

For the first time during the interview, Melissa's mother spoke. "May I ask you a question, Carl?"

"Of course, ma'am."

"Do you love my daughter?"

He leaned forward, his eyes filled with relief. Here was a question he was more comfortable with. "I sure do!"

Melissa felt her heart melt as she looked at him. It thrilled her that he felt that way too.

"Will you treat her right?"

"Yes, ma'am!"

Benjamin watched him for several moments, his face impassive. Melissa held her breath, then felt a tremendous surge of relief when she saw the corners of her father's mouth relax. Finally, he was smiling at her. "Is this the man you want to spend your life with, Melissa?"

She nodded quickly, her heart feeling as though it were going to burst. "Yes, Papa."

"Then it seems like that's what ought to happen." He stood and walked to Carl, hand outstretched.

It was the second day of August in the year of our Lord, one thousand eight hundred and thirty-one. It was a bright and glorious morning. A flock of crows was circling above the river some distance away, and their faint cawing joined in with the ever-present hum of a thousand honeybees busily servicing the dozen or more varieties of wildflowers that dotted the prairie landscape.

Nathan Steed stood shoulder-to-shoulder with Jessica Roundy Steed, who was flanked on the opposite side by Brother and Sister Lewis. Nathan was aware of the heat of the sun on his back, but his mind was on Jessica. It still felt strange to think that this quiet, resolute woman standing next to him was his sister-in-law. This was Joshua's wife.

It had been the hardest thing Nathan had ever done in his life when he sat down and wrote to his mother about Joshua and Jessica and what had happened. When the letter was posted, from that moment on Nathan had not spoken Joshua's name aloud again.

"Would the elders please step forward."

Gratefully, Nathan let his thoughts pull away from Joshua and back to the proceedings. The small group—close to a hundred, counting the older children who were present—was gathered in a half circle in front of a small patch of ground that had been cleared of its grass. The largest body was, of course, those who had recently arrived from the East. There were nearly sixty in the Colesville Branch group. Another half dozen had been in Joseph's party. The rest of the group consisted of new families baptized during the past several months by Oliver and his missionary companions.

Several men stepped forward, faces long with solemnity. Joseph led out, followed by Sidney Rigdon, Martin Harris, and Oliver Cowdery. Newel Knight, president of the Colesville Branch, stepped forward, as did his father, Joseph Knight, one of Joseph's earliest supporters.

Joseph stopped at the end of a long, freshly trimmed log cut from the timber near the river. Nathan counted quickly. There were twelve men, all elders in the Church. Joseph reached inside his breech coat and took out a folded piece of paper. After unfolding it, he had to hold it in both hands to stop it from flapping in the sharp breeze that was blowing.

"Brothers and sisters," he called, lifting his voice against the wind, "before we ever left Kirtland, the Lord promised that if we would gather to Missouri he would reveal to us the place where Zion was to be located."

An expectant hush fell over the group.

"Well, as you know, the Lord has kept his word. I received the following revelation the day after Martin and I and the others arrived here in Jackson County. I would like to read again to you the word of the Lord on the matter."

He found his place, then began to read in a loud, clear voice. " 'Hearken, O ye elders of my church, saith the Lord your God, who have assembled yourselves together, according to my commandments, in this land, which is the land of Missouri, which is the land which I have appointed and consecrated for the gathering of the saints.' "

He paused, then read more slowly and with greater emphasis. " 'Wherefore, this is the land of promise, and the place for the city of Zion. And thus saith the Lord your God, if you will receive wisdom here is wisdom. Behold, the place which is now called Independence is the center place; and a spot for the temple is lying westward, upon a lot which is not far from the courthouse.' "

He looked up. "On the morrow, we shall go to that site. It is at the knoll of the hill about half a mile west of the courthouse. There we shall dedicate the land for the building of the temple of the city of Zion, the New Jerusalem."

Nathan looked at Jessica and they smiled at each other. A temple on the earth again! The other night, around an open camp fire, Joseph had spoken of the prophets of old and how they had foreseen the days when Zion would again be built upon the earth. Prophecies millennia old were being fulfilled, and they were here to be witness to it. Nathan felt like crying and he felt like shouting aloud. It was a glorious day.

Joseph lowered the paper and put it back inside his coat. He let his eyes sweep across the crowd. "So it is, on this day, we are gathered to lay the first log for the first house built by the Saints on the land of Zion. Twelve of us—all elders of God, called and ordained of him to carry forth his work in the latter days—will carry and put this log in place. And why are there twelve?" He paused, letting his question hang in the air. Then he nodded slowly. "Because we represent the twelve tribes of Israel, whose gathering together again has now begun."

As one, the men bent over and lifted the weight of the log. There was a soft grunt or two, though Jessica could not tell from which men they came. They moved forward slowly, coming to the shallow trench which had been dug to receive it. They stopped. "With the laying of this log," Joseph said loudly, "we hereby signify that we are laying the foundation of Zion." He nodded and they lowered their burden and placed it carefully in place.

Instantly there were murmurs of approval. Some of the children clapped excitedly, and the group erupted into a spontaneous cheer. Several of the women were weeping.

The men returned to their places. "Brother Sidney," Joseph said, turning to his companion.

Sidney stepped forward. He looked over the crowd with great solemnity, then took a breath. "My brothers and sisters," he called loudly, "do you receive this land for the land of your inheritance with thankful hearts from the Lord?"

Nathan's thoughts suddenly turned to Lydia, and he wished she could be standing here with him at this sacred moment. "We do!" The group said it firmly, their voices in unison.

"Do you pledge yourselves to keep the law of God in this land which you never have kept in your own lands?"

"We do!"

"Do you pledge yourselves to see that others of your brethren who shall come hither do keep the laws of God?"

The answer went up a notch in volume. "We do!"

"Then, let us pray."

All heads bowed instantly, and the men swept off their hats. Sidney dropped to his knees and began to pray. It was a prayer of supplication, beseeching the Lord for his blessings on the little group of Saints gathered in response to his commands. But it was far more than that. It was a prayer of dedication. He described the beauty of the land on which they had gathered. He thanked the Lord for revealing the location of the city of Zion. And then he dedicated the land for the gathering of the Saints from across the nation and from around the world. Sidney was a master orator, but this was a prayer sprung from the depths of his heart. It was profoundly moving, and Nathan found himself stirred more deeply than he had ever been before.

Finally, Brother Rigdon was finished. He arose slowly, and the men in the congregation replaced their hats. Nathan glanced across to Jessica, curious as to what was going through her mind. Tomorrow they would travel the short distance to the Big Blue River and Nathan would baptize her. Sensing his look, Jessica turned and smiled.

Sidney's eyes moved from face to face. Finally he spoke again. "I now pronounce this land consecrated and dedicated unto the Lord for a possession and inheritance for the Saints, and for all the faithful servants of the Lord to the remotest ages of time. In the name of Jesus Christ, having authority from him. Amen."

"Amen!" With a hundred voices, the sound rolled across the prairie like distant thunder. Jessica's voice was raised as clearly as any of the rest.

As Sidney stepped back into his place, Joseph faced the group again. His voice was very solemn now. "My dear brothers and sisters, this is a historic occasion. After centuries of neglect and abandonment, the time has come at last for Zion to be redeemed. We are privileged to be chosen as part of those who shall see it come to pass."

Amen! Nathan felt like shouting praises of hallelujah and amens over and over. Joseph was exactly right. How many of the ancients had looked forward in vision and envied them the privilege of bringing forth Zion?

Joseph's voice brought him back to the present. "But as glorious as that privilege may be, it will not be without it's challenges." Again he reached in his coat pocket, this time to bring out another sheaf of papers. His eyes hooded for a moment as he opened them and glanced down.

"Yesterday I received the following from the Lord," Joseph said slowly. "I shall read only the first part now, though there is much of value here that I shall share with you at a later time." He opened the papers, using both hands to keep them from rippling in the breeze.

He glanced once more at the assembly, then began to read. " 'Hearken, O ye elders of my church, and give ear to my word, and learn of me what I will concerning you, and also concerning this land unto which I have sent you: for verily I say unto you, blessed is he that keepeth my commandments, whether in life or in death. . . .' "

Joseph's voice trailed off for a moment. Suddenly it was as if all sound had stopped. Every eye was locked on his face. He seemed to sense it and, if it was possible, continued with even greater gravity than before.

" 'Ye can not behold with your natural eyes, for the present time, the design of your God concerning those things which shall come hereafter, and the glory which shall follow, after much tribulation.' "

Tribulation? Nathan was startled by that. These were not words he had expected to hear. The jubilation that had gripped the group just moments before was suddenly gone. He felt a little shiver crawl up his spine as the import of Joseph's words struck him.

" 'For after much tribulation cometh the blessings,' " Joseph went on. " 'Wherefore, the day cometh that ye shall be crowned with much glory, the hour is not yet but is nigh at hand. Remember this which I tell you before, that you may lay it to heart, and receive that which shall follow.' "

For several moments Joseph stood motionless, his eyes seeing nothing. Then he shook his head slowly, as if finding it hard to say what came next. "My brothers and sisters, I know not what the Lord has in store for us, but I for one have determined to serve him no matter what may come. I am grateful to be here this day, standing on the very soil that God has designated as the land of Zion. I am grateful that you are here with me to share in this sacred moment."

This time it was not one chorus. It came as a soft murmur here, a determined affirmation there. But however it was said, one by one, the group that stood half surrounding their young prophet nodded and spoke the one word that said what was in their hearts. "Amen," they said. "Amen!"

———————

The home of Joshua Lewis was one of the few standing structures in Kaw Township. It was a simple log cabin with sod roof. Inside there was only one large room, partitioned off by blankets hung from ropes strung between hooks in the wall. The floor was hard-packed dirt, and the furniture was simple and handmade. The Lewis family had been one of the first to accept the message of the Restoration when the missionaries from New York and Ohio arrived in western Missouri. They had also been the ones to whom Oliver Cowdery had taken Jessica that morning after she had fled from Joshua's rage. They had taken her in without question, and she had been there ever since.

Jessica was helping to get the children settled in bed when a knock sounded at the door. Sister Lewis looked up in surprise as her husband went to answer it. He opened it and stepped back. To Jessica's surprise, Joseph entered, followed by Martin Harris, Oliver Cowdery, and Nathan Steed.

As they exchanged greetings, Jessica hung back. In a moment Joseph turned and walked over to where she stood. He reached out and took one of her hands, and without preamble began. "Sister Steed, I have somewhat to say to you."

"Yes?" He was peering deeply into her eyes, and she was more than a little disconcerted.

"As part of the law of the Lord, given in Kirtland earlier this year, the Lord instructed the Church about the healing of the sick."

"But—," she started.

Joseph held up his hand quickly, cutting off her protest. "The Lord said that the elders, two or more, shall be called and shall lay their hands upon them who need help, praying over them in his name. And he promised that if the person has faith, and is not appointed unto death, he or she shall be healed."

"Yes, I know," she said softly. "Nathan has taught me about that."

Joseph nodded. "Do you have the faith to be healed?"

She looked away quickly, her eye catching Nathan's gaze. He smiled encouragingly, his eyes filled with kindness. "I . . . I don't know," she finally stammered.

"Would you like a blessing at the hands of the priesthood?" Nathan asked.

"For the baby you mean?"

"For you *and* the baby," Oliver said.

"Do it, Jessica," Sister Lewis said from across the room. "I've seen it work. It's a wondrous thing."

Jessie stood there for several seconds, her eyes darting from one face to another. All of them were filled with love. For her. For the life that was in her. But could this help? It was too wonderful a possibility to even let herself dare hope.

Joseph squeezed her hand. "Look at me, Jessica Steed."

He was a full head taller than she was, and she had to tip her head back to meet his gaze.

"Do you believe in the Lord Jesus Christ?"

This time there was no hesitation. "Yes. Yes, I do."

"Do you believe he has the power to heal your body so that it can bear children?"

"Yes." It came out more firmly now. She was shocked to realize that she really did believe it.

"Would you like a blessing so that you can carry this child to full term?"

It burst out of her like a sob. "Oh, yes."

"Then, sit yourself down and it shall be done."

Joseph turned. Sister Lewis quickly pushed one of the chairs into the middle of the room. Joseph gently pulled Jessica toward it. When she sat down he gestured to the others. "Brother Lewis, as yet, holds only the priesthood of Aaron. This ordinance requires the higher priesthood, but Nathan and Oliver and I are all elders. Do you have a preference as to who you would like to act as voice?"

Jessie looked quickly from one to the other. Her eyes stopped on Nathan. He was so unlike Joshua, so different in temperament, and yet she could see Joshua in his face, especially when he smiled. She turned back to the Prophet. "Would it be all right if Nathan did?"

"Of course, if Nathan agrees."

"I would be honored," Nathan said.

Joseph nodded at Nathan to proceed. The four men gathered around Jessica, Nathan standing directly behind her. Nathan cleared his throat and laid his hands on her head. The others followed suit. Jessica felt a great sense of solemnity come over her as the weight of their hands pressed down upon her. As she closed her eyes she saw the Lewises bow their heads as well.

"Sister Jessica Roundy Steed," Nathan began, speaking slowly and reverently, "as elders who hold the holy priesthood we lay our hands upon your head in keeping with the instructions of the Lord. In the name of Jesus, I . . ." He hesitated, then corrected himself. "*We* give you a blessing."

Again there was a pause. Jessie had no idea what to expect and didn't know if this was usual or not. She felt a quick rush of concern. Maybe the Lord didn't have a blessing for her. Maybe he was displeased with her for her part in the card game in her father's home.

But Nathan went on, his voice suddenly husky with emotion. "Jessica, the Lord is aware of the sorrow that has been yours. He is aware of the struggles that you have faced with your husband and in your marriage."

At the mention of Joshua, Jessie felt her lower lip start to tremble and her eyes start to burn behind the closed lids. She pressed her lips tightly together, forcing herself to concentrate on what Nathan was saying.

"Do not despair. The Lord is mindful of you and of Joshua, and though he is not pleased with what your husband has done, the Lord still loves him and cares for him. Do not lose faith. Trust in the Lord, and even these things which have brought you misery shall eventually work to your joy.

"Now, my dear sister, the Lord would have you know that the feelings you have experienced in the past days have been from him. You were led to this home by the guidance of the Holy Spirit, and since that day, you have been prompted again and again by his influence. Do not resist these promptings. Follow them. Listen to your heart, for this is how the Spirit speaks to us, through the feelings of the heart.

"You have been given the Book of Mormon, and you have come to know that it is true. Tomorrow you shall be baptized for the remission of your sins and then shall be worthy to receive the gift of the Holy Ghost. This is pleasing to the Lord, Sister Jessica. He wants you in his kingdom."

Again the room fell silent for a moment, then Nathan continued. "Now, dear Jessica, there is one more blessing the Lord has in store for you. You are desirous of being a mother in Zion. You have longed with all the power of a righteous woman for the privilege of bearing children. As with Hannah of old, the Lord has heard your cries, and now grants you your petition."

Jessica stirred beneath the weight of their hands, feeling as though her whole body were suddenly on fire. Nathan seemed to sense it, for suddenly his voice became strong and clear.

"The life that is within you now shall be protected. You shall feel it swell and grow. Be at peace during the remaining time that you carry it, for the Lord's promises are sure. And when the time comes, you shall be delivered of a strong, healthy child. It shall be your privilege to live a long life and see this child grow to adulthood. Train her well, for she is one of God's chosen, and he has a mission for her in this life."

Jessica was barely aware that a tear had splashed onto her

hands, which were folded in her lap. The joy was like a massive force pushing from within, expanding her to the point where she was sure she was going to burst.

"These blessings are based on your faithfulness," Nathan went on. "But if you are faithful, they are sure, for this blessing is not of men, but of God. And we give it to you in the name of our beloved Savior and Redeemer, amen."

The hands lifted from her head. She sat there for a moment, dazed, overcome by the feelings that were exploding within her. Then she slowly stood. She saw Sister Lewis, who now had tears streaming down her face. She was trying to smile at her through them. Jessica slowly turned. Nathan's eyes were moist. With a sob she threw herself into his arms. "Thank you," she whispered. "Oh, thank you, Nathan."

He pushed her away so that he could look into her face. He smiled tenderly. "Don't thank me, Jessica. It wasn't *my* blessing."

Chapter Eighteen

February 3, 1832 Lexington, Ktky.

My dearest Lydia,

It having been now four months since my departure and more than a month since my last letter, I shall endeavor to catch you up on my activities since I last wrote. I am happy to report that my plan is to stay here in Lexington for the remaining two months of my labors, at which time I shall return to Kirtland. This means that for the first time since my departure, you can post a letter to me. Send it care of the Gould Mercantile Store and General Post Office. It would be ever so joyful to receive news from you. My heart longs to see you again, and I never close my eyes in sleep without you and young Joshua being the last ones in my thoughts. It has been a most difficult sacrifice to leave you and little Joshua. Nothing but a firm conviction that I am in the Lord's service would take me from your side.

Since leaving Kirtland October last, Elder Miller and I have traveled some six hundred miles without purse or scrip, most of that being on foot. We have preached 48 sermons, held 36 meetings, baptized 53 souls, and organized 3 branches of the Church. We have gathered little children and blessed them in the name of Christ. I have laid hands upon the sick and seen them recover. I have felt the power of the Holy Spirit more times than I can recount.

I have recently recovered from ten days of illness. In mid-January a raging blizzard left six inches of snow on the ground and caught us between towns. We were forced to wade through the snow for nearly twelve miles before we found a place that would take us in for the night. Shortly thereafter I was struck with a deep cough and high fever and was left so weak that I could not rise from my bed. To my good fortune, the family that housed us was kind enough to let us stay, and fed and sheltered us. In the last week the weather has improved somewhat, and though I am still very weak, I am now preaching and teaching again as before.

Lexington seems a welcome relief after traveling through the thinly settled areas of northern Kentucky. The people there were mostly very ignorant, but kind and hospitable. Some families dress entirely in animal skins without any other clothing. Houses are generally without glass windows, and the doors are left open summer and winter for light. Pigs, chickens, and cows often move in and out of the living quarters without restriction and make staying overnight an odorous and most unpleasant experience, especially since my normal bed is the floor and my cover a single blanket.

We are staying now with a family whom we baptized last week. They are most kind, and I have laundered my clothes for the first time in over a month. Also thanks to their kindness, I am finally eating well again, and I am sure this will help my health to continue to improve. For a time before Christmas, Elder Miller and I lived on nothing more than a few potatoes and salt for almost a fortnight.

Though we have had much success, often the people show

little interest in religion and the gospel message. Occasionally we find them openly hostile. A week ago last Tuesday, we stopped in a small community alongside the Ohio River. The town seemed filled with a spirit of lying and prejudice, and they would not hear the word of God. Elder Miller and I appointed a meeting in the open air, since no church or public hall or home was opened to us. Some came to hear, others to mock, and yet others to disturb. One man brought a mob of some fifty others, with drums, cornet, and other musical instruments. As I was trying to preach, they formed a line of battle around us and sought to drown out my words with the sounds of their drums and music. I had to break off my preaching several times, but did not give up. When they saw that we would not be put off by their attempts to disrupt our preaching, with one accord they rushed at us and began to pelt us with rotten eggs. In a moment we were both covered—forehead, bosom, and most of the rest of our bodies. As we departed and walked slowly away, drenched in the foul smell of their eggs, they followed behind, insulting and mocking us all the way out of town. We spent near half a day at a small stream trying to remove the results of this Christian benevolence.

The following day we had a more amusing experience. One of the rabble who treated us so shamefully was the owner of the house we stopped at later that same night and asked for lodging. He was of a mind to reject us outright, but the customs of hospitality in this part of the country are strong and required otherwise of him. So he reluctantly gave us bed. The next morning, his wife had set a wonderful breakfast of bacon, eggs, and plenty of bread. Brother Miller and I had not seen such a meal in over a week and set to the task of removing it as quickly as possible from their sight.

The moment we began to eat, the man lit into us for being Mormons, swearing at us and Joe Smith and the gold Bible and every other thing he could bring to mind. His swearing did not hinder our eating, for the harder he swore, the faster we ate, until we got our stomachs full. We then arose from the table and took our hats and thanked him for the breakfast, him swearing at us the whole time we did so. The last we heard as we took our leave was him still calling after us, swearing as fast as his tongue could form the foul words. I trust the Lord will reward him for the breakfast!

But there are wonderful moments of success as well, Lydia, and my heart rejoices in the privilege of spreading the message of the Restoration throughout the earth.

One example will suffice to share with you the joy that is ours. As we came to another town, not far north of Lexington, we were told by several of the inhabitants not to attempt a meeting or any religious instruction, for the town was inhabited by a hardened and irreclaimable set of blasphemers and infidels, given to gambling, drinking, and cursing. Elder Miller was not at all discouraged by such a report. Before entering the town, we found a secluded spot and knelt in prayer. We cried mightily to the Lord that he would open our way and soften the hearts of the people.

We then entered the town and called at a hotel. We told the landlord that we had come in the name of Jesus Christ to preach the gospel, being sent by him without purse or scrip. "Well," said he, "you are welcome to my house and such fare as we have, and we will meet together and hear your religion. If it proves to be better than ours we will embrace it."

When I asked what religion he embraced, he smiled and replied, "Our religion is to fiddle and dance, and eat, drink, and be merry, and gamble and swear a little; and we believe this to be better than priestcraft." A goodly crowd gathered, and we were treated with much hospitality and cordiality. Before we left the area we had baptized eight adults—men and women—and three children.

Well, my dearest Lydia, enough of this report. I long to know how things are with the family in Kirtland. I make mention of you always in my prayers. When I return I shall be much better prepared to speak with my father about the Church. I think I may also have some success with Melissa's husband, Carl. I have learned the value of bearing testimony by the power of the Spirit. Though I seek not to boast, I think I can now sway their hearts with more success than before.

Four months ago I started with nothing but a small valise on my back and twenty-three cents in my pocket. I shall return with the same valise, now well worn, and my pockets with nothing but holes. But I rejoice that I have been called as a missionary, for you know of my longings to preach the gospel. I can now say that if other Elders have gone hungry in traveling without purse or scrip, so have I; if they have traveled with sore feet, so have I; if any have been seized and put outside in the freezing weather for preaching, so have I; if any have been obliged, because of the hard-heartedness of the people, to lie out of doors at night, so have I; if they have been mocked and ridiculed and spit upon, so have I. Like Ammon in the Book of Mormon, I feel to glory in my God for the privilege of being one of his emissaries in the latter days.

Love,

Nathan

14th of February   Kaw Township, Missouri

Dear Steed family,

It still seems strange that I should write to you as my family, who I have never before met nor seen, except for Nathan. But as I said in my first letter to you, I feel close to you, like you were here. Your letter came about two weeks ago. I have read it over and over until I know it by heart. I wish I could write as good as you, Mother Steed. I am still learning and I read better than I write.

Thank you for telling me about each of the family members. It makes my heart happy and sad at the same time to think of

Matthew and Rebecca and Melissa, my family that I may never see. Perhaps someday I can come to Ohio and meet all of you. That would make me very happy.

I have not heard anything from Joshua. My father finally confessed that he sent Joshua to Santa Fe with one of the wagon trains so he would not be arrested. That was foolish because I would not have made trouble for him. In a way, I understand him better than anyone and know what drove him to it. It grieves me that he has not written or anything to ask after me.

But now for the best news of all. On the 24th of January, I gave birth to a healthy and strong little baby girl. She weighed about seven pounds and has dark hair. She is a Steed and not a Roundy. She has Joshua's long fingers, also his nose and mouth. She is a miracle and I have never known such joy in all my life. Grandpa Roundy is as proud as if he had given birth himself. The labor was long but not hard and there were no problems. I am feeling fine again now and back to helping the Lewises. That is the family that I live with.

When Nathan returns home, tell him for me what has happened. Also tell him that I thank God every night and morning for his coming to Missouri. He came to find Joshua and failed. But if he had not come, I would not have little Rachel now. (I shall name her Rachel after my mother who died when I was eight years old.) Now each day as I look at my little miracle, tears come to my eyes, something that has not happened to me very much in my life, only now they are always tears of joy.

In my first letter I had so many questions for you, I said little about how the work of the Church is going here. I should like to say more of that now, though I know that Brother Cowdery and Brother Pratt and others of the brethren have written of these matters.

It has not been an easy winter. As you know, by the time the group from Colesville and the others arrived, it was too late to put in crops for that season. We did spend much time cutting hay for the cattle and storing it for winter. The men worked hard to build cabins, but even with all their industry, they were not able to provide shelter for all. About ten families had to share an open, unfinished log room, without windows, and nothing but the frozen ground for a floor. Our food has consisted mainly of beef and a little bread, made of coarse cornmeal, made by rubbing the ears of corn over a tin grater.

Brother Parley was one of those who shared the open cabin and has been ill much of the winter. Yet his humor never lessens. When I asked him one day how they did it, ten families in one room, cold, no furniture, and him ill, he merely replied that it was an inconvenient way for a sick person to live.

But we have also enjoyed many happy seasons in our prayers and other meetings, and the Spirit of the Lord has been poured out upon us many times. Even some of the children—those eight, ten, or twelve years of age—have spoken and prayed and prophesied in our meetings or in our family worship. Yes, it has been hard, but there has been a spirit of peace and union, and love and goodwill manifested in our little Church in the wilderness. My faith feels like a seed that is growing so fast inside me that I cannot contain it.

Well, I must close. Please write again soon. You and the Saints here have now become my family. If we cannot see each other, at least we can get to know each other better through our letters.

With much affection,
Jessica Steed

3 March 1832   Jackson County, Missouri

Dear Joshua,

I have high hopes that this letter will eventually reach you. I hope you check the post from time to time in Santa Fe, if you are still there. As you know, I do not read nor write very well, so I am asking Judge Lucas to help write this for me. It is urgent that you get this and return to us as soon as possible. Yes, that is right. I am asking that you return at once. There are two reasons for this.

Wilson Everett, the gambler, left town before the turn of the year and has not returned. I trust he has gone to where there are richer pickings. He never learned anything about our device, and I shall say no more of that matter, if you get my meaning. The constable has dropped all charges and there is no more writ out for your arrest. Jessica does not want to make trouble and refuses to ask for vengeance. So you are not facing trouble if you return.

Mr. Cornwell, your foreman, has done a most praiseworthy job with the freight company. We had to sell much of the stock and all but four of the wagons to pay off your debts, but they did not take everything as we feared, and he has kept what you have left busy and profitable. I hear that you have used the wagons and teams that had already gone to Santa Fe to good service and are prospering there as well. That is good, but this is the place for you. New settlers continue to arrive almost daily, and the need for goods brought in from the East is great. Mr. Cornwell must be commended, but to be honest, he has not your sense of business nor your ability to organize. We need you. All is not lost as we first thought.

The second reason you must come back has to do with Jessica. As I said, she is not after revenge and will not press charges further. She lives out in Kaw Township with the accursed Mormons, and I regret to tell you that she has become one of them. Your brother Nathan came out last July seeking you. He arrived a short time after your flight. I understand that it was he who baptized her. I see her from time to time but she is not cordial, especially when I try to tell her that she has made a great mistake.

But here is the news that will be pleasing to you. As you know, Jessie was with child when you left. Always before, she could not carry a baby full term. But according to her, your brother gave her some kind of prayer and the laying on of hands. I don't believe any of that, but she does, and that seems to have been enough to change things. That's right! What I am trying to say to you is that Jessica carried the baby the full time and did not lose it. She gave birth to a baby girl about five weeks ago now. You are a papa! She has named the child Rachel, for my deceased wife.

For those two reasons, please return to us. All is well here.

Clinton Roundy

———◆———

March 16th, Kirtland, Ohio

Dear Mother,

I have little hope that you will acknowledge the receipt of this letter, or respond. I have written you and Papa many times in this last year, but you have never answered. I know I have hurt you deeply, but I still find it hard to understand why you cannot even write a short note to let me know if all is right with you and Papa.

It would be so good to hear from you, even a line or two. These last five months since Nathan has been gone have been very difficult ones for me. I told you in my last epistle that I am with child again. I am now in my sixth month, and this time it has been more difficult for me. I am often sick and find it hard to care for young Joshua. Fortunately, Mother and Father Steed are wonderful with him and do much to lift the burden. I believe I told you in my last post that when Nathan left I moved into town to live with his family. I am glad, for that breaks the loneliness somewhat, though Melissa has married now and I miss her companionship.

It seems like an eternity since Nathan left me. More and more at night now I cannot sleep. I get so lonely and often break into tears. I know the Lord needs him and that I shouldn't resent his absence, but I need him too! Little Joshua needs him! He is growing up without his father.

I need you too, Mama, and Papa. I know you can never condone my joining the Church, but it still hurts terribly to think that you will never even speak to me again. Sometimes, when I think of that day when Nathan and I were married and Papa was so cruel, it hurts inside so badly that I wish I could die.

I'm sorry. I did not start out to make this letter sound so discouraging. It's just that I can't talk to Mother Steed about this. Not now. She believes that Nathan has to answer God's call, even though it makes it difficult for his family.

Please write, Mama. Please!

> All my love,
> Your only daughter, Lydia

30th March, 1832, Hiram, Ohio

My dear Nathan,

When I was up last week visiting in Kirtland, your dear wife, Lydia, shared with me your recent letter from Lexington. How thrilling it was to hear your report of the missionary work! May the Spirit continue to accompany your labors and bring you the fruits of a bounteous harvest. I hope this letter reaches you before your departure to return to us. I look forward to sitting down with you and hearing of your labors firsthand. I will be leaving for Missouri the day after tomorrow, but should return to Kirtland not long after you get back, if not before.

I can report that all is well with your family. Lydia is now in the sixth month of her pregnancy and seems fine. She does get discouraged from time to time, but your return will do much to help that, I'm sure. She and Emma have become quite close. Emma seems to be able to cheer her up. Melissa and her new husband are very happy. Though he seems to have no inclination toward spiritual things, he is a man of integrity and gentleness. Perhaps in time he will change.

And speaking of change, your father continues to amaze us all. No, he hasn't consented to baptism, but he is now one of us in most other ways. He attends worship services regularly, and has been a great help to Bishop Newel K. Whitney in organizing the bishops' storehouse for the poor, as has Lydia. Her experience in her father's store has been most helpful.

Things here in Hiram have been both wonderful and terrible. Let me share some of the better news first, knowing that you have had no communication from us since your departure. Since we moved here to live with Brother John and Sister Elsa Johnson in Hiram, the work on the translation of the Bible has moved forward in good speed. We have also been busy compiling the revelations for publication, which now number over sixty. Last fall I instructed Brother W. W. Phelps to stop in Cincinnati on his way to Zion and purchase a printing press, which he did. In November last we held a conference for the purpose of making final plans for the publication of the revelations. The Lord was gracious and gave a revelation that is to serve as the preface to the book, which we shall call "The Book of Commandments," a phrase taken from the preface aforementioned.

We had a most interesting experience during that conference. As you know, in writing, my grammar is poor and my spelling far short of perfection. Fortunately, I have grown wise enough to use Brother Sidney and others as my scribes. In any case, some complaints were made about the language and style of the revelations. The Lord was displeased, and I received a revelation from him challenging the brethren to pick what they considered to be the "least" of the revelations and see if they could do better. William E. McLellin, a recent convert and a schoolteacher, was the wisest man present (in his own sight), and having more learning than sense, endeavored to write a commandment like unto one of the least of the Lord's. But he failed miserably. He learned that it is an awful responsibility to write in the name of the Lord. Thereafter, the brethren's faith in the revelations was renewed, and a testimony to that effect was written which will be placed in the front of the new book. Brothers Oliver Cowdery and John Whitmer have now carried the revelations to Missouri for printing.

In February, we received one of the most glorious revelations thus far. Brother Sidney and I were continuing our work on the translation of the New Testament. From sundry revelations already received, it was obvious that many points touching the salvation of man had been taken from the Bible, or lost before it was compiled. It appeared self-evident from what truths were left, that if God rewarded every one according to the deeds done in the body, the term "Heaven," as intended for the Saints' eternal home, must include more kingdoms than one. I know this is at strict variance with the doctrines of Christianity as now taught, but the Spirit seemed to testify that such was the case.

When we came to the twenty-ninth verse of the fifth chapter of John, which speaks of the resurrection of life and the resurrection of damnation, a vision burst upon our view. I can tell you without hesitation, Nathan, that nothing could be more pleasing to the Saints upon the order of the kingdom of the Lord than the light which burst upon the world with the opening of that revelation to our view. Every law, every commandment, and every promise touching the destiny of man, from Genesis to Revelation, witness that this revelation was in very deed a transcript from the records of the eternal world. Any honest man who reads must be led to exclaim, "This came from God!"

I have not the space to give you all the details—I shall let you peruse it at your leisure when you return. But suffice it to say that in that vision—or better yet, that series of visions, for different scenes were presented to our view—God's great plan for the salvation of his children was unfolded and we saw that there are differing kingdoms of glory to which men are sent after their sojourn in this life. As the Savior said, men are rewarded according to their manner of living and there are indeed many mansions in the kingdom of his Father.

I had to smile a little. There were close to a dozen men present in the translation room, here on the upper floor of the Johnson home, but only Sidney and I were privileged to see the vision. When the vision finally closed, poor Sidney was as pale and limp as a rag. The experience had totally drained him. I fear that he is not as used to this process of revelation as I.

Now for darker news. Satan continues to rage against our work. Just as the Savior foretold in the parables of the gathering, the gospel net brings in many kinds of fish. Some are stalwarts, like Oliver and Parley and Sidney and yourself. Others are as weak as a castle made of sand. Simonds Ryder, converted through the prophecy of a young girl about a great earthquake in China, apostatized when I misspelled his name as "Rider" instead of "Ryder" in a call for him to serve a mission. If the Spirit could not even spell his name correctly, he reasoned, then perhaps he had been mistaken about its promptings when he was converted. We lost another brother when I came down one day from the translation room where Sidney and I had been working, and immediately began to play with some children. It wasn't how a prophet should act, he said. Others leave because of economic difficulties, or because I do this or that which does not please them. Some of the Johnsons' own sons have turned bitter against me because I warned them that they must start living the gospel more diligently.

If it was simply a matter of them leaving the Church and kingdom, it would be a sad case; but they cannot simply walk away. The same spirit which leads them into apostasy drives them to fight against us.

Just about a week ago now, the opposition of these apostates came to a bitter and most tragic head. On the night of the 24th of this month, I suggested that Emma retire to her rest. Our twins, little Joseph and Julia, had been quite ill for a time with the measles and we had finally separated them, since the moment one would finally get to sleep the other would cry and wake the other. In the evening I told her I would watch with the sicker child so she could sleep. Later, when both babies finally took some sleep, she told me I had better lie down on the trundle bed also. I did so, and due to my state of exhaustion, quickly fell asleep.

The bedroom in which I slept was near to the front door. I awoke to the sound of Emma screaming murder from her room as about a dozen men came pouring into the house. I found myself going out of the door, in the hands of the men, some of whose hands were in my hair, and some who had hold of my shirt, drawers, and limbs. The men smelled of whiskey and were in an infuriated state.

I made a desperate struggle to extricate myself, but only cleared one leg. I kicked out with all my strength and connected with one of the men. He went sprawling and fell on the doorsteps. I was immediately overpowered again; and they shouted and swore at me. "By ——, " they screamed, "we'll kill you sure if you don't hold still." Frightened, that quieted me.

As they passed around the house with me, the fellow that I kicked came to me and thrust his hand, all covered with blood, into my face and with an exulting hoarse laugh, muttered: "—— —— ye, I'll fix ye." He then seized me by the throat and held on till I lost my breath and lapsed into momentary unconsciousness.

When I came to, we were about thirty rods from the house. I turned my head and saw a horrible sight. Elder Rigdon was stretched out on the ground, whither they had dragged him by his heels. I supposed he had been killed, and immediately began to plead with them, saying, "You will have mercy and spare my life, I hope." To which they replied, "—— —— ye, call on yer God for help, we'll show ye no mercy."

Now there were men coming from the orchard in every direction. About thirty rods further on, they stopped, and one said, "Simonds, Simonds," (meaning, I supposed, Simonds Ryder,) "pull up his drawers, pull up his drawers, he will take cold." Another replied: "Ain't ye going to kill 'im? ain't ye going to kill 'im?" A group of mobbers collected a little way off, and said: "Simonds, Simonds, come here"; and "Simonds" charged those who had hold of me to keep me from touching the ground (as they had done all the time), lest I should get a spring upon them. They held a council, and as I could occasionally overhear a word, I supposed it was to know whether or not it was best to kill me.

They returned after a while, when I learned that they had concluded not to kill me, but to beat and scratch me well, tear off my shirt and drawers, and leave me naked. They ran back and fetched the bucket of tar, when one exclaimed, with an oath, "Let us tar up his mouth," and they tried to force the tar paddle into my mouth. I twisted my head around so that they could not, which only infuriated them the more. Another one cried out, "—— —— ye, hold up yer head and let us give ye some tar." They then tried to force a vial into my mouth, and broke a part of one of my teeth. (You'll note upon your return that I now have a slight whistle when I pronounce certain words.)

All my clothes were torn off me except my shirt collar. At that point one man fell on me and scratched my body with his nails like a mad cat, and then muttered out: "—— —— ye, that's the way the Holy Ghost falls on folks!"

Finally the fiends left. I attempted to rise, but fell again. I was having difficulty breathing and realized that tar was covering my mouth. I pulled the tar away from my lips so that I could breathe more freely. I made my way back to Father Johnson's home. When I came to the door I was naked, and the tar made me look as if I were covered with blood. Emma, who was in a state of terror anyway, took one look at me and fainted dead away. In the poor light she thought it looked like I was all crushed to pieces.

My friends spent the night in scraping and removing the tar, and washing and cleansing my body; so that by morning I was ready to be clothed again. This being the Sabbath morning, the people assembled for meeting at the usual hour of worship, and among them came also the mobbers; viz.: Simonds Ryder, leader of the mob; one McClentic, who had his hands in my hair; one Streeter, son of a Campbellite minister; and Felatiah Allen, Esq., who gave the mob a barrel of whiskey to raise their spirits. Besides these named, there were many others in the mob. With my flesh all scarified and defaced, I preached to the congregation as usual, and in the afternoon of the same day baptized three individuals.

Oh, Nathan, how it burdens me to share this next piece of bitter news with you. When I was dragged into the night, with Emma screaming after me, the door to the house was left open, allowing the cold night air to pour into the room where little Joseph was resting. Because of that, our son contracted a severe cold in addition to the measles he already had. Nothing we did seemed to help, and he finally passed from this life yesterday, leaving Emma shattered and completely distraught. This is the fourth child we have lost.

I'm sorry, I cannot say more, for my heart is filled with sorrow. But I also rejoice in the work, good friend, and in your success. There is no need to write by return post, for as I said earlier, I will be gone to Missouri now for a time. I look forward to that time when we see each other face-to-face again, and you can tell me all that I long to hear.

Your dear brother,
Joseph

Opposition to the Work

Chapter Nineteen

J osiah, I would like to talk with you."

The owner and proprietor of McBride's dry goods store barely looked up. "Hannah, I have to get this stock put away and then take inventory of the tools. It can wait until tonight."

"No, it can't."

He straightened slowly, his small mouth tightening into a line. "Hannah, I said it can wait until tonight."

Hannah Lovina Hurlburt McBride would never be accused of wearing the pants in her family. Josiah McBride was a small man, but only in physical stature. He was a martinet in many ways, running his household with firm discipline and not much humor. Normally his wife, who tended toward austerity and primness herself, accepted his patriarchal role without complaint. But today was different. She stepped forward, hands on her hips, her eyes lowering like storm clouds scudding in from Lake Ontario.

"Josiah McBride, I said it can't wait. I want to talk to you now."

He blinked, taken aback. When he didn't protest further, Hannah McBride looked over her shoulder to where their clerk was working behind the counter. "Let's go upstairs."

"Hannah," he started, "I have . . ."

The look on her face was such that his voice trailed off. This was not the Hannah he was used to dealing with.

Wearily he wiped his hands on his leather apron and shook his head. "All right. But let's hurry."

He chose to go not to their living quarters, but upstairs to one of the stockrooms. He turned around. "Now, what is it that's so all-fired important."

She reached in her pocket and pulled out a letter. At the sight of it, his brows instantly furrowed and his eyes darkened. "I've told you before, until your daughter shows some remorse for the heartache and the hurt she has caused us I will neither read nor answer her letters. I wish you had the moral courage to take the same stand."

Ignoring that, she opened the envelope and took out the letter. "Read it!"

He snatched the letter, crumpled it up in one furious clench of his hand, and hurled it away. "Did you hear what I just said?" he shouted. "I will not read it!"

Surprisingly, his fury did not cow her. She walked over to the ball of paper, picked it up, and smoothed it out against her dress. When she came back she walked right up to her husband and stood toe-to-toe with him. "Josiah McBride, there's not much I'm ever asking from you, but this time I'm not asking you. I'm telling you. Read this letter!"

If she had burst into tears or stomped off in a huff or responded in any kind of similar way, she would have lost. But as it was, her brashness totally stunned him. For a long moment he stared at her, his mouth working, then finally he grabbed the letter from her again—only this time he turned slightly toward the light and began to read.

It was short, less than a page, and he finished it quickly. He thrust it back at his wife, who took it calmly. "So? What do you want? Do you want me to feel sorry for her? Well, she should have thought about that a long time ago. I told her that Steed boy was a no-good. He ran off right after their marriage and left her for a whole summer to work in Colesville. Then he was off to Missouri to look up that no-account brother of his. Now he's left her again to go out and preach the devil's gospel, leaving her and the child alone. It's no more than she deserves."

Hannah let him have his say without trying to stop him. When he finally finished, she simply folded the letter and put it back in the envelope. "I'm going to write her."

For a moment he just gaped at her, but only for a moment; then he exploded. "I forbid it!" he shouted. He spun around and strode across the room, then whirled back, his chest rising and falling. "There will be no contact, Mrs. McBride! No word! No concessions! None! Do you hear me?"

Again she completely shocked him by the unexpectedness of her reaction. She shook her head slowly, calmly. "Josiah, listen to me." She waved the envelope at him. "This is a cry for help. Your daughter is discouraged. She's depressed. She's lonely. For the first time since their marriage she is frustrated with her husband." She took a breath, amazed at her own daring. "If you ever want to win her back, get her away from all Joe Smith stands for, there will never be another time. Not for us."

Her husband had one fist raised, ready to shake in her face. Slowly he lowered it to his side.

"If we don't answer her now, we've lost her forever. Is that what you want?"

He didn't answer for several seconds, then stepped forward slowly. "Let me see that."

She handed him the envelope and he opened it again. This time he read slowly, read it clear through once, then again. Finally, his head came up. "She don't sound to me like she's ready for any change."

Hannah breathed a sigh of relief. He was thinking about it,

and that was a major step in the right direction. "She's not ready for a change. But she is ready to be loved."

"You tell her if she's ready to renounce that disgusting religion of hers, we'll write to her every day. Otherwise no."

His wife just shook her head, her eyes thoughtful now. "No, I won't tell her anything like that. For now I'm just going to write and tell her we love her, that we miss her, and that if there's anything we can do to make her feel not so lonely, I want her to let me know."

Her head came up and her eyes caught her husband's and held them, challenging, unflinching. "That's what I'm going to do, Josiah. I just wanted you to know."

Nathan Steed stopped in front of his father's home late in the afternoon of April twentieth, 1832. He was footsore, dusty, weary beyond belief, and hungry for anything more than the hard wheat bread and stream water they had lived on for the past five days since leaving Kentucky. He had no money in his pockets, had cast away all his clothes but those he wore (they had not been worthy of saving), and had given his knapsack to a young lad they met in Columbus who was on his way west.

As he reached the small picket fence that lined his father's yard, he stopped, blinking hard to fight the sudden burning in his eyes. He had left this spot during the first week of October of the previous year. He had raised a hand in farewell, then turned and walked away from his wife and his son. It had been almost six and a half months. *Six and a half months!*

He saw the curtain on one of the windows part slightly, then jerk back. A face was suddenly pressed up against the glass, nose squashing flat like a piglet's, the blond hair a flash of white through the window. Then he heard the faint cry. "Nathan! Nathan!"

He grinned, and opened the gate. The front door burst open as if it had been blown inward by a cyclone. Matthew came exploding out, his legs pumping. "Nathan! Nathan! Nathan!"

Becca was hard on his heels, pigtails flying, apron coming off one shoulder.

They nearly took his wind away, hugging him fiercely, jumping up and down, Matthew pounding his back. Then suddenly Nathan stopped. There were three figures in the doorway. His mother had her hand to her mouth, tears streaming down her face. His father, one arm around her shoulder, was nodding at his son, smiling broadly. But it was the third person who arrested Nathan's eyes. Lydia, heavy with child, held a young boy in her arms.

Nathan's heart lurched. When he had left, his son had been a baby. Now at eleven months, he was a little boy, with dark hair just starting to grow, light blue eyes, and his mother's fine chin and perfect nose.

Matthew and Becca stepped back. Lydia was crying now too. She stepped forward, coming off the porch, and stopped again. Slowly, with an effort, she lowered the child. He stood, a little wobbly, holding on to her one finger, gravely looking across the distance at the stranger who stood before him.

"That's your father, Joshua," Lydia whispered. "It's your father."

Nathan went down on one knee and stretched out his arms, a lump in his own throat all of a sudden making it very difficult to breathe. "Come, Joshua," he called softly, not wanting to frighten him.

Little Joshua turned, looking up, first at his mother, then at his grandmother.

"It's all right, Josh," Mary Ann smiled. "Go see your papa."

Matthew dropped beside Nathan and held out his arms. "Come on, Joshua," he called. "Come see Uncle Matthew."

The blue eyes appraised Nathan once more, then shifted to Matthew. A smile broke through the somberness and his eyes came alive. Then his short, stubby little legs began to move, and step by very tentative step, he toddled his way toward them.

With a sob, Nathan reached out and scooped him up, holding him to his chest, and burying his face against the small but wiry little body.

On April twenty-ninth, Melissa Mary Steed Rogers was delivered of a healthy, nine-pound baby boy. Though his hair was dark, almost everyone agreed that when the sunlight hit it, there was a definite touch of auburn in it. Predictions were common that he would be a redhead, most likely with freckles, like his father. They named him Carlton Hezekiah Rogers, being the first son for Carl and Melissa and the first grandson for the Rogerses.

Six weeks later, Carl Rogers traveled out with Melissa to the schoolhouse near the Isaac Morley homestead for a worship service. There Nathan, uncle to the new baby, named and blessed young Carl by the power of the holy priesthood.

The night before, Nathan went to Melissa's home and spent some time talking with Carl about the ordinance. Carl stated that he had no objection to Melissa's having the child blessed however she wished, but he resisted, amiably but firmly, when Nathan tried to talk with him about the Book of Mormon.

After the services were over and the blessing done, Melissa pulled Nathan aside and quietly suggested he not try and talk religion any further with her husband.

It was the fourteenth of June, and the mosquitoes swarmed in the lingering heat of the evening air. The horse kept its tail moving constantly, but Joshua Steed paid the insects no mind, brushing at them absently as he pulled to a halt in front of the small sod hut. "Excuse me, neighbor."

The man was at a grindstone, his leg pumping on the lever to keep the stone wheel flying. Sparks showered from the ax blade that he was sharpening. He lifted the ax, but his foot kept moving up and down out of habit. "Good evening."

"Could you tell me where I might find the home of Joshua Lewis?"

The man took his foot off the grindstone lever and let the

wheel come to a stop. He stood, taking off his hat to brush at the sweat on his brow. "I'm Joshua Lewis. What can I do for you?"

Joshua swung off the horse and tied the reins to a small bush. He didn't move any closer. "I'm looking for Jessica Steed. I understand she lives with you."

The man, definitely a sodbusting farmer, nodded slowly, his eyes suddenly suspicious as they carefully took in Joshua's trail garb, his heavy beard, and the tired, weary eyes. "And who might you be?"

Joshua's eyes didn't move from the man's face. "I'd like to speak with her. Ask her to come out please."

The man was half a head shorter than Joshua and probably weighed forty or fifty pounds less, but if he was intimidated by Joshua's size, or by the pistol that was stuck in his belt, his expression didn't show it. Again he sized Joshua up and down, then stuck one hand in his pocket. "I'll be happy to fetch her if I know who it is I'm tellin' her to come out and see."

There was a flash of irritation, but Joshua pushed it down. He had arrived in Independence around noon, taken time only to bathe and eat, then started out to find her. All the way out he kept seething over the fact that Jessica had become a Mormon. Somehow Joseph Smith was seeping into his life again, messing things up. He didn't like it. Not one bit. But he kept promising himself he would keep his temper in check, so now he forced a brief smile. "My name is Joshua Steed. I'm Jessie's husband. I'm just in from Santa Fe today."

Lewis's eyes narrowed. Whatever friendliness had been there was instantly gone. "I'm not sure she'll want to see you, Mr. Steed."

In an instant Joshua's irritation flared into full anger. "She's of age," Joshua said coldly. "You just go tell her."

The hostility was unmistakable now, but the farmer finally turned and went into the house.

Twice Joshua saw the door open a crack and small, curious eyes peer out at him, but it was almost five minutes before Jessica finally stepped out. He saw instantly that she had on her best dress and had hastily brushed through her hair. He also saw that she carried a little bundle in her arms.

Behind her, Lewis stood at the door. He glared at Joshua for a moment, a child peeking out from behind his legs, then touched Jessie's arm. "You need me, Jessica, you just holler."

"Thank you, Brother Lewis. I'll be fine."

He nodded, then slowly shut the door behind her. For a moment she stood there, her eyes wide and unreadable. Then, she came forward a few steps. "Hello, Joshua."

"Hello, Jessica."

"Pa said he wrote you and told you to come back."

"Yes."

"He was afraid you'd gone on somewhere else, hadn't got the letter."

"I was up in Pueblo with a load of mercantile goods. I didn't get the letter until about two weeks ago." For a moment he was angry with himself for feeling that he had to explain. Then he let his eyes drop to her arms, and he softened a little. "Your pa told me about the baby. I couldn't believe it."

"Yes, it's wonderful, isn't it?"

He made a rueful face. "No Doctor Hathaway, I assume."

She laughed softly. "No, no Doctor Hathaway."

Jessie stepped up to him, pulling the blanket away from the baby's face. She was sleeping, the tiny features peaceful in repose. He bent over, peering at his daughter in wonder. "Clinton told me you're going to call her Rachel," he murmured. He reached out and tentatively touched the slender fingers.

"Yes, for my mother."

"She's beautiful."

Jessica smiled down at her daughter. "I think so too. Would you like to hold her?"

He fell back a step.

"Go ahead, it's all right. She sleeps well when she's full."

Gingerly he took her, cradling her in his arm. He pulled the blanket away from her body so he could see her full length.

Jessica watched him, her eyes soft. "She's growin' real good. Sister Lewis says she eats like the strongest pup in the litter. And she's got a real good disposition. She hardly ever fusses."

A mosquito buzzed in and circled for a moment over the baby's head. Joshua flicked his hand at it, then wrapped the blanket around her again. "She's real sweet, Jessie. I'm real happy for you. You always wanted a baby so bad."

"So did you," she whispered.

He stood there uncomfortably for a moment, then handed Rachel back to her mother. "Yes," he finally said. "Yes, I did." He took a deep breath, then let it out slowly. His hands plucked at the bone buttons on his deerskin jacket. "Jessie, I . . ."

She waited, watching him steadily.

"I'm sorry about what happened that night. I was so out of my head drunk. When I lost everything, I went crazy. I . . ." He shook his head and looked away.

"What's done is done. I'm not bearing a grudge, Joshua."

"I should never have hit you."

She thought about that, then shook her head. "No, you shouldn't have. But I healed."

He looked down again. "And now you have a baby."

She smiled. "Not a baby, Joshua. Our baby."

"I know."

"Did Pa tell you why I have the baby? why I was able to go the full time?"

He frowned. "He said Nathan came."

"Yes, he gave me a blessing by the priesthood—"

"I don't want to hear it."

Her head came up slowly. "Nathan also baptized me a member of the Church—"

He spoke sharply. "I said I don't want to hear it. I know all about Joseph Smith and his wild tales. It angers me, Jess, that my own brother would come out here and fill your head with all that nonsense—"

"Joseph Smith was here, Joshua."

He stopped. "He was?"

"Yes, not long after you left. I met him. I watched him. I listened to him, Joshua. By the time Nathan came, my mind was already made up, so there ain't no use you blamin' your brother for this."

"That don't surprise me none. Joseph's always had a way of swaying people with his lies and foolishness."

"I've been baptized, Joshua. It's done, and I won't have you talking about Brother Joseph that way."

"Brother Joseph?" he hooted. "Brother Joseph? Is that what we've come to now?"

Jessica half turned back toward the house. "Sister Lewis," she called.

In a moment the door opened. A farm woman in a plain dress and no shoes stood there.

"Can you take Rachel and put her back to bed?"

"Of course."

She came to Jessica, keeping her eyes averted away from Joshua, lovingly took the baby, then returned into the house. When she was gone, Jessica turned back to Joshua, her face calm and serene. Joshua fought down the anger, cursing himself for letting it get away from him. For several moments, neither spoke, then he cleared his throat. "So, what now?"

Jessica gave a soft laugh, not without a bitter edge to it. "You tell me, Joshua? What now?"

"Well, I'm back. We still have the house. It needs some cleaning up but—"

She was shaking her head.

"What?"

"I'm not unhappy here, Joshua."

He looked incredulous. "A one-room sod hut on the prairie, ten, twelve miles from anything?"

"These people took me in. They've been good to me."

"What about us?"

Her chin came up, and now there was anger in her eyes. "Yes, Joshua, what about us? It's been almost a year. This is the first time I've heard that question in all that time."

He looked away, knowing it would come to this. "I had to run, Jess. I had no choice."

"And what about a letter, Joshua? Did you even once think about me? Where I was? If I had a place to stay? If I had any money?"

His shoulders lifted, then fell. "I didn't dare write," he said lamely. "I didn't know if they'd send someone out after me."

"I see," she said, making no effort to hide her feelings. "Well, I'm sorry if I'm finding it a little hard to throw myself into your arms."

"Look, Jessie," he said, his voice rising, "I told you I'm sorry for all that. I know what I did was wrong, but I want to make it right now."

"Do you?" she cried softly. "Do you really, Joshua?"

"Yes."

"Have you stopped drinking?"

He rocked back slightly. "I—"

"Are you still gambling?"

His brows furrowed into a deep crease and his jaw tightened. "Now, look, I said—"

"And what about Joseph Smith and the Mormons? I'm one of them now, Joshua. Are you willing to accept that if I come back."

"I won't have no talk of Joseph Smith in my house," he said darkly. "And I certainly won't have my daughter raised to be one of them."

Jessie turned away, folding her arms and hugging herself. "My house. My wife. My daughter. That's how it's always been, hasn't it, Joshua?"

He let out his breath. It was always like this, the twisting of his words, the sharp, jabbing attacks. He stepped forward and touched her shoulder gently. "Look, Jessie, I ain't said nothing about you causing me to lose everything I owned. I'm willing to forget what's past."

She spun around, and he saw tears in her eyes. But they were not tears of hurt, they were tears of frustration. "So am I, Joshua.

You don't believe that. But what about the future? If things go bad again, what promise do I have you won't get ugly drunk and mean again? How do I know that a year from now you won't throw another year's worth of work into the center of a poker table on the hopes you're better than the man across from you?"

"Jessica—"

She rode right over him. "And what if I'm not willing to give up the first decent thing that's come into my life? I didn't become a Mormon just because the Lewises were nice to me, Joshua. I believe it. I've accepted it. I can't just turn my back on it. I won't!"

Inside him, all the images of Palmyra flashed across his mind: the rainy night when he, the Murdocks, and Mark Cooper had been made to look like fools; Lydia's going to get his father and Nathan to stop him from getting the gold plates; his father slapping his face. Joseph Smith was at the heart of all that, and on this issue there was no bending in him.

Each word came out hard and flat and final. "I will not have my daughter raised to be a Mormon."

She gave a curt nod. "Then, I guess it's settled. Good-bye, Joshua." She turned and started for the house.

He leaped forward and grabbed her shoulders. He jerked her around roughly. "Don't you walk away from me! I'm talking to you."

"No, you're not. You're shouting at me." She yanked free of his grasp and turned again.

"Jessie!" This time when he grabbed her arm his fingers dug into her flesh and she gasped with the pain. "You listen to me—"

The front door to the sod hut flew open and Joshua Lewis stood there with a double-barreled shotgun pointing at Joshua's head. "Let her go!"

For a moment Joshua just gaped at those two huge holes staring down at him.

"I said, *let her go!*" Lewis barked sharply. "I mean it."

Joshua released his grip and stepped back, his eyes narrowing. Jessica stumbled quickly over to stand beside the farmer.

"Mister, I'd suggest you get on your horse and ride on out of here."

"This woman is my wife," he cried hoarsely. "That's my child in there. I've got my rights."

"I saw your wife the morning after your so-called poker game," Lewis said in utter contempt. "I saw her black eyes and her battered face." The shotgun lowered to point squarely at Joshua's chest. "You got no more rights, mister. Now I suggest you git."

On June twentieth, 1832, after being home only two months, Nathan Steed received a call to preach the gospel in eastern Ohio and western Pennsylvania. He left almost immediately in company with three other brethren. Two weeks after his departure, on the fifth of July, Lydia McBride Steed gave birth to a baby girl. It was a prolonged and difficult labor. Lydia was bedfast for two weeks. Before Nathan left, he and Lydia had discussed possible names. If it was a girl, Nathan favored Sarah, Lydia wanted Emily. In the press of Nathan's leaving, the question was never finally resolved. Lydia named the baby Emily.

Benjamin found the Smith brothers—Joseph, Hyrum, William, and Samuel—in a woodlot, cutting and chopping wood for their winter firewood needs. The air was cold and crisp, frost still visible where the pale November sunlight did not reach the ground.

"Ho, Brother Benjamin," Joseph called as he saw Ben coming through the trees. He set down his ax and stuck out his hand. "How are you, good friend?"

"Fine, Joseph. I just learned this morning that you and Bishop Whitney had returned from your trip to Albany, New York, and Boston."

"Yes, we returned two days ago."

"And did you get the funding for the new store?"

"We did. We negotiated a loan for the goods. We shall open the mercantile establishment immediately."

"So you returned in time for the birth of your new son?"

Joseph's face fell a little. "No, I returned shortly thereafter."

Hyrum walked over to join them. "Hello, Brother Steed."

"Good afternoon, Hyrum. How are things with you and yours?"

"Fine, thank you."

Benjamin turned back to Joseph. "Mary Ann made some stew for you and Emma."

"How thoughtful of her!" Joseph exclaimed.

"Emma was asleep, so I just left the food." He sobered. "How is she doing?"

"It was a difficult labor, and she is still very weak, but she will be fine. To have the baby"— his eyes were suddenly moist— "to have one finally live, that is the most wonderful medicine she could receive."

"Yes, we are all very happy for the both of you. What shall you name him?"

Joseph beamed proudly. "Emma thinks we should name him Joseph Smith the Third."

Benjamin nodded his approval. "I think that would please both you and your father."

"It does, thank you. And thank your wife for the food. She's an angel, you know."

"Yes, I know."

Joseph clapped him on the shoulder. "And what can we do for you?"

Benjamin smiled as he shucked off his outer coat. "The question is, what can I do for you? I have nothing at home waiting. Do you have an extra ax?"

Little Joshua shrieked with delight as his Uncle Matthew rolled him on his back and buried his head in his tummy.

"Matthew!" Lydia cried.

He looked up, a little surprised at the sharpness in Lydia's voice. Joshua stopped laughing too and looked at his mother, his eyes suddenly grave.

Lydia took a breath, and forced a faint smile. "Melissa and I are trying to talk, Matthew. Can you take Joshua in the bedroom and play?"

"Sure." He scooped Joshua up, ruffling the dark, curly hair. "Come on, Josh, I'll be a tiger, and you can be the goat."

Off they went, already starting to giggle as they started into the adjoining room.

"Matthew!" Melissa said sharply, pointing towards the loft above them, "you'll wake the babies."

He turned, waved an acknowledgment, and clapped a hand over his mouth in mock horror, which only sent his nephew into peals of laughter all over again.

Lydia shook her head, wanting to be angry but smiling in spite of herself. Matthew would be thirteen this coming July and was fast becoming a man. The little boyishness in him was gone, and he would likely pass both Lydia and his mother in height by his birthday. Young Joshua was twenty months old, and loved his Uncle Matthew with unswerving devotion. In large part that was due to the fact that when Matthew and Joshua got together, Matthew reverted to all boy again. No wonder young Joshua so loved him.

Melissa sighed as she watched them disappear into the back bedroom that Benjamin and some of the brethren had helped Nathan add on to the young couple's little cabin a few weeks earlier. "If it weren't so cold out, we could send them outside to play."

She turned back to her sister-in-law and watched her for a moment, trying not to let the dismay show in her eyes. Lydia's appearance had really shocked her. She looked worn and haggard. There were dark circles under her eyes, and she seemed listless and without spirit. It was so unlike Lydia that Melissa felt a stirring of alarm.

And guilt. She and her mother had talked about the change

in Lydia more than three weeks ago, and Melissa had been vowing to come out to the Morley farm and visit with her ever since. But it seemed that nowadays little Carl took so much of her time, and getting him all bundled up against the cold and everything . . .

"So, where is Nathan?"

"Oh, didn't Mother Steed tell you? He's been invited to participate in the School of the Prophets that started a week ago."

"That's right. I forgot. She did tell me."

"He leaves about four in the morning. Usually they don't finish much before supper time."

"So you're alone all day?"

Lydia shrugged. "I'm used to it now." She looked wistful. "And he's having some wonderful experiences. Did you hear about the meeting they had a couple of days before the school started?"

"No." Melissa looked down at her hands. "With Carl not being a member, I don't hear everything like I used to."

Lydia was suddenly animated, and her words came in a rush. "It was in that room above the store, the same where they hold the School. It wasn't just priesthood holders. There were sisters there too. Emma was there. Sister Rigdon, Sister Whitney. Nathan said it was wonderful. After they opened with prayer, Joseph got up to speak—only suddenly he began to speak in tongues."

That brought Melissa's head up with a jerk. "Tongues?"

"Yes, just like in the Bible on the day of Pentecost. Nathan said it was an incredible experience. After Brother Joseph finished, Zebedee Coltrin stood. Then William, Joseph's brother. One after another—the sisters too. Emma prophesied. So did Sister Whitney. They spoke and prayed and sang hymns, all in tongues."

Melissa was stunned. She had not heard any of this, which showed just how much she was losing touch with things.

"Nathan said that at first he didn't understand anything. Some of the others did, though, and interpreted, but near the last, he began to understand too. He said it was really strange—hearing something totally incomprehensible with your ears, but suddenly feeling your heart listening, understanding!"

Gradually the enthusiasm in Lydia's eyes died, and she went quite still. "It must have been wonderful. Nathan had asked me to come with him. But with the children . . ." Her voice trailed off, and she turned to stare out of the window.

Melissa leaned forward. "Are you all right, Lydia?"

Lydia snapped around, for a moment looking frightened, like a nocturnal animal suddenly caught in the lamplight. But then she nodded, her eyelashes dropping to cover her eyes. "I . . . I'm fine."

"Lydia," Melissa said gently, "since you married Nathan you and I have grown as close as any sisters. So put away your public face. This is Melissa asking you, remember. Are you all right?"

There was a sudden sheen of tears and Lydia looked away, embarrassed that her emotions were so transparent. The breath came out of her slowly, as if it were painful to let it go.

"Please, Lydia. Please tell me."

Now the tears began to flow freely. "I don't know, Melissa. That's just it. I don't know."

Melissa stood quickly and moved over to sit beside her. She reached out and took a hand in both of hers. She had never seen Lydia like this, so bleak, so desolate.

After a minute, Lydia forced a tiny smile. "I got another letter from my mother," she volunteered.

"Really?"

"Yes. She wants me to come see them this summer."

That really rocked Melissa. "Back to Palmyra?"

Lydia nodded.

Melissa again had to fight not to look too shocked.

"I can't, of course. Nathan would never agree to it. He and my father are like ax blade and grindstone. There's always sparks when they get together." She paused, her eyes suddenly forlorn and empty. "Maybe a year from this summer. Josh would be three then, and Emily nearly two."

Melissa felt as if someone were clanging a bell somewhere in her mind. "Are you and Nathan having problems?"

Lydia's eyes widened and she shook her head vigorously, but not until there had been a moment's hesitation.

"Lydia," Melissa chided gently. "Is that it?"

"No."

"Then, what?"

Lydia swallowed back the tears. When she finally began to speak, it came out slow and measured, almost halting, as she sought for the right words. "I . . . I don't know. I feel like . . . I don't know how to describe it. It's like . . ." Her shoulders lifted and fell. "Like I've stopped growing. Like I'm rooted to one spot, while everyone just . . . I don't know. Like they're passing me by. Like life is passing me by."

"Does Nathan know any of this?"

Lydia shook her head quickly. "That's part of the problem. He's so . . . so alive. He's so excited right now. He came back from his missions so filled with enthusiasm, so full of . . ." She groped for the right word. "I don't know, so on fire."

"A little too much on fire," Melissa said tartly. "I finally had to tell him to leave Carl alone."

Lydia laughed in spite of herself. "I know. Your mother also told him to stop pushing your father so hard. He keeps wanting him to be baptized. The other day Father Steed nearly dunked *him* in the river to cool off a little of his ardor."

Melissa chuckled at the image. "Might do him good."

Lydia sobered slowly. "I envy him, you know."

"You do? Why?"

"He's feeling all these things. Having all these experiences. Teaching the gospel. Feeling the Spirit. Interpreting tongues. That little miracle where he blessed Joshua's wife and she was able to carry the baby." She stopped and looked at the floor. "I would love to have something like that happen to me. I would love to feel something again."

The pain in Melissa was suddenly so sharp and intense that she had to stand. She turned away from Lydia and stepped to the window, feeling her chest constricting, fighting back the burning in her own eyes.

Lydia misinterpreted her reaction. "Do I shock you, Melissa, talking that way?" There was soft bitterness in her tone. "Lydia the faithful, Lydia who left her family for the gospel's sake now becomes Lydia the lifeless, Lydia the doubter."

Melissa swung around. "Shocked?" She gave a soft hoot of self-derision. "Let me see if I can describe what you're feeling." Her eyes took on a deep sadness. "Is it like you know exactly what you ought to be feeling, need to be feeling, but you can't seem to recapture it anymore?"

Lydia's eyebrows went up in surprise.

"Is it knowing that you ought to care more about the things of the Church, of God, than you do? But simply knowing doesn't seem to make any difference?"

"You too?" Lydia said, standing slowly.

Melissa turned away, talking to no one now. "Is it knowing that you need to go to Sabbath services every week, but not having the energy to pull yourself together and go alone? Or when you try to say your prayers, you start, but you know your husband is lying there waiting for you, wondering what's going on in your head, not understanding this part of you, and you finally give up because you're not feeling much of anything anyway. You leave the Book of Mormon on the shelf now, not because your husband would ever say anything if you spent time reading it. But you know it's something you don't share together, and he's so good, and so gentle, and so kind, that you're not sure you want to have things you don't share."

Lydia walked to Melissa and put an arm around her waist. For several moments they stood there, not speaking, each lost in her own pain.

Finally, Lydia spoke. "I know Nathan is doing what God wants him to. I know he needs to be a missionary, and go to the School, and all the other things. But I miss him so terribly when he's gone. And then the resentment starts growing in me, like some ugly weed I can't ever get to and pull out." Her lower lip started to tremble, and tears welled up in the corners of her eyes and started a slow trickle down her cheeks. "He wasn't here when Emily was born, Melissa. He didn't even get to see Joshua take his first step."

"Then, say something to him!" Melissa burst out. "I know the Lord needs him, Lydia. But so do you."

Lydia shook her head, the sorrow in her eyes nearly breaking Melissa's heart. "That's the very worst thing."

"What?"

"Knowing in your head—absolutely knowing—that you're wrong, that you're being selfish and faithless." She stopped and dropped her face into her hands. "It's knowing that in your head, but not being able to make your heart accept it."

———————

"Jessica, it's your father."

"My father?"

Sister Lewis nodded quickly. "I asked him in, but he said he needs to talk to you outside."

Jessica had been nursing Rachel, but the child had had her fill now and lay asleep, the long lashes lying on her cheeks, her mouth drawn into a tiny little pout as she slept. Jessica leaned down and kissed her forehead softly. "Can you put her to bed for me?"

"Of course." The plain farm woman was not much more than five years older than Jessica, but in the last eighteen months she had become sister, mother, and friend to Jessica. She lifted Rachel from Jessica's arms and cradled her, smiling down at her. It was the last of January. A week ago Rachel had had her first birthday.

Jessica stood, reaching for the shawl that hung over the chair. Sister Lewis shook her head quickly. "You'll need a coat, Jessie. It's very cold out there." But Jessica shook her head and went out.

When she came out, her father was standing next to his horse, smoking a cigar. He quickly dropped it and there was a soft sizzling sound as it hit the thin layer of snow that covered the ground.

"Hello, Pa."

He turned, nodding. "Hello, Jess."

"This is a surprise." She had neither seen nor heard from her father or Joshua since that night the previous summer when Brother Lewis drove Joshua off at the point of a gun. Clinton Roundy was clearly uncomfortable. He shifted his weight from one foot to the other, and he jammed his hands into the pockets of his trousers to stop them from fluttering.

"Joshua made me—uh, asked me to come."

"Joshua?"

"Yeah."

She kept her face impassive, not wanting him to see the emotions that suddenly swirled inside her.

Now her father was clearly in pain. "I told him it weren't right for me to be the one. But he wouldn't listen. You know how he can get sometimes."

She laughed bitterly. "Yes, I know that, Pa."

"He said there weren't anyone else who could do it."

"Do what, Pa?"

He pulled off his gloves and fumbled inside his heavy winter coat. When his hand came out, he was holding a sheet of paper folded over twice. He thrust it at her, not meeting her eyes.

She took it slowly, gingerly. "What is this?"

He took a quick breath. "It's the divorce paper."

Her mouth opened, but the pain was too sharp and it shut again.

"He said it's all legal and everythin'. You can get a lawyer to look at it if you want."

She jammed the paper under her arm, feeling as if it were suddenly burning the palm of her hand.

Her father's eyes were watching her closely. Now his face softened. "At first he was talkin' about tryin' to take little Rachel away from you." He stopped as her head came up sharply.

"But," he went on hastily, "I told him that wasn't right. Besides, I told him if you wanted to make trouble it could be bad business. Even the worst Missouri wildcat don't take much to a man beating up a woman, especially a woman with child."

It was as if he were speaking to her from across a wide field. She felt herself nod, her lips pressed tightly together. She turned and started back toward the house, walking slowly, without looking down.

"Jessie, it ain't too late."

She stopped.

"Leave this religious foolery you've got into your head. Come back to him. He's better now. He hardly ever drinks anymore. You can make it work again. I know you can."

She didn't turn. "Did he tell you to say that?"

"No, I . . ." He stepped forward and took her by the shoulders. "Jessie, listen to me. Feelings are running high in town against the Mormons. The old settlers don't like what's happening. Hundreds of you Mormons are here now, and more coming all the time, buying up the best land, putting on airs like you was better than the rest of us. There's gonna be trouble, sure as men drink whiskey. You've gotta git yourself outta here."

"Thank you for troublin' yourself, Pa. I know it's a cold night and a long ways to ride."

"Jessica!" His fingers dug into her shoulders. "Why are you bein' like this? You know these Mormons are just a bunch of empty-headed fools. It ain't like you to be so blind."

"Good-bye, Pa." She pulled free from his grasp and started toward the door.

"Jessica!"

She kept moving, her head held high, her step sure.

"Joshua has met a widder woman."

Her hand was reaching for the rope that pulled up the inside latch on the door. It froze in midair.

"She's a real looker. Got two young'uns. She's got marriage on her mind."

Jessica turned slowly, remembering the night she stood behind a bedroom door peeking through a tiny nail hole. It all came flooding back. "Your wife a looker?" the gambler had asked Joshua. She would never forget the look in Joshua's eyes as he wrestled with that one. Jessica knew, without being hurt by it, that she was a plain woman, without much of what men called beauty. If Joshua had simply said, "No, she's not," it would have been infinitely less painful. Instead he had glanced in panic at the door where she stood, then looked away and not answered. It was that look, coupled with the shame she felt in helping her husband cheat, that had finally given her the courage to turn around and walk out of the bedroom, leaving Joshua to win his own poker games.

"Good-bye, Pa." She turned again and entered the house, shutting the door firmly behind her.

Y ou're asking *me* what I think?" Benjamin said in disbelief. "I wouldn't do that if I were you."

Joseph laughed. "You think I can't handle a little disagreement?"

Mary Ann watched her husband, the anxiety clearly written on her face. She had feared this from the beginning, when Benjamin had insisted on inviting Joseph and Emma over for supper. She could tell something at the temple ground-breaking had put a burr under his saddle and that he was itching for a chance to have at Joseph.

They had finished supper and left the kitchen to Matthew and Becca for cleanup. Now they were in the sitting room. Emma was on the sofa beside her husband, content for the most part to listen. Across from them, Mary Ann and Benjamin sat on matching chairs that flanked a lamp table.

"Ben, if the Lord wants us to build a house to his name, then build a house to his name is what we shall do. And I would appreciate any advice that you have to give. I have come to realize that you have an uncommon amount of good sense. I trust your judgment."

"Then, abandon this project," he said bluntly and with hard finality.

"Benjamin!"

He glanced at his wife, his face stubborn. "Well, he said he wanted to know what I think. That's what I think."

Joseph sighed. "But that's the problem, Ben. That's not an option. The Lord has commanded that it be done, and when the Lord commands something, my motto is to do it."

Emma stirred beside him. "The Lord is displeased that we have not started sooner. Joseph received a stern rebuke last week."

"You did?" Mary Ann asked.

The Prophet nodded soberly. "It was last December when the Lord first told us that we were to build a house to his name. We heard, but we did not really listen. During the ensuing months we managed to purchase the land for the building of the temple, but we didn't get started on the construction. Well, about a week ago, the Lord gave a revelation of chastisement. He said we have sinned a grievous sin because we have not taken seriously enough his commandment to build his house. It's been about five months now, and we have accomplished little."

Benjamin hooted. "So you send two men out to start digging a trench for the foundation? I'll bet the Lord is impressed."

Emma was stung by the sarcasm more than Joseph. "Joseph's cousin, George A. Smith, the one who moved here last month with his father, he hauled the first load of stone from the quarry south of town today."

"Good," Benjamin said dryly, "*three* men."

Now Mary Ann understood what had set Benjamin off. This morning she and Benjamin had gone to look at some land south of town. As they passed the site where the new temple was to be built, they had seen Hyrum Smith and Reynolds Cahoon digging the trench for the foundation in the midst of a wheat field. They also noticed that a pile of stone had been dumped at the site. Later that day when they returned, the trench was nearly done. Benjamin had insisted they stop and ask Joseph and Emma to dinner. Now it was clear why. He was not a man to let something that was bothering him go unsaid.

But Mary Ann decided she was not going to let her husband's negativism be the only voice heard. "I think it's wonderful that the construction is getting under way. It's started now, and that says to the Lord that we are taking his commandment seriously at last. I felt a real witness from the Spirit that what Hyrum and Brother Cahoon were doing this morning was pleasing to the Lord."

Benjamin harrumphed his disgust. "Well, the Spirit isn't going to build those walls or put on no roof."

He was trying to bait her a little bit, and Mary Ann knew it. Instead of responding in kind, she simply looked at him steadily.

He began to squirm a little. "What?" he finally asked.

"I watched you this morning, Benjamin Steed, when those brethren told us what they were doing," she said quietly. "I watched your face. I watched your eyes. You felt something, just like I did. And you can't deny it."

He looked away quickly, not answering, and Joseph chuckled for a moment at his discomfiture. Then the Prophet quickly sobered. "That's why we need your help, Ben," he began eagerly. "Look at you, farmer turned businessman. You shocked us all a little when you decided to buy land and develop it into lots for the new people moving in rather than buy another farm. Now, in little more than a year, you've become one of Kirtland's more successful businessmen. You're prospering. We need that kind of expertise, that kind of good judgment. Ben, help us. Help us build this temple."

Benjamin was embarrassed but obviously pleased by Joseph's sincere praise. But still his head began to move back and forth.

"If I have any good sense, as you say, then I'm telling you, you have taken on an impossible task." He threw his hands up in the air. "You're not talking about a church house here, Joseph. This building you've planned is huge." He shook his head in disbelief. "Three stories high?"

Joseph was smiling. "And with a tower that rises even higher than that."

"And Hyrum said today you won't even consider using logs. Even with logs I'd say you were mad."

Emma reached out and took Joseph's hand, her face glowing with pride. "Joseph can't build it of logs," she said.

Benjamin looked suddenly suspicious. "Why not?"

"Yes," Mary Ann came in, "why not?"

Emma looked at Joseph as if asking his permission. He smiled at her and nodded. She turned back to them. "Because he knows exactly what the building is to look like."

"You do?" Mary Ann asked, looking at Joseph.

"You do?" Benjamin echoed.

"Yes," Emma rushed on, "he's seen it in vision. Tell them, Joseph."

Her husband leaned back, his eyes watching Benjamin with some amusement. "I'm not sure Ben believes in visions."

"Oh, tell us, Joseph," Mary Ann pleaded.

Benjamin watched Joseph through half-hooded eyes, wary now but very curious as well. "Go on, Joseph," he finally said. "I'll try to keep an open mind."

Satisfied with that, Joseph nodded; his face became serene and his voice took on a faraway quality. "Not long ago, Brother Rigdon and Frederick G. Williams and I knelt in prayer as the First Presidency. God had asked us to build a house for him. But we had no idea what it should look like. He had given us the dimensions, but nothing else. Where did we start? What did we do? So, we asked him to help us, to let us know what his house should be like." He stopped, then looked right at Ben. "Suddenly, there it was, right in front of us, within easy viewing distance, as if we were gazing out of a window at it. We saw it in every detail. It was a magnificent structure, a fitting house for our God. It was white, three stories high, with arched windows and with a great tower on the east. I can still see it in my mind's eye in every detail."

Mary Ann felt a little thrill course up and down her spine. Ben did not speak, but his eyes were not filled with doubt as she had expected. He seemed almost stunned by Joseph's words.

Joseph was watching Ben closely now too. "Now, I ask you, Benjamin, do you really feel it is appropriate to build God a house made of logs?"

Mary Ann felt a great rush of relief when her husband finally shook his head. "No," he said quietly.

"Do you believe that such a project deserves less than the finest of materials and workmanship, even though we are poor and unskilled?"

Again Mary Ann held her breath. Again her husband amazed her.

"No, if it truly is God's house, then it must be the finest of buildings." But then it was as though he shook off the spell that gripped him. "But on the other hand, Joseph, you must also be practical."

Joseph laughed aloud at that. "Emma's not sure that *practical* is a word that fits me well."

"That's what I mean," Benjamin bored in, glad to be on safer ground now. "Take your store, for example."

"Ah, yes," Emma sighed with some pain, "the store."

"You would have to bring that up," Joseph said ruefully.

In the fall of 1832, Joseph and Newel Whitney had taken a short trip to Albany, New York City, and Boston to raise funds for the establishment of a general store owned by the Church and run by Joseph and Emma. They were successful in acquiring a considerable amount of mercantile goods on loan, and returned and established the store. But very quickly there was trouble. Many of the Saints pouring into Kirtland were poor, some destitute. They requested that Joseph extend them credit, though clearly they had no prospects of ever paying him back. At first, Joseph refused, but to his dismay many members turned hostile and bitter. How could he, they demanded, who was a prophet, who preached Christian discipleship and charity, refuse them help in their direst hour of need? Some walked out—out of the store and out of the Church. Soon Joseph was extending credit to everyone, and within a few months the store failed miserably.

"How much did you and Bishop Whitney borrow in order to buy all those supplies?"

"Benjamin!" Mary Ann cried. "That's not our affair."

"It's all right, Mary Ann," Joseph said. "If I'm asking for Benjamin's help, he's got a right to ask me questions in return." He turned to him. "Between fifteen and twenty thousand dollars."

Benjamin whistled softly. "And that's all gone now?"

Joseph nodded glumly.

"That's what I mean, Joseph. You needed to stand firm with those freeloaders."

The Prophet's face looked suddenly wistful. "Most of the Saints are people of integrity, Benjamin. But even when they fail in their duty, I decided that the worth of a soul was greater than the worth of dry goods. I could not refuse the Saints credit and risk them losing their testimonies on my account."

"You make a better prophet than businessman, Joseph."

Joseph laughed softly. "Was that meant as a criticism or a compliment, Benjamin?"

Benjamin started to answer, then just shook his head.

"Businessmen are easier to find than prophets, Joseph," Mary Ann said softly. Then, before he could respond, she turned to her husband. "Benjamin, you are a businessman. A good one. An honest one." Her eyes were pleading now. "You know this temple is of God. You may not be willing to admit it, not even to yourself. But you know it is."

He didn't look up, not at her, not at Joseph.

She reached across the table and touched the sleeve of his shirt. "Ben, you know the Spirit has borne witness to your heart about this work. So I'm asking you, Ben. Will you help Joseph? Will you help us build this temple?"

For almost a full minute, the room was completely silent. Even the sounds of the children in the kitchen had quieted and the hush was complete. Finally, Benjamin looked up, turning to Joseph. "And what if we fail?"

Those clear blue eyes that could seem so gentle one moment, and so piercing the next, calmly took the measure of Benjamin Steed.

"You admit yourself that the Church is deeply in debt. You've got so many poor people pouring into Kirtland, the citizens are saying you're going to break the county through pauperism. You tell me, Joseph, how can you not fail?"

Joseph's eyes clouded with pain for a moment. "Years ago I gave in to Martin Harris and let him take the hundred and sixteen pages of manuscript even though the Lord told me not to. And as you know, he lost them."

"I remember," Ben nodded. "Martin's wife was making things difficult for him."

"Well, at that time God taught me a great lesson, something I've never forgotten, Ben. It is the answer to your question. He said, 'Remember, remember, it is not the works of God that are frustrated, but the works of men. The works and the designs and the purposes of God cannot be stopped, neither can they come to naught.' "

He took a breath. "This temple is God's work, Ben," he went on. "I bear my witness of that. Your good wife has just borne her witness of that. She said that you have received your own witness from the Spirit of that." He stopped, and then a smile began to play at the corners of his mouth. "I did not hear you deny it."

There was no answer. Benjamin seemed a little dazed by this turn in the conversation.

"Do you deny it?" Joseph demanded, his voice suddenly like that of a lion.

Mary Ann had come forward on the edge of her chair. She was staring at her husband. *Oh, please, Ben, look inside your heart!* She cried it to him across the silence.

He looked at her, as though he had heard. "No," he whispered.

The atmosphere in the room was suddenly electric, filled with tension. "Then," Joseph asked softly, "will you give us your assistance in building the house of the Lord?"

Mary Ann held her breath.

"Yes."

She felt her shoulders sag and tears spring to her eyes.

But Joseph was not through. For what seemed like an eternity, he just gazed across the room at Benjamin, holding his eyes with his own. Then with slow and measured words, he went on. "I have one other question, my dear brother Benjamin."

"What?" Benjamin said, his voice barely a whisper.

"There is another work, Benjamin, a work even more important and more grand than building a house of God."

"What?" Again it was barely audible.

"Building the kingdom of God."

Time seemed suspended before Benjamin finally nodded slowly.

"I am but a man, Ben. I have many weaknesses, many failings. But this is not my work, this is God's work."

Joseph rubbed his hands across his eyes, as though suddenly weary, and continued speaking. "People are so quick to question sometimes. Why do we have to move to Ohio? Why are you trying to set up another Church center in Missouri? How can you govern a church whose members are separated by almost a thousand miles? How can you build a temple when you're so poor? How can you ask people to consecrate all their material wealth and live as one? Sometimes I don't know how to answer them, Benjamin. I don't know what to say. Except this."

Now the weariness was gone, and the power in his voice sent little shivers up and down Mary Ann's spine again. "God is in this work, Benjamin. We do not always see—I do not always see—the pattern he is weaving, the purposes he has designed. But pattern there is, and purpose there is. God will build his kingdom and no hand shall stop it, no man or combination of men can stop it. Do you believe that, Brother Benjamin Steed?"

Ben was mesmerized, as were Mary Ann and Emma, and the question caught him by surprise.

"I . . ."

"Do you believe that, Brother Benjamin?" Joseph thundered.

Benjamin jumped. His mouth was working but nothing came out.

Now Joseph was suddenly pleading. "Search your heart, Ben. The Spirit is striving with you. Listen to it! Give heed to it! There is a greater work to be done than building God's house, a far greater work, and the Lord wants you to be part of that too. You know that in your heart, don't you?"

Mary Ann was staring at her husband, stunned at what was happening. He turned to her, his eyes wide. For the longest time he did not move. Then, with what seemed like imperceptible slowness, he turned back to Joseph and his head bobbed once, then again.

Mary Ann nearly leaped into the air. Emma let out her breath in a rush of air that sounded like an explosion in the still-ness of the room.

Joseph sat back, drained and yet beaming. "I knew you did. I knew you did."

Benjamin sat back now too, looking as if he'd been struck an unseen blow.

"To help—to *really* help, Brother Ben—you must have the right tools. The gift of the Holy Ghost. The power of God's holy priesthood. Those tools only come after baptism, Ben. Are you willing to be baptized and come unto Christ so you can better serve him in his kingdom?"

There was no answer. Then, finally, Ben slowly turned his head to look at his wife. Her eyes flew open in disbelief, then in-stantly filled with tears. His eyes were glistening. He was crying.

For the first time in the nearly thirty years she had known him, Benjamin Steed was crying!

In an instant she was to him and kneeling by his side. She took his hand in hers and laid it against her cheek, looking up at him with tear-filled eyes. Slowly, so slowly that she thought her heart would burst with joy before he finished, he nodded. His eyes never left hers as he whispered, "Yes, Joseph. Yes, I am."

With the coming of the summer of 1833, the Mormon migration to Zion in western Missouri recommenced in earnest. The five missionaries to the Lamanites had arrived near the beginning of the year 1831. The Colesville Branch arrived in the latter part of July of that same year in time to join the Prophet Joseph and the other brethren in the laying of the foundation of the first log cabin in Zion. Incredibly, just one year later there were nearly eight hundred Mormons in Jackson County, with more families arriving almost weekly. By July of 1833, the number had gone up half that much again. There were nearly twelve hundred Latter-day Saints in western Missouri.

For the most part these emigrants were a homogeneous group, though they came from diverse backgrounds and locations. With few exceptions, they were from the East, many of them bringing with them a strong New England heritage. They were industrious, educated, and, for that day and time, quite used to the refinements of society. Though there was a fair share who had lived in simple cabins and homes along the frontier, just as many came from the established towns, villages, and cities of expanding America. They left well-crafted and finely furnished homes with fenced yards and neat flower and vegetable gardens. Carpenters, glaziers, potters, coopers, blacksmiths, merchants, hatters, and tailors could be found as commonly as the men of the soil. The literacy rate was remarkably high, and the education of their children highly valued.

The homogeneity of these Saints was clearly tied to the faith they had all embraced. From the very beginning, the Church which Joseph Smith restored to the earth demanded the highest moral standards of its members. They were constantly exhorted to eschew evil and seek godliness, to worship God and love their neighbors, to care for the poor and to be industrious. "He that is idle shall not eat the bread nor wear the garments of the laborer," one revelation said plainly. This was not to say that the Latter-day Saints didn't have many of the foibles and pettiness of other people, but the very nature of the Church tended to create a spiritual oneness unusual among most churches. This unity made it easy for total strangers to bond together quickly and gain a sense of communal identity.

It was inevitable that this body of Saints—diverse and varied in their own right, but unified and similar in so many ways—should come into direct conflict with the Missourians living in Jackson County. The "old settlers," as they were called, came largely from the mountainous areas of the Southern States. For the most part they had settled along the forested areas that lined the rivers and streams rather than taken the open prairie lands, which required some difficulty to plow but were fertile and rich when cultivated.

Many of these old settlers were content with their simple lives and lack of conveniences—happy to live in what the "snippety Easterners" had a tendency to call poverty and squalor. They would clear a small farm plot and build a simple log cabin or sod hut. These often had no windows or doors and nothing but dirt for floors. Many did not have chimneys, and the inside walls would be dingy and gray with the accumulated soot and smoke of the daily cooking fires. Pictures, knickknacks, wallpaper—such adornments were rare. Pigs, chickens, and geese wandered in and out of the houses as freely as did the children, who commonly looked as wild as any animal of the forest. A large majority of the families were unschooled, and those who could read and write were the exception.

Other factors contributed to the boiling pot that was starting to simmer in Jackson County. At this time in America's history,

Missouri's western border, which lay just twelve miles beyond Independence, was also the western edge of the United States of America. Beyond that lay Indian Territory, and further on, the great, largely unexplored regions of the Rocky Mountains and the great Southwest. Many a blackheart who ran afoul of the law in the East fled west and settled in Independence. If trouble threatened, within an hour these outlaws could be across the border and out of the jurisdiction of constituted authority.

With this combination of the lawless and the uneducated poor in Missouri, it was not surprising that behavior which the Saints looked upon with horror and disgust was accepted among most Missourians as a matter of course. Profanity, horseracing, gambling, drunkenness, whoring, and other forms of debauchery were viewed by many Missourians as their natural right, and they deeply resented anyone who looked down their long and proper noses at them for thinking that way.

Further complicating matters was the fact that Missouri had come into the Union under the great "Missouri Compromise" of 1820. Although many of the old settlers were not slaveholders, still there was strong pro-slavery sentiment and bitter resentment against any abolitionist tendencies. Since the Saints were mostly from the North and the East, they rejected slavery on both social and moral grounds. Feelings on this issue were running especially high at this time. In Virginia the previous year, Nat Turner had led a rebellion in which over seventy whites and a hundred slaves were killed before it was put down. An irrational but primal fear swept across the slave states, causing deep and pervasive paranoia.

The rapid influx of Mormons did little to resolve these deep and divisive differences in Missouri. One did not have to be particularly astute to see that, with more than a thousand Mormons already present and hundreds flocking in monthly, the political balance in Missouri would quickly swing to the Saints, and the Missourians would lose their political control.

Once in Missouri, the Saints quickly established their own

mercantile store. A. Sidney Gilbert, partner with Newel K. Whitney in the dry goods business, was called by the Lord to Missouri for that express purpose. Such a store would help the Saints economically, and provide badly needed goods. Once the store was established, the Saints naturally preferred to trade there whenever possible. Also, many of them had little cash money, and Gilbert allowed them to do business in trade. This deprived other merchants in Independence of the benefits of the burgeoning population. Worse yet, Gilbert chose his location well, placing his store next to the square that was considered the eastern terminus of the Santa Fe Trail. In a short time, the Gilbert store was siphoning off much of the lucrative trail business formerly handled by Missourians.

It was indicative of how high feelings were running when in the spring of 1833 the Saints took a large share of the blame for a trick of nature. After heavy snows in the Rockies and considerable rain on the Great Plains, the Missouri River flooded. It wiped out the steamer landing in Independence and eventually carved a new river channel some distance away from the town. A new village with a better landing was established at Westport (later Kansas City) upstream a few miles, and Independence business sharply declined. Rumors began to fly that somehow the Mormons were responsible for the disaster, though no one ever attempted to provide a rational explanation as to how that was possible.

During this time, the Saints were having their own internal problems. Seven high priests, with Oliver Cowdery as the head, were appointed to lead the Church in Zion. They were to select elders to preside over the five branches of the Church that were established, and were to regulate the affairs of the kingdom. But many of the incoming members ignored the direction of the leadership, and chaos quickly resulted. Others refused to accept the law of consecration and sought to gain property through some other means than properly constituted inheritances. Having the Prophet Joseph some eight hundred miles away did not help. Some even accused Joseph of caring only for the Saints in Kirtland and of seeking "monarchial power."

Learning of these problems, Joseph wrote a letter of rebuke to the Church in Missouri in January of 1833. "The Lord will have a place whence His word will go forth, in these last days, in purity," he warned them; "for if Zion will not purify herself, so as to be approved of in all things, in His sight, He will seek another people." Orson Hyde and Hyrum Smith were appointed to write a letter to the Saints in Zion. "Repent, repent," they cried, "or Zion must suffer, for the scourge and judgment must come upon her."

For a time it worked. Solemn assemblies were held in the various branches in Zion and the two letters read to the congregations. A spirit of contrition swept over the Saints. On April sixth, about eighty Saints gathered at the ferry on the Big Blue River to rejoice and thank God for the restoration of his church which had taken place exactly three years earlier on that day. It was a happy time, and for a few weeks harmony and peace prevailed in the land of Zion. But quickly the problems started all over again, and neglect of their godly duties began to creep into the Missouri branches of the Church again. The Lord's warning had been given; the Lord's warning had been mostly ignored.

This was the state of affairs in Jackson County on July twentieth, in the year of our Lord one thousand eight hundred and thirty-three.

<hr />

Joshua stood at the bar of Clinton Roundy's saloon on Main Street, watching the noisy rabble around him. The tavern was jammed, and with the liquor flowing freely it was pandemonium. One could sense the rage simmering just below the surface. *Good*, he thought. That was one of the purposes for starting in the saloons before moving to the courthouse. Every tavern and saloon in Independence was jammed at this moment, and that was not accidental. The committee of leading citizens that was formed to deal with the "Mormon problem" knew full well that liquor would play an important role in the day's proceedings.

Clinton Roundy, Joshua's father-in-law—or rather, his ex-father-in-law now—came up to him, a tray of empty beer mugs on his arm. "Do you want them to have another round?" he asked.

Joshua shook his head quickly. "No."

In April a similar meeting had been called, but someone had furnished a free barrel of whiskey. Before they could settle on any action, the men were blind drunk and the meeting erupted into a good old-fashioned "Missouri row." They had accomplished nothing more than giving each other some good bruises and a few black eyes. This time the committee wanted to make certain that the liquor stoked the fires, not doused them. Joshua himself held a mug of beer, but he had barely touched it.

He looked over to the table in the corner where four of Jackson County's leading citizens sat. The most important of these was Lilburn W. Boggs, *Lieutenant Governor* Lilburn W. Boggs. This was a coup of the highest order, to have Missouri's second highest government official present for the events of this day, and Joshua was justly proud of his role in it. Joshua and Judge Lucas had made a trip to the capital of Missouri, Jefferson City, specifically to persuade Boggs to come back for the meeting. It had not proved to be a difficult task. The lieutenant governor was a resident of Independence and one of Jackson County's largest landowners. Joshua also knew that the old fox was interested in buying additional land owned by the Mormons, who were refusing to sell. A hint that the land might become available at "a very reasonable price" was sufficient to convince Boggs to lend his support. He kept saying he wanted to "keep a low profile," which, as near as Joshua could determine, meant he was willing to do everything needed except stand before the public. That was fine, for the word was out that Boggs was there and in full support. It would be enough.

The other three men had been selected to lead out as catalysts in the day's events. Colonel Richard Simpson was to serve as chair, and James Flournoy and Judge Samuel Lucas as secretaries. Simpson had appointed seven men to a committee whose task was to draft a statement that would be read to the public, then presented to the Mormon leaders. The committee had finished and brought the statement to Boggs for his approval. Boggs finished reading it and sat back, obviously pleased.

Joshua caught the eye of the lieutenant governor and lifted a questioning eyebrow. Boggs shoved the papers back to Simpson, then pulled a pocket watch from his vest pocket and looked at it. He said something to the others, then abruptly pushed his chair back and stood, giving Joshua a quick nod.

Joshua swung around. "Gentlemen," he shouted.

It took only a moment for quiet to sweep across the room. Every eye turned to Joshua, the expectancy lighting their faces. He let the silence hold for a moment, feeling the tension building like smoke billowing from a blacksmith's bellows. Then, raising his fist, into the hush he cried, "To the courthouse! Let's deal with the Mormons once and for all!"

The crowd exploded with a roar and made a rush for the door. Boggs and the other three came over to join Joshua.

"Who's going to read the statement?" Joshua asked.

Colonel Simpson glanced at the others and they nodded. "Robert Johnson," Simpson said. "He was chairman of the committee that wrote it. He's quick with words and well respected."

"He'll do the job," Lucas said flatly.

"Good," said Joshua. He turned to watch the men clogging the doorway, almost fighting each other to be the first out.

Simpson clapped Joshua on the shoulder. "This time, Steed, there ain't no one going to stop us."

"That's right," Boggs said with satisfaction. "Gentlemen, let's be off. You have business to attend to."

They poured from every saloon and tavern along Main Street, every shop and business. Farmers had come from as far away as twenty miles. For weeks now a "secret constitution" had been circulating. The document denounced the Mormons and called for all concerned citizens to meet at the courthouse on July twentieth. The Mormons were going to be removed, "peaceably if we can, forcibly if we must."

In moments, the fifty or so from Roundy's saloon swelled to a hundred, then two hundred, then five. They milled about the new brick courthouse, talking angrily, shaking their fists, filling the air with their threats. It was evident that the liquor had done its job. The crowd had been transformed into a mob. All that was needed now was someone to crack the whip and point them in the proper direction.

Robert Johnson was that man. As he stood on an overturned crate, the crowd instantly quieted.

"Citizens of Jackson County," Johnson cried, waving the sheaf of papers he had received from Colonel Simpson, "we are gathered here together to deal with a problem of the greatest magnitude." He paused for effect. "I speak of the problem of the Mormons."

The crowd erupted with jeers, catcalls, angry insults. Johnson did not try to stop it. He nodded, letting the noise of the crowd rumble outward.

"As you know, we have formed a committee to deal with this problem. You know us, the men on that committee. We consider ourselves to be loyal, concerned citizens of Jackson County."

He raised a hand, acknowledging the smattering of applause and a cry or two of good-natured acceptance.

"We have done our work." He tapped the papers with his other hand. "This is our statement."

Joshua watched the man with open admiration. It was not hard to see why Simpson had recommended him. Johnson knew people, and played to a crowd like one of those traveling dramatists that went through the countryside from time to time. He read slowly, pronouncing the words distinctly and carefully, sometimes dropping his voice for emphasis, but never to the point where the men on the periphery of the crowd could not hear him.

The document started with a catalog of all the evils which the Mormons represented. They were a lazy and an indolent people. They came to Missouri in the most abject poverty, wishing to get their "inheritances" without money and without price. They were interfering with the practice of slavery, stirring up trouble like that which had occurred in the East, inviting free people of color to settle in Jackson County.

At each charge there was an answering cry from the crowd, but at the last one the rage exploded, and for almost a minute Johnson had to let it run its course. This was a particularly sensitive issue, and the committee knew it. The statement had been deliberately calculated to capitalize on it.

Earlier in the month, the *Evening and Morning Star*, a newspaper printed by the Mormons in Missouri, had run an article on "free people of color." Free people of color were Negroes and mulattos who had either purchased their freedom somehow or been freed by the kindness of their masters. The article, written by W. W. Phelps, editor and proprietor of the paper, outlined the laws of the state concerning these freed slaves and counseled the Saints to use prudence in dealing with them. Instantly, the populace of Jackson County interpreted that as a call for all free people of color to settle in Jackson County.

On the sixteenth of the month, a special issue of the *Star* was printed which denied the charge and tried to explain that just the opposite was true. But the damage was done. The emotions had been triggered, and the retraction fell on deaf ears.

Johnson stood silent and majestic as the rage vented itself. His expression managed to convey sympathy, outrage, understanding, and determination all at the same time. When the noise finally quieted, he lifted the papers again, but now he didn't bother to read; he knew what was written on them.

"It is further obvious," he cried, "that the evils which threaten our community, brought on by the rapid influx of these Mormon settlers, could not have been foreseen. Therefore our laws are not prepared to deal with these problems." His face hardened. "And if we wait for legislation to resolve them, the delays will put the mischief beyond all remedy."

Again the muttering and cries from the crowd began to rise, but this time Johnson rode over them, his voice rising sharply with indignation. "If the migration of these Mormons to our community is not dealt with forthwith, the day will not be far distant when the civil government of this county will be in the hands of the Mormons."

He dropped his arm to his side. "Is that what you want?" he shouted.

The answer was instantaneous. "No!"

"Do you want your county judges to be Mormons?"

."No!"

"Do you want your sheriffs and your constables to be Mormons?"

"No!"

His voice dropped almost to a whisper, tinged now with horror. The crowd leaned forward together, as if they were one man, as they strained to hear his words. "Think for a moment, my good friends. What would be the fate of our lives and our property in the hands of jurors and witnesses who do not blush to declare, and do not hesitate to swear, that they have wrought miracles, that they have been the subjects of miraculous and supernatural cures, that they have conversed with God and his angels, that they possess and exercise the gifts of divination and of unknown tongues?"

He lifted his head and screamed out the next question, causing many in the crowd to jump in surprise. "*Is that what you want?*"

The answer was an animal roar, and the sound battered at the speaker. "No! No! No!"

Johnson nodded, breathing hard, his face showing the depths of his own outrage at such prospects. Finally he lifted the papers again. "Then, be it resolved," he read, "one, that no Mormon shall in the future move to or settle in this county; two, that those now here, who shall give a definite pledge of their intention, within a reasonable time, to remove out of the county, shall be allowed to remain unmolested, until they have sufficient time to sell their property and close their businesses without material sacrifice; three, that the editor of the *Star* be required forthwith to close his office, and discontinue the business of printing in this county; four, that in the case of all other stores and shops belonging to the sect, their owners must, in every case, strictly comply with the terms of this declaration; five, that upon failure to do so, prompt and efficient measures will be taken to close the same; and finally, six, that the Mormon leaders here are required to use their influence in preventing any further immigration of their distant brethren to this county, and to counsel and advise their brethren there to comply with the above requisitions."

Virtually every head in the crowd was going up and down now as each phrase in the resolution was read. Johnson stopped and raised his head. "All in favor?"

It was a thunderous response. "Aye!"

"Those opposed, if there be any?" His eyes swept the crowd, daring any to raise a contrary voice. There was not a sound.

"Then I propose that a committee of twelve men, led by none other than our chairman, the honorable Colonel Richard Simpson, immediately and forthwith take our demands to the Mormon leaders and that we wait here for their response. All in favor?"

"Aye!"

He swung around, his eyes glittering with satisfaction.

Boggs nodded his approval, then turned to Joshua and the others. "Go. You have your mandate from the people."

Chapter Twenty-One

W illiam W. Phelps was obviously frightened. "We do
not represent the full leadership of the Church in Zion," he said
quickly. "Brother Oliver Cowdery, the leading elder here in Missouri, is out at Kaw Township."

The six Mormons had evidently known of the gathering at
the courthouse, for they were huddled in conference in the office of the *Evening and Morning Star* when the delegation of
twelve Missourians stormed into the building.

Colonel Simpson turned to Joshua. "Is that true?"

Joshua had thought carefully about this moment every day
since the big gathering in April had degenerated into a drunken
brawl. Shortly after that, he had met Oliver Cowdery on the
streets of Independence. Joshua had the widow Martin on his
arm and couldn't pass up the opportunity to parade her before
Cowdery a little, knowing it would get back to Jessie. In actuality, the widow was much more serious about marriage than
Joshua was, but Cowdery didn't have to know that. He also took

the opportunity to let Cowdery know about the meeting and the sentiment against the Mormons. But his little moment of triumph turned sour when Cowdery informed him that the Mormons had heard of the gathering of the Missourians and had fasted and prayed. In their minds, the breakup of the meeting was a direct result of God's intervention and not the result of some fool's miscalculation about the effects of too much whiskey.

From that point on, Joshua set about to know everything he could about the hated sect. He became an active voice in the committee that was formed to drive the Mormons from the county. He learned the names and faces of the Mormons' leadership. On a county map he charted the places where every Mormon had settled. He made note of which houses were isolated, how many people were known to be living there, what arms they had, and so on. The next time, he vowed, he and the other Missourians would be ready, and the Mormons would learn which God could save them and which could not.

Now that time had come. He looked on the six men with contempt and answered Simpson's question. "Not quite. Joseph Smith appointed seven high priests to direct them out here. Oliver Cowdery is the leader of the seven, and it is true that he is not here. But the other six who join with him are here." He pointed at each of the men in turn as he said their names. "William Phelps, who publishes the *Star* and operates the printing establishment; A. Sidney Gilbert, owner of the mercantile store across the street; John Corrill; John Whitmer"—his lips curled in disgust—"he's one of those that signed his name to the Book of Mormon; Isaac Morley; and Edward Partridge. Partridge here is the so-called Mormon bishop. He's the one who assigns out the land and gives the people their 'inheritances.' "

"And you're Nathan Steed's brother," Isaac Morley said with a touch of contempt of his own. He was the oldest of the six, but not cowed at all by the delegation of Missourians. Joshua's head came around, his eyes narrowing, but Morley went right on. "Your brother and his wife now live on my farm back in Ohio. He would be shamed to know of your role in this."

"My brother is a fool!" Joshua snarled. "And his wife's no better." He turned to the others. "These men represent six of the seven leaders of the Church here. They can speak for the Mormons."

Simpson stepped forward, holding the same sheets of paper from which Robert Johnson had read to the crowd. "We have been appointed to inform you of the following resolution which has been adopted by the will of the people."

John Corrill snorted in derision, and Lucas stepped forward menacingly. "You're to listen," Lucas warned, "nothing else."

Simpson read the statement through, slowing down at the end to emphasize the final demands of the group for the exodus of the Saints from Jackson County. Joshua watched with a deep satisfaction as he saw the shock and numbness spread across the faces of the six Mormons.

"This is an outrage!" Gilbert cried when Simpson finished. "We are not guilty of those vile and ridiculous—"

"Enough!" Simpson roared. "We are not here to listen to your defense, but only to take your answer back to the people who await us. What is your response?"

"But . . ." Phelps stammered, "but we can't answer a demand like that. Our leader, Joseph Smith, is in Ohio."

"You lead here!" Joshua snapped. "That's good enough."

"Please," Gilbert broke in again, "you've got to give us some time. We will need to send word to Joseph Smith and ask for his counsel. May we have three months to consider these demands?"

Joshua reached out and grabbed the man by his shirt. Gilbert was an older man, small of stature, and Joshua was almost a full head taller than he. Joshua pulled him up close until they were nose-to-nose. "We don't want none of Joe Smith's counsel out here," he hissed. "Do you understand that?" He released him, giving him a hard shove backwards. Gilbert stumbled into Corrill and they both nearly fell.

Partridge stepped forward now, not frightened by the numbers confronting them. "You must give us time. Even if we decide to leave, you must realize that it takes time to close down a printing shop and a store, to sell our land and houses. We have twelve hundred people. We can't just wave our hands and make them all disappear."

Simpson was shaking his head even as Partridge spoke. "Three months is too long."

"Then, ten days. We must have at least ten days," Phelps pleaded.

Simpson turned to his party, waving the papers. "Do you think it takes ten days to agree to a reasonable demand such as this?"

There were raucous bursts of laughter and angry rejections. "No!" "Ten days is too long!" "They're stalling for time."

Simpson spun around. He looked at the six men haughtily. "You have fifteen minutes. We'll await you're decision at the courthouse."

And with that they turned around and trooped out.

———◆———

"What'd they say?" men called as the delegation returned to the crowd milling around the courthouse. "What happened?" "Are they going?"

Simpson and Lucas walked directly to Lieutenant Governor Boggs and began to report quickly and quietly on the meeting. The other members of the delegation began mingling with the crowd, muttering quick reports of their experience. Joshua, emboldened by the rage that was smoldering in him, moved up to join Boggs and the three leaders of the citizens' committee.

"Ten days is out of the question," Boggs was saying.

"That's what I told them," Simpson nodded. "We gave 'em fifteen minutes."

"Fifteen minutes is too long," Joshua said quietly.

All three men snapped around. "But we said—," Lucas started.

Joshua cut him off harshly. "In fifteen minutes these men will start wandering off to find another beer or put their backs up against some building and fall asleep. The time is now or you're gonna lose 'em."

"He's right," Simpson said, turning to look at the men. Timing was important when it came to whipping a group into action, and he could sense that the conditions were right.

Lucas was still wavering, but Boggs for the moment seemed content to hear both sides. Joshua threw up his hands in disgust. "You want another farce like that one we had in April? The Mormons are already saying we ain't good enough to fight anyone but ourselves."

That hit a soft spot in Lucas, as Joshua knew it would. Lucas had been decked by some drunken bum that night and spent three days at home with a swollen jaw. Now his lips tightened into a hard line. "That ain't true."

"Then, let's show 'em!" Joshua urged. "Now's the time. They ain't gonna give us an answer. They're stalling."

Boggs gave him an appraising look, then laid a hand on his shoulder. "All right. Get up on that box and tell 'em that."

In an instant Joshua was up on the crate, his hands raised high in the air. The silence swept across the crowd like a stiff breeze moving through a field of grain. He waited for the last voice to die and every eye to fix on him.

"Men," he shouted, "we've been to the Mormons and we've given 'em our demands."

"What'd they say?" someone called from the back.

"They said they wanted three months"—his voice mimicked that of a woman—"to think about it."

"No!" came the cry; it was ragged and scattered, but the anger in the voices was clear.

"Then they asked for ten days!" Joshua shouted. He clenched his fist and jammed it skyward. "You want to give them ten days?"

"No!" They were quickly getting the idea, and this time almost three-quarters of the men roared their answer in unison.

Judge Lucas jumped up beside Joshua. "They're just stalling," he shouted to the crowd. "They wouldn't give us an answer."

Joshua watched their reaction, exulting in the power he suddenly felt. The crowd was like the ground in an earthquake zone.

The underlying forces were there, starting to strain and rumble as they ground together. It just needed the right moment, the proper trigger.

"You've seen these Mormons come in here and take away our business, haven't you?" he shouted.

"Yes." "That's right." "They're stealing us blind."

"And you've seen them come in here and take up the best land, haven't you?"

"Yes!"

Joshua's voice rose in both volume and pitch. He hurled the words at them like missiles flung from a catapult. "And you've read their newspaper that calls on colored people to come in and take over our state, haven't you?"

This time the roar was deafening. "Yes! Yes!"

"Well, that place where the article was printed is no more than one block from here. That store that is taking away our business is no more than one block from here." He was pointing, and the men turned as a body, eyes riveted on the two buildings up the street from them. Together the men were like a hound with the smell of blood in its nose, straining at the leash, baying to be set free.

Joshua looked down at Boggs, whose nostrils were flaring in and out with the excitement. The fever pitch was in his eyes too. He caught Joshua's look and nodded curtly. "Do it!" he mouthed.

Joshua swung back around. "Let's make a new resolution," he screamed. "I resolve we tear that print shop apart! Now!"

He leaped off the box and plunged into the crowd, his fist raised high like a banner of attack. A howl went up, like some primal scream of rage, and the men surged in behind Joshua, Simpson, Lucas, and the other delegation members. In a rush, they made their way straight for the two-story brick building that housed the offices and print shop for the *Evening and Morning Star* and the residence of W. W. Phelps and his family.

Phelps and the other Mormon leaders evidently had been watching anxiously out of the windows, for as Joshua and his army approached, the six men came stumbling out, hands raised high, as though to ward off a blow. Phelps was in the lead. "No, no!" he pleaded. "Please!"

It was like using a twig to stop a flood. Joshua shoved him roughly aside, and in a moment the six men were swallowed by the crowd. "Don't leave anything," Joshua shouted.

Miraculously, Phelps broke free of the encircling crowd. He hurled himself forward enough to clutch at Joshua's shirt. "No!" The man was stricken with panic. "My wife and children are in the house. My baby's sick. I beg of you, please don't hurt them."

Joshua reached out and grabbed the collar of the man next to him. "You!" he shouted, his voice nearly drowned out by the shrieking of the crowd. "Get the family out of there."

The man darted ahead.

Coming to the building now, Joshua leaped over the low picket fence and up onto the small porch. There was a sharp crash as the picket fence went down beneath the feet of the mob. Joshua raised his hands again and the crowd quieted momentarily. Emerging from the front entrance of the building was Sally Phelps, escorted by the man whom Joshua had sent inside and by Colonel Simpson, who had also gone in. She was holding a screaming infant, and two other small children, also crying, were clutching at her skirts. She was white faced, terrified almost into immobility. Simpson shoved her roughly into the arms of her husband, who had finally burst through the crowd to reach her side. Phelps led his family stumbling and sobbing across the yard and out into the street.

Joshua now turned to the crush of men that surrounded him. "All right," he shouted in triumph, "I don't want to see anything left standing. Do you hear me, boys! Nothing!"

He jumped back to get out of the way of the surging mass that poured into the building.

———————

Mary Elizabeth Rollins was fifteen years old. At age ten, she with her widowed mother moved to Kirtland, Ohio, to live with her uncle, A. Sidney Gilbert. There, in October of 1830, she listened to the testimony of four missionaries who had come from New York. She, along with some of her family, was baptized.

Even at twelve, this was a remarkable young woman. When her family learned that Father Isaac Morley had a copy of the Book of Mormon in his possession, the only one in that part of the country at the time, Mary Elizabeth determined she wanted to see the book for herself. She went out to the Morley farm one afternoon to see if she could at least look upon it. When she saw it, she was so filled with a desire to read it that she begged Father Morley to let her take it home with her.

At first he refused, but she was so persistent, he finally agreed, on the condition that she return it before breakfast on the following day. She ran all the way home. "Oh, I have got the 'Golden Bible,' " she exclaimed to her uncle. The family stayed up long into the night, taking turns reading the treasured book. At first light, Mary Elizabeth was up again. She set out in time to return the book to Father Morley as promised.

When she appeared at the Morleys' with the book, Father Morley was kindly but a little condescending. "I guess you did not have a chance to read much in it," he said to her. She opened the book and showed him how far they had gotten, then handed it to him. "Oh," he said in surprise, "but I'll bet you cannot tell me one word of what you have read."

"To the contrary," this little twelve-year-old said, and she proceeded to quote to him the first verse of the book, which she had memorized that morning, and then outlined for him the history of the family of Nephi. When she finished, Father Morley was staring. He held the book out to her. "Child," he said with a new respect, "take this book home and finish it. I can wait."

The Rollins family were among the number of Saints who emigrated to Missouri in 1831. They chose to build a small home in Independence rather than move out on the surrounding prairies. So it was that Mary Elizabeth Rollins and her twelve-year-old sister, Caroline, were on the streets of Independence this day as the mob of five hundred angry men stormed the printing offices and home of William W. Phelps. As the Saints scattered before the mob, there was no time for the two sisters to find their family. Like the others, Mary Elizabeth and Caroline fled in terror before the blind, mindless fury that had been unleashed upon them.

As the animal roar of the mob filled the air, the two girls darted around a building and across a vacant lot. A stand of corn, now four or five feet high, provided safe haven, and they ducked into it. For several moments they huddled there, shivering with fright, listening to the foul oaths of the shouting men, growing ever more horrified as they heard windows being shattered and the crash of furniture being smashed to pieces.

"Come, Caroline," Mary Elizabeth said, taking her hand.

"Where are we going?" her sister cried in fear.

"I just want to see." Mary Elizabeth crept forward to where the cornfield ended. A short distance away was a wooden slat fence. Two boards had been knocked out, providing a gap large enough to slip through. The grass along the fence line was knee high and thick enough to hide them. "Come on." Mary Elizabeth, with her sister in tow, ran in a low crouch to the fence, where they dropped to the ground and peered through the gap at the chaos before them.

It was as if the very doors of hell itself had been thrown open and every demon set free to rush out. Fiendish shouts rent the air. Sister Phelps stood with her husband and children, guarded by several men and forced to watch as piece after piece of their furniture came flying out of the windows and doors of the building that served as their home and as the printing offices for the *Evening and Morning Star*. Any piece of furniture that survived that treatment was instantly destroyed by the men outside. Men with sledgehammers were battering at a side door of the building, splinters of wood flying in every direction. In one of the upper-story windows the figure of a man appeared. The glass had already been ripped away. He held a long wooden tray, and Mary Elizabeth groaned. She loved the print shop and had been there many times to watch Brother Phelps set type. This was one of the trays that held the thousands of pieces of lead type used to print the newspaper. She watched, feeling physically sick, as the man at the window began to scoop handfuls of type from the tray and fling them across the yard.

At another large upper-story window, an object that nearly filled the entire opening was teetering on the sill. "Push!" came the faint cry from inside. There was a terrible screeching sound, and in a moment, the press, bought in Cincinnati and carried to Independence at great cost, came out of the window. With a thunderous crash it hit the ground. There was a cry of triumph from several men at the window from which the press had fallen. Like men possessed, those surrounding what was left of the machine fell upon it with axes, shovels, hammers—anything they could lay hands on.

"Oh, look Caroline!" From where they sat, the sisters could see the west side of the building. There was a flash of white at one of the windows. A man was carrying armfuls of large sheets of paper to the opening and tossing them out onto the ground.

"What is it?"

"It's the Book of Commandments," Mary Elizabeth cried. Brother Phelps had been working on the printing of the revelations for more than six months now, and it was nearly ready for binding. Now the unbound sheets were being dumped into a pile. *For burning!* The thought flashed into Mary Elizabeth's mind like a jab of a knife. They were going to burn the Book of Commandments!

"We've got to save those sheets, Caroline."

"No," her sister cried. Her eyes were wide and filled with terror. "They'll kill us, Mary Elizabeth."

Mary Elizabeth swallowed hard, her heart pounding as though it would burst. Caroline was right. There was no question about the fury of the mob. Even as they watched, they saw a group of men on the roof. They began to rip off the shingles and smash at the ribbing underneath them. Two men with horses, having attached ropes to the front wall of the building, now only waited for the signal to pull it down. Other men had crossed the street and were smashing their way into the store of their uncle, Sidney Gilbert. Boxes, tools, cloth goods came flying out, one after the other, into the ankle-deep dust of the roadway.

But something inside Mary Elizabeth would not give way to the fear, as terrible as it was. These were the revelations that were being tossed out of that window. These were words that had been given to the Prophet. It was God's word. Could she simply sit and watch them burn?

The fifteen-year-old Mary Elizabeth reached out and took both of her sister's hands. "Caroline, I'm going to try and save some copies. Will you help me?"

For a moment Caroline was about to shake her head—her lips were trembling and her hands shaking violently—but she didn't. She merely closed her eyes and nodded her head.

Mary Elizabeth turned back. The man brought one more load of sheets and tossed them onto the pile. She waited for a moment. He did not reappear. "Let's go!" she cried.

In a moment they were through the fence and running low, hair flying, skirts dragging through the long grass. They circled out and around the back of a nearby house, pausing only long enough to see that the man had not come back to the window.

"Grab everything you can carry!" Mary Elizabeth hissed. In an instant they were to the pile, scooping up bundles of the large sheets into their arms. Caroline turned and started away. Mary Elizabeth began to follow, then swung around to add another handful.

"Hurry!" Caroline wailed. "They'll catch us."

They made it halfway back to the fence line before they heard the startled cry. "Hey! What are you doing?"

The girls looked over their shoulders even as they redoubled their speed. A man near the Phelps home and printing office was pointing in their direction. "Hey, come back here!"

"Quick, into the cornfield," breathed Mary Elizabeth.

"They're taking the book!" the voice shouted. "Stop them!"

Just before they ducked through the fence, Mary Elizabeth's

heart plummeted. Out of the corner of her eye, she saw some men break into a run toward them. One had something in his hand, and with a lurch, she realized it was a rifle.

Like two prairie dogs being chased by a hawk, Mary Elizabeth and Caroline scampered into the welcoming thickness of the cornstalks. "Don't stop!" Mary Elizabeth cried. "Go in deeper. Stay close."

When they were twenty or thirty yards in, Mary Elizabeth suddenly stopped, holding her finger to her lips. Both were gasping for breath, hugging the unbound sheets of paper to their bodies. Behind them they heard muttered oaths, then the crashing sound of men entering the corn.

Mary Elizabeth dropped to the ground, throwing her body on top of the papers. Caroline instantly followed suit, her head touching her sister's feet. "Pray, Caroline, pray!" Mary Elizabeth whispered hoarsely.

They did, faces buried in the soft, warm earth, eyes pinched tightly shut. They prayed with a fervency known only to those in deepest need. For ten minutes they listened in terror as men crashed back and forth through the cornfield, crossing and crisscrossing as they looked for the girls. Twice, Mary Elizabeth's heart almost stopped beating as one of the men came so close that she could see his legs and feet just a row or two away. But then he moved away again.

Finally, to their immense relief, the two sisters heard one of the men call out. "Those little nits have got away. Come on, we're missin' out on all the fun."

Slowly the sounds of the men died away, and all became silent except for the distant cries of angry men and the noises that accompanied a two-story building being totally razed to the ground. Then, and only then, did Mary Elizabeth and Caroline Rollins sit up. They threw themselves into each other's arms, and began to cry.

Like blood lust that cannot be satiated, the mob's desire for action was not spent when the printing office and home of W. W. Phelps was completely leveled. They fell to destroying the goods being hurled from the Gilbert and Whitney store and only desisted when a frantic Sidney Gilbert promised that he would close the store, pack the goods, and be gone within three days.

They swung around, like a pack of wild dogs looking for their next victim. Someone cried out, "Let's find the leaders!" They fanned out, shouting and cursing. The Saints, who had watched the destruction from shuttered windows or from a distance with frightened faces and pinched lips, now scattered like sheep before a coyote. Women grabbed their children and ran screaming. Men ducked into buildings or fled for the cornfields and the wheat fields.

Bishop Edward Partridge, who had watched from his home in numbed shock as the Church properties were demolished, had no time to react to the swift change of targets. Suddenly his house was surrounded. The door burst open and men poured into the room. He was dragged out at the point of a rifle, leaving a sobbing wife and terrified children. Across the street, Charles Allen, a twenty-seven-year-old convert from Pennsylvania, was also caught.

"To the square!" Joshua shouted.

The two men were driven through the crowd toward the public square. People leaned forward to scream in their faces. Men clutched at their clothes or clawed at their bodies. A woman, her face twisted like some demented and pathetic hag, leaped forward and slapped Partridge across the face. Someone threw a clod of fresh horse droppings and hit Allen alongside the head. A thirteen-year-old boy stuck out his foot and tripped Partridge. The crowd roared its approval as he went down hard, tearing open his trousers and badly skinning his knee.

Dragging, shoving, cursing, swearing, spitting, and threatening, the mob moved their two captives to the square. In an instant, the crowd gave way enough to make a circle around the Mormons. Joshua stepped into the circle and raised his hands. The noise level dropped, but there were still angry mutterings and cries for action.

"Friends," Joshua yelled, letting his eyes sweep the crowd, "here we have two of the Mormon leaders."

"Yes!" "Stone them." "Don't let them get away!" "Somebody get some tar and feathers."

A neighbor of Joshua's, named George Simpson, pushed through the crowd and stepped out beside Joshua. He had been one of those who led the mob to seize the two Mormons. He looked at the two men now with utter disgust as he walked around them slowly, eyeing them up and down. Their clothes were now soiled and disheveled. Allen had a dark smear where the foul missile had hit his cheek. He looked frightened, but Bishop Partridge stood straight and tall, calm and serene. The people, sensing that something was about to happen, gradually quieted.

"So you are the leaders of the vaunted Mormons?" Simpson sneered.

Allen started to protest—he was not actually part of the leadership—but Partridge warned him to silence with his eyes.

"Well, where's your God now?" Simpson cried. He pointed over the heads of the crowd toward the spot where the print shop once stood. "There won't be any more newspapers calling for rebellion amongst the slaves."

Angry muttering rippled through the crowd. Joshua stepped up to Simpson and whispered something in his ear. Simpson looked surprised for a moment, then pleased. He clapped Joshua on the shoulder and turned to the two men.

As the noise died out again, he spoke loudly. He wanted all to hear. "We don't want to seem unreasonable in these matters, but"—his voice rose sharply—"you Mormons have done us irreparable harm."

"Yeah!" "That's right!" "Make 'em pay!"

He smiled—an evil, leering smile that would have sent chills into the heart of any normal man. "But there is a way you can now make restitution."

"What is that?" Partridge asked quietly.

Simpson swung around, calling to the crowd. "What if these

men were to renounce their ridiculous faith and tell us they were sorry for being Mormons? Would we forgive 'em then?"

The question caught the crowd by surprise, but only for a moment. The thought delighted them. "Yes!" someone shouted. Others nodded. "Yes. Let them renounce their faith."

Partridge started to shake his head. Joshua was to him in two strides and thrust his face close to the bishop's. "Deny the Book of Mormon," he cried, "and you shall go free this moment. Refuse, and we shall drive you from the county."

"I cannot do that," Partridge answered, almost in a whisper.

Joshua grabbed the front of his shirt. "What?" he screamed into his face. "What did you say? I don't think the people heard you."

Bishop Partridge's chin came up. "I said I cannot deny the Book of Mormon," he said loudly and firmly.

Charles Allen swallowed twice, staring straight ahead at nothing, not daring to meet the eyes of either Joshua or the crowd. But the courage and serenity of Bishop Partridge had obviously strengthened him, for he spoke with the same conviction. "Nor can I," he said.

Simpson swung around. "Did you hear that, people? Is that the answer you wanted?"

"No!"

Suddenly there was a cry from the back of the crowd. "Let us through! Let us through!"

Heads turned and people inched back to make a passageway. Two men came pushing through and entered the circle. The first carried a wooden paddle in one hand and a large bucket of tar in the other. The other had two pillows tucked under his arm. "I say we tar and feather them!" the first shouted.

Here was something tangible, some way for the group to express their rage. Instantly cries of acclamation rent the air.

Simpson raised his hand and waited for quiet. He turned back to Partridge. "You have two choices. Either you deny the Book of Mormon or you leave the county. And if you choose the latter"—he gestured toward the two men—"we shall see that you leave us in style. Which shall it be?"

Edward Partridge took one step forward. When he spoke it was loud enough for all to hear, but his voice was perfectly clear and calm. "I cannot and I shall not deny that which I know to be true, nor can I agree to leave the county. The Saints of God have suffered persecution and mockery in all ages of the world, and I am willing to suffer for the sake of my Lord and Savior, Jesus Christ."

His head swung around and his eyes met the sullen and angry stares of the crowd. "I have done nothing to offend anyone here, and if you choose to abuse me, you abuse an innocent person."

That brought an instant response from the crowd. Someone near the front began to curse and swear at anything Mormon. Another man shouted, "Tar and feather him, then let him call upon his Jesus." Others were crying, "Let him speak. Let him speak. We can't hear him." In a moment the noise had swelled to the point that it drowned out Partridge's words.

Bishop Partridge stepped back, his head high, his arms at his sides. Joshua just stared for a moment. He didn't like the sudden cries of sympathy Partridge's courage and demeanor were eliciting. Raw anger surged up inside him. This man before him exhibited exactly the kind of blind fanaticism he saw in Jessica now. Their attitude was: "I'm the faithful. I have done no wrong. Let me suffer for my Jesus." This was the end product that Joseph Smith and his wild stories produced. This was the final result. When he thought of his own daughter being raised to this—

He whirled around. "Strip them of their clothes!" he commanded.

Three men jumped forward and ripped off the Mormons' hats, coats, and vests.

"All right," Joshua hissed at the two men who had pushed their way through the crowd and stood ready with the tar and the feather-filled pillows. "Do it!"

Giggling wildly, the first man jumped to the task. He scooped from the bucket a large blob of tar, now sticky and oozing in the heat of the July afternoon, and gleefully smeared it on the left side of Bishop Partridge's face. He had to lean hard to get the tar off the paddle, and the movement pushed Partridge off balance. But only for a moment. The Bishop planted his feet more firmly, clasped his hands behind his back, and turned his head so the man could more easily get at him.

This submissiveness caught the crowd by surprise. There were a few whistles, an oath or two, and some catcalls, but they had expected resistance, cries for mercy, or at the very least, anger and cursings in return. But Partridge stood without flinching as the tar was smeared into his hair, on his face, over his arms. He did not even so much as grimace, just stood there in calm repose, gazing out over the heads of the crowd, peace written across what little could now be seen of his face.

To Joshua's dismay, the cries of the crowd quickly died. As the second man took out his knife and ripped open one of the pillows and dumped its contents over the head of Bishop Partridge, there was not a sound. Charles Allen submitted to the indignities in the same submissive spirit, as the somber crowd watched in silence.

The Mormons stood there together when it was done, two figures covered with black smears and chicken feathers, looking like some strange, unrecognizable bipeds taken from some child's nightmarish dreams. They should have looked utterly ridiculous, but the effect was just the opposite. Their meekness gave them majesty, their resignation in the face of revilement a dignity that even Joshua could not deny.

In silence, one by one, the members of the mob turned away, some glancing back over their shoulders at the work they had wrought, the shame evident on their faces. Joshua and Simpson sensed that there was nothing more to be done here and walked swiftly away. In a few minutes, Edward Partridge and Charles Allen stood alone in the public square.

Three days later, the mob spirit exploded again. About five hundred men—waving a red flag and armed with rifles, pistols, whips, dirks, and clubs—gathered from every direction. On signal they went looking for the Mormons. This time their violence was not restricted to Independence. They spread out across the countryside, torching haystacks, setting fire to the ripening grain fields. Men were caught and threatened with whipping. Houses, barns, and businesses were ripped apart and their remains left scattered across the ground.

Six of the Mormon leaders offered themselves as ransom if the pillaging would stop. But it was not enough. Threatening to whip every man, woman, and child in the Church, the Missourians thrust an agreement before the six men. In the starkest of terms it outlined their demands. By April following, there would be no more Mormons in Jackson County. The choice was capitulation or terror, surrender or rapine. With heavy hearts, the leaders took up the pen and signed the agreement that declared they were to leave the land of Zion.

Ironically, on the very day the six men were putting their names to the contract of expulsion, in Ohio another group of Saints were gathered, this time under happier circumstances. Benjamin Steed, newly ordained as an elder in the Church, was privileged to be a participant. His wife and family looked on happily, Mary Ann with tears in her eyes. In great solemnity, led by Joseph Smith and following the order of the priesthood, the officiating elders grasped the ropes on the block and tackles and hoisted four large blocks of stone. These had previously been brought from the stone quarry south of town and carefully dressed and finished. Now the elders swung them into place and lowered them onto the four corners of the footings that had been completed a short time before.

The cornerstones for the house of the Lord, the first built in nearly two thousand years, were in place. A great shout of joy went up from the assembled throng.

A day or two following the outrages of July twenty-third, Oliver Cowdery was dispatched to Ohio to inform the leadership of the tragedy unfolding in Missouri. On August second, several days before Oliver would arrive in Kirtland with the terrible news, Joseph Smith received a revelation concerning the "brethren in the land of Zion." Among other things it said:

> Therefore verily thus saith the Lord let Zion rejoice, for this is Zion, THE PURE IN HEART: therefore let Zion rejoice, . . . for behold and lo, vengeance cometh speedily upon the ungodly, as the whirlwind, and who shall escape it: . . . for the indignation of the Lord is kindled against their abominations, and all their wicked works: nevertheless Zion shall escape if she observe to do all things whatsoever I have commanded her, but if she observe not to do whatsoever I have commanded her, I will visit her according to all her works: with sore affliction; with pestilence; with plague; with sword; with vengeance, with devouring fire.

Nathan and Lydia sat side by side with Nathan's parents in one of the upper rooms of the Newel Whitney store. They were crowded in with another fifty or sixty Saints who had gathered in response to a hurried call from the Prophet. Oliver Cowdery had arrived that afternoon. It was a bittersweet reunion, for Oliver brought news of the situation in Zion.

Oliver Cowdery stood near the front of the room. He spoke quietly and slowly, his voice filled with immense pain and horror. It was as if he had been struck with the center beam of a hay crane and hadn't fully recovered. The press? Destroyed. The printing office and W. W. Phelps's home? Razed to the ground. The Book of Commandments? Gone, save for a few copies. The Gilbert and Whitney store sacked, Bishop Partridge tarred and feathered, the Saints shocked and filled with fear. It was a grim report. Horror and stunned disbelief filled the room. Joseph, who sat on the front row with Emma, just kept shaking his head, the pain etching deep lines around his eyes. Emma was weeping silently, as were many of the other women.

When Oliver finally finished and slowly sat down, Joseph stood and let his eyes sweep across the faces in the room. "Brothers and sisters, this is terrible news indeed." He stopped, looking dazed. There wasn't a person in the room who didn't have someone close—a brother or sister, a parent or child, other relatives, close friends—living in Zion. "I recommend we adjourn this evening. I trust that thoughts of our brethren and sisters in Zion will weigh heavily in your prayers tonight. I would like a council of the priesthood to convene here tomorrow morning at ten, so we can consider what course of action we now should take."

The moment Joseph was finished, Nathan was up and over to Oliver. Nathan was shocked at the other man's appearance. He had aged five years. His eyes were dull and listless, and there were dark circles under them. Part of that, Nathan knew, could be attributed to trail weariness. Oliver had just completed a journey of over eight hundred miles, a goodly portion of it on foot. But it was more than that. He was drained, spiritually, emotionally, physically.

Others were starting forward, and Nathan had no time for preamble. He had to know. He took Oliver by the arm and turned him half around, so they were not facing the group. "Oliver," he said in a low voice, "tell me. What is the news of Jessica and the baby? Were they hurt in any way?"

Oliver managed a wan smile. "No, that is one happy thing to report. Jessica is safe."

"Thank heavens," Nathan breathed.

Oliver brightened a little. "Rachel, her baby, is not really a baby anymore, you know. She's nearly a year and a half now. She has beautiful, dark curly hair, and the brightest, perkiest pair of blue eyes you've ever seen."

"And what about my son?" Benjamin Steed asked from behind Nathan.

Nathan turned, his heart falling. Both of his parents, along with Lydia, were standing next to them now. That was the question he had hoped to ask before his parents came up to hear. Now it was too late. His father, face as grim as though he were waiting for a pronouncement of a death in the family, looked steadily at Oliver. "What of Joshua? Did he have a part in this?"

Oliver looked first at Benjamin, then at Mary Ann. His shoulders rose, then sagged. "Joshua Steed is a member of the citizens' committee that was largely responsible for what happened. He helped draft the secret constitution that called for the expulsion of the Saints."

Nathan was watching his mother and felt a piercing stab of pain. Mary Ann fell back a step, as though she had been struck in the face. He had never seen her so stricken, so vulnerable to the pain that swept across her soul.

But Benjamin wasn't satisfied with Oliver's answer. "Was he there? On the day the mob destroyed the press? Was he part of that?"

Oliver hesitated, then finally nodded slowly. "Yes."

Benjamin nodded, his jaw tight, his lips pressed into a hard line. Blindly, Mary Ann turned and stumbled away.

———————————

Lydia whirled around, fighting to keep her voice under control. "Why you, Nathan?"

He threw up his hands. "Because Jessica is our family, like it or not."

"Your father said he was going to send money. What else can you do?"

"I can make sure she's safe, that she has a home."

Lydia had a hairbrush in her hand. She had been brushing her hair when Nathan had returned from the council meeting held at the Whitney store and announced that Joseph was going to send a delegation to Zion to investigate the situation. When he told her he planned to volunteer himself, she exploded. Now she slammed the brush down on the chest of drawers with a sharp crack. "Oliver said that Jessica was safe."

"She was when he left. We don't know what's happening

there now." Nathan walked over to her. He reached out to take her into his arms. "Lydia, let's not fight about this."

She jerked away angrily. "Don't, Nathan!"

He stepped back, hurt. "Lydia, I don't understand you. If that were you there in Jessica's place, would you want—"

"No!" she cried, flinging the words at him. "Don't try to make me feel guilty. You know I care about what happens to Jessica and little Rachel. But you don't have to be the one who rushes off to save them. Not you, Nathan."

He threw up his hands. "I don't believe this." He blew out a quick breath of frustration. "I just don't understand you anymore, Lydia."

"Well, that's obvious enough," she snapped.

He was stung. "What more do you want from me?" he burst out. "Nothing I do anymore seems quite good enough for you."

"I want you home!" she cried. "I don't want you to leave me again. I don't want you in Missouri." She spun around, not wanting him to see the tears.

For a moment he stood there, wanting to hold her, not daring to. His hands came up, then dropped again.

She finally turned around, brushing at the corners of her eyes. "I need you here, Nathan," she whispered, "as much as Jessica needs you there."

He reached out again for her, and this time she came into his arms. "I don't want to have another baby without you," she said, choking back a sob. "Is that too much to ask?"

"But Lydia," he said, speaking carefully, "you're not due till early March. I'll be back in a month."

"Will you? Back from Missouri maybe. Then where? Off on another mission to the East? Or on to Canada?" Joseph and Sidney were making plans for a mission to Upper Canada.

Nathan fought back a flash of irritation. They had had this discussion too many times before. "I have to go where the Lord calls."

She pulled away from him sharply. "The Lord has also called on the Saints to finish building his house here."

"I've been working on the temple."

She softened a little. "I know that, Nathan. So why can't you just stay here? There's work enough to do for the Lord right here in Kirtland."

He sighed, fighting a hurt of his own. This had become an ever-present barrier between them now, and it frustrated him that he could not help her see it from his perspective. He missed her fiercely when he was gone. He missed the children. But other men left. Other men preached the gospel and their wives weren't knocked off balance by it.

She looked up at him. "If Jessica had been hurt or something, then I wouldn't stop you, Nathan. You know that. But she's all right. And I need you, Nathan. Please don't leave me."

For a long moment he just held her. Then finally he nodded slowly, staring out of the window. "All right. I won't say anything to Joseph."

On the twenty-first day of August, 1833, a council of priesthood holders met in Kirtland and determined to send Orson Hyde and John Gould as special messengers to Zion. Upon their arrival they instructed the Saints not to dispose of their property or move from the county unless they had specifically signed an agreement to do so.

Not all Missourians agreed with the depredations going on. In August a Missouri newspaper ran a series of articles censuring the mob and encouraging the Saints to seek civil protection and redress from the state authorities. Heartened by this nominal support, the Saints spent much of September documenting the outrages committed against them and denying the charges of the old settlers. In early October, a petition having been drafted, Orson Hyde and W. W. Phelps journeyed to Jefferson City to present it to Governor Daniel Dunklin.

The petition asked for three things. The Saints wanted the state to raise troops to defend their rights. They sought the right to sue in the courts for damaged and lost property. And they asked that the mobbers be brought to justice. Governor Dunklin consulted with his attorney general for several days, then received the Mormons once again. He was not unsympathetic to their plight, he said. He abhorred the acts of the lawless elements in Jackson County, but he felt that force was not necessary to see justice done. He advised the delegates to seek redress through the local courts and law officers. If this failed, he promised to use other means to solve the problem.

The brethren went home greatly discouraged. Appeal to the local judiciary and legal officers? How bitter the irony. The signatures on the "secret constitution" that demanded the removal of the Saints from Jackson County included, among others, those of Samuel Lucas, judge of Jackson County; Samuel Owens, county clerk; Russell Hicks, deputy county clerk; John Smith, justice of the peace; Samuel Weston, justice of the peace; William Brown, constable; and Thomas Pitcher, deputy constable. And all of these were secretly assisted by none other than the lieutenant governor of the state himself, Lilburn W. Boggs. In a word, the very men who had pledged their lives and their honor to the task of driving the Saints from the county were now to be petitioned for redress? When they tried to convince Dunklin of that, their accusations fell on deaf ears.

Perhaps their journey to Jefferson City had been in vain, but with the return of the delegation an important corner was turned. The Saints had followed the admonitions of the Savior. They had turned the other cheek and submitted meekly to injustice. They had gone the second mile, and gone it again. "Now," they said, "we cannot patiently bear these wrongs any longer; according to the laws of God and man, we have borne enough." Members were counseled to arm themselves and protect their women and children, even with force if necessary. A group of brethren went north into Clay County and purchased powder and lead.

On October twentieth, three months to the day after the destruction of the *Evening and Morning Star*, the Church leaders formally declared their intentions to defend themselves against any more physical violence. They would not be the aggressor in any case, but the Missourians were given fair warning. The Saints were no longer to be idle spectators to their own demise.

With that declaration, the die was cast, fate was set and locked. The final confrontation between saint and settler in Jackson County was about to begin.

It was October thirty-first, 1833. On the morrow it would be what some Christians called "All Saints' Day." In ancient Europe, on that day, a special mass, called "Allhallowmas," was said. The night before the mass came to be called "All Hallows' Eve," or more commonly, "Halloween." An ancient Celtic festival that was also held on October thirty-first came to have an influence on the Christian celebration of All Hallows' Eve. While many of the Celtic customs were left behind by the religious immigrants who came to America, some survived. One of the most common was the pulling of pranks and the working of mischief on Halloween night. The Celtic peoples believed that the souls of the dead were allowed to return to their homes for only one evening a year—Halloween—and when forced to return to their graves, would vent their frustration by tipping over gravestones, soaping windows, pulling down outhouses, and so forth.

Though Joshua Steed knew nothing of the origin of Halloween or why behavior that was normally forbidden was winked at on this night, as he reined his horse to a halt along the edge of the tree line he couldn't help but chuckle at the irony. They were no longer boys, these forty or so men who rode with him and Colonel Pitcher, but they were about to do a little mischief of their own tonight.

The night was still and clear, cold and already frosting. There was a quarter moon but the night was quite dark, and he heard men curse and swear as they bumped into one another or got slapped across the face with low-hanging tree branches.

"Quiet!" Pitcher hissed. "You'll have every Mormon in the settlement awake and waiting for us."

Gradually the men quieted down. Beneath him, Joshua's horse was dancing a little, sensing the tension in the humans around him. Joshua leaned down and patted his neck. "Steady, boy."

"All right, Steed, where do we go?"

Joshua had specifically chosen to ride with Pitcher, because although Pitcher was only deputy constable of Jackson County, Joshua found him to be much more decisive and prone to action than Constable Brown. And it was action that Joshua was looking for this night. He wasn't interested in a night of hard riding and a lot of bluster.

He prodded his horse forward a little, pointing. In the pale moonlight thin streams of smoke could be seen coming from several chimneys. Four or five dim lights glowed, outlining the windows of those cabins in which there were people still awake; but other than that, the cabins were not visible in the darker shadows of the trees that lined the Big Blue River.

"This is called the Whitmer settlement," Joshua said to Pitcher. "The cabins are mostly on the edge of the trees that line the river. The ferry is to the left, there where the trees are thinnest."

Pitcher half turned in his saddle. "All right, men," he said, "you all know that the Mormons have been told to resist, to fight back." He grinned, a look of pure enjoyment crossing his face. "That's what they've been told. Do you think they've got the stomach to actually do it?"

There were soft cries and a bark of raucous laughter.

"Do *you* have the stomach for it?"

"Yeah!" It came out as one cry.

"Then, let's go!" Pitcher lifted the reins and put the spurs to his horse.

"Hee yaw!" Joshua yelled. He jerked forward, laying his face next to the horse's mane, giving it its head. Behind him the men erupted. There were screams and yells, shouts, cursings, oaths, and a pistol shot or two as they thundered across the meadows and up to the little cluster of cabins. Pitcher pulled his horse up hard and Joshua nearly ran him down.

"Fan out!" Pitcher yelled.

Joshua leaped off his horse even before it came to a halt, and hit the ground running. "Get the menfolk!" he shouted. "Don't let any of them escape."

Without waiting to see if he was obeyed, he pulled out his pistol, darted up to the door of one of the cabins, and threw his shoulder against it. It was made of wood slabs, loosely nailed and lashed together with strips of rawhide. It shattered inward, spewing wood everywhere. There was a woman's terrified scream and sounds of frantic scrambling. By the light of a dying fire, he saw a woman in a white nightshirt and cap sitting up in bed, clutching the blankets around her. The whites of her eyes were like two small lamps against the surrounding darkness.

"Mama! Mama!" A three- or four-year-old girl came stumbling out from behind a blanket used as a room divider. At the sight of Joshua, she screamed and burst into tears.

In an instant the woman was out of the bed and clutching the child to her. Joshua looked around quickly. "Where's your husband?" he demanded.

"I . . . I don't know. He ran." But her eyes darted momentarily to where a large, hand-hewn log table sat in the corner. In two steps Joshua was there, the muzzle of the pistol pointing beneath it. "Out!" he barked.

For a moment there was silence, then a scuffling sound. Joshua stepped back and let the man come out. When he stood, Joshua jerked him around so the firelight would catch his face. He nodded in satisfaction. "Why, Mr. Whitmer," he said, "how good of you to join us."

They found eight men all told. The rest had scattered into the night, and no amount of threatening could make the frantic women tell where their husbands had gone. Now the men stood before the mob. Standing there in their nightshirts, barefooted and with their hair disheveled, they looked small and ridiculously vulnerable.

Pitcher was gleeful as he marched back and forth in front of them. He turned to his men, who formed a half circle around their captives. "Do these look like the men who promised to fight for their women and children?"

There was a roar of laughter and cries of derision.

Joshua stepped forward. "Do you know who these men are?" he shouted.

"They're Mormons," one man yelled back, "that's good enough for me."

"They're more than that," Joshua said, turning to let his eyes sweep along the line. "Some of these men are Whitmers."

Now the men of the mob seemed a little puzzled. What did they care who they were?

But Joshua cared. "The Whitmers are close friends of Joe Smith. The Whitmers helped Joe Smith with the Book of Mormon." He stepped to the last man in the line. "Take this man here, for example." He reached out with his riding crop and lifted the man's head. "This here is Hiram Page. He married a Whitmer girl. Mr. Page is one of them that claims he saw an angel, the same angel that Joe Smith said he saw."

"No," Page said, "I saw the plates, but I never said I saw—"

But he never got a chance to finish. Suddenly the Reverend Mr. Pixley, a man sent out west to Christianize the savages who inhabited Indian Territory, leaped forward. "Blasphemy!" he cried in horror. "Blasphemy!" He hurled himself at Hiram Page, slashing across Page's cheek the short stick he carried.

It was like a signal to the pack. The men swarmed over their captives, screaming, shouting, kicking, jabbing. Whips and clubs flashed in the pale moonlight. Joshua stepped back to stand beside Pitcher, a little shocked by the fury that he was witnessing.

Pitcher leaned over slightly. "You were right about Pixley," he said.

Joshua nodded. The deputy constable had objected to having the good reverend ride with them, but Joshua had persuaded him otherwise. Not that Joshua had found religion. He had little more respect for these men than he did for the Mormons, but war made for strange bedfellows. Pixley and the Reverend Finis Ewing of the Cumberland Presbyterian church had been in the forefront of the opposition to the Mormons. Joshua knew that Pixley would not blanch when it came to violence, and sensed that he might be an important influence in prodding the men to action. Besides, Joshua had told Pitcher with a chuckle, the preachers lent a certain air of respectability to the whole affair.

With their fury finally spent, the men stepped back, chests heaving, the madness slowly dying in their eyes. The Mormons were all down now. Some lay still, moaning softly. Others writhed in agony. Blood poured from several noses, and one man had an ugly two-inch gash over his eye. Hiram Page lay crumpled in a heap, his face deathly pale. He had been whipped savagely.

At that moment, from behind them, there was the sound of a gunshot. Joshua and Pitcher whirled around. It had come from a cabin down near the edge of the settlement. They broke into a run, the men falling in behind them. As they came pounding up to the cabin, two men came out, one jamming a pistol back into the belt of his trousers. Through the open door, Joshua could see a woman kneeling at the side of a man in a low bed, sobbing hysterically. As she swayed back and forth, Joshua saw that the man's head was covered with blood, as was the front of the woman's nightdress where she had held him to her.

"What happened here?" Pitcher demanded.

The man with a pistol, a farmer who lived south of Independence, swung around and glared belligerently back into the cabin. "We told him to get up and come out, but he wouldn't."

The woman whirled around. "My husband is very ill," she sobbed. "He can't get up."

The other man laughed, a little nervously. "In bed or out—if you're gonna get a beating, I guess it doesn't make a lot of difference where."

"We heard a shot," Joshua said. His eyes kept being drawn to the sight of the man's head.

"I told him to get out of that bed or we'd blow his brains out," the man with the pistol growled. "He didn't, so I shot him."

"Don't look like you killed him," the Reverend Mr. Pixley

said. And with that the men quickly lost interest. Pitcher turned and started back toward the horses. The men followed him.

For a moment Joshua stood there, listening to the shuddering sobs from the woman. Finally, he stepped inside the cabin. "Get back," he commanded.

Frightened, the woman moved away from her husband. "Don't hurt him!" she cried. "Don't hurt him."

Joshua bent over, peering at the man's head. He grimaced, then felt his jaw relax. The man with the pistol had been standing just a few feet away, but fortunately he was a lousy shot. The ball had grazed the top of the sick man's skull, taking the hair and the flesh with it, but it had not pierced the bone.

Straightening, Joshua was surprised by the intensity of his relief. His hatred for the Mormons and his desire for vengeance burned as hot as anyone's, but he stopped short of murdering a sick man in his bed while his wife watched.

He turned and strode to the door. "It's just a flesh wound," he said gruffly. "He'll be all right." He plunged out of the door and into the night.

As he headed back toward the main body of men, he stopped. Pitcher had his horse backed up to Hiram Page's cabin. A rope snaked upward to the topmost pole that formed the roof. The horse strained as the rope tightened and the animal took the full load, hooves clawing for a grip on the frozen ground. There was a tortured screeching sound, then an explosive crash. Even in the darkness Joshua saw the clouds of dust billowing upward. When the other men saw Pitcher's success, they darted to their own horses, whooping their approval.

Joshua nodded in satisfaction. Now, this was more like it. Let the Mormons dig out their furniture and personal belongings from that mess and maybe they'd start getting the message.

Ten minutes later, as they reached the same spot where they had stopped earlier, Joshua turned back to look. There were no lights now, and he could not make out any of the cabins in the darkness. But he knew there were ten or twelve of them unroofed, and at least eight men who were likely to be wiser and more amenable to counsel. He smiled faintly toward the darkness. It was not a bad night's work for this Halloween.

———————

In spite of the noise that filled the room, Rachel had finally fallen asleep in the corner along with three other of the smaller children. Jessica watched her for a moment, her eyes warm with love. The last four nights had been hardest on the children, and it was good to finally have them feel secure enough to sleep soundly.

The night after the Halloween raid against the Whitmer settlement, the leaders of the Church counseled the members living in isolated homesteads to come to where there were greater concentrations of members. In Kaw Township the main settlement was the Colesville Branch. Though the Joshua Lewis family lived no more than a mile from there, Brother Lewis still decided to heed the call. They moved to the settlement that next afternoon, taking Jessica and Rachel with them. Though circumstances were challenging—three or four families in one- or two-room cabins—Jessica did not regret their decision. The previous night they had stood outside and watched the night sky lit up with the eerie glow from burning haystacks and barns. One of the fires came from the Lewis homestead.

She turned away from Rachel as Parley P. Pratt raised his hands. "All right," he called, "let's have a little order here."

As the group gradually quieted, Jessica looked on this gentle and humorous man with admiration and respect. Over the past two years she had watched "Brother Parley" cheerfully bear sickness and hardship, walk barefoot six miles to teach the School of the Prophets in Zion, preach sermons that made her cry, and tell stories that left her sides aching with laughter.

As Parley waited for the crowd to quiet, one hand absently stole to his forehead and rubbed gingerly at the ugly red scab that was there. That was yet another thing which added to Jessica's immense respect for this man. Three nights before, the guards posted to watch the settlement had discovered two armed Missourians. A fight erupted, and when Parley, who was unarmed, stepped forward to help, one of the Missourians whipped out his pistol and struck Parley a savage blow to the head. Parley staggered back, blood streaming down his face, as the other men angrily seized the mobber and pinned his arms. The next morning, at Parley's urging, the two men had been given back their guns and released without harm.

Finally, as Parley now called for order again, the group quieted. Newel Knight, who was the branch president for the settlement, stood next to Brother Parley. "Brothers and sisters," he said, "we have some news, but there is still no report from our brethren who went to aid the Whitmer settlement."

There were murmurs of disappointment, and instantly the tension in the room shot up. About midmorning, more than four hours ago now, a brother from the Whitmer settlement, which was three or four miles east of their location, had ridden in to raise an alarm. The mobbers had returned. A ferry on the Big Blue River operated by the members there had been seized and the owners driven off. Rumors were also flying that the mob was on the rampage, destroying homes and property located east of the river. Brother Knight had called for volunteers and nineteen men had left immediately. It was not hard to tell which women were wives or daughters of the volunteers, for their faces were deeply etched with concern now.

"We do have news from Independence," Brother Parley spoke up. Immediately the murmuring stopped and the room went quiet. "As you know, three nights ago in the city, the brethren drove away a mob who were in the midst of destroying the Gilbert and Whitney store. One man was captured in the very act of brickbatting the store, a man by the name of Richard McCarty."

There were some mutterings from some of the men. This was something that chafed at all of them. Sidney Gilbert and others had taken the man before the justice of the peace and asked for a warrant against him. Though McCarty had been caught in the very act of destroying the store by three or four witnesses, the justice blandly refused to act and released the man.

"Well," Parley said, grim faced and angry, "guess what happened today? Mr. McCarty went to that same justice of the peace this morning. He has obtained a warrant for the arrest of Brother Gilbert, Brother Corrill, and others. They have been placed in the county jail and will be tried this afternoon."

A gasp of shock swept through the room. "On what charges?" someone cried.

"Assault and battery, and false imprisonment." Parley shook his head in amazement. "We cannot get a warrant against a man for breaking into the store, but he can get a warrant against us for catching him at it!"

Newel Knight spoke up. "The brethren are—"

He was cut off as the door flew open and a man burst into the room. It was one of the nineteen men who had left earlier. "We're under attack!" he cried. "At the Big Blue! The mob are after our men!"

It was now nearly sundown on November fourth, the day that would come to be known as the "bloody day," and Joshua Steed was highly frustrated and in a foul mood. Early that morning, he and Colonel Pitcher had led another group of men out from Independence. They had taken the Mormon ferry at the Whitmer settlement on the Big Blue without firing a shot. All they had done was wave their pistols and the Mormons who were operating it fled.

Once the ferry was secure, they moved on to a small store run by a Missourian named Wilson, about a mile west of the river. There they stopped to rest and refresh themselves. But unbeknownst to the Missourians, marching up the road toward them were the nineteen volunteers from the Colesville settlement. Before these volunteers reached the store, however, they met some Saints who reported that while the ferry had been lost, the rumors about the rampages east of the river were false. They also told the Colesville group that the mob was at the store.

Upon hearing this news, the nineteen men decided to return home and avoid a confrontation.

Unfortunately, two small boys caught sight of the band of re-treating Mormons. They ran pell-mell to the store and reported to Colonel Pitcher that the Mormons were on the road west of them. Eager for action, the Missourians dashed for their horses. When the Mormons saw forty or fifty men thundering across the prairie towards them, they fled in every direction. That had been in the afternoon, but it provided only a temporary diversion. When Pitcher's men had seen the Mormons scatter, they had gone after them with relish, driving their horses back and forth through the cornfields, hoping to flush them out. When that failed, they began to break into the houses of the nearby Mormons, terrorizing the women and children. That had been going on now for more than two hours.

Disgusted and tired of it all, Joshua walked to his horse and swung up into the saddle. He walked it over to where Pitcher was talking with several of the men. The deputy constable looked up. "What do you think, Steed?"

"I think I'm going back to Independence and getting a beer."

Some of the men chuckled, nodding. One stood up. "That'll be the first good thing to happen today. I'm goin' too."

"I guess you're right," Pitcher said in disgust. "There ain't nothin' goin' on—"

A cry from off to their right brought them all around sharply. A man was gaping, his arm pointing toward the west. "It's the Mormons!" he shouted.

Joshua stood up in the stirrups, peering into the low-lying sun. He felt a leap of exultation. Sure enough, there was a whole body of men—thirty for sure, maybe more. They were coming toward them; the sun was at their backs, and Joshua could see several rifles silhouetted against the horizon. The Mormons had come to fight!

"To arms! To arms!" Pitcher was shouting. Joshua dug his heels into the horse's flanks and sent it leaping forward. All around him pandemonium erupted. Men were scrambling for their weapons, shouting and yelling. Some, he noted in disgust, ran for cover.

As Joshua pounded past the few men standing amidst the dried, brown cornstalks, he yelled at them. "Form a line! Form a line!"

"Fire, fire!" Pitcher was screaming. He had one foot in the stirrup of his saddle, but his horse was frightened and the colonel had to keep hopping on one foot to keep his balance as the horse kept skittering around in a circle. Off to Joshua's left, someone fired a rifle. The explosion sounded muffled and distant as it rumbled across the open fields.

"Hold your fire!" Joshua screamed, racing toward the men nearest the road. "Let 'em get closer."

But panic was the commander now, and no one gave Joshua heed. He saw a man throw his rifle to his shoulder and fire. One of the Mormons in the lead file jerked backwards, slamming into one of his companions, then crumpled to the ground. A cry of triumph went up from the Missourians.

They were firing wildly now as Joshua joined them. He saw a flash across the fields, followed instantly by a puff of smoke. The Mormons were firing back.

"Take your aim!" he screamed at the men. "Make your shots count." Joshua pulled out his own pistol but didn't fire. They were in good rifle range now, but a pistol was still useless.

He reined his horse around to see if Pitcher and some others were mounted yet. A good charge would send the whole lot of them scattering. But just as his eye found the colonel, his horse stumbled and Joshua went flying. Instinctively he rolled as he hit, trying to hold his pistol away from him. For a moment he lay there, dazed, shaking his head, letting his mind register that there was no serious pain. He swung around. His horse lay flat, one hind leg kicking weakly in its death rattle. It had taken a ball just below its left eye, and the ball had gone straight into the brain.

Joshua leaped up, a rage seizing him. He had bought that horse from a breeder in Kentucky and brought him all the way out to Independence. He fired at the men, now no more than fifty yards away, then fired again. The Mormons had spread out now and formed a skirmish line. Flashes of rifle fire were coming fast now. He instinctively ducked as he felt a ball whistle over his head.

Just behind him there was a sharp cry, and Joshua whirled around in time to see a man five or ten yards from him drop his rifle and clutch at his stomach. He had a shocked look on his face as he slowly sank to his knees, then pitched forward on his face without a sound. The man next to him stopped, gaping in horror.

Now things were happening so fast that it was impossible to follow them. An inhuman shriek rent the air, and Joshua knew that another horse had been hit. Somewhere behind him, he heard Pitcher screaming, though whether to attack or retreat he could not tell. Men were cursing and yelling. Clouds of smoke from the gunpowder hung like little puffs of cumulus in the still air, swirling wildly when men ran through them, otherwise just slowly dissipating.

Directly in front of Joshua a man was running towards the Mormons, firing blindly as he ran. Then, as though he had been hit at knee level with some giant scythe, he went down, sending up little clouds of dust as he hit the dry soil. For a moment there was a violent twitching, then he lay still.

"Oh no," someone screamed hysterically. "Hugh's down."

"We can't hold 'em!" another cried. "Run! Run!"

"No!" Joshua tried to scream the word, but it came out as a hoarse cry, barely more than a croak. But it wouldn't have mattered either way. The man who yelled had already done the damage. Everywhere he looked, men turned and ran. There was no attempt to stay low, no attempt to dodge back and forth. They ran blindly to their horses with no thought but escape. It was not a retreat, it was a rout, and Joshua stood there shaking with rage as he watched the battle evaporate before his eyes.

He swung around, suddenly realizing he was vulnerable, un-horsed and standing straight up in the open as he was. But the

Mormons, seeing their opposition in flight, had also had enough. They too were moving backwards, more cautiously, but nevertheless eager for disengagement. The sound of gunfire had ceased.

Joshua watched the retreating Mormons until they were well out of rifle range, then he put his pistol away, trying to ignore the keenness of his disappointment. Slowly he walked to the body of the first man who had fallen. He knelt down and felt at his neck for a pulse, then stood slowly. The man was dead. He walked to the second man, the one whose fall had been the turning point for the Missourians. He knelt down beside him and turned him over. He didn't even check for a heartbeat. The bullet had caught the man squarely in the left side of his chest.

Joshua straightened slowly. The irony was not lost on him. This man's name was Hugh L. Brazeale. That very morning, after they had taken the ferry, Brazeale had been one of the most vocal in the spate of braggadocio that followed. "Give me ten fellows," he boasted, "and I will wade to my knees in blood and drive the Mormons from Jackson County."

Joshua turned his head and watched the last of his men whipping their horses at full flight for the line of trees along the river. "There's your ten men, Hugh," he said bitterly. "Go get 'em."

———◆———

Jessica Steed pulled back the curtain and tiptoed quietly into the sleeping area that the curtain separated from the main room of the cabin. It was about half an hour before sunset on November fifth, and the late autumn sunlight streamed through the shuttered windows in narrow shafts. She stopped, her eyes softening. Sister Dibble sat beside the still form of her husband, Philo Dibble, who was stretched out on the one bed in that corner of the room. Her head had dropped to her chest and she was breathing heavily, still clinging to her husband's hand.

Thankful Pratt, wife of Parley, was standing near the window, gazing at nothing. She sensed Jessica's presence and turned around, quickly lifting a finger to her lips. Jessica motioned to her and Thankful tiptoed quietly across to her. They both moved out of the sleeping area, letting the curtain drop again.

"Did you find any medicine?" Thankful asked.

Jessica held up her hand. She had a wad of clean rags. "No, I found some more bandages, though, and Sister Anderson and Sister Lewis are checking some of the other families for medicine."

Thankful had spent most of the previous night and all this day helping Sister Dibble and attending to Philo's needs. She looked as if she could easily fall asleep even as she stood there.

Jessica closed her eyes for a moment. "By the way, I didn't get a chance to tell you earlier. Brother Barber died early this morning."

"Oh no!" Tears sprang to Thankful's eyes.

"Yes," Jessica said, fighting her own emotions. "He was such a fine young man."

When the Missourians opened fire on the approaching Mormons at what would come to be called "the battle of the Big Blue River," Andrew Barber and Philo Dibble had both been hit almost instantly.

Jessica reached out and took Thankful's hand. "The brethren wanted to administer to him, but he wouldn't let them."

Parley's wife looked up in surprise. "Why not?"

"He said—" Jessica's voice caught and she had to swallow quickly. "He said there were angels in the room waiting to take him home." She managed a smile through her tears. "He was a little put out with us that we couldn't see them too." Jessica had spent the better part of the day with the Barbers, helping to comfort them, assisting in preparing the body for burial. It had been emotionally draining. Only when that was done had she and two other sisters come to see if they could help at the Dibbles'.

Thankful had a faraway look in her eyes. "He is the first martyr killed in battle defending the kingdom in this dispensation."

Jessica's eyes widened a little. She had not considered it in that light before.

There was a noise behind them, and they turned to see that

Sister Dibble was standing at the curtain. "Will my husband be the second?" she cried in an anguished whisper.

Jessica and Thankful rushed to her side. "No," Thankful said fiercely, "no, you mustn't lose faith."

"But you heard what the doctor told us," she said, fighting to stop her voice from becoming a wail of despair. "He said Philo was a dead man."

Philo had taken a ball and two pieces of buckshot squarely in the abdomen. Amazingly he had grabbed his rifle and powder horn and walked away, in spite of the excruciating pain. He had finally found his wife and children in a cabin not far from the Whitmer settlement. Since the mob was threatening to kill anyone who aided the Mormon militia members, they had tried to hide him, but he was in such agony that they were able to take him no more than a short distance to another cabin. As the night passed and the day wore on, his condition worsened.

When Jessica arrived, both Sister Dibble and Sister Pratt were nearing exhaustion. She and the two sisters who came with her set about cleaning the cabin, cooking a meager meal. Then the doctor had come. Jessica went in to watch. She had gasped when the doctor pulled down the blanket and revealed Philo Dibble's horribly distended stomach. There was little question but what he was steadily bleeding to death internally, for his abdomen had swollen to the size of a bread basket. His face was mottled and his breathing shallow and labored. Grimly, the physician had finally stepped back and made his terrible pronouncement: Philo's death was certain. Brother Dibble, still conscious at that point, writhing back and forth in agony, had heard the diagnosis. It was as if he had accepted the inevitability of the verdict and surrendered to his fate. The writhing had stopped, and in moments he lay deathly still, his face a ghastly gray against the pillow.

That's when Jessica and two of the other sisters had gone to the house of David Whitmer looking for medicine, leaving Thankful to stand watch with Philo's grieving wife. Now Jessica reached out and took both of Sister Dibble's hands. "I told

Brother Whitmer what the doctor said. He said to tell you that Philo shall not die. That he should live."

For a moment Sister Dibble brightened, but almost instantly her face twisted again. "How can he?" she moaned. "He is nearly dead now."

There was a sound on the doorstep, and all three women turned as the door to the cabin opened. In burst one of the sisters who had gone with Jessica. She quickly stepped aside, opening the door wider. "Look," she said. "Brother Knight has come."

Newel Knight stepped into the room and immediately crossed to Sister Dibble. "I have come to help," he said quietly. "With your permission I would like to give your husband a blessing by the hand of the priesthood."

Her voice broke and she choked back a sob. "Oh, yes, please."

Jessica stepped to the curtain and held it back, and the five of them entered the small area where Philo Dibble lay. Newel Knight spoke not another word, but he moved to the bed and sat down carefully beside Brother Dibble. There was a soft moan, then nothing more. Newel glanced at the women for a moment, then reached out and laid his hand on Philo Dibble's head. Again he said nothing, just sat there in great solemnity, his eyes half-closed, his hand resting gently on the wounded man's forehead.

Suddenly, Philo Dibble's eyes fluttered open. He stared at the ceiling, seeing nothing, but his chest started to heave up and down, his stomach distending and extending with it. His wife was so startled, she just gaped at him in shock.

"The chamber pot!" Newel Knight cried, jumping up. "Get him the chamber pot."

Jessica leaped to the bed, reached under it, and grabbed the unused chamber pot. As she pulled it up, Philo groaned and rolled over on his side, grabbing at his stomach. His wife snatched the pot from Jessica and jammed it in front of him just as a violent spasm shook his body. There was a gagging sound, then he vomited, and vomited again. Time after time his body convulsed and expelled great quantities of a dark and bloody liquid.

Jessica was dumbfounded. The chamber pot could hold several quarts, and by the time Philo collapsed back on his bed, his body finally at peace, the pot was better than half full. Beneath the blanket, his stomach was flat again. Jessica stared at him in amazement. His face was still very pale, but even as she watched the grayness was swiftly taking on color.

Thankful took the pot from Sister Dibble, who was gazing at her husband in wonder. He smiled weakly and reached out for her hand. With a sob of joy, she threw her arms around him, burying her head against his chest.

He touched her hair, then turned to face Brother Knight. "When you laid your hands on me?" he said. He stopped for breath. "I felt . . ." Now his eyes filled with tears and he could not finish.

Newel took his other hand. "What, Brother Philo?"

"I don't know how to explain it. It was like fire, only not terrible. It was wonderful. I could feel it flowing all through me, purifying every part of me. It was like I was being purged of the corruption that filled my body."

Newel nodded soberly as Sister Dibble straightened. "Your mission on earth is not yet completed, Brother Philo," he said. "The Lord has chosen to spare you so you can fulfill your mission in life."

Philo Dibble considered that for a moment; then, turning to his wife, he managed a wan smile. He merely nodded as he clasped her hand to his breast.

While the Colesville settlement spent the night of November fourth watching over their wounded and their dying, the news of the battle of the Big Blue spread through Jackson County like a prairie fire fanned by high winds. And with each telling the story grew more horrible. Two Missourians had been killed, but by morning, in the telling that number had swelled to more than a dozen. The Wilson store, only a temporary stopping place for Pitcher's men and totally untouched by the action, now figured into the expanded accounts. The Mormons had attacked it. Wilson's young son had been shot down in cold blood.

In reality, the Mormons had returned to their homes to mourn their loss; in rumor, they had ridden into Indian Territory and persuaded a massive war party to join them. They were on their way to put Independence under siege.

By ten o'clock on the morning of November fifth, Independence was at a fever pitch. Armed men from every part of the county poured into town, looking for whiskey, trouble, and Mormons. A hasty war council was called. Lieutenant Governor Boggs decided this was a perfect opportunity. He formally called out a unit of the Missouri militia to "preserve the peace." "Formally called out" in reality meant that he deputized the armed crowd who flooded the town. Colonel Thomas Pitcher, deputy constable of Jackson County, was named militia commander.

From mob to militia, from lawlessness to legitimacy, in one stroke Boggs had turned the citizens of Jackson County into the law. The Saints were outmanned, outgunned, and outmaneuvered. Pitcher demanded that the Saints surrender their weapons. They agreed on the condition that the militia do the same. Pitcher cheerfully accepted and pledged his honor, along with that of Lieutenant Governor Boggs, that the Saints would be left unmolested and given ten days to leave the county. The Saints gave up what few weapons they had in trade for peace.

It was a brilliant move on Pitcher's part, a coup of the highest order. He had no intention of disarming his own followers, didn't even so much as make a show of doing so. Within hours of the "treaty" he unleashed his men on the countryside with orders to drive the Mormons from the county. Disarmed now, the Mormons were powerless to stop them.

"Listen!"

All heads in the room, women's and children's, instantly jerked around. Conversation, already hushed and filled with tension, was cut off as sharply as though severed with a knife.

"There's a rider outside!"

Sister Lewis gripped Jessica's arm, her fingernails digging into the flesh. It had been Newel Knight's wife who cried out. She was nearest the door, dressing a small child for bed. Now every head was half-tipped, listening intently. Earlier a sleet storm had raced across western Missouri, leaving the ground covered with a thin sheet of slush. But the sky had cleared and the slush had frozen into ice that covered everything. It was impossible for anything to move across the prairie without a sharp crackling sound. And there was no mistaking it now—a horse was walking slowly outside, each step echoing sharply in the stillness of the night.

"Blow out the candle!" Jessica hissed as she sprang to her feet. Jeremy Lewis, just turned twelve, leaped across the room and blew sharply. Instantly the room was plunged into darkness, and several of the children started to whimper.

"Hush, children!" Sister Knight hissed.

Jessica reached out in the darkness toward the bed. "Rachel?" She felt a little hand come up from the bed. "Mama's right here. You stay with Martha. I'll be right back."

In a moment she stumbled across the room to the window, barking her shin on a footstool near the table. Jessica pressed her face to the glass, aware of the sounds in the cabin—mothers shushing their children, trying to calm them, ready to throw their hands over their mouths if it became necessary. Outside, the moon shone, but clouds were scudding across the sky, and the landscape was, for now, in dark shadow. Her field of vision was too restricted to see much, and for a moment she could make out nothing. Then she jumped as a large, dark object crossed her view. It stopped, about thirty feet from the cabin. It was a man on a horse.

She swung around. "Shhh!" she urged. "There *is* someone out there."

There were soft gasps, and a choked sob from one of the women. There were about six women and perhaps eighteen or twenty children crowded in the little cabin. The scene was the same in half a dozen other cabins in the Colesville settlement. Earlier that afternoon, all able-bodied men—all but three old men, too frail to be of assistance—had left the village in search of wagons and carriages sufficient to move their families and belongings from the county. The women had banded together in small groups, no one wanting to be alone once darkness came. Now they waited anxiously for their men to return.

"Jessica!"

The faint cry spun her back around and she stared at the shuttered window.

"Jessica Roundy Steed."

"Who is it?" one of the sisters whispered.

Jessica straightened slowly. "It's my father."

———————

"I'm telling you, Jessica, you've got to get you and little Rachel out of here."

Jessica hugged herself against the bitter cold. She had grabbed only a shawl to wrap around her shoulders before walking out of the cabin, and had nothing more on her feet than a thin pair of moccasins. The clouds had temporarily blown away from the face of the moon, and the night was filled with a soft, silvery glow, so she could see her father's face clearly. There was no mistaking the fear she saw in his eyes.

"Joshua can't hold them back much longer," he went on when she didn't answer. "Supposedly he's in command of this company, but they're headstrong and thirsting for blood."

"What are you saying, Pa? That I can't expect Joshua to do anything to protect his own daughter and wife?"

"Former wife," he corrected without thinking.

"And former daughter?" she said bitterly.

He shook his head, unable to cope with this kind of feminine stubbornness. "Jess, I'm tellin' you that Joshua can't stop them. They nearly mutinied when he told them I was comin' in to check things out."

"How many are there?" She had never felt so bleak in her entire life.

"Close to a hundred men. All of them armed."

She wanted to grab him by the shoulders and scream, "But the Missourians promised us ten days to get our things together and leave." But she didn't. The two days following the so-called treaty had been filled with one depredation after another.

She shook her head. "Pa, there are no men here. They've all gone after wagons. There's only women and children."

"You think that will stop them!" he asked incredulously. "Their orders are to drive the Mormons from the county. All Mormons!"

"I'm a Mormon," she cried. "Is that what you want?"

He took a step forward, his face twisted with pain. "You don't have to be, Jess. Get little Rachel and come with me now, before it's too late."

"And deny all that I believe in?"

He shook his head in frustration. "No, just say you don't believe Joe Smith. That's what's got 'em all riled up. You can believe in Jesus and all that stuff if you want."

Her head came up slowly. "I can't do that, Pa." Her shoulders lifted and fell. "Tell Joshua I'm grateful that he would care enough to try."

He flung an arm outward. "Did you hear what I said?" he shouted. "These men don't care about women and children. You're in danger. You've got to get out of here. Now!"

Suddenly there was a sound behind them, off to the east. Clinton Roundy jerked around, his eyes wide. Across the prairie, from a dark mass of trees, a line of horsemen was thundering toward them in a hard run.

"Oh no!" Roundy breathed. "Here they come!" He whirled back to her. "Run, Jess, run!"

The next few minutes would ever remain a nightmarish blur of horror in Jessica's mind. She darted back toward the cabin as her father ran for his horse. Inside it was utter chaos—women screaming in terror; children shrieking and running blindly in the darkness; infants, torn from sleep, wailing and howling;

people bursting out of the cabin into the night, some with enough presence of mind to grab a coat or pull on shoes, but most bolting madly, like fawns before a charging grizzly.

She found Rachel still sitting on the bed with little Martha Lewis, both of them screaming hysterically. Someone knocked against Jessica, groping wildly in the darkness. "Martha! Martha!" It was the voice of young Jeremy Lewis.

She reached out and grabbed his arm. "Jeremy, it's me, Jessica. Martha's right here." She guided his hand and heard him sob in relief. "I've got Rachel. You get Martha."

She felt him reach out and sweep the three-year-old up in his arms. Jessica did the same with Rachel, then leaned down to yell in Jeremy's ear. "Where's your mother?"

He started to cry. "I don't know. She had baby Ellen. She told me to get Martha."

The sound of horses was deafening now, and she knew that their time was gone. "Hold on to my dress, Jeremy. Don't let go!" She leaped for the square of light that was the open door, hesitated only a moment when she thought she heard Joshua's voice, then slipped outside and started to run.

Dawn came quickly that morning. The clouds had moved east during the night and left the sky crystal clear. Once first light pierced the eastern horizon, the landscape quickly began to lighten and reveal the pitiful column strung out across more than a half mile of prairie. There were nearly a hundred and fifty women and children plodding along, heads down, spirits broken. The crying and the whimpering had long since ceased—it took energy to protest, and energy was too precious to be wasted now. Behind the column, two men slowly rode escort, one on either side. Their bullwhips were now looped around their saddle horns, and the men sat silent and low in their saddles, huddled in their warm woolen coats and scarves. But earlier those whips had cracked like pistol shots over their heads as the men herded the refugees into a line and pointed them toward the northeast and the Missouri River. That had been somewhere around nine o'clock the previous night. Now it was just past six o'clock in the morning.

Jessica swung Rachel down, grimacing as the pain in her back shot through her like fire. "Rachel, I'm sorry, you've got to walk, just for a minute, so Mama's arms can rest.".

Rachel clung to Jessica's arms, refusing to put her feet down. "No, no! Mama!"

Jessica groaned with the pain. "Just for a minute." She forced Rachel's hands from her arms and set her down, the wailing cry of her daughter as painful to her as the ache in her body.

Rachel dropped to her knees and buried her face in her hands. "Mama, no! Mama!"

Behind them, Jeremy Lewis was coming with Martha. His eyes were open, but it was as though he saw nothing. He almost bumped into them before he blinked and something registered. Without a word, he swung Martha down beside Rachel. She didn't even look up, just collapsed into a heap and started to cry softly.

Jeremy sank to his knees slowly, his arms hanging at his sides like wooden stumps. In the last nine hours this twelve-year-old had passed from boyhood to manhood. He had run out of the cabin without shoes. Sometime early in the night, Jessica had torn her shawl into two pieces and wrapped them as best she could around his feet. Now, in the light, she could see that the cloth was wet and filthy and shredded in places. The prairie grass, stiffened by the thin sheet of frozen sleet, had ripped at their feet all during the night. As she looked closer, she could see that Jeremy's ankles were a mass of scratches and cuts. The bottoms of his pant legs were dark with blood.

Jessica sat down beside him and reached out to touch his face, tears welling up in her eyes. "How are your feet?" she asked softly.

His eyes came open and he looked down. He shrugged. "I don't know," he replied with simple honesty. "I don't feel much down there right now."

She nodded, knowing exactly what he meant. Everything below the knees was a dull, fiery pain, but it had long since taken second place to the exhaustion and the pain of carrying Rachel. But her eyes dropped now to her own feet. In spite of what she expected, she gasped, shocked by what the morning light exposed. Her moccasins had long since split open, and her feet were a mass of raw, bleeding flesh.

As they sat there in the snow—Rachel now barely whimpering, Martha curled up on the icy prairie grass—they looked at each other. Jeremy's eyes were grave. Finally, he gestured with his head behind them, down the trail where they had come. Most of the prairie glistened under its covering of ice, but a broad path marked where the column had broken through as they walked along. Soon the sun would be up and melt the ice, and their trail would disappear. But there was one thing that would not disappear. Here and there, clearly seen against the light brown of the prairie sod, were spots and streaks of bright red. They would darken quickly in the cold air, but they would not go away.

Jeremy smiled sadly. "I don't think Pa and the other men will have much trouble following us," he said.

———•———

Joshua Lewis was shaking his head even before he was fully inside the makeshift home, which was part tepee, part tent, part lean-to. His hair and beard glistened with drops of water. It had been raining steadily all day and the water still came down in a dreary drizzle. His clothes were wet, and his cheeks red with the cold.

His wife looked up in alarm. "What?"

"The ferryman will not take us over unless we have the fare."

Jessica did not look up. It was exactly what she had been told, in no uncertain terms, by the same man. She had not expected anything less.

"But the Missourians are threatening to whip anyone left on this side of the river," Sister Lewis blurted out, her voice strained to the breaking point. "We can't stay here another night."

"It's fifty cents, or there'll be no crossing," Brother Lewis said flatly. He moved to the boxes that were serving as their table and chairs, and sat down heavily. He leaned forward, putting his head in his hands.

Jessica watched the two of them for a moment, her heart heavy. They had done so much for her. If she had owned one thing of earthly value, she would gladly give it to them now, but she did not. They did not. That's why they were facing a crisis with no solution in sight.

Jessica glanced over to the blanket in the corner where Rachel's dark hair shone dimly in the candlelight. The little girl's chest rose and fell in a steady rhythm, so Jessica stood up. "I'm just going to step outside for a moment. If Rachel wakes up, call me."

"It's raining," Brother Lewis mumbled, not looking up.

"I know. I'll be all right."

She moved outside gingerly, hobbling on her battered feet. The night was hushed and still, the only sound being the soft plunking of the raindrops in the myriad puddles that filled the now practically empty campground. It was very dark, and she stood still, feeling the coldness of the rain on her cheeks, letting her eyes gradually adjust to what little light there was.

It was so quiet now. The first two nights had been chaos. The straggling column of women and children from the settlement, having been driven across twenty to twenty-five miles of prairie, finally reached the river shortly after sunup. There they huddled, lost and frightened, until their men finally found them later that day. By then, the river bottoms were a teeming mass of humanity. Refugees poured in from every settlement in Jackson County. Many families had been separated in the panicked flight, and there was the constant call from men looking for wives, women searching for their husbands or children, and children with wide and forlorn eyes desperately looking for any family member. Dogs barked, oxen lowed, cattle bellowed, hogs squealed.

Some families had been fortunate enough to escape with their household goods and even managed to save their livestock and bring it with them. Others had grabbed food and tools and shelter of some kind. But many, like the Lewises, fled with nothing but what they could carry. Makeshift shelters were erected by cutting down long branches and stacking them together in tepee form, then covering them with whatever could be found. Some camped around open fires, taking whatever the weather chose to send them. The Lewises had spent the first two nights out in the open, then moved into one of the shelters vacated as the Saints were ferried across the river.

During that first night after they reached the river, in one makeshift tent a woman gave birth to a baby boy as water dripped down upon her. Exposed to the cold and damp, she lived for a short time, then died quietly. The next day the camp had stopped to watch in somber silence as another sister was carried onto the ferry, stiff and still. There had been no pitched battle with rifles firing and balls flying this time, but these two were casualties of battle as surely as had been Andrew Barber. Jessica had looked away, not able to bear her sorrow. Two more names had now been added to the roster of the martyrs.

Jessica turned and looked north. Across the river, now jet black in the darkness, she could see the faint gleam of lamp or candlelight. There were hundreds of Saints still camped along the river bottoms on the north side, waiting for an opportunity to move inland into Clay County. That was something, she thought; one bright spot in an otherwise dismal landscape. The residents of Clay County were not in sympathy with their cousins across the river, and offered some degree of hospitality to the Mormon exiles. They made it clear that they did not want the Mormons making permanent settlement there, but in the meantime they responded with true Christian charity to their plight. Empty slave huts, barns, sheds—whatever was available—were offered as shelter. Men were given work so they could earn money or food for their families. Some provisions were just given outright to the destitute Saints.

Jessica hugged herself, looking with longing across the river. There, at least, lay some semblance of peace and refuge. That was why it was so frustrating—and so frightening—to still be camped here on the south side. There were only three families—the Lewises and two others—left now, and none had the necessary fare to cross. And none of those who had crossed could help now. Their own resources were exhausted, or they knew not that others were stranded.

A sudden movement off to her left caught Jessica's eye. Someone was there. She felt a start for a moment, but then saw the dark shape and could see it was a woman. Jessica walked across the open area toward the riverbank, stepping carefully to protect her tender feet.

The figure ahead of her stopped and whirled around. Jessica called out softly. "It's Jessica Steed."

"Oh." There was tremendous relief. "Mary Elizabeth Rollins."

Jessica smiled to herself and moved over to join the girl. Mary Elizabeth Rollins and her sister, Caroline, were heroines among the Missouri Saints. Word had spread quickly of their courage on that July day when they had braved the mob to save several copies of the Book of Commandments. Since then, Jessica had gotten to know Mary Elizabeth better and had come to love her pluck and her persistently positive outlook on life.

"Evenin', Sister Steed."

"Evenin', Mary Elizabeth. What are you doing out on a dark and rainy night like this?"

"Putting out some lines for catfish."

"You're fishing? Tonight?"

"Brother Higbee suggested we might catch enough to give to the ferryman tomorrow. Maybe he'll take that as payment."

"Oh." Jessica felt bad that the thought had not occurred to her.

"If we have faith, the Lord will provide."

Jessica laughed softly. "You really believe that, don't you, Mary Elizabeth?"

"Yes'm." There was not the slightest hesitation in her voice.

"There are some who are saying the Lord has abandoned us."

Mary Elizabeth tossed something and there was a soft plop.

"I know," she said matter-of-factly. "They're some of the same ones who refused to humble themselves when Joseph told us that we in Zion would have to repent or suffer."

She walked another few feet down the riverbank, Jessica following, and looked for a proper spot. Again she leaned over, tied a line to a tree, then tossed the hook and bait out into the river. She stepped back, wiping off her hands on her dress.

Jessica had a sudden thought. "Would you mind if we prayed together? Before we go to bed?"

Mary Elizabeth nodded emphatically. "I wanted to pray anyway. We need some fish if we're goin' to get across this river tomorrow."

Jessica reached out gratefully and touched her hand. It was so refreshing to stand in the presence of such simple and direct faith. They both bowed their heads, unmindful of the rain, and Mary Elizabeth began to pray.

———————

"Sister Steed! Sister Steed! Come quick! Come quick!"

Jessica stooped down to glance out through the low opening to their shelter. Mary Elizabeth Rollins was coming on the dead run, pigtails flying, hands waving frantically.

Sister Lewis gave Jessica a questioning look, but Jessica could only shrug.

"Watch the children, Jeremy," Sister Lewis said. Then she and Jessica both ducked through the door and went outside. Brother Lewis was out chopping wood. He moved over to join them as Mary Elizabeth came running up.

"What is it?" Jessica asked.

"You've got to see this. Come on." Without waiting for a reply, she turned and hurried back in the direction from which she had come. Still puzzled, the three of them fell in behind her.

Suddenly Jessica understood. "Did you catch some fish?" she asked eagerly, catching up to the girl now.

Mary Elizabeth just smiled and shook her head. "You've got to see it."

They came to the lean-to where the Higbee family was staying. Brother Higbee was standing with a huge catfish in his hands. It was easily two feet long, and Jessica guessed it weighed close to fifteen pounds. She had never seen one quite that big.

As they came up to Brother Higbee, Jessica was awestruck. "You did it!" she said to Mary Elizabeth. "It's a miracle."

Mary Elizabeth's eyes were wide as she shook her head slowly. She stepped to Brother Higbee, who lifted the fish higher as she did so. Now Jessica could see that the fish had been slit up the gut. Brother Higbee had started to clean it. Curious, she and the Lewises stepped closer too.

Mary Elizabeth reached out and put her hand on the fish's stomach where it had been slit. "No, Sister Steed," she said triumphantly, "*this* is the miracle!" She lifted the skin.

For several seconds Jessica just gaped, not believing what her eyes were seeing. She heard a gasp behind her and realized that Sister Lewis was staring too, as dumbfounded as she was. There in the midst of the blood and entrails, lying in what had been the stomach sack, were three bright, shiny silver half-dollars. At fifty cents per family, it was exactly enough to get the Lewises, the Higbees, and the Rollinses across the river to join the rest of the Saints.

Joshua Steed looked up as Clinton Roundy entered the saloon. Roundy gave him a quick glance and motioned with his head. Joshua took a drink from his glass, then stretched. He laid down his poker hand. "Count me out of this one," he said to the others seated at the table.

Casually he got up and walked to the bar. After a moment, Roundy sidled over to join him.

"Well?" Joshua asked.

"They're gone."

"You're sure?"

"Yes. The ferryman said he took the last three families across this afternoon."

"And Jessica was with them?"

Roundy shrugged. "He said there was a single woman with a little dark-haired girl."

Joshua nodded, finally satisfied. For a long moment they stood there in silence. Then Joshua looked at Roundy, his eyes darkly bitter. "I hope I live long enough," he said softly.

"Long enough for what?" Roundy asked.

"Long enough to see every Mormon rotting in hell."

On the twenty-fourth day of February, 1834, three things took place almost simultaneously, though at the time none of those involved were aware of the other happenings.

In Missouri, Governor Dunklin finally agreed to prosecute those who had perpetrated the lawlessness against the Saints. Charges were sworn and twelve of the Church leaders living in and around Liberty in Clay County were subpoenaed as witnesses for the state and called to come to Jackson County to testify. The governor agreed to provide military protection to assure that the Saints would not be harmed. W. W. Phelps, John Corrill, Bishop Edward Partridge, and others crossed the river from Clay County under the escort of Captain David Atchison and fifty men from the "Liberty Blues." By the time the group arrived, the citizens of Jackson County, fueled by considerable stores of whiskey, were in an ugly and violent mood. Attorneys, judges, law officers—anyone associated in any way with the trial—were threatened with the direst of personal consequences if they took the Mormon side. Lacking the courage to stand up against such opposition, the court dismissed the case and ordered the witnesses and their escort to march out of town at quick time to the tune of "Yankee Doodle."

———————

Conditions in Kirtland were, at this time, not particularly wonderful either. There was much that was positive to be reported—continuing success in the missionary work, the building of the temple moving ahead, the Saints sacrificing their time and goods to help the poor and move the work forward. But the construction of the temple and taking in hundreds of newcomers had also left the Church deeply in debt. The poor continued to flock to Ohio, bringing little more than additional hungry mouths and a desperate need for immediate shelter. Opposition from the enemies of the Church was on the rise. Feelings were running so high that it became necessary to put a guard on the temple site during the night. In early January, an unknown group had fired thirteen rounds of cannon shell at the site one night. Because of threats to his life, Joseph now had appointed some of the brethren to serve as his bodyguards around the clock.

Within the Church, petty jealousies, selfishness, and general disregard for the commandments were cropping up. Some of these things were not much more than minor annoyances, but reflected a spirit not compatible with the requirements of discipleship. Joseph was arrested on a writ sworn out by a salesman who tried to get Joseph to try out a newfangled cooking stove and then convince the Saints to purchase them as well. When Joseph refused, the man used the writ as a ploy to make Joseph change his mind.

On another occasion, Joseph finally had to put a public notice in the newspaper that he could no longer accept COD mail. Postage in America was very expensive at this time—twenty-five cents for a letter, or about half a day's wage for some folks. Usually that was paid by the sender, but it was permissible to send a letter COD and have the postage paid by the receiver.

People began to flood Joseph with mail, much of it filled with the most trivial questions, some of it sharply critical of him. Of course, they sent it COD.

But there were things of much greater consequence. With increasing frequency the members fell into squabbling with one another or began to transgress the laws of the Church. One man brought charges against Bishop Newel K. Whitney because, according to him, he had been treated rudely by Bishop Whitney while in his store. Another man was charged with selling "revelations" to the members. Some bitterly criticized the Prophet for not doing enough for the poor, others because he was doing too much for them. Even Martin Harris was brought before a council for claiming that Joseph was drunk while he translated the Book of Mormon. He apologized and admitted the charges were not true and was forgiven, but this case was indicative of some of the challenges facing the Church in Ohio.

That was the climate in Kirtland when Parley P. Pratt and Lyman Wight arrived from Missouri on the twenty-second day of February. Commissioned by the leadership in Zion to go to Ohio and report on the condition of the scattered and destitute exiles, the two men had traveled eight hundred miles in the dead of winter, with virtually no money and little food. When they arrived, they were emaciated and exhausted, their clothes ragged and their boots in tatters. Joseph called for a meeting of the Kirtland high council, formed just the week previous, along with other priesthood holders to hear Parley and Lyman's report.

So it was on the afternoon of the twenty-fourth that a most somber group of priesthood brethren gathered in Joseph Smith's home and heard the full extent of the tragedy that had befallen the Saints in Missouri. It was a disturbing report they brought, and it caused much consternation among the Church leadership. What could and should be done to restore Zion and get redress for her children? When the two men had finished their report, Joseph inquired of the Lord: What is thy will concerning Zion?

In a previous revelation received in December, the Lord had

given a parable in which he compared Zion to the vineyard of a nobleman. The nobleman, the lord of the vineyard, instructed his servants to build a tower so they could be prepared for the time when the enemies came to spoil the vineyard. But the servants fell into discord and did not heed the warning of their master. While they were thus contending amongst themselves, the enemies overran the vineyard. After rebuking the servants for their slothfulness, the nobleman called on one of his servants to gather all "the strength" of his house and return to the vineyard and redeem it.

Now, on this afternoon of the twenty-fourth, a second revelation came. "Verily I say unto you, my friends," it began, "behold, I will give unto you a revelation and commandment, that you may know how to act in the discharge of your duties concerning the salvation and redemption of your brethren, who have been scattered on the land of Zion." What followed was electrifying. Joseph Smith was specifically identified as the "servant" in the parable who was to rally the strength of God's house and redeem Zion. The call was to go out to the "young men and the middle aged" of the Church and ask them to volunteer to go to Zion and support the governor of Missouri in restoring the Saints to their lands. Joseph and seven others were instructed to leave immediately and extend the call throughout the various branches of the Church in the East. If five hundred could not be found, then four hundred; if not four, then three. But in no case, the Lord said, should there be less than a hundred men go up to Zion.

When Joseph finished reading the revelation to the assembled body, he gazed at them for several moments, then said solemnly: "Governor Dunklin of Missouri has promised to reinstate the Saints if they can find a way to protect themselves once they are back. God has called upon us to lead an army of righteous priesthood holders back to Zion for that purpose. I am going to Zion to help redeem it. Are there others present who will volunteer to join me in this?"

Thirty to forty men raised their hands. One of the first hands up belonged to Nathan Steed.

———•———

The third event that unfolded that afternoon took place in a cabin out on the Isaac Morley farm. Earlier that morning, Lydia Steed had given in to Nathan's suggestion that she stay in bed and not worry about fixing breakfast. She was heavy with child now, the baby being due in less than two weeks, and had had a difficult night. He would feed himself, he promised. He would also see that little Joshua and Emily were dressed and fed before he took them to a neighbor who had volunteered to tend them so Lydia could get some rest. Then he left for town to join in the meeting at Joseph's home.

Shortly after noon, the neighbor, worried that she had not heard any word from Lydia, went to the cabin. She found Lydia collapsed on the floor just inside the door, hemorrhaging badly. Lydia reported later that she had awakened with severe stomach cramps, managed to get out of bed and pull herself to the doorway, but there fainted with the pain. As the word went out and sisters rushed to Lydia's aid, one of the brethren was sent to town to find Nathan. Unfortunately it was mistakenly reported that he was working at the temple site. So it took the messenger almost an hour to finally locate him at the Prophet's home.

By the time Nathan rushed back home, Lydia had already delivered a six-pound baby boy. He was perfectly formed in every respect, with a thin sheen of dark hair, dark eyelashes, and tiny little fingernails. But it was not enough. He never took a breath; his eyes never opened. The boy they had planned to call Nathan Morgan Steed was stillborn.

———•———

Mary Ann looked around the table with pride. It was the afternoon of the last Sabbath in April, and she had every one of her children with her. *Except for Joshua, of course*, she reminded herself. It had been so long, sometimes it seemed he wasn't part of the family anymore. Even though her children lived in the Kirtland area, this was the first time they had all been together in almost three months. Lydia's pregnancy, then near death and the loss of the baby had precluded any big family get-togethers until now, and so Mary Ann was grateful to have everyone finally gathered around her again.

The smell of roast turkey, sweet potatoes, fresh bread, and half a dozen other foods still lingered in the kitchen, but few were mindful of it. They were nearly finished with supper now, and were satiated and content. They were listening to Melissa's husband, Carl, report on how things were going at the livery stable. His father had pretty well turned the business over to him now, and Melissa watched him proudly as he talked.

Mary Ann smiled as she watched Carl and Melissa's son, little Carl, now two, working diligently to get the last of some peas onto his spoon. His eyes were grave and his mouth was pulled into a little frown of concentration. He could have done it easily if he used his other hand to hold the peas in place, but he was determined to do it with the spoon alone. Melissa and Carl lived only a few houses away from Benjamin and Mary Ann, and little Carl was a common visitor to Grandma's house. Mary Ann always loved to watch him. He was so serious, and looked so much like his mother. He had not favored his father's red hair and freckled complexion as everyone had predicted. He was Melissa from head to toe—dark hair; dark, somber eyes; the bewitching little smile when he was secretly pleased.

Finally he succeeded and the peas were captured. Triumphantly he put them in his mouth; then, when he saw that his grandmother had witnessed his success and was nodding her approval, his face split into a wide grin.

Lydia and Nathan sat beside Melissa. Lydia still looked pale and drawn, though she seemed more like her normal self today than she had since that terrible February afternoon. Young Joshua was between his parents, propped up on two pillows so he could reach the table. Lydia held baby Emily on her lap. Mary Ann felt a little pull of sadness as she glanced at her granddaughter—Emily would be two in July and was really past the age at which she would normally be called "baby Emily." But her mother continued to use the term, and no one had the heart to suggest otherwise.

There was no mistaking that Joshua and Emily were siblings, for both had inherited their mother's fine-cut features and thick, black hair. Emily, just a couple of months younger than little Carl, had large dark eyes much like her mother's, and was already such a beautiful child that whenever Lydia took her out, people invariably stopped to ooh and aah. Young Joshua, not quite three yet, had the same qualities, except that his eyes were a disarmingly light blue. He was full of fun, and mischievousness constantly danced across his face. Both children were completely and irrevocably adored by their father and grandfather.

Mary Ann turned slightly and watched her own youngest children with a special glow of affection in her eyes. Matthew, now close to fourteen, sat straight and tall next to his father. His blond hair was finally darkening, and the first hint of stubble was starting to darken his upper lip. His maturing had not lessened the striking resemblance between him and Nathan, however, and it was like looking at the past all over again whenever she watched him.

On Mary Ann's left, Rebecca was primly finishing off the last of her potatoes. *How like her*, Mary Ann thought. Though she loved to have a good time and often still romped with Matthew when they were alone, Rebecca was quite serious minded by nature and loved to have things in order. She had turned into a young woman in the last two years and was now as lovely in her own way as Melissa and Lydia were in theirs. Mary Ann had noted on more than one occasion lately that the eyes of young men turned to follow Rebecca as she passed. Two more years and she would be eighteen. Mary Ann suspected that it wouldn't be much longer than that before she lost another of her children from the home. An inexplicable sadness suddenly swept over her. Then there would only be Matthew. And then, in a few more years, she and Benjamin would be alone in the house.

The conversation had lagged and Mary Ann came back to the present. She looked over at Nathan. "Has Joseph said how many men have volunteered for Zion's Camp by now?" she asked.

Nathan shrugged. "I haven't seen Joseph for a couple of weeks."

Benjamin spoke. "As of a few days ago, he had approximately one hundred men."

"Is that all?" Mary Ann said in surprise. "What about from the branches in the East?"

"A very disappointing response. There are some who have promised to join the company soon, but so far only about a hundred total are actually committed."

"Soon!" Melissa cried. "I heard that the first wagons are to leave on Thursday. Isn't it about time they made up their minds?"

Mary Ann saw Nathan's eyes drop to his plate. He began to saw at the last of his turkey with his knife. Lydia was watching him closely, her eyes wide and filled with sorrow. Mary Ann instantly regretted bringing up the subject. It was a poor choice on her part.

But matters instantly got worse. Because Melissa's husband was not a Church member, the family often avoided talking about Church subjects in his presence, so that he wouldn't feel left out of conversations. Clearly Melissa had not told him of the situation between Nathan and Lydia, because he turned to Nathan and asked, innocently enough, "Are you going, Nathan?"

Mary Ann winced and Melissa jerked around, her eyes wide and trying to warn her husband off. Immediately after the death of Nathan and Lydia's child, Nathan had gone to Joseph and withdrawn his name from the list of volunteers. Though he never said anything about it, those close to him knew the pain that not going was causing him.

Instantly Carl sensed his mistake, but before he could speak, Nathan looked up. "No, I'm not going," he said.

Lydia's eyes were on her husband's face. "Yes, he is," she said softly at exactly the same moment.

They left Nathan's parents' home immediately and walked to the temple site. There Nathan brushed off one of the large stone blocks that had been cut and dressed for placement during the coming week. He took Lydia's elbow and guided her to it. "Let's sit down."

She nodded, sweeping her skirts around in front of her. When they were settled, he reached out and took her hands. "Look, Lydia," he began, without preamble, "this is all settled. I've talked to Joseph and he understands perfectly why I can't go with them on Zion's Camp. Until you're stronger and feeling—"

She moved quickly, putting a finger up to his lips. "No, you listen to me for a moment."

"But—"

She pressed her finger more firmly, cutting him off. "Please, Nathan. Just listen for a few moments. This will be difficult enough for me."

He finally nodded and she took her hand away. For a moment she let her eyes wander across the construction site, collecting her thoughts. Finally she took a breath and began. "You've been wonderful these past two months, Nathan. You've rarely left my side. You've been attentive to my every need and wish."

Suddenly her voice broke and she had to stop. She shook her head, angry at herself for losing control. "If you hadn't—" She took a quick breath. "If you had insisted on going to Zion at that point, I don't know what I would have done. Fallen completely apart, I guess."

She forced a short laugh. "Not that I didn't anyway."

"Lydia, what you went through was not an easy thing."

"No," she whispered, "it wasn't." For a long moment she was still, except for a slight trembling in her lower lip. Finally she looked up at him. "But it means a great deal to me that you were willing to tell Joseph that you couldn't go. That you knew how badly I needed you."

She laid her head against his shoulder and he put his arm around her. "I know this past year has been a hard one for us," she went on, choosing her words with care. "I don't know what's happening to me, Nathan. It's like things are slipping between my fingers, no matter how hard I clench my fists to try and stop them."

She began to rub his arm with her hand. "I've been a real witch. I'm sorry."

He turned to her fully now. "Lydia, you haven't been a witch. It's not just you, you know. I haven't made things any easier for you."

She smiled at him. "No, you haven't," she agreed ruefully.

Laughing, he gently poked at her shoulder. "You were supposed to disagree with me, at least a little."

Sobering again quickly, she shook her head. "But I'm stronger now, Nathan. I'm not out of it completely yet, but I'm stronger."

"Not strong enough."

Now it was she who slugged him. "Well, *thank you!*"

"I didn't mean it that way, I—"

"I know. But I am better. Really." She took a quick breath. "You need to go to Zion, Nathan. I know that. When I think of what those families are going through—Jessica and her baby, the Knights, Thankful Pratt, all the people we know and love—how can I ask you to stay here and watch over a blubbering wife who can't seem to get her life in order?"

"There are others who can go—"

She shook her head. "Right," she mocked him. "That's why the Lord asked for five hundred men and only a hundred have volunteered."

Now he looked anguished, but he said nothing.

"You have to go, Nathan," she said earnestly. "I've come to accept that. I couldn't live with myself if you don't. Will you go to the meeting Joseph has called for tonight?"

"But what will you do?" he said. "We'll be gone for two or three months. I can't just leave you alone. You still don't have all your strength back."

Lydia stood up abruptly and walked a few steps away from him. For several moments she stared at the partially raised walls in front of her, then she turned her face toward the sky. "The weather has finally turned warm now."

That unexpected turn caught Nathan off guard. "Yes, it has," he said slowly.

"That means the canals are open again."

His head snapped up.

Now Lydia turned to face him, her face eager and excited. "Nathan, what if you took me and the children to Fairport Harbor before you leave? You could see us off and make sure we had safe passage and—"

He blinked. "Safe passage?"

She came and crouched in front of him, taking his hands. Her words came in a rush, tumbling over each other in her eagerness to get them out now. "Yes. I know we don't have the money, but Father Steed would help. I know he will. The children and I could take a steamer to Buffalo, then catch one of the canal boats. We'll be all right. It's only about a week to Palmyra."

"Palmyra?" He was still stunned.

"Yes, to visit my parents. Mother has begged me to come, to bring the children so they can see them. It would occupy me while you are gone. Then I wouldn't miss you so terribly." She paused for a brief moment, looking at him intently. "Nathan, when we left Palmyra I thought I would never see my parents again. Now I have another chance with them. Joshua and Emily need to meet their other grandparents. And I could see some of my old friends."

Nathan watched her, his heart sinking. The very thought of Josiah McBride—hard, cold, unbending—made him clutch up inside. But as he looked into her eyes now, eyes that were alive—really alive—for the first time in months, and her face so filled with excitement, he knew he had no choice. How could he dash her hopes?

And there *was* the other part of it. Telling Joseph that he would not be joining Zion's Camp had been one of the hardest things Nathan had ever done. He felt as if he were betraying the Prophet and the Lord, and yet there had been no other choice but to stay; he knew if he left Lydia the damage could be—almost certainly would be—irreparable. But now if she went . . .

"Oh, please, Nathan," Lydia pleaded. "You know it's the perfect solution for both of us. You have to go to Zion. *You have to!*

I know that now. But, as I told you, I think this will help me pass the time so I don't miss you so terribly."

"I . . ." He searched her face for several moments. How he loved this woman! How he ached for her pain! He reached out and laid a hand on her cheek. "All right, Lydia. I think it's a wonderful idea."

She leaped up and grasped his hands. "Oh, thank you, Nathan. I need this. I need some time to try and find myself again."

For the moment, Nathan was content to sit back and listen to the discussion going on around him. They were gathered in the little log schoolroom, the room where meetings were often held. Final plans for the departure of Zion's Camp were under way. Joseph had led the meeting for a time, but currently, under the direction of Parley P. Pratt, the group was discussing which men would accompany the baggage wagons that were to leave four days hence. A moment ago Parley had turned to Joseph to ask a question, and as they talked, the room quickly broke up into a dozen different conversations. Nathan didn't join in. In his case the decision was already made. It would take every moment between now and the fifth of May to get Lydia and the children packed and taken to Fairport. There was no way he could be ready in four days.

So he listened idly, watching the men around him, the men who would march together on a trek of nearly two thousand miles by the time they returned. There was Wilford Woodruff, a convert of less than four months. Woodruff was one of the notable exceptions to the rather disappointing response the Eastern Saints had made to the call for volunteers. When Parley Pratt had arrived in Richland, New York, seeking funds and recruits, Woodruff immediately declared his intent to answer the call. He settled up his affairs, and he and two companions had departed for Kirtland, arriving just a few days before.

Across the aisle sat those with more familiar faces—Parley Pratt, Newel Whitney, Frederick G. Williams. Oliver Cowdery and Sidney Rigdon were there too, but they would not be going. They would stay in Kirtland to supervise the continuing work on the temple and regulate the affairs of the Church. Nathan glanced sideways out of the corner of his eye. His father was trying not to show his keen disappointment. He too would be staying, at Joseph's request, to help maintain things in Kirtland.

"I'm telling you, Brigham, if we are not willing to fight when we get there, then we may as well stay home." The voice rose above the noise in the room, and Nathan turned around to see who had spoken. It was Heber C. Kimball, and as usual he was punctuating his words with his hands. "I'm not afraid of a little fight."

Brigham Young bowed his neck a little. "You didn't listen, Heber," he said forcefully. "I didn't say we shouldn't fight, I said the Lord may come to our aid so we don't have to fight."

Nathan smiled a little. It was always an experience to watch these two converse. Brigham was slight of build and slim of waist, though he had broad shoulders. He wore his hair in a pageboy cut, brushed back away from his face, which gave him a little bit of a boyish look, even though he was four years older than the Prophet. Heber C. Kimball, on the other hand, was the son of a blacksmith, and fit the part to perfection. Though he had later become a potter, his early years had been spent learning his father's trade. He boasted that he was the only man alive whose chest measured the same front to back as it did from side to side. He was already balding and, though the same age as Brigham, looked several years older. Brigham was five feet ten inches tall, Heber six feet. Heber looked a little like a stout oak tree that had been lopped off where the foliage starts to grow.

If a person who didn't know them listened to them talking, he might be led to conclude that there was some friction between them, but just the opposite was true. One of Brigham's older sisters—Brigham was the ninth of eleven children—was stepmother to Heber's wife. In addition to being related through marriage, back in New York they had been next-door neighbors and the closest of friends. In fact, it was a measure of their closeness that they could speak their feelings with complete honesty.

Brigham and Heber's discussion had become vigorous enough now that the other men were turning around to listen. Parley Pratt had finished with Joseph. He watched for a moment, then moved over to join them. Joseph, for the moment, seemed content to listen.

Brigham's older brother Joseph Young had still not agreed to go to Missouri, and Brigham was trying to convince him to accompany them. He saw all this talk of fighting as being counterproductive to his efforts. But Heber's dander was up and he wasn't about to back down. "And what if some Missourian sticks his gun in your face and tells you to get out of town?" Heber demanded. "Are you just gonna turn around and walk away?"

Someone from the back spoke up. "I don't think we should be going if we're expecting that kind of trouble."

Parley exploded. This was not a matter of abstract theorizing for him. He had been there. "How can we redeem Zion if we back down from a confrontation? Those farms are ours. We paid for that land. And God has said we can use force if necessary to get back what is rightfully ours." He turned and appealed to the others. "Zion is part of our destiny. How can we carry out God's purposes if we don't go in there and redeem it?"

Joseph Smith now stirred from his place near the front of the room. The men quieted as he walked back and stood between the two Young brothers. He laid a hand on each of their shoulders. "Brother Brigham and Brother Joseph," he said firmly, "if you will go with me in the camp to Missouri, and keep my counsel, I promise you, in the name of the Almighty, that I will lead you there and back again, and not a hair of your heads shall be harmed."

The room fell deathly quiet now as the men sensed that the spirit of prophecy had settled on Joseph. Every eye was on him or on Joseph Young. Finally, Brigham's brother looked up, then slowly he nodded. "Then, accompany you I shall, Brother Joseph. I accept your promise as a promise from God."

"Good." The Prophet turned and surveyed the group. His face had grown very solemn now, and a little thrill shot through Nathan. This was the look Joseph took on when the Spirit of God was upon him.

"Brethren, I want to say to you, before the Lord, that you know no more concerning the destinies of the Church and kingdom than a babe upon its mother's lap."

His voice rose in power and majesty as he saw the shock register in their eyes. "You don't comprehend our destiny. It is only a little handful of priesthood you see here tonight, but this church will fill North and South America—it will fill the world. It will fill the Rocky Mountains. There will be tens of thousands of Latter-day Saints who will be gathered in the Rocky Mountains, and there they will open the door for the establishing of the gospel among the Lamanites."

Nathan turned and looked at his father. He was stunned, as were all the rest of them in the room. The Rocky Mountains! They had been talking about Zion. No one had said anything about the Rocky Mountains.

"Now," Joseph continued, his voice dropping to a more mild tone again, "I suggest we turn our attention to the business at hand and conclude this meeting. We have much to do on the morrow."

———◆———

Lydia clung to Nathan, feeling the power in his arms as he hugged her tightly. "Please be careful, Nathan."

"I will." He let her go and stepped back. "*You* be careful."

"I will."

"I've talked to the captain. Once you arrive in Buffalo, he'll see that you are taken to the dock where the canal boats come in. From there it's straight to Palmyra."

"I know. Thank you." Suddenly she started to cry. She brushed quickly at her eyes with the back of her hand.

He took her in his arms again. "Good-bye, my darling Lydia. I'll miss you."

There was a muffled cry, a choking sound. "I'm sorry, Nathan."

He pulled back in surprise. "Sorry?"

Great sobs now began to rack her body. "I wanted so much to be perfect for you. I've tried so hard."

He encircled her in his arms. "Lydia, Lydia, please. Don't say that. You're all that I've ever wanted. All that I hoped for. I love you."

She just shook her head against him, as her body shuddered convulsively over and over. He stood there, gently stroking her hair, helpless, not knowing what else to do. People on board the steamer and those passing them to go up the gangplank watched them with open curiosity.

Gradually the shaking subsided and the sobs stilled. But it was a full minute before she dared to look up. "I'll be better when you come home," she whispered. "I promise."

"Lydia, I don't—"

But the blast from the boat's steam whistle shattered the air, cutting off his words. "All aboard," a man's voice shouted. "All nonpassengers ashore."

Lydia turned. Matthew and Rebecca were hurrying along the deck of the boat, pushing through the people, young Joshua in tow behind Becca, and Emily in Matthew's arms.

Lydia went up on tiptoe and her lips brushed Nathan's cheek. "Good-bye, Nathan. I love you."

"Good-bye, Lydia. And I love you!"

She nodded, the tears welling up again, then turned and bolted up the gangplank, not looking back until she had the children safely in hand.

The boat was far out into Lake Erie, the people no longer distinguishable, when Becca finally tugged at Nathan's sleeve. "Come on, Nathan," she said. "We'd best be getting back."

———◆———

It was early morning on the fifth of May when Joseph gave the signal. They had gathered in front of the Whitney store, a huge crowd come to see the men off. The last farewells had been made, the last desperate kisses for wives and children given. Now everyone stood back. Joseph looked up and down the line of the company of about eighty-five men, nodding proudly (an advance party of about twenty had left four days earlier). He turned to the crowd. "As we, the men of Zion's Camp, prepare to depart in obedience to God's commandment, we invoke the Lord's blessings on our endeavors and on you who remain behind. May we all be kept, as the prophet Isaiah has said, in the hollow of His hand."

"Amen!" came the murmured cries from throughout the crowd. Joseph turned to Emma, took her into his arms and kissed her good-bye, then mounted his horse and turned it around to face eastward, their route taking them that direction to Chardon, then south to New Portage before turning west. He raised an arm high. "Forward!" The arm dropped.

"Ho, you team!" the wagoner shouted. There was the crack of leather and harnessing, then the lead wagon began to move, creaking and groaning under the weight of its cargo.

A ragged cheer went up. "Good-bye, Papa!" "Godspeed." "Good-bye." "Good-bye."

Handkerchiefs waved. Women turned away, wiping at their eyes. Men kept their eyes to the front, trying to look brave, trying to look untouched by their emotions.

Nathan was near the rear of the column. As he came by the store, he saw his family standing on the porch. Mary Ann's cheeks were wet, as were Melissa's. His father, face grave but steady, slowly raised his arm in a salute. Matthew did the same but could not hide the quivering of his lip and the glistening eyes.

"Good-bye," Nathan murmured. Then he turned his eyes to the front and fell into step with the man just ahead of him.

Monday, May 5th

I have determined that I shall keep a journal, and record the experiences which shall be mine on this important trek to redeem Zion. I know from my previous experience as a missionary that important things are quickly forgotten if not recorded. This will provide me an opportunity to share in some small way this Zion's Camp experience with Lydia upon my return.

We departed Kirtland at approximately 8 o'clock this morning to a fine crowd come to wish us farewell and godspeed. I am not much given to emotions, but this week has brought them close to the surface more than once. Parting with my wife and children at Fairport was almost more than I could bear. I still have deep misgivings about sending Lydia off to her parents. They seem to have relented much in their feelings toward me and the Church of late, but I cannot yet feel good about her going, though I cannot begrudge her the chance to return to her home and introduce our children to their grandparents.

The sorrow of that parting was only compounded this morning when I marched past my family, come to bid me farewell. Knowing that we go to the land where our enemies are sworn to exterminate our kind from off the earth leaves me wondering if I shall ever see my wife and children and the rest of my family again. O Lord, let it be so if it be thy will! Through thy Prophet, thou hast promised Brigham and Joseph Young a safe return. May I be worthy of the same.

Our column is a stirring sight. At the lead, we carry a white banner with the word "Peace" written thereon. Brother Joseph is finely dressed and rides a good horse. He is perhaps the best armed of any of us with good sword and a fine pair of pistols with brass barrels. He has also brought along his dog for guard duty. It is a massive bulldog which looks as though its face and the flat side of an anvil iron have met company on more than one occasion.

We made 27 miles today. Most of our feet are not up to such a walk as yet. Brother George Albert Smith (Joseph's young cousin) purchased a new pair of boots for the march and did not take time to break them in. By mid-day his feet were blistered and bleeding badly. Joseph removed his boots and gave them to George A.

We are now camped in the barn of a Mr. Ford not far from the town of Streetsborough, Ohio. Brother Brigham Young rode away upon our arrival in company with his brother, Joseph Y., to the home of a member near here, an Israel Barlow. He will seek additions to our company and perhaps food for our stores.

There is the trumpet blast—one of our number has an old French cornet—the signal for group prayer, lights out and bed. It will be welcome this night.

Tuesday, May 6

Trumpet called us awake at 4:00 a.m. for prayers. This will be our usual schedule. We marched to New Portage, about 50 miles south and west of Kirtland. Met with wagons and men who departed previously. Others continue to join us. Israel Barlow joined our camp this morning as did two other families brought by Brother Brigham.

Wed. 7th

Had difficulty getting to sleep after lights out last night. Was very tired, but could not get my thoughts off Lydia and my children. They should be in Palmyra by now. I pray all is well with them.

Spent the day under Joseph's direction organizing the camp. Leaders were appointed including as paymaster, Frederick G. Williams and commissary general, Zerubbabel Snow. With our consent, F. G. Williams collected all moneys from individuals and will disburse them from a common pot as needed.

Our number is above 130 now with 20 baggage wagons. Most are young and nearly all are Elders, Priests, Teachers or Deacons.

Joseph split us into companies of approximately twelve men each. We are to select our own officers, including two cooks, two firemen, two tent men, two watermen, one runner, two wagoners and horsemen, and one commissary. I am in the same company with Brother Brigham and HC Kimball. I rejoice in that for their faith is strong. Brother Brigham was chosen as our captain.

Spirits are still high. The day spent in organizing was good. Our feet are very thankful.

Th. May 8th

Made 12 miles today. Camped in a beautiful grove at Chippeway, Ohio.

Sunday, 11

Sabbath today. Last three days have passed without incident

save it be the tedious marching. Last night shortly after our arrival here (near Mansfield, in Richmond County) we were joined by several elders from the north part of Vermont. Joseph was much pleased to have their company. This morning, eight more came from Richland and Stark Counties. They are mostly Germans but a welcome addition to our numbers which now approach 150. A few men have brought wives and children now, something which I did not expect. We have eight or ten sisters and about that many of their children. These sisters will serve as cooks and washerwomen, but having women and children with us slows our march somewhat. This is a trek for the strongest only and we worry what will happen when we reach Missouri and may have to fight. But Joseph evidently knew all along, since these men and their families plan to stay in Missouri once this is all over.

Received the sacrament of bread and wine. Elder Sylvester Smith preached a fine sermon. He is not related to Joseph.

My thoughts are constantly with Lydia, young Joshua and Emily. I miss them terribly. I also long for the company of my father and mother and all.

Monday, May 12

Made thirty-five miles today after yesterday's rest. We are now in Crawford County camped on the plains of Sandusky. Brother Parley P. said that it was among Wyandot tribes near here that he and the other missionaries to the Lamanites stopped in the winter of '30-'31.

May 13th

Very difficult passage today. Made our way through a long range of beech trees. Roads very bad with deep sloughs and mud holes. Many times had to hook ropes to the wagons and aid the teams in getting them out. Horses and men are both exhausted. P. P. Pratt broke his harness and we had to pull him with ropes three miles, but he went onward singing and whistling.

Settlements are thinning now and food is harder to come by. Must be more cautious of what we use.

Had Matthew been two or three years older, would have brought him along. George A. Smith is just sixteen and holding up well. This is a grand experience to know we are marching in the Lord's cause under the direction of a prophet of God.

Wd. 14th.

Reached Bellefontaine today. Abt. 175 miles from Kirtland now. Some grumbling. Sylvester Smith complains about the shortage of bread. He can be a sour man and short of temper. My own company fares well. Brother B., our captain, has sent two men ahead to procure supplies.

Friday, May 16

Last night, Brother Moses Martin fell asleep on guard duty and was discovered. This is viewed as very serious, knowing the number of our enemies. Court-martial held this evening. Brother M. said he was so overcome with fatigue, he could not keep his eyes open. Joseph recommended acquittal, but gave him and all of us stern warning to be alert henceforth.

As we passed through a growth of woods this morning, Joseph surprised us somewhat. He was speaking to his brother Hyrum and said he felt much depressed in spirit and lonesome in that place. We all felt the same, though knew not why. He then remarked that there had been a great deal of bloodshed near there and said that whenever a man of God was in a place where many have been killed he will feel melancholy and sink in spirit.

As the wagons passed on, not more than forty rods further from where Joseph had spoken, we came through the woods upon a farm. There on our left was a large mound, sixty or more feet high. We could see the remains of human bones and saw that this had been a burial place of some sort, though how long ago we could not tell. Joseph's feelings were proved to be correct.

Many of the brethren are worried about "milk sickness"

which seems prevalent hereabouts. Many are afraid to use the milk and butter obtained from local settlers. We inquired of Joseph what he felt, some even fearing that perhaps our enemies would sell us tainted milk to do us harm, but Joseph told us not to fear and promised if we would follow his counsel none would be harmed. Thus far, though we pass through areas where many are afflicted, Joseph's promise has held true.

We passed through Dayton, Ohio this day. There was much curiosity about our company and many inquiries about where we were from and whence we journeyed. As per Joseph's instructions, we give no specific information about where we are from or where we go, but remain vague. Joseph has instructed us that when those not of our number are around us, we are to call him Squire Cook. We know we have many enemies who would love to do us harm and we must be ever diligent.

May 18, Sabbath

No march today as it is Sunday. Yesterday we crossed the border into Indiana after a march of close to forty miles. The weather has been very warm and our feet were sore and badly blistered. Many stockings soaked with blood when our boots were removed. I thought my feet were strong after two weeks of trekking. I was wrong. There was considerable murmuring and I confess for a time this afternoon I was possessed of the same fault.

Sylvester Smith continues to be a bad apple in the barrel. He manifests a rebellious spirit and last night got into difficulty with one of the brethren. Joseph was called to give judgment. He rebuked Smith and others who showed the same spirit to a lesser degree. He gave the camp solemn warning, telling us that if we do not manifest a more godly spirit, we will meet with misfortunes, difficulties and hindrances, and that such would be so before we left the place in which we were camped.

This morning when we woke, a most singular occurrence lay before our eyes. We found almost every horse in the camp so badly foundered that we could barely lead them to water to drink. This was of great concern as we have twenty wagons filled with baggage for our companions in Zion and can go no further without the aid of the teams. Immediately our minds were taken back to Brother Joseph's warning of the night previous and a somber spirit fell upon us all. Joseph called us together and proclaimed that as a witness that God ruled over all things and also that he had His eye upon us, if we would humble ourselves, the horses would be restored to health immediately.

We were inclined to heed his counsel with all diligence and I felt keenly to repent of my own failings of the day previous. To our complete amazement, by noon the horses were as nimble as ever, with one exception. Sylvester Smith's horse died shortly after the rest were restored.

Mon. 19th

We have now struck the National Road, which makes the going better, though we must often detour around muddy holes and bogs. Hope all is well with family in Palmyra and Kirtland.

Wednesday, May 21

We passed through Indianapolis without incident. This was a small miracle of sorts. We learned that the residents of that city knew of our coming and had vowed we would not be allowed to pass. We were told that the governor of Indiana had declared that he would have the Mormons dispersed. There was some contention in the camp about whether to go through, as many of the brethren were filled with fear. This looked like it might be the first test of our mettle, and I admit I was filled with much anxiety too.

Brother Joseph declared in the name of the Lord that if we would exhibit faith in God we should pass through Indianapolis unmolested. Before entering the city some of us got into the wagons and separated from one another at some distance. Those who went through the city on foot walked down different streets. We all passed through without incident, then camped some miles west of the town, leaving the inhabitants to wonder what had become of the "large company" they had been expecting.

As I passed down a narrow street, I came upon a group of young children playing a game with a stick and a ball. A young lad about four was on the sidelines watching. He had dark hair and bright blue eyes. For a moment my heart leaped inside my bosom, for he looked much like my own Joshua. But it was not he, of course, and I marched on. My heart is heavy tonight because of being separated from those I love best.

Sunday, 25th

No worship service today, but spent the day washing, baking and mending clothes and equipment. We crossed the Wabash River yesterday and continued on until we entered Illinois. Estimate we are 375-400 miles from Kirtland and not much more than that from Independence. Nearing the halfway point. Tonight completes our third week on the trail. People still suspect we are "Mormonites" as they call us, but we tell them nothing. (We object to the title "Mormonites." In the conference held just prior to our departure, it was decided we should call ourselves the Church of the Latter-day Saints.)

Had a bad dream during the night. It was about Lydia, but could not remember any details by morning except that I felt a great sadness and a sense of dread.

Monday, May 26th

Very hot and difficult today but several things of interest. Today we entered the first real prairie country we have seen thus far. It was a great curiosity to many of the brethren who have not been west before. The ground was so level that we saw deer a long way off. Some of the men got excited and started after them, only to realize their mistake in assessing the distance. We who have been on the plains before had some fun with them over the matter.

At noon we stopped at a slough, the only water within five or six miles. We had nothing else to drink and this water was filled with living animals, commonly called "wigglers." We had to strain them out before we could drink it. Most felt inclined to wait a little longer. Some time later we found the house of a settler named Mr. Wayne who had a well of sweet water. It was received with great rejoicing as we were nearly famished by that time.

We crossed the Embarras River late this afternoon and made camp not far away. In pitching his tent, Brother Joseph discovered three prairie rattlesnakes which the brethren set about immediately to kill. Joseph rebuked us for this attitude. He asked how the serpents will ever lose their venom while the servants of God make war upon them. Taking sticks we carried the serpents—very carefully!—across a small creek and let them go on the other side. He said we should kill animals during our journey only when necessary for food.

Joseph later shot a squirrel from a tree and then passed on leaving it on the ground. Brother Orson Hyde picked the animal up and suggested it be cooked so that nothing be lost. Joseph commended him, for it showed he had learned the lesson Brother Joseph sought to teach us earlier.

Others continue to join us. Our numbers are now a little under 200. Will it be enough to throw down the watchtowers of the wicked? I do not know.

Tuesday, 27

Last night the prairie played another trick on our company. There is much concern about our enemies as reports are frequently received of their intent to harm us. The pickets were therefore much on the alert. Well after we had all retired to our couches, the guards ran and woke Brother Joseph. There were enemy camp fires to the southeast of us. A mob was approaching.

The Prophet, who has traveled to Missouri now more than

once and is used to the landscape, immediately discovered the truth of the matter. The moon was just rising, and its reflection struck some trees along a creek, making them appear as an enemy encampment. But Joseph is not one to miss his fun and so he discharged his gun at any rate.

I am happy to report that while we awoke with some panic, we quickly came to arms in order. Joseph then told us what had happened, much to the embarrassment of the pickets. But he said the scenery was most delightful and well worth the trouble of any man who had not seen the broad prairie before to rise from his bed to witness. As we retired, Joseph was much amused, as were most of the camp, save perhaps the pickets.

This afternoon, Brother Solomon Humphreys, one of our more aged brethren, became so overcome with weariness that he lay down on the prairie sod and fell asleep. When he awoke, he found a rattlesnake coiled up asleep between his head and the hat which he tossed on the ground when he lay down. Much alarmed, the brethren wanted to kill it. But Brother Humphreys refused to harm it. "You shan't hurt him," he said. "He and I had a good nap together and I shall protect him."

Thurs. May 29

The trip starts to wear on us now and tempers are growing thin. Some are not at all reluctant to let others do their work for them and this results in grumbling. Several times now I have had to help with the fire duty since Brother John K. always manages to be somewhere else when it is time for the work to be done. I have spoken to him thrice now, once quite sharply, but he tells me that I am to mind my own affairs and leave his to him.

Joseph seems to sense that our patience is being tried with the daily monotony of the journey. Today he divided us into three companies and we had a sham battle. It was good diversion and buoyed us up. Some of our captains show good judgment in directing their troops. There was one mishap, however. Brother

H. C. Kimball had the skin cut from the palm of his hand when he grabbed a man's sword while attempting to deflect his charge.

Tonight Brother Joseph rebuked the cook (Z. Coltrin) for serving him sweet bread while the rest of his company were given sour. Brother J. said he wanted no partiality shown to him in this regard. It is a joy to be in the company of Brother Joseph. He is unfailingly of good cheer and exhibits traits of great leadership. Again and again he demonstrates his prophetic gifts and shows that he has truly been called of God. Any man with eyes to see cannot help but exclaim, "There is a man of God!"

Friday, June 6

It has been some time since my last entry and since there is near an hour before trumpet call tonight, I shall seek to repent of my sloth.

We are now camped on the west bank of the Mississippi River, having spent the last two days ferrying all across, there being only one ferry at this place. As always, the river leaves one feeling quite insignificant as it is nearly a mile and a half wide here. The muddy currents swirl darkly and carry huge logs and much debris south toward the sea.

Some things of note since I last wrote. On June 2nd we crossed the Illinois River and camped on its banks until Tuesday the 3rd. There were some large mounds nearby, of which there are many in this area. Joseph says they were thrown up by the ancient inhabitants of the area—Nephites, Lamanites, etc. Many of us went with Joseph to the top of one of the largest. On the top were stones which appeared to be ancient altars, now in a state of ruin. There were also the remains of bones on the ground. Some of the brethren procured a shovel and a hoe and scraped down the dirt to the depth of about a foot. There we uncovered the skeleton of a man, almost in its entirety. Between his ribs was a stone arrow point, which had obviously caused his death.

After we left the mound, we inquired of Joseph who he

thought this might have been. Joseph said that while he was on the mound, the visions of the past had been opened to his mind by the power of the Almighty. He discovered the man was named Zelph, a white Lamanite who had died in battle with the Lamanites. We rejoiced to think that God was so mindful of us that he would give us this information through his servant Joseph.

About noon of that same day, Joseph gathered us again. He climbed upon a wagon wheel and said he wished to deliver a prophecy. He gave us much good advice and exhorted us to faithfulness and humility, then said that the Lord had revealed to him that because of the fractious and unruly spirit some in the camp were manifesting, a scourge would come upon the camp and that we would see the men die like sheep with the rot. With the most tender entreaties, Joseph begged us to repent and humble ourselves so the scourge might be turned away, but feared it would not be so, because so many members are filled with an unruly temper.

We were much subdued for a time, but alas, I must say that the same spirit now fills our camp again. Much of it comes through the person of Brother Syl. Smith (I can hardly call him brother. He carries such a rebellious spirit I have little patience for him.) Recently Brother P. Pratt called upon Sylvester to share his provisions as he had none and they were scarce in the camp. Smith had plenty and more than enough, but he refused Parley and sent him off to ask others. Parley finally went to bed hungry. When Joseph learned of this, he sharply reproved Sylvester, who did not take it well. Since then he finds every excuse to criticize Joseph's leadership and his spirit is influencing others in a bad way.

Joseph's bulldog is a mean-tempered animal and often snaps or growls at the men. We have found this to be quite objectionable, but Joseph says the beast is but responding to the treatment he receives. There are considerable feelings against it. The dog and Sylvester especially do not get along. I wager it is because they are both alike in temperament.

This morning Joseph again spoke with us. He said he was much alarmed about the spirit which was in the camp. To help us drive it from the camp, he would show us what we were like now. Then raising his voice, in a surly tone he said: "If any man insults or abuses me, I will stand against him even at the expense of my own life."

At that moment, Syl. Smith returned from the meadow where he had been caring for his horses. Overhearing the last statement, and thinking Joseph made reference to him alone, he went into a fury. "If that dog bites me," he yelled, "I shall kill him."

Joseph whirled around. "If you do, I will whip you."

He then turned to us and lowering his voice said, "Now, brethren, I have descended to that spirit which fills our camp. Are you not ashamed of it? I most certainly am."

Though we all knew what Joseph was trying to do, it did not set well with many. I, myself, have thought a great deal about it. I think it was unwise. I'm not sure this was the best way to deal with us. Tensions are high. There are reports that 400 men from Jackson County are in the area looking to stop our march. Dear Brother Joseph, we don't need your rebukes as much as we need your support and your encouragement.

Tues. 17th

It has been nearly a fortnight now since I last wrote. Between long marches in the day and double picket duty on many nights, I have little energy for writing. I also accept the fact that much of my enthusiasm for this journey seems to have died. We have been joined by more volunteers from Michigan, which brings our numbers to about 207 (not counting women and children) with 25 baggage wagons. This is as strong as we have ever been, and yet a spirit of despair seems to pervade us all.

There is now almost no hope that Governor Dunklin will keep his promise to reinstate the Saints to Jackson County, even if we provide them protection. Orson Hyde and Parley Pratt have returned from a visit to Jefferson City. They got nothing but sympathy and not enough of that. Gov. D. says he has no power and there is little he can do. He counseled the delegation to have the Saints sell their land and abandon any claim to it. This, of course, we cannot do, for the Lord forbids it.

O Lord, have we come all this way for naught? What purpose do you have for us if we cannot prevail and redeem Zion?

The men behave more strangely each day. Yesterday, Brother Martin Harris was boasting that by the power of the priesthood he could handle snakes with perfect safety. To prove his point, he removed his boot and began to tease a black snake he had found. He provoked it until it bit him on the heel. When Joseph learned of it, he was angry and rebuked Brother H. We are not to trifle with the promises of the Lord, he said. It is true men may be healed if accidently bitten by a poisonous snake but we should not seek such a thing simply to test the Lord. Mr. Harris is fortunate this snake was not poisonous.

Part of this comes from low morale, I'm sure. Conditions are hard and there is little to rejoice over. We have been six weeks on the trail and memories of our families seem more and more dim. I know I should think more often of Lydia and the children, but my thoughts are consumed with the daily needs of our existence. The weather is very hot with hardly a breeze to stir the air and good water is now difficult to come by. Yesterday a heavy thunderstorm came and we caught as much water as possible in the brims of our hats and drank it. But this was not sufficient and some were forced to drink water from the horses' tracks. Likewise our food is scarce and of poor quality—much of it rancid or moldy.

Today, the spirit of dissension reached a climax amongst us who call ourselves "brethren." We reached the Wakenda River, it being high and requiring that we ferry over, always a labor that exhausts both man and beast. A man informed us that a large body of Missourians were gathering and would attack us that night. He also said that the prairie ahead of us was twenty-three miles long with no timber or good water. Some of the brethren suggested we camp there on the river where there was an ample supply of good water and firewood. Joseph was worried that the woods left us vulnerable to being ambushed and suggested we take wood and water with us out onto the prairie.

There was considerable disagreement on the matter. I voted to stay in the timber but suggested we be especially diligent. Then Brother Hyrum Smith said he felt impressed to say, in the name of the Lord, that we should camp on the prairie and not at the river. Joseph felt to heed the counsel of his older brother and said the prairie it would be. I hesitate to murmur, but why should Hyrum be allowed to decide our camping place? Is Joseph our leader, or is he not?

Well, be that as it may, as we set to the march once again, Lyman Wight, who has been elected general commander of our company now that we are in Missouri, was still arguing for the river. Brother Sylvester Smith stood in the roadside as the men passed and cried, "Who shall you follow, your general or some other man?" Meaning of course, Joseph Smith. About twenty heeded the call and stayed behind with Syl. Smith and Wight. I was sorely tempted, but finally felt I should follow Joseph. Although Lyman Wight has been elected general, Joseph is still our commander in chief. I went reluctantly with many misgivings. Is Joseph doing right?

When we reached our campsite here, about eight miles from the river and out of sight of timber, we found only a slough with putrid water filled with some kind of little red living things. The water we had brought from the river had been put in two empty powder kegs and proved to be undrinkable. Thus our situation was almost intolerable, and this only furthers the complaints against Joseph.

Lyman Wight and the others finally rejoined us just a few minutes ago. Joseph rebuked Bro. Wight for not obeying counsel and for tarrying behind. He told him not to do so again. Bro. W. showed a repentant spirit and promised Bro. Joseph he would never forsake him again but would stand by him forever.

I was pleased to hear that, for I have admired Bro. W. He

strikes me as being a man of great courage. I wish I could say Syl. S. exhibited the same spirit but he did not. He was his usual difficult and fractious self.

I would be dishonest if I did not say that I too struggle with this problem. Joseph has warned us about having a fractious and rebellious spirit, but I find myself filled with bitterness towards those who have brought this upon us, especially Syl. Smith. Brother Brigham, my captain, and HC Kimball, Wilford Woodruff and others have sensed my flagging spirits and have worked much to buoy me up.

What is worse for me, with each passing day we draw closer to Jackson County. While I yearn to know if all is well with Jessica and my young niece, my mind is increasingly filled with thoughts of my eldest brother. I know that our Savior says we are to have love for all men, even those who despitefully use us, but my heart is filled with the blackest feelings for Joshua. I pray nightly that God will help me find it in my heart to forgive him, but as yet, I wish only to face him and say he is not worthy to be called a Steed. God forgive me for this bitterness, but I cannot help it.

Chapter Twenty-Six

W hat darling children, Lydia!"

"Thank you, Mrs. Roth."

Hannah Lovina Hurlburt McBride smiled proudly and lifted little Emily higher in her arms. "This is Grandma's girl, this one, aren't you, sweetheart?"

Emily—always one to know when she was on parade, and also very much aware of the benefits of pleasing Grandma— bobbed her head. "Yes'm," she said demurely, the large brown eyes appraising the other woman quite openly from beneath the long lashes.

"Oh," gushed Mrs. Roth, "she is such a little angel. How old are you, darlin'?"

Emily held up four fingers, then carefully reached out with her other hand and folded two of them back down again.

"Two?" Mrs. Roth cried in mock amazement.

"Almost two," Grandma McBride amended. "About three more weeks. July fifth."

Joshua sensed what was coming—it happened almost every time they went out—and so he cut it off. He looked up at his mother. "Mama?"

Lydia looked down. "Yes, dear?"

"Can we have some candy?"

She nodded absently. "I suppose. We'll have to ask Grandpa."

They were standing on the boardwalk, just two or three doors down now from the McBrides' mercantile store, so Joshua immediately saw his escape. "I'll take Emily," he said, like the little man that he was. "We'll go see Grandpa."

That was enough for Emily. Immediately she squirmed her way out of Grandma McBride's grasp and slithered down to join her brother. As they moved off, the three women watched them go.

"They are such angels, Lydia."

"Thank you, Mrs. Roth. We do find great pleasure in them."

"And when will you be going back to Ohio?"

Lydia was caught off guard by the question. Hannah shot her neighbor a sharp look and cut in quickly. "Not for a while yet. Why, she's only been here barely a month. That's hardly any visit at all."

"We'll probably stay for Emily's birthday," Lydia said hesitantly. "My husband's still in Missouri and—"

"And then Lydia's birthday is in August, you know," her mother went on smoothly. "He very likely won't be home before then anyway."

"Well," Mrs. Roth said quickly, sensing she had kicked over the beehive, "it's very good to have you back home again, Lydia. You look absolutely lovely. Come over and visit us before you go. Won't you please?"

Lydia smiled. "I will, Mrs. Roth, thank you kindly. It's good to see you again."

As Mrs. Roth hurried away, Lydia watched her go, a wistful look on her face.

"Now, Lydia," her mother said firmly, "the letter you got from Nathan said they weren't even halfway to Independence yet, and that was almost the first of June. Heaven only knows how long that Joe Smith will keep them in Missouri once they get there."

"Joseph Smith," Lydia corrected automatically.

"Well, there isn't any point you going home to an empty house, now, is there?" She didn't wait for an answer, but started after the children.

"I need to be there when Nathan gets home—," Lydia began.

Hannah McBride stopped and turned back. "Well, he isn't home now," she said in a tone that closed the matter once and for all. "There'll be plenty of time to find out when he's coming. Now, let's get in that store before your father gives those children every piece of candy in the store."

"Do you see him?" Newel Knight whispered anxiously.

"No."

"Then, let's get out of here." Brother Knight made no attempt to hide his nervousness as he eyed the crowd that pushed in around them.

Next to him, Jessica was up on tiptoe trying to see above the crowd. She shook her head. "I've got to know, Brother Knight."

Newel sighed and shook his head, wondering who had ever been foolish enough to suggest that men were the stubborn ones of God's creation. "Sister Steed," Knight whispered, "we cannot stay. This is a very foolish thing we are doing."

"Just another minute. Please."

She understood the foolishness as well as he, and felt the danger and the fear also. But she had to know. Was he here? Had he come?

They were standing outside the courthouse in Liberty, the county seat of Clay County. Seven or eight hundred people jammed the square; another hundred or more were inside watching the proceedings. It was hot. It was humid. And Jessica could feel the sweat trickling down her back inside her dress.

But none of that mattered. When they learned that a delegation from Jackson County was coming to Liberty to negotiate peace with the Mormons (a peace which, given the Missourians' unrealistic proposals, would more than likely not be reached), Jessica had determined to come into town and see if Joshua had come with them.

It had become an obsession with her now. Twice during the winter, since the terrible exodus from Kaw Township, money arrived in Liberty for Jessica Steed. The sender's name was never given. The money never came with a message. But between the two deliveries, there had been more than a hundred dollars. The gift had been a godsend. Food was scarce, shelter barely marginal. The children in the camp were like little derelicts, castaways from society, gaunt faced and hollow ribbed. With the money Jessica received, she and some others had rented a group of huts previously used for slaves, enough for five families, and bought flour and sugar and even two slabs of bacon. Everyone in their little group said it was a miracle, and Jessica did not dispute that. But she thought she knew by whose hand the miracle had come. Now she had to see him and find out if it was true.

Then suddenly she froze. A face in the crowd was turned toward her. It was Joshua! His mouth dropped open as he recognized her, and for a moment their eyes locked. She ducked her head, the shock taking her breath away. "There he is!" she cried in a hoarse whisper.

Newel raised his head. "Where?"

Jessica couldn't resist. She went back up on her toes to see if she had been mistaken. She gasped. He was coming toward her, pushing his way roughly through the crowd, face as grim as though he were death itself.

Jessica spun around. "He's coming!" she hissed. "He's after me!" She looked around wildly, seeking escape.

"But I thought—," Newel Knight started, but before he

could finish, Jessica plunged into the crowd, elbows up, pushing her way through with urgency. "Jessica, wait!" he called.

But the crowd had swallowed her up, and so Newel plowed in after her.

By the time Joshua reached the opposite side of the square, Jessica was nowhere to be found. He searched quickly, scanning the hundreds of faces. Nothing. Disappointed, he slumped back against one of the buildings.

"What is it, Joshua?" Clinton Roundy had come up to join him.

"I saw Jessica."

Roundy's jaw dropped. "Here?"

"Yes!" Joshua looked at Roundy, then rubbed a hand across his eyes. "I wasn't going to hurt her. I just wanted to ask about Rachel."

———◆———

"All right, men," Joseph said quietly, "I don't want anybody firing unless I say. Just keep your guns ready." He walked along the line, touching their shoulders momentarily.

The men of Zion's Camp were standing in a half circle around the edge of a bluff that had been formed by two different branches of the Fishing River. Below them, at the fording place across the main stream, five heavily armed horsemen were crossing and starting up the hill toward them. Beyond that the land stretched out in a flat run to the Missouri River, about two miles south of them. The wheat fields and cornfields of early summer provided a rich patchwork of various shades of green.

Nathan stood next to Joseph's young cousin, George Albert Smith. Out of the corner of his eye, he saw George A. lick his lips, then wipe first one hand and then the other on his trouser legs. Nathan did not smile at the boy's nervousness. Suddenly his own throat was dry, and he found himself breathing a little more rapidly. His stomach also felt as though he had eaten something that disagreed with him and was thinking about parting company with it. He had heard men talk about the "taste of fear." Now he knew what they meant.

The bluff was not an ideal defensive position, though it held the only high ground in the vicinity. But their wagons had broken down again and again during the day's march, and they had not made Liberty as they originally planned. So Joseph had picked this site, and they had made do. Now there were armed men approaching. Only five, it was true, but they certainly wouldn't be so brazen as to ride into an armed camp unless they had more men somewhere behind them.

As the horsemen approached the line, Joseph spoke quietly again. "Hold steady, boys. If they want trouble, we'll give it to them, but we'll not be starting it."

Nathan swallowed, then swallowed again, trying to ignore the squeezing sensation in his gut.

The five riders topped the hill and pulled up a few yards short of the line. They were mean looking, bearded and unkempt. One swayed unsteadily on his horse, and Nathan guessed they had all been drinking, probably a lot.

Lyman Wight—general commander of the camp, and a man of considerable courage—stepped out from the line, his rifle cradled in one arm. "That's far enough," he said.

"This the Mormon army?" one of them sneered.

"What do you want?" Wight demanded.

The man looked up and down the line with contempt. "You mean this is it? This is what we've been hearing about for over a month now?" He threw back his head and laughed raucously.

Joseph stepped between the line of men and came forward to stand next to Wight. "If you have business with us, I suggest you get on with it. If not, I suggest you leave." He spoke with mildness, but there was a hardness along the line of his jaw that Nathan could clearly detect.

The man's face twisted with anger. "Oh, we got business with you, all right," he said. "Our business is to see you in hell before morning."

Another man leaned forward in his saddle and spit a stream of tobacco juice at Joseph's feet. "Know this, Mormon," he muttered. "We've got two hundred of the best boys of Jackson

County at Williams Ferry. They're coming across the river now. We're goin' to meet them, then we'll bring them back here."

"And there's seventy men coming from Liberty, and sixty more from Richmond," cried another one of them. "Before mornin', we'll have four or five hundred men here. Then we'll show ya a thing or two."

Nathan felt his stomach plummet. *Four or five hundred!* That was double their number.

The one who was apparently the leader of the five horsemen grinned evilly. "We got cannon too! That'll let hell know you're coming."

Lyman Wight looked up at them calmly. "When you think about it, I guess you boys would know a lot about hell, now, wouldn't you?"

The man next to the leader uttered a curse, and his hand grabbed for the pistol jammed in the belt of his trousers. Instantly a hundred rifles and pistols jerked up. There were several sharp clicks as hammers were pulled back.

The leader's hand shot out and he grabbed the man's arm. "That's all right, Eb. Let it go. We'll have our fun soon enough." He wheeled his horse around. "Come on, boys, let's go get the others and show these Mormon boys how to die."

Howling with glee, they set spurs to horseflesh and went hurtling down the hill. For a long moment, no one moved. The riders crossed the river ford in a grand spray of water, disappeared for a few moments in the trees, then reappeared again. They skirted a cornfield, then cut south toward the dark line of green that marked the bottomlands of the Missouri River.

"Joseph," somebody finally said, "we can't fight them here. We'll all be killed. I say we march quick time to Liberty."

Lyman Wight whirled around. "Liberty, my fat eye!" he cried. "Let's follow that scum to the ferry, and catch the lot of them while they're crossing the Missouri."

Another man turned and looked toward the east. "If there's men comin' from Richmond, we could be trapped. Ambushed."

Brigham Young snorted in disgust, as several men swung

around and anxiously scanned the prairie. "Don't matter much which direction they come from. We'll be ready."

The camp erupted. Everyone started talking at once, some calling for action, others for prudence, others for full retreat. Suddenly Joseph raised his hands. "Brethren," he called. "Brethren, please."

Immediately the noise died away and the group fell silent.

"Brethren, let us remember that we have come here in response to God's commandment. We are here on his errand. We have a right to his protection, and protect us he will."

He turned and gazed out over the broad expanse of prairie, his eyes grave and his face filled with solemnity. "Brethren, stand still and see the salvation of God."

For several moments, the men stood around, a little bewildered, expecting more from the Prophet than that. But he finally turned to them, smiled, and walked back to his tent. After a moment, others began to disperse, and the tension started to die.

About five minutes later, as Nathan was cleaning his rifle, there was a cry off to the left. He looked up. One of the pickets was standing near the edge of the bluff and pointing toward the south. With a lurch of fear, Nathan leaped up and ran, along with others, to join the man. What he saw sent the adrenalin pumping through him all over again. From the Missouri River bottoms, about two miles away but clearly seen in the bright sunshine, a large group of riders had broken out of the trees and were coming directly toward them. There were thirty men, maybe forty. Instantly, the fear was back. The first ferryload of men was across the Missouri!

As men jumped for their weapons, and pandemonium broke out in the camp, there was another shout. This time it was Orson Hyde who was pointing, only now it was to the west. "Look!" he cried, his voice tinged with awe.

Nathan swung around. In the western sky, where just minutes before there had not even been so much as the wisp of a cloud, a small dark cloud was forming. Even as they watched it billowed upward and outward, doubling in size in less than a minute, then doubling again.

No one moved. The riders to the south were forgotten. Every man, woman, and child in the camp stood rooted in place, watching the heavens darken with a speed that was both frightening and eerie. In less than five minutes the sun was blotted out. In ten, the dark clouds filled the entire western sky and rolled toward them with astonishing swiftness.

A little chill shot up and down Nathan's spine as he watched. The thunderheads were literally exploding upwards, towering mass building upon towering mass, the underside as black as night itself. The band of clouds was spreading in every direction, and coming toward them rapidly, unrolling like some massive black scroll. He had never seen anything quite like it before.

Several men jumped as a jagged shaft of lightning streaked downward, forking out to hit the ground in several places. A moment later there was an ominous rumble of thunder. "See to your tents, men," Lyman Wight hollered, "there's a real gully buster coming."

———◆———

Joshua Steed had his back to the west as he helped the ferry operator get the lines straightened out and the raft ready for the return trip. He cursed steadily and passionately, including in his tirade every Missourian who lived south of the river in Jackson County.

They had ferried across the first load of men and wagons with no problems. But five men who had already been to the Mormon camp were waiting for the new arrivals, and began hollering and bellowing about where the Mormons were camped and how few they were. Before Joshua could stop them, the men from Jackson County had jumped on their horses, whipped the wagon teams into action, and thundered off, leaving him and the ferry operator shouting after them.

The raft was a big one, made of long logs lashed together, with boards nailed over them to provide flooring. It had brought across the river two wagons and more than thirty men, so it was heavy enough that one man couldn't get it launched again without help. It would be no easy task for the two of them, Joshua and the ferry operator. But no one had thought of that. Not one of the stupid idiots had paused long enough to consider that if they didn't get the raft launched again for the next group, there wouldn't be enough men to cause the Mormons any more than a minor sweat. And so he cursed as he tugged and shoved the big raft.

"What the . . . ?"

He straightened. The ferry operator had turned and was looking across the river where a dark shadow was moving swiftly across the face of the muddy water. It was moving faster than a man could run.

Joshua whirled around to the west, and his jaw dropped open. Now it was he who was stunned. A massive thunderhead darkened the whole western sky, like a wall thrown up by some fantastical giant. Even as he watched, a shaft of lightning flickered between two of the massive thunderheads, lighting up the dark underside of the cloud mass for a moment.

Joshua stared, dumbfounded. As the ferry was coming across, some of the men had been bragging about having the "Mormon business" done by nightfall. Joshua was more realistic than that and had looked to the west to check the sky, thinking in terms of a night battle. He had grunted in satisfaction when he saw that the sky was perfectly clear. That had not been more than five minutes earlier. Maybe ten. He passed a hand across his eyes, his mind refusing to accept what his eyes were telling it.

"Balls afire!" the ferry operator gasped. "Would you look at that!"

That jerked Joshua out of his trance. He whirled. "There's a storm comin'!" he shouted. "Get that ferry back across the river."

The man backed up a step, still staring towards the heavens.

Joshua grabbed him roughly. "Hurry, man! We've got to get the rest of the men across before it closes in."

Finally the man leaped into action. He raced to the tree

where the line secured the raft, undid it, then jumped onto the raft and began to pull on the rope with all his might. Joshua waded in to his ankles, giving the ferry one last shove so that it cleared the grassy bank. Across the river—which was close to a hundred yards wide at this point—a man leaped to that end of the rope and began to pull in rhythm with the first. The raft slid out into the water, it's tail swinging around slightly as the current caught it.

Joshua saw a man, near the landing, waving frantically at the others on that side. Several leaped to the rope and began to pull now too. There was a soft sighing above him, and Joshua looked up. The air had been perfectly still until this moment; now the leaves and branches above his head were starting to stir. Even as he watched, the breeze stiffened and started to blow, bending the branches back.

He swung around, amazed at how rapidly the wind was rising. Even as he did so, it picked up in velocity again. It was blowing straight out of the east, which caught the raft broadside. Now the wind and the current fought for dominance over the ungainly craft.

"Pull!" Joshua screamed. "Hurry!"

The ferryman's hat went sailing out over the water. He made a wild grab for it just as a heavy gust caught the raft and jerked it around sharply. The man lost his balance and nearly pitched into the water before he was able to steady himself on the ropes.

Across on the far side, Joshua saw someone cup his hands to his mouth. There was a faint shout, but it was snatched away as quickly as Joshua heard it. Above him now, the wind was howling through the treetops, and the great trunks creaked back and forth in protest. The water was fast getting very choppy, and the wind was starting to whip the tops of the waves into a fine spray. As Joshua turned to check the western sky again, the first raindrops stung his cheeks. They came slashing in, nearly horizontally, feeling like pebbles being hurled against his face.

Pulling his own hat down hard, Joshua darted for the place where he had tied his horse. The horse reared as lightning flashed again, followed almost instantly by a deafening clap of thunder. Joshua fought to control the horse's head, and finally got the animal calmed down enough to mount it. It was insanity to ride out onto the open prairie in a storm like this, but he had no choice. He had thirty men riding hell-bent for a confrontation with the Mormon army, thinking they had four hundred and fifty more coming as backup.

He didn't even bother to look back over his shoulder. He knew there would be no one else coming across in this weather.

———•———

They sat in the old Baptist meetinghouse, some on the rough-hewn benches, others on the floor. No one tried to sleep, though many were near exhaustion. The whole canopy of heaven was one continuous series of lightning flashes, often one coming so hard on the heels of another as to keep the room lit bright enough to see by. Nathan had long since stopped flinching at the terrible claps of thunder. It was as if they had moved inside the center of a huge bass drum that someone now beat on constantly with a vengeance. So they talked quietly, or sang hymns. One or two had candles lit and were trying to write in their journals, but it was a hopeless task.

The door flew open, bringing with it a blast of cold, wet air. The figure, dressed in a long black slicker, had to lean against the door to get it closed again. Every head came up as the man turned around and pulled off his bedraggled hat. Joseph shook the water from his coat, then grinned at them. "I'm telling you, boys, there is some meaning to all this. God is in this storm. We have nothing to fear from our enemies this night."

Nathan looked up. Water streamed underneath the doorway and across the floor and out again. For a moment he listened to the pounding roar on the roof. "Well," he said to no one in particular, "if the Lord used anything like this with Noah, I don't see why it took forty days to get that ark launched."

Brigham Young laughed from the bench where he sat whittling on a stick. "I like that idea," he said. "Here we are in the ark. And out there are all the wicked, wishing they could get in."

———◆———

Joshua had no idea where the "wicked" were at that moment. Nor did he care any longer about the Mormons. He only had one thing on his mind, and that was finding refuge from the storm. As the lightning flashed again, he scanned the country around him, trying to get his bearings. More than once he had hunted deer and elk along this side of the river. He knew the country fairly well. But he saw nothing familiar now.

Wiping, or rather washing, his bloody hands on his shirtfront—he was as wet as if he were standing in a river—he stumbled off again. He had lost his horse over an hour ago. Lightning had struck the ground no more than fifty yards away from him as he rode, blinding and stunning him. Neighing wildly, the horse reared back. Joshua grabbed for the saddle horn, but missed. The saddle was soaked, his clothes were soaked. He slid off like an otter going down a mud slide. He had managed to hold on to the reins, and fought desperately to keep control of the animal. It nearly cost him his life as the horse bucked and fought wildly to free himself. With one sharp jerk of the mighty neck, the horse had pulled the reins through Joshua's hands, making him scream as the searing-hot pain tore at the flesh.

As he stumbled on through the alternating blackness and flashing light, slogging through the mud and water, Joshua suddenly realized that something had changed. Now the rain, which had been pelting him unmercifully, began to sting sharply. With a moan, he realized the rain was changing to hail. Even as he focused his mind on this new threat, he felt the pellets go from tiny, stinging darts to sharp missles the size of his thumbnail. He threw his arms over his head and began to run, feeling as if he were running through the line of fire of a thousand young boys slinging rocks at one another.

There was another flash of lightning. Off to his right, about a hundred yards away, there was a black line against the horizon. Trees! It had to be the river. Now he ran with the pain driving him faster and faster. The hailstones were the size of plumbs now, and they slashed at him relentlessly.

Joshua plunged into the shelter of the trees, arms outstretched now against the blackness. Above him the sky was lit again, and in that moment of light he saw the dark mass of a cottonwood tree. With a cry of joy, he dove to its leeward side and out of the pounding hail. Never had anything seemed so wonderful.

For several moments he lay there, savoring the respite. Then he forced his mind to begin to think again. These trees had to be along the river, probably the Big Fishing River, judging from how he thought he had come. That meant that if he crossed it and followed it upstream, he would come to the bluff. He knew that there were two old buildings up there somewhere—a church and an old school. He was not proud; in this storm he would take any refuge.

But then gradually his ears became aware of a new sound. It was nearly drowned out in the din of thunder and the pounding of the hail that was cutting branches from the trees around him and sending them crashing to the ground. He focused, concentrating. It was a dull and steady roar, like that of a herd of buffalo stampeding across the plain. Puzzled now, he straightened a little, turning toward the sound. He waited for the next flash of lightning, straining to see.

When the lightning came, what he saw was so startling that his eyes refused to believe it. He waited for another flash of lightning, this time going up on his knees, leaning forward. When the next lightning flash came, he fell back. There was no mistaking it. The Big Fishing River, which normally about this time of year ran a foot or two deep and maybe five or six across, was now a raging torrent that filled the thirty- or forty-foot gully that contained it. He slumped back. It was the final blow. Cursing the storm, cursing his luck, cursing the stupidity of his men, and most of all cursing the Mormons, he curled into a ball against the trunk of the big cottonwood, and settled in for what he knew was going to be the most miserable night he had ever spent.

When the people of Zion's Camp came stumbling out of the old church house the next morning, they stopped and gaped. It was as though they were standing in the center of a ring, around which the furies of hell itself had been unleashed. There were a few tree branches down here and there around the church, and the ground was muddy and covered with puddles. But the area had had no hail. Now, in the light of morning, the group saw that this was the only place that hadn't. In the distance, cornstalks that were green and lush the night before, now stood like stripped willow sticks stuck in rows. Grainfields were flattened. Tree limbs were broken and shattered. It was like a scene from the Apocalypse, and it chilled them to see it.

"Look," Parley Pratt cried.

They all swung around to where he was pointing. Below them the river was a churning caldron of brown. Logs, parts of trees, debris of every kind hurtled along in its grasp.

Joseph came over to stand by Parley. Lyman Wight came to join them. For a moment all were silent, then Joseph turned to the men. Unconsciously, they came to some semblance of attention before him.

"Brethren," he said. "I think we can pick up camp and move out. I think it safe to say that the men whose purpose last night was to find Joe Smith and see him dead found other things to worry about."

There were no chuckles or smiles. The landscape before them, the roar of the river were too real, too awesome to be treated lightly.

"We'll find a safer place to camp," Joseph concluded. "Then I'd suggest you get out your journals and record what you have seen here this night."

July 3rd, 1834

I sit tonight in the hut in which my sister-in-law and two other families live. This shall be the final entry in my journal. We are some four or five miles west of the town of Liberty. Joseph called many of the brethren together and organized a High Council. He also authorized General L. Wight to give us our discharge. Zion's Camp is disbanded. Zion's Camp is no more. We are given leave to return to Kirtland.

Though it is a great disappointment, there is nothing to be done. Governor Dunklin and the other weakling officers of the state of Missouri refuse to call out the militia and restore our people. Without that, how can we act? In spite of all attempts to negotiate with them, the Jackson County settlers are sworn to die before they let us return. Sadly, the Lord has revoked the commandment to redeem Zion because of our own unfaithfulness. The Saints in the east largely ignore the plight of their brothers and sisters, and fail to share their means with them. We in the camp itself have brought upon ourselves grave consequences because we have failed to be obedient. God commands, and God revokes. Now he has revoked. The redemption of Zion must wait for a season.

Some of the camp members will stay on with the Saints here in Missouri, but most will return to the East. I am happy to say that I have persuaded my sister-in-law, Jessica Steed, and her daughter, Rachel, to return with us to Kirtland. There she can be with our family and perhaps find some measure of peace. She will leave two days hence with Brothers Brigham Young and Heber Kimball. If all goes well, I shall be with them by the time of their departure or shortly thereafter. If not, I have asked that Jessica carry this journal back to Lydia and my family and explain why I did not return. But of that I cannot speak more, for my feelings now are too tender. I shall simply try to complete the record of our trek so my family has it in its entirety.

It was not long after the storm of which I have already spoken that Joseph received the revelation saying that the Lord no longer wanted us to redeem Zion. The revelation was greeted with much dismay. A great murmuring swept through the camp. Some said Joseph had lost his courage, others that God did not change his mind and therefore the revelation must be false. I will not go into detail on where I stood in this matter except to say that I did not stand firmly with Joseph. That shames me now, but alas, it is true. I stood with those whose faith wavered.

Joseph called us together and reminded us that before we ever crossed the Mississippi he had warned us about our fractiousness. He had prophesied then that if we did not repent and show a more humble spirit, the Lord would send a scourge among us and we would see men die like sheep with the rot. This only made some of the men angrier still and the murmuring continued. It was a sorry time.

On the 24th of June the prophecy came to pass. On that night a cholera epidemic struck the camp. It has been a most fearful thing. Never have I seen anything strike with such swiftness. It seizes upon men like the talons of a hawk. First one and then another collapsed. Men would be standing around talking one moment, then writhing on the ground in another. Sister Betsy Parrish, one of the women in our camp, was in good health and spirits at the midday meal. I sat beside her. Shortly thereafter, she began to feel distressed. By supper she was in a coma and by trumpet's call, she was dead.

I myself was standing guard duty early on the second evening of the scourge. I was much alarmed by the situation and, speaking frankly, had undertaken some serious personal reflection and repentance. I felt to mourn for my own murmurings and saw that the hand of God was upon us because of what we had done. But to that point I felt well and fit and was rejoicing in my good fortune in being spared. Suddenly it was as though I was struck with a flat iron. I dropped to my knees, my rifle still in hand. The next thing I knew I awoke in my tent in the most severe distress. For three days and nights I hovered between life and death, many times not caring which took me so long as I could escape the anguish I was in.

Joseph tried to lay his hands on the ill and rebuke the

disease, but was stricken himself. He later told me it was clear that when the Great Jehovah decrees judgment upon a people, no man should attempt to stay his hand.

Yesterday morning, Joseph called us together, those who could get about. I was starting to recover by then, though I was still very weak. Joseph told us that this was the scourge of which the Lord had spoken. He then promised us that if we would humble ourselves before the Lord and covenant with a most solemn covenant to keep his commandments and follow Joseph's counsel, the plague should be stayed from that very hour and there would not be another case of the cholera among us.

By then, any spirit of rebellion had long since vanished and we listened with open hearts and accepted with willing minds. We united in common prayer that the Lord would turn away his wrath from us. That was about thirty-six hours ago now as I write. Happily I report that Joseph's promise is fulfilled. The disease is leaving us. There have been no further outbreaks since yesterday and we are recovering now quickly. But all told, sixty-eight have been stricken. Of that number, fourteen are dead.

How that should give us pause for reflection. Though we have marched nearly a thousand miles, we have lost not a man to accident. Though we faced a hostile enemy sworn to kill us, we lost not a man in battle. Only two out of over two hundred men have deserted us on the march. Yet because of our own foolishness, fourteen of our number now lie beneath the prairie sod. May Jesus bless them to come forth in the morning of the first resurrection, and may we, the living, never forget the lessons of this day.

And that brings me at last to the task which I have set for myself. Earlier I wrote of the terrible feelings I have harbored in my heart for my brother Joshua. It has become an obsession of late, like a canker in my soul. I see now that my whole outlook has become darkened with bitter feelings toward him. I know this darkness was largely responsible for the mean spirit which has possessed me of late and caused me to murmur. If I would follow the example of the Master, I must purge my heart of this ugliness toward my own flesh and blood.

I have therefore determined that I shall ride to Jackson County this night and seek out my brother. Many try to dissuade me, for Jackson County still seethes with hatred for all that is Mormon. Jessica informs me that about a month ago a young lad went across the river in search of some of his livestock. He was caught and beaten unmercifully. Threats of death to any Mormons are commonplace. But this matters not to me. I cannot rest until I have sought him out and tried to make peace with him.

My dearest Lydia, if I do not return to your side, know that my last thoughts were of you and the children. I love you, and will forever.

Nathan Steed.
Written in my twenty-sixth year of age.

———◆———

"He's a Mormon, I'm tellin' ya. I can see Mormon written all over him."

The man closest to Nathan reached out and grabbed Nathan's hair, yanking back on it hard. His face was next to Nathan's, no more than an inch or two away. Tobacco juice oozed out of one corner of his mouth and into his beard. His breath was foul, his eyes bloodshot and wild. With his other hand he whipped out a pistol and laid it up alongside Nathan's head. "Are ye a Mormon!" he shouted. "Tell me or I'll blow your brains out."

They were in a small room above a saloon in Independence. The four men who had intercepted Nathan shortly after he crossed the river had brought him here via some back stairs. One of their number had gone downstairs. Now the rest interrogated Nathan angrily.

Nathan began again, speaking slowly, patiently. "My name is

Nathan Morgan. I have just recently come from the East. I am from the state of New York. I am a friend of Joshua Steed. We lived in the same town. Send for him, he'll tell you—"

The man shoved hard, sending the chair crashing backwards against the table. Nathan's arms were lashed down tightly to the chair, and so he could do nothing as the chair spun on one back leg, then toppled over, slamming the back of his head against the floor.

The door opened. "Steed's comin'," a man said.

"Good," said the first man. "Get him up."

Two men lifted the chair and sat Nathan upright. He turned his head and wiped a trickle of blood from the corner of his mouth against his shirt. There were footsteps on the stairs, and the man who had shoved him stepped forward toward the door, blocking Nathan's view.

"What's going on here?" a voice demanded harshly. Nathan felt his heart leap. It had been almost seven years since he had last heard that voice. "What's this about some man who—"

The man standing in front of Nathan stepped aside and Joshua Steed stood face-to-face with his brother. Nathan looked up slowly, not speaking, not moving, just looking up at his brother's face. Joshua blinked, then blinked again. It said something about his poker playing ability that only his eyes registered the fact that he was totally stunned.

"This man claims he knows ya, Steed," one of the men said. "Claims he's from New York State."

Joshua didn't respond, just kept looking at Nathan through eyes suddenly hooded.

"Hello, Mr. Steed," Nathan said evenly. "Do you remember me?"

Again there was no response. Nathan thought that Joshua looked as though they had pulled him from sleep. His hair was tousled, his eyes rimmed beneath by dark circles, his chin covered with a dark beard. He looked very weary.

"I think he's a Mormon," one of the men said. "He won't say yes or no, just kept askin' for you."

Joshua reached inside his jacket pocket and retrieved a cigar. One of the men sprang to where two candles were in a holder on the wall. He pulled one loose and held it for Joshua, who leaned forward, sticking the tip of the cigar into the flame. Through it all, his eyes never left Nathan's.

When he had the cigar glowing, he took it from his mouth and blew a stream of smoke into the air. He turned to the other men. "I ain't been back East for nearly seven years now. Let me have a few minutes alone with him, boys. I'd like to question him a little."

"Yes, sir, Mr. Steed. We'll be right downstairs if you need us."

Without answering, Joshua watched them go, then stepped to the door and shut it firmly. Finally, he turned around. He pulled out one of the other chairs, turned it around, and sat down slowly. "Well, well, well," he said slowly, shaking his head. "This is a surprise."

"Hello, Joshua."

"What are you doing in Missouri?"

"I came with Zion's Camp, to help the Saints."

His head came up slowly. "You're with the Mormon army?"

"Yes."

"Were you at Fishing River?"

"Yes."

Joshua looked away, a sudden shadow crossing his eyes.

"Why?" Nathan said. "Were you?"

Joshua laughed bitterly. "Kind of."

"So if the storm hadn't come . . . ," Nathan started slowly. He didn't finish. Brother against brother? He felt a little chill.

"Why have you come here? Didn't your people tell you what they're doing to Mormons on this side of the river?"

"Yes, they did. I had to see you, Joshua. They've disbanded Zion's Camp. We're going back. I couldn't leave without seeing you."

"Why?" It came out blunt and hard. "I ain't part of the family anymore."

"You are to us."

There was a grunt but Nathan couldn't read it one way or the other.

Nathan sighed. "I couldn't go without at least trying to see you."

Putting the cigar down, Joshua softened a little. "How's Ma?"

"Fine. Melissa's married now, you know?"

Joshua looked up. "Ma wrote me, remember?" he said.

Nathan couldn't keep a touch of tartness from his own tone. "We weren't sure you ever got the letters. You never answered, remember?"

Joshua brushed all of that aside curtly. "You were a fool to come here."

Nathan nodded. "That's what everybody over there said too."

"Did Joseph come with the group?"

Nathan hesitated, remembering Joseph's caution about revealing their identity, but a week ago he had announced himself to the Missourians, so it was no longer a secret. "Yes."

"Why don't you send him across the river?" Joshua asked, his voice softly menacing. "Then we'll see how long he keeps telling them stories about angels."

Nathan shook his head in discouragement. "Oh, how little you know him. Besides, what's with you and Joseph anyway? He never did anything to you. Why do you hate him so?"

Joshua nearly snarled out the answer. "What do you know? Joe Smith ain't done nothing to me except cause trouble. Every time I turn around I got Joe Smith sticking in my face."

"Joseph's——," Nathan started, then he changed his mind. He hadn't come to fight over Joseph Smith. "Look, Joshua, we don't have to battle over this. I didn't come to try and make you a Mormon."

Joshua hooted, the very idea so ludicrous to him as to make him laugh. "Then, why did you come?"

"I came because . . ." Again he let it go without finishing, realizing suddenly how foolish it would sound to start talking about forgiveness. He shrugged. "I told you, I came to see you."

"No," Joshua said, boring in. "You started to say something. What?"

"Nothing. I just wanted to see you before we left."

Joshua pounced on that. "We? Is Joseph going back with you?"

"Not with us particularly, but yes, he's returning to Ohio." Nathan took a quick breath. "I'm taking Jessica and Rachel back with me, Joshua."

Joshua had started to reach for his cigar again. His hand froze in midair, then lowered slowly.

Nathan rushed on. "It's been hard for her, Joshua. She has no one to care for her, no way to make a living. Back in Kirtland, we'll see that she's taken care of."

Joshua picked up the cigar and jammed it in his mouth. "What are you telling me this for? She's not my wife anymore. We got a divorce, or didn't she bother to tell you that?"

"She told me. Have you remarried yet?"

That brought Joshua's chin up a notch. "You always were nosing around in other people's business, little brother."

"You haven't, have you?"

"That ain't got nothing to do with Jessica," he snarled.

Nathan took a quick breath. This was not going how he'd hoped. "She also told me about the hundred dollars you sent over to her."

Joshua jammed the cigar down on the tabletop, crushing it against the wood. "I don't know what you're talking about."

"Suit yourself, Joshua," Nathan said wearily. "But I think you're carrying one great big load of guilt because of the way you treated her. Well, she don't hold no grudge against you. That's hard to believe. Heaven knows I have for long enough. But she don't."

"You got a grudge against me, spit it out."

"I didn't come for that. I came to put it behind me, let you know we still care, that we miss you."

Joshua snorted in disgust. "I'm touched."

Nathan's mouth tightened, but he fought down the anger.

He leaned forward as much as his bonds would let him, peering at his brother. "She still loves you, you know? She'd come back in a minute, if you'd stop your drinking and gambling and let her be a Mormon in peace."

Joshua came straight up out of his chair, his eyes blazing. "Oh, really?"

"Yes, really," Nathan snapped, losing the last of his patience.

Joshua gave Nathan's chair a savage kick. "And who appointed you as the official mediator in this matter?"

"No one, I just—"

"Then butt out, mister," he said coldly. "Jessica made her choice. She changes her mind, she knows where I live."

Nathan just stared at him, hardly believing his ears. "After what you've done, you want her to make the first move?"

With the speed of a striking rattlesnake, Joshua's hand flashed out and grabbed Nathan's shirtfront. "You listen to me, my Mormon little brother," he shouted. "Everything that was ever important to me, Joe Smith and the Mormons have destroyed. You took my life in Palmyra. You took my wife and turned her against me. You took my daughter. Don't you be talking to me about what I've done."

Nathan hooted incredulously. "*We* took your wife?"

"That's right. You and Joe Smith and the rest of the Mormon maggots that live in those hovels out on the prairie."

Straining forward against the rawhide lashings that bound him, Nathan was livid. "You've got a short memory, big brother." The last two words were filled with all the insolence he could put into them. "Remember, I was here that summer. I saw Jessica's face after you beat her up—and her in the third month of being with child."

Joshua let go of Nathan's shirt, as if it were suddenly hot. He recoiled as though Nathan had struck him.

"And just two nights ago, I saw her feet. They're covered with scars, Joshua. Scars from walking twenty-five miles across a sleet-covered prairie, carrying a child. Your child, Joshua Steed! And you at the head of the mob that drove them out." He shook his head in utter contempt. "And you have the gall to stand there and tell me it's the Mormons' fault that you lost your wife?"

"I couldn't stop them that night," Joshua whispered, his voice suddenly stricken. "They were out for blood. I sent Clinton to warn her. I—"

Nathan turned his head and spit contemptuously. "You must be some kind of leader, big brother."

Joshua whirled, his fist cocking back, his face a mask of fury.

Nathan tensed, but he did not turn away. "Go ahead, Joshua. That's always your answer to everything, isn't it?"

Gradually Joshua's face smoothed and the hand finally lowered. Without another word he turned and walked toward the door.

For years afterwards, Nathan would always regret what happened next. He had come, hoping to purge away his anger and hate. Instead, he gave full vent to them in his blind desire to hurt, to wound, to strike at this infuriating man who should have been his brother.

"For seven years now," Nathan said slowly and evenly, "Ma has prayed for you. Every night and every morning. She's prayed for your safety. She's prayed that you would someday come back to us. Even when she heard about you beating Jessica. Even when she heard that you were right there helping everyone else to drive out the Mormons. She never quit."

Joshua had stopped at the door, but didn't turn.

"Well, I'll tell you something, Joshua." Nathan was flinging the words at his brother's back now, like stones hurled from a sling. "When I return, I'm going to beg Ma to stop those prayers. Because you ain't worth praying for anymore."

Joshua slowly turned. His eyes were like glacial ice and his face was as hard as granite. Then, suddenly, he started to laugh softly. Nathan had never heard anything that chilled him more. "Is that it, Nathan? Is that your best shot?" He threw back his head and roared. Then, as suddenly as it had begun, the laughter was cut off. He jerked the door open and stuck his head out. "Abner?" he bellowed.

Instantly the sound below them quieted. "Yes, Mr. Steed?" came a man's voice.

Joshua turned and gave his brother one last look, then stepped out of the door. "I ain't ever seen this man in my life," he said. "He's lyin' his head off to you."

It was nearly two o'clock in the morning when Brigham Young sat straight up in his bedroll, which was stretched out on the floor of the tiny hut. "We got company," he cried in an urgent whisper, reaching out for Heber Kimball.

Instantly, Heber was up and grabbing for his rifle. The sound of hoofbeats was clearly heard, four or five horses, coming hard.

From the corner, Jessica jerked awake. She looked around for a moment in panic. "What is it?"

"Shhh!"

The horses slowed to a canter, but they were closer now, almost to the hut. Heber darted in a crouch to the door, then straightened and leveled his rifle at it. Brother and Sister Lewis were also sitting up now, their eyes wide and frightened in the darkness. Jessica reached out and pulled the sleeping form of Rachel toward her.

There was a heavy thud against the door. Then the horses exploded into a lope again, but they were moving away now, fading rapidly.

"Careful, Heber," Brigham called softly as his companion moved to the door. Heber peered out for a moment, then threw the door open and dropped to one knee before the still form that lay on the doorstep.

Gently he turned the figure over. There was a faint moan. "Heaven help us," Heber exclaimed softly, "it's Brother Nathan."

"God is in this storm"

The river was more beautiful than anything Lydia had ever seen. It came cascading down from the heights of the verdant mountains, its waters as clear as the finest of European crystal. And everywhere, its waters enriched the land around it. There were lush meadows, carpets of wildflowers, trees and shrubbery of every kind. She longed to tarry in this beautiful place, but as always, she could not. The path was clearly marked and she knew it well, for she had walked it numerous times before. Something always prodded her on, even though with each step the dread began to grow.

As she rounded a bend, there stood the mighty oak tree, just as she knew it would. It was magnificent, standing there in solitary splendor, its trunk so massive that five men could not link hands around it. Beneath its spreading branches the air was cool, the grass like velvet. Again she longed to pause, to rest and partake of the oak's beckoning shelter, but the unknown something drove her on.

The other trees came into sight one by one as she walked on. Here was a mighty conifer, as tall as ten buildings would be if stacked one on top of the other; then came a shimmering birch, a mighty chestnut, a delicate maple, a more slender black willow. Each was resplendent in its own right, and each provided its own degree of refuge.

Her feet were moving faster now, against her will, and the landscape changed as quickly. The meadows and parkland gave way to sagebrush and dry, brown prairie grass. Then even that gradually thinned until there was nothing but the starkness of a vast desert. A dust devil danced off in the distance. Part of the rib cage of some animal long since dead lay half-buried just off to her right. Here the river was no longer a torrent, but spilled out of its channel and began to flood out across the broad plain. In moments the parched ground swallowed it up and there was nothing left.

She turned, as she always did at this point, filled with inexpressible horror. And even as she turned, the desert spread outward, faster than the eye could follow, shriveling grass, shrubbery, vegetation. Her beloved trees were transformed into silent skeletons silhouetted against the brazen sky. The river became a dry, rock-strewn channel, with only a few stagnant pools here and there. The mountainside, which moments before had been green and lush and beautiful, was now a barren crag, as bleak and lifeless as was the desert.

With a moan, Lydia fell to her knees and began to sob uncontrollably.

"Mama! Mama! Wake up!"

Lydia awoke with a start. Little Joshua was on his knees beside her on the bed, shaking her shoulders. He was half crying. "Please wake up, Mama."

She looked around wildly for a moment, then sobbed in relief as she recognized the outlines of her bedroom in her parents' house in Palmyra. In the soft moonlight, she could see Emily standing in her crib, wide-eyed, whimpering softly. Joshua sat back, relieved now, sniffling back the tears. "Are you all right, Mama?"

She reached out and swept him into her arms, hugging him fiercely. "Yes, Josh, I'm all right now. Get Emily."

As she took her daughter in her arms and began to rock her back and forth, trying to soothe her, the door to the bedroom opened. Her mother stood there with a candle in her hand. "Lydia?"

"Yes, Mama?"

"Are you all right? I heard you cry out."

"I'm fine now, Mama. I'm afraid I also woke the children."

Hannah McBride watched her daughter for a moment. "Was it the dream again?" she finally asked.

Lydia was unable to suppress a shudder. "Yes. It was the dream again."

———————

It was the second day of August, not quite a full month from the day they had left Clay County and started east. Nathan stood for a moment in front of his father's house and felt a lump well up in his throat. Beside him stood his sister-in-law, Jessica Roundy Steed, and her two-year-old daughter, Rachel. Night had fallen more than an hour before, and in Kirtland there was no one about.

He turned and lifted a hand to the three men who were moving on up the street. "Thank you, Brother Brigham. Thank you for a safe journey home."

Brigham, his brother Joseph, and their longtime neighbor and friend Heber C. Kimball all turned. "Thank you for traveling with us," Heber said. "You can put your bedroll in my tent anytime you wish, Brother Nathan."

"Thank you all so much for your help with Rachel," Jessica said. She spoke wearily, but with much emotion. "I couldn't have made it without you."

"You bring that little lady around to the house when she gets rested," Joseph Young said. "I'd like the missus to meet her."

"I will."

They lifted their hands and trudged on, eager to reach their own homes.

Nathan turned to Jessica and smiled. "Are you ready for this?"

She brushed a hand nervously across her hair, then pulled at the skirt of her dress. "No," she finally said, "I think I'll go back."

He laughed. "Come on, you're going to love my family."

He walked to the door and rapped sharply, then stepped back and swept Rachel into his arms. There was a sound inside, the scraping of a chair, then footsteps coming across the floor. Nathan found his own heart suddenly beating a little more quickly.

The door opened and a large figure stood in the frame. The light was behind him, so his face was in shadow, but even then Nathan could see the eyebrows suddenly shoot upwards as he fell back a step.

"Hello, Pa."

"Nathan?" It came out as a shocked whisper.

"Yes, Pa. We're back." He reached out and brought Jessica forward. "Pa, this is Jessica Steed, your daughter-in-law. And this is Rachel." His voice broke, and he had to swallow quickly. "She's your granddaughter."

"You have such beautiful hair, Rachel," Rebecca cooed as she ran the brush through it again and again.

Rachel looked up and gave her head a little toss, making the dark curls bounce and dance in the lamplight. She beamed proudly. She had always been loved, but in Missouri she had never been pampered. During the last fifteen minutes, she had been pampered shamelessly.

"So," Matthew said eagerly, watching as Nathan finished a slice of bread smeared with butter and raspberry preserves, "did you get to fight, Nathan?"

Nathan looked up, his face suddenly grave. "No, Matthew, we didn't have to fight. The Lord fought our battles for us."

"But Joseph said the Lord withdrew his command that you save Zion."

"He did." Now his eyes dropped completely. "We weren't worthy of it."

Mary Ann watched her son with anxious eyes. Though there was a great joy in him at being home again, there was also a deep melancholy. There was so much she wanted to ask, so much to learn, but she sensed that it wasn't the time yet.

Nathan turned to his father. "When did Joseph get back?"

"Day before yesterday."

"So you know about what happened?"

"Only in the broadest detail. There's a meeting this Sabbath. Joseph promised to give a full report."

Nathan stood wearily and looked at his mother. "Thank you, Mother. That should sustain me enough to get me through the last two miles."

Both father and mother suddenly looked at each other. Matthew looked away. Rebecca's hand froze with the brush in midair.

Nathan was too tired to notice any of it. He turned to Jessica. "Lydia is going to be so anxious to meet you. We'll come back into town tomorrow." He turned to Rachel. "And you, you'll get to meet your cousins."

Benjamin stood slowly. "Nathan?"

"Yes?"

"Lydia's not there."

Nathan jerked up sharply. "What?" Then he nodded. "Oh, is she staying here in town somewhere?"

Benjamin shook his head slowly. Nathan just stared at him, not comprehending. Mary Ann stood and walked to the small china hutch she kept in one corner of the room. She opened it, took out an envelope, and walked over to her son. "Lydia's still in Palmyra, Nathan," she said quietly. She handed him the envelope and turned away. "Come, children," she said, "let's find a place for this little girl and her mother so they can go to bed and get some rest."

———•———

My dearest Nathan,

If you are reading this letter, then you must now be in Kirtland and know that I am still in Palmyra visiting at the home of my parents. How it saddens me that I am not there for your return. How I wish I were, not only to see you again—something for which I long most desperately—but so we could speak face to face about the situation and not through a letter.

Little Joshua and Emily are doing fine. They are the apple of their grandparents' eyes and they have been spoiled greatly. They love Palmyra and have made many friends here. Last month Papa purchased Joshua his own pony and he is already learning to ride with ease. He is so proud and eager to show you his accomplishments.

I am not quite sure how to put into words my own situation. Coming to Palmyra has been wonderful for me. I am revived in spirits in many ways, and have rejoiced to have my time filled with activities so that my thoughts are not always of you. I suppose this largely explains my reluctance to return to Kirtland. I know not how long it shall be before your return. I cannot bear the prospect of returning to an empty house and an empty life.

I received a letter from Melissa. She told me about being with child again. I am so happy for her. I miss her and your family very much. Will you tell them that? Please tell them that my staying in Palmyra has nothing to do with them. They have been more than wonderful to me and I love them as I do my own.

Papa still has many bitter feelings about Joseph Smith and the Church, but he has softened much. A few weeks ago I even took the children to the small branch of the Church that meets in Manchester Township, not far from here. Papa would not drive me, but he did not forbid it. Mother has told him that he cannot be too rigid.

I hesitate to mention this next thing, but it is something to consider, and perhaps telling you of it now will give you time to carefully think about it before we meet again. Papa is growing older and speaks often of what will happen to the store when he can no longer run it. Mother and I have spoken much of this, and your name has been discussed between us several times. To my amazement, when Mama talked to Papa about it, he did not reject the idea. He loves the grandchildren dearly, and it would mean he would not be alone in his old age. And while you and he differ on religious matters, he knows you are a good worker and a man of integrity.

I have warned him that if we ever did move back to Palmyra, he could not seek to restrict our choices in matters of religion. I think he can accept that. Now that Joseph has moved away, much of the tension towards the Mormons has disappeared. I know that it would mean your being away from your family, but travel between here and Ohio improves all the time. The financial remuneration would be much better from the store than from farming, and we could better afford to travel to see your parents from time to time.

I know you will have many questions and concerns about this matter, but don't dismiss the idea immediately. I shall most anxiously be awaiting word from you, dear Nathan. The moment you return to Kirtland, post me a letter, so that I can know of your safe return. Until then, may the Lord keep you safe and bring you home to us again. For this I pray continually.

All my love,
Lydia

"You look wonderful, Melissa."
She leaned back, patting the protruding roundness of her stomach. "You always were more kind than you were honest,

Nathan." They sat in Melissa's kitchen together. It was the first Nathan had been alone with his sister since returning to Kirtland.

"No, I mean it. You look great. Are you happy?"

Melissa nodded instantly. "Yes, I am."

Nathan gave her a sharp look. The answer had come a little too quickly. "That's good. Carl is a good man."

She smiled. "I think so too."

Nathan knew he should let it go, but he wanted to know. "Is he showing any interest toward the Church?"

She looked away, and Nathan felt a deep sadness sweep over him. "Is he fighting you on it?" he asked quietly.

Melissa shook her head. "Not really. His father has turned quite sour against the Mormons. Carl still lets me do what I want."

"But he doesn't really like it?" Nathan guessed.

Again there was the quick shake of the head and the sorrow in her eyes.

Nathan decided to change the subject. "What do you think of Jessica?"

Melissa immediately brightened. "She's wonderful! I think it will take some time to really get to know her, but I like her."

"She's much more of a private person than you or me," he agreed. "She's been through a lot."

Melissa nodded, then pushed aside the tray that held the plate of cookies and the pitcher of milk. She leaned across the table, putting a hand on his arm. "Will you tell me about it? About Missouri? About Joshua?"

He shook his head quickly. "Maybe some time," he said quietly. "Not now."

"All right," she said softly, wanting to cry when she saw the depths of the pain in his eyes.

With an effort, Nathan pulled himself out of his thoughts. He gestured toward the letter that lay on the table. It was Lydia's letter. Melissa had read it, then put it back into its envelope without comment. Now her eyes went to it too. She sighed. How honest could she be, when he was hurting like this?

She took a quick breath, then plunged in. "Nathan, Lydia is—" She let the air out slowly, shaking her head. "It's hard to put into words. Lydia is having a hard time of it. When you were gone on your missions, it was very difficult for her."

"I know that," he said. "It was difficult for me, too. Do you think I wanted to be away from her?"

"No. But that doesn't change things. You were still gone."

He looked very glum. "I know."

"You've got to remember that Lydia is an only child. She had only one source of love and that was her parents. Then you came along and she had a second thing to love. Unfortunately, she was forced to choose between your love and that of her parents. I think it was very much harder for her to be rejected by her folks than any of us know."

"Yes, I suppose you're right."

"But you helped fill the void. You were more important to her anyway, so she was able to live with it. And then, suddenly, you weren't there anymore."

"But Lydia said she wanted me to go."

"Of course she did. She loves the Lord too. She meant it."

"But it was harder than she expected?" he asked.

"Your being gone was only part of it, Nathan. That made it harder, of course, but it was more than that. Even when you were home, things were different. You were filling your life with other things—the School of the Prophets, working on the temple, blessing the sick. You were having all these wonderful, fulfilling experiences, and all Lydia was feeling was that more and more she was losing you."

He threw up his hands. "But she wasn't. I never loved her any less."

"I know that, and Lydia knows that. But in a way, that didn't help. You were doing everything right, at least on the surface. You were serving the Lord. You were being faithful. This only added to Lydia's sense of guilt, because now she felt resentment, and she knew that wasn't right either. She started to feel like a millstone around your neck."

His eyes narrowed a little. "What do you mean, I was doing everything right 'on the surface'?"

Melissa looked him right in the eye. "Can I be honest with you?"

"Of course."

"There for a while, you got pretty pompous. You were a successful missionary. You were in tune with the Spirit. You were going to convert the world. It was like the rest of us didn't quite measure up."

He looked at her sharply.

"Oh, you never said anything directly, but . . ." She sighed. "Well, that doesn't matter anymore. I'm happy to say you pulled out of that stage."

He was staring at his hands. "Did I?" he whispered.

"Yes, you did," she said firmly. "There for a while, I wasn't sure you were going to. But you did. But by then, Lydia had begun to doubt herself, started to wonder about her own worth. Then, to add to her problems, she lost the baby."

"I know. I've never seen her so forlorn."

"It was a heavy blow when she was already staggering."

"Then why did she insist that I go on Zion's Camp? I had decided not to go."

Melissa smiled sadly. "Because by then the guilt had become unbearable. She knew what had to be done. She couldn't bear to hold you back. We all saw the pain in your eyes. But, at the same time, she couldn't bear to be alone again, especially not when we all knew that this time you were marching off to possible battle, not just to preach the gospel."

"So she went to Palmyra."

"Yes. By then her parents were calling for a truce. It came at an opportune time. Here was a chance to rebuild what she had lost. When they totally rejected her for joining the Church, that left only one leg on her stool, and that was you. But the Nathan leg was leaving, going into danger. If that leg collapsed on her, she would be left with nothing. So, yes, she went to Palmyra."

For a long moment he just stared at Melissa, then slowly he nodded. "I think I understand. So what do I do?" He laughed with soft bitterness. "Move to Palmyra? Take over her father's store? I can just see it now. Me and Josiah McBride working side by side. Me calling him Papa and him calling me son."

Melissa clapped her hands and laughed aloud. "Oh, now there's an image for you." But she sobered instantly. "Nathan, can't you see? The fact that Lydia is even considering something so ridiculous shows how desperate she's become. She feels terrible that she's abandoned you. But until she finds something to anchor herself to, she'll grasp at any piece of driftwood to hang on to."

Upstairs there was the faint sound of a child's cry. Melissa looked up. "There's young Carl."

Nathan stood. "I've got to get going." He walked around to his sister as she stood awkwardly. He gathered her into his arms. "Thank you, little sister. You are a gentle and a wise woman."

She looked up, touched by the sudden emotion in his voice. "Why, thank you." She reached up and touched his face. "Just love her, Nathan. That's what she needs right now."

He nodded, then suddenly he pulled her to him fiercely and buried his face against her shoulder. "It should've been you," he whispered hoarsely. "It should've been you."

Caught completely off guard, Melissa tried to pull back to look at him, but he would not let her go. "What, Nathan? What should've been me?"

Suddenly, great, racking sobs began to shake his body. Stunned, totally bewildered, she clung to him, trying to steady him as the sobs swept over him in violent shudders. "It should have been you that went to see Joshua," he cried. "It should have been you."

N athan Steed?"

Nathan looked up in surprise. A man was standing at the front door of McBride's dry goods store, staring at him. With the light at the man's back, Nathan could not see his face clearly, but as the man strode across the room toward him, Nathan recognized the roundness of the body, the rolling gait.

"Parley?" he cried. "Parley Pratt?" In a moment they were in each other's arms, pounding each other on the back. Then Parley encircled Nathan with his big arms and lifted him right off the ground, nearly crushing his ribs. "I can't believe it's you," he roared in delight. "Let's go break the heads of a few Missourians, just for old time's sake."

Josiah McBride was at the counter helping a lady select some yard goods. He kept looking up at the two of them, peering over his spectacles in disapproval. The lady kept looking over her shoulder nervously.

Nathan ignored them both. It was as though spring had suddenly burst into the room in the middle of a January day. He couldn't believe his eyes.

"What are you doing here in Palmyra?" Nathan said breathlessly, when Parley finally freed him.

"I'm on my way east to preach the gospel. Your family asked if I would stop and say hello."

"How are they?"

"Fine. Your mother said to be sure and tell you that Melissa had her baby. Another boy. Everything's fine." He looked around. "Where's Lydia?"

"Upstairs. We live above the store."

Parley reached in his jacket and extracted a long white envelope. "Will you give this to her? It's from Emma."

"Of course, she'll be thrilled to hear from Emma." Nathan leaned forward. "And how is Thankful?"

A shadow crossed Parley's face. "Not well. As you know, she has long been in delicate health. The trip back to Ohio did not help. But she is recovering. We are living in New Portage now."

"And the temple? How is it coming?"

"Slow. There is so much to do, so little money."

"How long does Joseph think it will take?"

"At least a year, maybe a year and a half."

"I wish I could be there to help."

"Me too. New Portage is just too far to get up there very often."

A sound behind Nathan brought him around. Josiah McBride had finished with his customer and had come up just behind them. He gave Nathan a sharp look, then folded his arms and took a rigid stance.

"Parley," Nathan said quickly, "this is Lydia's father, Josiah McBride. Josiah, this is Parley P. Pratt, an old friend of ours from Ohio."

"And Missouri," Parley boomed. He stepped forward and took McBride's hand, which was belatedly offered. He pumped it up and down enthusiastically. With obvious distaste, Nathan's father-in-law murmured something, then started back toward the counter.

Nathan instantly forgot him and turned to Parley. "Have you seen Joseph?"

Josiah McBride whirled as if he had been jerked with a rope. "Nathan!" he said sharply.

Nathan looked up. "What?"

"There's to be no talk of Joseph Smith in this store. That was our agreement."

For a moment Nathan was dumbfounded—not only at the suddenness of the attack but also at the incredibly poor taste the man was showing in front of a guest. He fought to keep his voice even. "I agreed that I would not try to talk to anyone about Joseph Smith or the Church of the Latter-day Saints. But Parley is already a member of the Church. We're just talking about a mutual friend."

"You're talking about Joseph Smith." McBride spat it out with contempt. "Our agreement was that his name would not be mentioned in this store."

"Look, Nathan," Parley said hastily, "it's all right. I'm going east on the canal boats. We don't leave until morning. We can talk later tonight."

Nathan shot a withering look at his father-in-law. "No," he said, starting to untie his apron, "we'll go outside and talk."

"You're in the midst of taking inventory, Mr. Steed," Lydia's father snapped. "You talk on your own time."

Nathan looked at him for several moments; then a great calm came over him. He finished untying the apron and slipped it over his head. With great deliberateness he turned and dropped it over the back of a chair. "I *am* on my own time, Mr. McBride. I no longer clerk in this store." And with that, he took Parley's arm and both men walked out into the early September sunshine.

"Please, can't we talk this out like adults?" Lydia's mother was on her feet in the midst of the sitting room, poised between Nathan and Lydia, who sat on the sofa, and her husband, who was perched on the edge of the large overstuffed chair across from them.

Nathan shook his head. "I'm not trying to be stubborn, Hannah. It just became very clear today. We've been lying to ourselves for the last two weeks. This partnership thing is not going to work."

"Not if you won't honor the agreements you made," Josiah blurted. "You gave me your word."

"Papa," Lydia started, "Nathan was just talking with a long-time friend. He wasn't trying to preach about Joseph Smith or anything."

Josiah lowered his head. "Either a man's word is his bond, or it isn't. He promised! You sat right there and heard him."

"Josiah," Lydia's mother began, her tone soothing, "I don't think it helps to—"

"No!" he shouted. "You listen, Mrs. McBride. I've bent far enough. I will not bend any further. Either Nathan honors our agreement or I will not have him in the store."

A great despair swept over Lydia. "Papa—," she started.

But he leaped to his feet, glaring at her with so much venom in his eyes that it stunned her into silence. "I will not hear anything further," he thundered. "Either Nathan honors our agreement or it's over."

Lydia started to cry. Nathan touched her knee, then stood slowly. She looked up and grabbed for his hand, trying to ward off the explosion. But he stepped away, as though he wanted to disassociate himself from her so that what happened next would be his responsibility alone.

"You are right, Josiah," he began. There was no sarcasm, no animosity, just a great calmness. "This is your house. Your store. You have a right to set the conditions which prevail in them. And as long as we live here, we are obligated to honor them."

Josiah McBride blinked. He had gone up on the balls of his feet when Nathan stood, tensing for the confrontation. This was not what he had expected.

"On the other hand, I have the right to believe as I choose. And I believe Joseph Smith to be a man of honesty and integrity."

He stopped. Josiah McBride had started to splutter. Nothing in Nathan's face changed, nor had his voice altered in pitch. But something in his look stopped his father-in-law's outburst before it cleared his throat.

Nathan went on with that same wonderful calmness in his voice. "I believe Joseph Smith was called of God to be his prophet, just as Abraham, Moses, and other prophets in the Bible were called of God. I believe Joseph Smith to be an Apostle of the Lord Jesus Christ in exactly the same way that I believe Peter and James and Paul to be Apostles."

He turned, so that now Lydia could see his face. His eyes were filled with great sadness. "I believe that I dishonor the Lord and I think I dishonor Joseph's name when I refuse to acknowledge my beliefs publically or speak of what I know."

Lydia felt hot shame shoot through her like fire.

Nathan turned back to his father-in-law. "Since your wishes and my commitments are totally incompatible, I shall move out of your house first thing in the morning. Lydia and I will discuss at that time what that means for us and our children."

"No," Hannah whispered.

If he heard, Nathan didn't respond. He turned to Lydia fully now. "I am going to visit with Parley now. I may be late. I will see you in the morning."

"Nathan, I—"

"Parley brought a letter from Emma for you. I left it on the dresser." He turned and walked to the door.

But Josiah McBride wasn't through. The spluttering now exploded. "Prophet? Apostle?" he shouted. "How dare you blaspheme in my house?"

Nathan turned. "Good night, Josiah. Good night, Hannah."

Lydia's father's face had gone bright scarlet. His eyes were bulging with the fury that drove him. "The prophets gave their lives for God," he screamed at Nathan's back. "Paul was whipped and stoned and beaten. He said he bore in his body the marks of Jesus. That's what it means to be a true Apostle. What has your precious Joe Smith done that he dares to claim apostleship?"

Nathan's hand was on the doorknob. He stopped, then slowly turned. Josiah McBride fell back a step. Lydia felt as though she had been slapped. It was the most haunted look she had ever seen on a man's face.

"I am not an Apostle," Nathan said quietly. "I don't think I will ever be one. But if it's the marks of discipleship you are looking for, then please accept mine."

In one swift, savage move, he grabbed his shirtfront and ripped it open, sending the buttons flying. He threw the shirt off, then reached for the long cotton undershirt tucked into his pants and yanked it upwards, baring himself from waist to neck.

Lydia gasped. Her hand flew to her mouth, and for a moment she thought she would be sick. Somewhere, far off, she heard her mother cry out too. The pattern of the bullwhip was there for all to see, each scar a long stripe, some running from shoulder to belt line. And all of the wounds were still new enough that they were dark and red and ugly.

Nathan turned around. Lydia gasped again, and bit down on her lower lip so hard that she drew blood. There was no pattern now, no single, distinguishable lines like those on his chest. From shoulder to waist, the whole expanse of flesh was one obscene, horrible mass of crisscrossing scar tissue.

Lydia pressed her fists to her eyes, trying to blot out the vision of what lay before her. As she did so, she suddenly remembered something. Since he had come to her two weeks ago, Nathan had never removed his undershirt in her presence. She had thought it very peculiar at first, but he had brushed aside her comments, saying something about the discomfort of being in her parents' house. She had finally dismissed it and said no more about it, though it had continued to trouble her.

The sound of the door brought Lydia up. She opened her eyes in time to see that Nathan had dropped his undershirt and gathered up his shirt and tucked it under his arm. He looked at her and smiled faintly. "I'll be late, Lydia. Don't wait up."

A moment later he pulled the door softly shut and left the McBride family sitting there, staring at the door.

It was close to midnight when the door to her bedroom opened slowly. She didn't move as Nathan stepped inside, moving on tiptoe so as not to wake her. She lay on her side, watching his shape move about in the darkness. He took off his shoes, then his shirt and trousers. Now she could see the lighter color of his undergarments. Unbidden, tears sprang to her eyes again and began to trickle down the side of her face.

Carefully, he lowered himself onto the bed beside her, trying not to bounce the bed with his weight. He adjusted the covers for a moment, then lay still. But in a moment he raised again and turned and felt the pillow with his hand. He turned it over to its other side.

"I'm sorry," she whispered. When her pillow had become soaked with tears she had traded hers for his dry one. That had been over an hour ago. "I forgot it was still wet."

He turned his head. "I didn't mean to wake you."

"I've not been asleep."

"Oh."

She waited for a moment, to see if he would say more. When he didn't she spoke again. "How's Parley?"

She could sense that he smiled in the darkness. "Parley is Parley. It's wonderful to see him again."

She felt a pang. There hadn't been many things that were wonderful in Nathan's life lately.

"I'm sorry about tonight," he said slowly. There was a long pause. "I shouldn't have done it. It proved nothing."

Her heart twisted inside her, as though it were going to break. "Why didn't you tell me, Nathan?" she whispered, her voice trembling.

"There's not much to tell. Once the camp was disbanded, I went across the river into Jackson County to try and find Joshua. I—"

"Joshua did this to you?" she cried in horror.

Again there was a long silence before he spoke. "No. It was my fault. I did something very stupid."

In an instant she slid next to him and buried herself against his side. She choked back a sob. "I never knew, Nathan. I'm so sorry."

He brought his arm up and pulled her into his protective embrace. He rubbed her shoulder over and over. "It's all right, Lydia. There's nothing for you to be sorry about. It's all right."

After a long time, she lifted her head and looked at him. "I'm sorry about Papa."

"Don't be. He's doing what he feels is necessary."

"I'm sorry that I made you come here, that I made you take the store. I know how you've hated—"

He reached out and gently put his hand over her mouth. "I said it's all right, Lydia." He pulled her closer and held her tightly. "I love you. That's all that matters. We'll talk about it in the morning."

She pulled her head away from his hand and came up on one elbow. "No, it's not all right. I've been a fool. We need to talk about what we're going to do."

"I'm the one who's been the fool," he murmured. "In so many ways. I'm sorry that I didn't understand what you were going through, that I was so blind. I'm sorry."

Suddenly she started to giggle softly.

He looked up in surprise.

"If either one of us says, 'I'm sorry,' one more time, I think I'm going to be sick."

He laughed in spite of himself. "I guess we do sound pretty awful."

She sat up and crossed her legs, brushing at the last of the tears that were still in the corners of her eyes. "Can you get a candle from the hallway? I want to read you something."

He looked puzzled, but nodded and went out to where they kept the candle burning in the hall to provide some night light for the children. When he came back Lydia had retrieved the letter from Emma and was sitting back on the bed again. He wedged the candle in a holder on the desk, then got in bed again, sitting by her side.

"Emma is such a dear," Lydia began. "With all she's got going, she still takes time to write."

"What does she say?"

She held up the paper. It was only a third filled with writing. "Very little. She inquired after the children. Asked how we were doing." Her voice broke and she shook her head quickly, fighting for control. "She said that she and Joseph pray for us every night and morning. Other than that, it wasn't much." She looked up at him. "Except that she sent me a copy of the revelation the Lord gave her back in Harmony."

"The one where he told her to compile a book of hymns?"

"Yes." Lydia pulled the second sheet of paper out from behind the first. This sheet was nearly covered with Emma's neat, precise handwriting. But Lydia laid it in her lap again and stared out at the room. "She could have said so much, you know."

"Like what?"

"Like the fact that she has buried four of her children, I have only lost one. Like the fact that Joseph is gone three or four times as much as you have been. He's always gone here to this branch to preach, or off to that town to ordain someone to the priesthood. It's a mission here, then Missouri there. He's gone all the time." Her shoulders lifted and fell. "It makes my problems look pretty small compared to hers."

"Emma's problems don't make yours any less real."

She reached up and touched his face. "Thank you for saying that. But I've lain here for the last three hours thinking about this, thinking about Emma. And I feel pretty small right now. Just take one example. Living with others. My parents have really opened their house to us here, but I still hate it. I hate not having my own house, my own kitchen, my own flower garden. I hate having to worry about Emily crying in the night and waking my parents.

"Yet look at Joseph and Emma. For most of their married life, they've lived with others—her parents, his parents, the Whitmers in Fayette, the Whitneys in Kirtland, the Johnsons in Hiram. How she must have detested it, being passed from family to family, depending on their charity, never being alone."

She reached out and took Nathan's hand, interlocking her fingers with his. "I came to Palmyra because I couldn't face the possibility that you might be killed in Missouri. But Emma"—she blew out her breath in amazement—"she's seen Joseph arrested, hounded, tarred and feathered, insulted, abused. They have to have bodyguards sleep in the house with them. It must leave her constantly terrified."

Nathan was nodding, remembering a day in Palmyra, several years ago now, when he had intervened in Emma's behalf, stopping a group of men from mocking and insulting her. "She's come in for a fair share of abuse herself."

"I know," Lydia answered bleakly. "She told me one day what it's like to be the Prophet's wife, always on display, always being criticized for this thing or that thing which doesn't measure up to people's expectations."

Lydia turned to him now, her eyes shining. "That was a good part of my tears tonight, I guess. Thinking about Emma. She has challenges so much worse than mine, yet she continues on, standing by Joseph's side, always so gracious, always so beautiful."

"*You* are gracious. *You* are beautiful," he said gallantly.

"Will you stop being so nice?" she laughed. "I'm trying to do some repenting here."

His eyes filled with mock gravity and he nodded. "Yes, ma'am."

She picked up the second sheet of the letter from Emma, the one that contained the copy of Emma's revelation. "Let me read you some things."

"All right."

"The Lord starts out by calling her his daughter. He also calls her an elect lady."

"Hmm. That's a nice title." He smiled at Lydia. "Elect lady? Yes, I like that. You are an elect lady, too, you know. I knew that that very first day when Joshua introduced us right outside the store. Do you remember?"

She laughed. "Of course I remember. I can even tell you what I was wearing that day. Can you?"

He gestured toward the paper in her hands. "It's getting late. Tell me what the Lord said to Emma."

She laughed, taking his hand again. It had been so long since they had laughed together like this. It felt wonderful. She looked down, found the place she wanted, and started to read. " 'Behold thy sins are forgiven thee' "—she squeezed his hand, and he squeezed it back—" 'and thou art an elect lady, whom I have called.' "

She took a quick breath. This was going to be harder than she thought. Slowly now, she continued, her eyes finding the lines and words she wanted. She chose only those things that had impacted her with such force earlier.

" 'The office of thy calling shall be for a comfort unto thy husband, in his—' " Her voice caught, and instantly tears filled her eyes again. She swallowed quickly, forcing them back. " 'The office of thy calling shall be for a comfort unto thy husband, in his afflictions with consoling words, in the spirit of meekness.' "

She lowered the paper. "You read it," she said, her voice husky.

Nathan reached out and took it from her hands. She pointed at the spot where she wanted him to go on.

" 'Continue in the spirit of meekness,' " he started, his voice steady and firm, " 'and beware of pride. Let thy soul delight in thy husband. Keep my commandments continually, and a crown of righteousness thou shalt receive.' "

"Don't you just love that phrase?" Lydia whispered. " 'Let thy soul delight in thy husband.' "

His eyes were thoughtful. "Yes. The same would be true for a man, I think. I know that my soul delights in you, Lydia."

"And mine in you," she breathed. Straightening, she took the paper from him. She folded it carefully and placed it back in the envelope.

"Those are beautiful words, Lydia."

"They are, but they are more than that," she said softly. "They are my answer, Nathan." She looked up at him, her eyes wide and filled with love. "They're also *your* answer."

"My answer?"

"Yes. Don't you think I know what you've been praying for?"

"I've been praying that I can make you happy again."

She reached up and kissed him softly. "I know. And now you have your answer."

"I do?"

"Yes, I'm happy." She kissed him again. "I'm so very happy."

He seemed a little dazed.

"So let's go back to Kirtland."

That brought his head up with a snap, then he immediately frowned. "You don't have to do that for me, Lydia. I can be happy here if you wish."

She shook her head, then moved around so she was partially behind him. Slowly she reached down and grasped the bottom of his undershirt. His eyes widened, but he did not move as she lifted it enough to expose his chest. Tears streamed down her face now as she began to trace, ever so softly, the welts with her fingertips. "They did this because you were a Mormon?" she asked, her voice barely audible.

He closed his eyes, then finally nodded.

She let the shirt drop back into place, and put her arms around him. "Then, how can I not go back to Kirtland? I have things to do, covenants to keep."

He whirled around to face her. "Do you mean that?" he cried. "Do you really mean that, Lydia?"

Her chin came up and she smiled through the tears. "How else can I ever expect to become an elect lady?"

The eighteen months between the fall of 1834 and the spring of 1836 provided a much-needed time of peace and relative tranquility for the Church of the Latter-day Saints and its members. For the most part, the Saints in Missouri lived in harmony with the citizens north of the river, though all agreed this would not serve as a permanent solution and Church leaders there began looking toward the northern, uninhabited areas of the state as a possible settling place. In Kirtland, the swelling numbers of Mormons pouring into Ohio still created some tension between member and nonmember, but at least for a time, in both states, there were no serious outbreaks of violence.

With the return of the men from Zion's Camp, work on the temple intensified. The walls, only about four feet high when Zion's Camp returned, went up quickly thereafter. Men gave a "tithing" of their time, most working at least one day a week on the building. During the winter, when farmers were idle, they donated much more. Each Saturday, the brethren would gather with their teams and wagons at the stone quarry south of town and, with Joseph acting as foreman, would cut and haul enough stone to the temple site to keep the stonemasons busy for the coming week.

Benjamin Steed was called to serve as a member of the building committee and began to play a more and more prominent role in the erection of the structure. By now one of the leading land developers in Geauga County, Benjamin had purchased several blocks of property around the city, as well as two farms, one out south of town beyond the stone quarry, and the other east on the Chardon Road. When Nathan and Lydia returned from Palmyra, Benjamin persuaded them to leave their little homestead out on the Morley farm and manage both of Benjamin's farms. This freed Benjamin so that he could spend his time developing his town properties into prime building lots. It also left him considerable free time, all of which he spent at the temple.

Mary Ann was nearly as involved, for it was not just the men that labored on the Lord's house. The women gathered frequently to sew, knit, and weave: first they concentrated their efforts on making clothes for the temple workmen; then later they made the carpets and the long curtains, or veils, that were designed to partition off the large assembly rooms into smaller compartments.

By November of 1835 the plastering of the exterior began. Crushed glassware was added to the stucco to make the walls glisten in the sunlight. Under the direction of Brigham Young, who was a skilled carpenter and glazier, the interior was finished during February of 1836. The large assembly rooms were furnished at each end with elaborate and beautifully crafted pulpits for the presidencies of the priesthood quorums.

The settling of affairs in Missouri freed many of the brethren for missionary work. They fanned out in every direction, carrying copies of the Book of Mormon in their knapsacks and the fire of testimony in their hearts. In 1830 the Church had been organized with six official members. By the end of 1835 there were nearly nine thousand Latter-day Saints.

Nathan Steed was one of the many who contributed to this missionary effort. He and Lydia returned home in time to help his father harvest the fall crops, then he left on a two-month mission to Pennsylvania. He left for a month in the early spring of '35 and visited the nearby settlements in Ohio, then left again the following fall, this time traveling more extensively through New York, Connecticut, Vermont, and Massachusetts. In his journal he recorded that, in all now, he had walked over two thousand miles, preached seventy-nine times, laid hands on the sick and blessed them over one hundred times, blessed over fifty children, and baptized nearly a hundred converts.

This eighteen months was a time of many important developments in the Church. Changes in organization were made, additional scriptures published, new doctrines revealed. In February of 1835 the Three Witnesses to the Book of Mormon, following the Lord's instructions, chose twelve men to form a Quorum of Twelve Apostles. Two weeks later Joseph organized the Quorum of the Seventy. Some said that Zion's Camp had been a failure, but it was interesting to Nathan to see that of the Twelve, all but three had marched to Missouri to redeem Zion; of the Seventy, without exception every one had been a member of Zion's Camp.

In the summer of 1835, Kirtland was electrified by a visitor from the East who brought some Egyptian mummies and some scrolls of papyrus filled with the mysterious hieroglyphic writing used by the ancients. Desirous to know what the writings contained, the Saints purchased the mummies and the scrolls for twenty-four hundred dollars, and immediately Joseph began work on the scrolls. To his joy, the Prophet discovered that they contained the writings of Abraham and of Joseph of Egypt.

Later that same year the Saints received a second work of latter-day scripture to serve as companion with the Book of Mormon. A revised and expanded version of the Book of Commandments was published; it was called the Doctrine and Covenants. The first section of the book contained seven lectures on faith prepared by Joseph Smith and others and given at the School of the Elders. This section was called "the doctrine." The second and much larger section contained "the covenants and commandments," or the revelations Joseph had received from the Lord over the previous seven years. More than a hundred were included.

But while these developments were exciting and gave the members much to talk about, for the most part life went on in the daily routine of making a living and raising families. For the Benjamin Steed family, it was a much-needed time for restoration as well. When Nathan accepted the task of running his father's two farms, his mother persuaded him to move with Lydia and the children into town rather than live on one of the two farms.

It proved to be one of the wisest things Nathan could have done, for it not only kept them in the mainstream of Church life but also united the family in an unusual way. Jessica and her young daughter moved into a small cabin next door to Benjamin and Mary Ann's place, and was quickly welcomed and fully accepted into the Steed family circle.

A month or two after Jessica's arrival, Melissa prevailed upon her husband, Carl, to let Jessica work at the livery stable keeping the books. Carl at first agreed only reluctantly; but Jessica's previous work experience with Joshua's freight company in Independence proved invaluable, and thereafter Carl was pleased to have her work for him.

When Lydia and Nathan returned from New York and agreed to live in town, the circle was completed. Jessica had dreaded this time, the time when she and the legendary Lydia met face-to-face. But any fears she had were quickly put to rest. Jessica understood now why Joshua had continued to nurse his fantasies about Lydia, but she also knew they had been nothing more than that.

Mary Ann was thrilled with the way things worked out, of course. To have both of her daughters and both of her daughters-in-law around her was wonderful. And then there were the grandchildren! There were six now. Jessica's little Rachel, a sober child with wide, vulnerable eyes and a pensive spirit, quickly became her grandfather's favorite and went everywhere with him, her tiny little hand always reaching up to grasp his. Melissa had two sons now—young Carl, who had taken her dark hair and eyes, and David Benjamin, destined to be as redheaded and freckle-faced as his father. Lydia and Nathan's oldest, young Joshua, would turn five in May of '36. He was a frequent visitor to his uncle's livery stable, where he and young Carl had the most wonderful romps. Little Emily, who had fully inherited her mother's beauty, took a special liking to her Grandmother Steed, and they became fast friends. The baby, born in the fall of '35 and named Nathan Joseph, was a strapping youngster with an insatiable appetite and, as long as he was fed, a wonderful disposition.

It was a frequent occurrence to have all the Steeds gather at Grandma and Grandpa's house for a cornhusking, or to work on temple projects, or for dinner. There was not a day that went by but what Mary Ann and Benjamin gave thanks to the Lord for the blessing of having their family around them.

Things were looking up for Nathan and Lydia; not only had they weathered their crisis, but their marriage entered a phase now in which their relationship deepened and was strengthened. Part of that stemmed from the promises Lydia had made to herself and to Nathan. Part of it came from the more reflective and mature Nathan who had returned from the experience of Zion's Camp. When Joseph opened the Kirtland School in the winter of 1834-35, William E. McLellin was hired to teach geography, penmanship, arithmetic, and English grammar to the more than one hundred students—old and young, male and female—who enrolled. Nathan went to McLellin one day and suggested he consider Lydia as a substitute on those days when he got sick or had commitments he could not set aside. McLellin liked the suggestion, and Lydia took to teaching as if she had been born to it.

Then, in January of '36, when Joseph hired a professor from Hudson, Ohio, to come to Kirtland and teach the brethren Hebrew, Nathan immediately enrolled in the classes. Each night, when he wasn't on guard duty at the temple, he would bring his notes home, sit Lydia down, and teach her what he had learned. At first it was just Lydia. But quickly Jessica and Rebecca and Mary Ann were part of these evening "classes" as well. Lydia and Becca were especially quick to pick up the Hebrew words and constructions, and soon were going around the house reciting: "Aleph, bet, gimmel, dalet, hay. . . ." They would almost never make it clear through the Hebrew alphabet without breaking into gales of laughter.

Worship was another thing that bound the Steed family together. No meetinghouses were constructed while the work went forward on the temple, so the Saints met wherever they could. During the winter it was usually in homes or in the school. In more pleasant weather they preferred to gather outdoors in some shady and grassy spot. Since Benjamin and Mary Ann had one of the larger homes in Kirtland, theirs was often the site of Sabbath services. Sunday meetings were simple. They would begin, usually at ten o'clock, with a hymn and a prayer, followed by sermons, then another hymn and a prayer of closing. The afternoon service was the same, only it also usually included the administration of the sacrament of the Lord's Supper.

Weeknights were often filled with priesthood quorum meetings or other preaching services. The first Thursday of the month was "fast day." The food saved by fasting was brought and distributed to the poor, then they had a "testimony meeting." These meetings lasted much longer than Sabbath meetings, sometimes as long as six hours. The members would rise to their feet and bear testimony of their beliefs, or tell of manifestations of God's good will in their lives. Often they would exhort one another to live more Christlike lives. "Physical fasting, spiritual feasting," was the way Mary Ann described the fast meetings.

There was another meeting of a more unusual nature that was held from time to time. In the first months of the Church's organization, many people began to ask Joseph to petition the Lord for their own personal revelations. He did so, but as the Church grew in numbers this became more and more difficult for him to keep up with. In December of 1833, while giving blessings to his own family, Joseph was inspired to call his father as the Patriarch to the Church. In Old Testament times, the patriarchs—Adam, Abraham, Isaac, Jacob, Joseph—gave blessings to their children and others. These blessings gave the person counsel from the Lord, promised blessings if the individual was faithful, and warned about weaknesses or problems that the person should avoid.

Soon Father Smith was traveling to the various branches of the Church, where he would hold special "blessing meetings." He would gather a group of Saints together and, one by one, give each a patriarchal blessing.

On the night of February second, 1836, while a winter storm raged outside, Nathan and Lydia Steed, along with Jessica and Rebecca, sat in a blessing meeting inside the home of Joseph Smith, Sr. For over an hour Joseph's father, white haired and dignified, now in his sixty-fifth year, had stood in his place behind the chair placed in the center of the room. One by one, each person went to that chair. He would lay his hands on the person's head and in quiet reverence, speaking slowly so his wife or son could transcribe the words, pronounce the blessing upon the individual. He had now gone almost all the way around the circle. Lydia was next.

"You go first," she whispered to Nathan, as Father Smith finished and the other person stood and shook his hand. For some reason, she was suddenly nervous.

Nathan smiled and shook his head.

"Sister Steed," Father Smith said, beckoning to her.

Nathan squeezed her hand, then gave her a gentle push. "Go on."

She went to the chair and took her place, then turned and looked up into the kindly face. "Lydia McBride Steed," she said. He always asked for the person's full name. He nodded. As she turned back to the front and bowed her head, she felt the gentle hands with their long slender fingers come upon her head.

"Sister Lydia McBride Steed, in the name of our Lord and

Savior, even Jesus Christ, and as a patriarch called of God and ordained to that office by one of the Lord's anointed, I lay my hands upon your head and give unto you a blessing."

He paused for a moment, to listen to that still, quiet, inward voice that was prompting him. His voice deepened. "Sister Steed, you have been called of God to enter his church and kingdom in this the last of the dispensations, the dispensation of the fulness of times, even that dispensation that shall bring about a restoration of all things in preparation for the coming of him who is Lord of lords and King of kings.

"Sister Steed, the Lord is pleased with your willingness to enter the waters of baptism and take his name upon you, and he will bless you throughout your life with a multitude of blessings as long as you continue faithful to his word."

A multitude of blessings? They have already come. Her heart sang with joy as a list quickly ran through her mind: Nathan and their love. Three beautiful children. Good health. A comfortable home. The Steed family. Membership in the Church.

"Sister Steed, you are a member of the house of Israel, coming through the loins of Ephraim, who was the son of Joseph, who was the son of Jacob. This is a noble lineage, and you have been born into it because of your faithfulness.

"The Lord would have you know that your calling in this mortal life is to be a righteous mother in Zion. You have already chosen a good and faithful man as your husband. Stand by his side in his endeavors, and you shall be the queen in your home. You have already been blessed with children, and you shall yet be blessed with sons and daughters. These spirits that have now and will yet be entrusted into your care come from the presence of God, where they lived with him. Take them into your home with love and care. Train them in the way they should go, teaching them the principles of the gospel and the importance of serving Jesus Christ. This is a sacred and holy trust that you are given. If you fill it well, you shall come forth in the morning of the first resurrection with all the holy angels and there behold the face of God."

A thrill shot through Lydia as the image of his words filled her mind. *Sons and daughters! The first resurrection!* Her mind was reeling with the wonder of it.

Again there was a pause, only longer this time. When he continued—more slowly now, speaking clearly and distinctly—his voice rose in power. She felt the pressure of his hands bearing down more firmly on her, as though to impress his words into her mind.

"You are to devote your time and your talents and your energies to being a righteous mother in Zion. If you are faithful in this calling, you shall be as a river of pure water which rushes down from the mountain, bringing life to all that is nearby."

Lydia started slightly and her eyes almost flew open. *A river? Mountains?* The images of her dream flashed into her mind. She had not had the dream for over a year now and had almost put it from her mind. Because of the terrible dread she always felt during the dream and afterwards, she had never told anyone of it, not even Nathan.

Her sudden movement beneath his hands caused Father Smith to stop, but when she steadied he went on. "Your children shall be blessed by your influence. They shall be as trees planted in a goodly land, by a pure stream, and they shall be most comely and exceedingly fruitful. In your old age, your children and their children and their children shall rise up and, with a joyful noise, shout praises unto your name."

Lydia felt a hot, scalding sensation on her cheeks and realized she was crying. It was her dream. The mountain, the river, the majestic trees. But he had not spoken of the desert, of the terrible desolation, the rushing horror that always swept over her. But she didn't feel horror now. Or dread. She was infused with joy, with a tremendous, surging sense of relief.

Startled, she realized Father Smith had finished and removed his hands. Trembling slightly, she stood and turned around to face him, brushing quickly at her cheeks. In one step she was to him and embraced him. "Thank you, Father Smith. Thank you."

Far to the west of Kirtland, Joshua Steed stood alone on the streets of Independence. Night had fallen, and most of Jackson County's citizens were in their homes, or else gathered in the saloons for a last beer before going home. The latter had been Joshua's plan as well. He found nothing at the house now to hold him. The emptiness was depressing. And so, when he had finished his work at the freight office, he had started for Clinton Roundy's saloon on the main street of Independence. A beer or two, maybe a friendly game of low-stakes poker—it would help pass the time.

With a frown, he reached in his coat pocket and took out the envelope again. Now he wished he hadn't passed the dry goods store. The proprietor had seen him going by. "Mr. Steed!" he had called. "A letter came for you today."

He opened it again slowly, smoothing the brown paper against his chest. Nathan's neat handwriting filled both sides. There was a postscript in his mother's hand. In the moonlight, Joshua could not read any of it. But he didn't have to. He had stood there, outside the mercantile shop, and read it over and over, until the words seared his emotions like a blacksmith's fire.

Suddenly, with one savage twist of his hands, he tore the letter in two. "I don't want your forgiveness, little brother," he hissed. He ripped the paper again. "I don't need it." With deep satisfaction he shredded the paper into tiny pieces and flung them away.

As they fluttered to the ground, his mouth tightened into a hard line. "And get it out of your head that you're coming back to Missouri." His chest lifted and fell. Now the bitterness made his voice go soft and cold. "That would not be a wise move on your part, little brother. Not a wise move at all."

With that, he turned and strode back down the street toward Roundy's saloon and the company that awaited him there.

Usually on a Sunday morning in Kirtland, the streets were mostly quiet and deserted until about seven-thirty or eight o'clock. But such was not the case on this morning of March twenty-seventh, 1836. Saints had been streaming into Kirtland from miles around for the past two days. They came from Painesville and Chardon, Mantua, Hiram and Thompson, New Portage, Orange, Warrensville, Amherst and Ravenna. They slept with friends and relatives, put bedrolls in the backs of wagons, pitched tents, or in some cases just rolled out their bedding on the ground in whatever vacant lots were available. By dawn they began to stir and prepare for a Sabbath that would be different from any one thus far in their history.

Benjamin Steed stepped out of the doorway of his house at ten minutes before seven. He stopped and stared in amazement. The street was teeming with people, all moving northward toward the temple block and the massive building that dominated the bluffs of upper Kirtland. The sun was not quite up yet, and in the softness of the morning light, the white walls gleamed almost translucent and the great eastern tower seemed even higher than it was.

"My goodness," Mary Ann blurted as she came out of the door, "would you look at that! And it's not even seven o'clock yet."

Benjamin nodded. "I knew people would start coming early." The services were not scheduled to start until nine, but Joseph had suggested they get there well before that if they wanted seats.

Rebecca stepped outside and joined them. "Are they ready?" Benjamin asked her.

Rebecca nodded. "They're just giving Matthew some last-minute instructions about the children. Rachel wants to go, and Jessica's trying to explain things to her."

Mary Ann smiled. "They'll be fine." Joshua, Emily, and Rachel adored their Uncle Matthew, and given the fact that he was almost sixteen, Mary Ann did not worry for a moment about his competency. Lydia's baby was just six months old and still had to stay with his mother, so Matthew would only have the three older children to look after. Melissa and Carl were only two blocks down if there should be problems.

"Becca," Benjamin said, "tell them we'll go on ahead and get in line. We'll save them a place."

Joseph Smith and the other members of the First Presidency came outside about eight o'clock to let the people in and to begin seating them. By then the crowd was approaching a thousand in number. Clearly, if they kept coming at this rate, not everyone was going to get a seat this day.

As the Steeds neared the front door, taking their turn in line, Joseph came out again and spied them. "Well," he said, "and here are the Steeds. Good morning, good morning."

"Good morning, Brother Joseph."

"Come with me. I have a place for you near the front."

Benjamin looked up in surprise. "Are you sure, Joseph?" he said quickly. "We don't want any special favors."

"No special favors," Joseph said just as quickly. "But there is a place reserved for the building committee, and the Lord knows, Benjamin, you surely did your part on the building committee."

As they went inside, Joseph stopped for a moment in the large entryway as he saw the Steed women look up, their eyes widening. Benjamin and Nathan had both been in the temple within the last few days for meetings held on the upper floor, but the women had not. They had been inside previously to help hang the large canvas veils that hung from hidden rollers in the ceiling, but that had been before the last of the finishing work and painting had been completed.

"Oh, Joseph," Lydia exclaimed, "this is beautiful!"

He nodded in satisfaction. "Come inside and see what you think."

As they entered the large hall that filled the entire main floor, they stopped again, their eyes wide. "Oh!" Jessica breathed.

"It's marvelous!" Mary Ann echoed.

The hall was wonderfully bright. Large, Gothic-arched windows let plenty of light into the room, which was huge—sixty-five feet long by fifty-five feet wide, with high ceilings. It would have seemed cavernous except that along the full length of the north and south walls the ceilings had been lowered, leaving only the center section vaulted. A series of gracefully fluted columns supported these lowered ceilings, breaking up the expanse of the room without taking away anything from its spaciousness. Lydia's eyes lifted to examine the delicately carved motif of interlocking circles that capped each pillar.

The room was filled with sectioned-off pews, a little lower than waist high. In each of these compartments there were backless benches, this so the congregation could face either way, depending on which end of the room was used by the person conducting. And it was to those two ends of the room that the eye was drawn and held. Here, filling the entire center sections of the east and west walls, were the pulpits of the priesthood—the west being for the Melchizedek, the east for the Aaronic. They rose in four graceful tiers from the level of the floor, so that the highest pulpit was eight or ten feet above the congregation. The lowest tier was a large table with drop-down leaves designed for use in the administration of the sacrament. Above that, each tier held three places for the presidencies of the various priesthood quorums. These tiers were flanked by other benches on both sides so that additional members of the quorum leaderships could be seated.

The workmanship was exquisite, and here the master craftsmanship of Brigham Young and those he had supervised was instantly evident. In the four corners of the hall, placed so as to face the pulpits, were additional tiers of choir seats, more simply finished but still blending in perfectly with the overall feeling of the room. Everything was painted white and gleamed in the morning light. The effect was to make the whole room airy and bright, which immediately lifted the spirits and gladdened the heart.

Rebecca said it all for them when she simply turned and said, "Oh, Joseph!"

Joseph was much pleased by their reaction. "It is a fitting house for the Lord, don't you think?"

"Indeed," Nathan said fervently. They were all touched with a sense of reverential awe.

Joseph led them to the pew that was four rows back from the western pulpits. "Sit here," he suggested. "Lydia, you can take the outside; then if the baby needs nursing you can get out more easily."

"Are you sure this is where we belong?" Mary Ann asked.

Joseph laughed and nodded. "Remember that day when I was trying to convince Benjamin to help us build the temple?"

She nodded, but Ben shook his head, somewhat embarrassed. "I remember," he said. "I was being a little pigheaded as I recall."

"A little?" Mary Ann said, poking at him with her elbow, but unable to keep the pride from her voice.

"Well," continued Joseph, "that day, after you agreed to help, I vowed that I would see that you got a good seat for the dedication. Now I look back on what you've done, Benjamin—" Suddenly his voice caught, and he reached out and grasped Benjamin's hand. "Thank you, my good friend. Your contribution has been enormous."

Benjamin's voice was suddenly husky too. "It has been the greatest joy in my life, outside of my family, Joseph. Thank you for not giving up on an old fool."

"The Lord didn't give up on me," Joseph laughed. "I guess that's where I learned my patience."

Mary Ann reached out and touched his arm. "Thank you, Joseph. It is a great day."

"It *is* a great day, friends. A day of Pentecost. The Lord is pleased with our sacrifice and shall pour out his Spirit upon us in great abundance here today."

At precisely nine A.M., President Sidney Rigdon stood, and instantly the soft murmur of people whispering quieted. Every seat on the main floor was filled. The great doors had been pulled shut. Even with nearly a thousand people seated, the ushers had turned people away. Some had been sent to an overflow meeting at the schoolhouse to the west of the temple. Others were promised there would be a repeat session on Thursday next. Nathan looked at his father and mouthed a word of thanks. Waiting until Thursday would have been heartbreaking. It was worth the two-hour wait in order to be here.

"I would like to begin these services," President Rigdon was saying, "by turning to the book of Psalms. I shall first read from Psalm ninety-six."

He opened a Bible, turned the pages until he found his place, then began to read. " 'O sing unto the Lord a new song: sing unto the Lord, all the earth.' "

A thrill shot through Nathan. *Yes!* he thought. He felt like singing. He felt like shouting out praises to his God. He looked down. Lydia had gone out and nursed little Nathan Joseph just before the meeting had begun. Now he slept peacefully in his father's arms. He saw Lydia smiling at him and reached out and took her hand.

" 'Sing unto the Lord,' " President Rigdon continued, " 'bless his name; shew forth his salvation from day to day.' "

Nathan smiled back at his wife and clasped her hand more tightly.

Next President Rigdon turned to Psalm twenty-four. Nathan's head came up. This was one of his personal favorites. But as Sidney boomed out the question asked therein, it startled Nathan. He had heard it, read it a hundred times or more. He had never applied it to himself in quite the way he did on this day.

" 'Who shall ascend into the hill of the Lord?' " Sidney cried, " 'or who shall stand in his holy place?' " He paused to let his eyes meet the hundreds of eyes that watched him steadily. " 'He that hath clean hands, and a pure heart; who hath not lifted up his soul unto vanity, nor sworn deceitfully.' "

Nathan winced, his mind flashing back to that night almost two years ago now, in the room above a saloon in Jackson County. He had lost his temper and deliberately goaded Joshua into a rage. Did that leave him with clean hands? And what did it mean to swear deceitfully? He had sworn to cross the river so that he could make peace with Joshua. Instead, . . . He looked away, his face burning with shame.

Nathan's head came up as he realized that Sidney was through reading.

"We'll now hear from our choir," he was saying, "under the direction of Brother M. C. Davis. They will sing from our new hymnal prepared by Sister Emma Smith, hymn number nineteen, 'Ere Long the Veil Will Rend in Twain,' a hymn written by our beloved brother, Parley P. Pratt."

Surprisingly, Jessica's thoughts at that moment, like Nathan's, were turned to Missouri and to Joshua Steed.

> Ere long the veil will rend in twain,
> The King descend with all His train;
> The earth shall shake with awful fright,
> And all creation feel His might.

Was that what it would take to restore the Saints to their rightful place in Zion? The Lord shaking the earth until the Missourians felt the power of his might?

> Lift up your heads, ye Saints, in peace,
> The Savior comes for your release;
> The day of the redeemed has come;
> The Saints shall all be welcomed home.

Jessica sighed inwardly, a deep sadness coming over her. What power could soften Joshua's heart to the point where he could be welcomed home in the presence of God? She shook her head. She was not sure there was any.

The choir finished and sat down. President Rigdon stood and bowed his head. Jessica followed suit, as did the rest of the congregation.

"Our Father who art in heaven," he began, his voice now somber and filled with awe, "hallowed be thy name."

Suddenly Jessica stiffened. As President Rigdon continued, invoking the Lord's blessings on the proceedings of the day, it seemed that his voice suddenly changed. Then she realized it wasn't him. It wasn't his voice at all. It was something inside of her. She was feeling the most peculiar sensation. It started in her chest and radiated outward rapidly, going out to the tips of her fingers, and shooting down into her feet. It was the most wonderful thing she had ever experienced. Her whole body was tingling.

She felt Mary Ann stir beside her, and cracked one eye open for a moment. Mary Ann had her hands out in front of her, staring at them. Immediately Jessica understood. Mary Ann was experiencing the same thing she was. Then she saw that Becca, on the other side of Mary Ann, was looking at the two of them, her eyes filled with wonder. She felt it too. Without a word, the three of them were suddenly holding each other's hands. On the other side of Jessica sat Lydia, who now leaned against her. Jessica turned. Lydia was crying, tears of joy streaming down her face. With her other hand, Jessica reached out for her.

As President Rigdon continued, they sat there like that, these four Steed women, sitting shoulder-to-shoulder, holding each other's hands tightly, thrilling to the sensation that was sweeping through each of them.

———•———

Becca Steed caught a movement out of the corner of her eye and started a little. President Rigdon had closed his sermon, and stepped back for a moment. Beside her, her father was reaching into the pocket of his vest. He pulled out his watch and flipped back the cover. She stretched a little, then stared in amazement. It was nearly twelve o'clock!

She couldn't believe it. After his invocation President Rigdon had announced another choir number. When they finished he stood to deliver his sermon. That would have been—she calculated quickly—about nine-twenty. She sat back, almost stunned. He had spoken for two and a half hours!

President Rigdon had been, at one time, a Campbellite preacher before the missionaries had come to Ohio, and he was well renowned for his oratory gifts. But if anyone had tried to tell Rebecca before this moment that she would sit for two and a half hours so mesmerized that she was barely conscious of the passage of time, she would have laughed aloud. Now she simply sat and marveled.

President Rigdon chose as his text the scripture from the eighth chapter of Matthew in which it is recorded that Jesus said, "Foxes have holes, and the birds of the air have nests; but the Son of man hath not where to lay his head." He developed it powerfully, showing that in spite of the many meetinghouses which were built by the various denominations to provide worship places, there was nowhere a house that the Lord could call his own.

Becca had wept as Sidney recounted the sacrifices and the hardships the Saints had experienced as they built out of their poverty this magnificent structure so that the Lord would have a house he could call his own. He also pointed out that for the most part the people of Jesus' time had rejected him and ignored his teachings. The same was happening now. That really hit Becca hard. Had she lived in Jerusalem back then, would she have followed the Master? Would she have been one who listened? Or would she have been part of the crowd that screamed, "Crucify him! Crucify him!" Right then and there she vowed that she would make it her lifelong goal to listen to the words of Christ and accept them, no matter where they took her.

Mary Ann was also deeply stirred by President Rigdon's message. When he stepped back she felt a pang of disappointment. How she loved to hear the gospel, especially when it was taught with such power and clarity.

President Rigdon took a sip from a glass of water, then stepped forward again. "Brothers and sisters, we will now sustain Brother Joseph Smith as our prophet and seer," he said. "We will do this by calling upon the quorums of the priesthood to manifest their support, followed by the full congregation."

As President Rigdon called for the quorums to stand one by one, Mary Ann's mind jumped back to those first days in Palmyra and Fayette. She still remembered the distinct thrill of being in the home of Peter Whitmer, Sr., on the day the Church was organized. She had looked around at those assembled, and marveled. There had been about fifty there. Fifty! She turned her head as another group of priesthood brethren rose to their feet, a great sense of awe swelling inside her. Here in one room there were nearly twenty times that number, and this only represented about half of those who wanted to get in, and a tenth of the total membership of the Church. What would six more years bring? Ten? Twenty?

"The sustaining of Brother Joseph by the priesthood quorums has been unanimous in the affirmative," Sidney was saying. "Will the congregation now signify your willingness to accept him as our prophet and seer."

As one, the entire congregation, about a thousand people, came to their feet.

"Thank you." President Rigdon waited until the noise of the

congregation being seated again died. "Are there any who oppose this?"

His eyes swept around to watch, but no one stood. Sidney grunted his satisfaction. "Thank you. We shall now ask the congregation to join with the choir in singing another hymn by Brother Phelps, one of our leaders in Zion. It is hymn number eighteen in your hymnals, 'Now Let Us Rejoice in the Day of Salvation.' It will be sung to the tune of 'Hosanna.' After the song, we will take a twenty-minute intermission before proceeding."

Mary Ann opened the small book and found the place. None of the hymns had music, only words. They were sung to various familiar tunes, sometimes the same hymn being sung to different music. This is why the tune had to be designated. This particular hymn was rapidly becoming a favorite among the Saints. It was definitely one of Mary Ann's favorites. And as the choir director raised his arms, then led out, she could not follow. Her eyes suddenly blurred as she read the first two lines. "Now let us rejoice in the day of salvation, no longer as strangers on earth need we roam."

She turned and glanced at Jessica and Nathan and Lydia. *Oh, yes!* she thought. *Now let us rejoice!* Here she stood, in Kirtland, in the temple of God, with her family around her.

Not that everything was perfectly in order. Her rejoicing was always tempered with a touch of sorrow. Mostly that sorrow came for Joshua. He was far away, in every sense of the word. She had been shocked into numbness when Nathan finally told her what had happened that night in Jackson County. He had not asked her to stop praying for Joshua, as he had threatened. In fact he begged her to continue. She did, of course. How could she not? She and Nathan had written a letter to Joshua over a month ago. But she was without hope, for whenever she closed her eyes in prayer for Joshua, the image of Nathan's scarred flesh came back to her, and she knew that something down deep inside Joshua had died. But she had Jessica and Rachel. That meant a lot.

Melissa was another source of concern. Carl, who had been so patient, so accepting when first they were married, was becoming difficult about the Church. At first it had just been quiet resentment at Melissa's being gone, but in the last few months he had started to openly oppose her involvement. When Melissa requested permission to accompany the family to the temple dedication, Carl had flatly refused. They were going to his parents' church services this Sabbath. They had already promised. Normally Melissa did not push these things, but the dedication meant a great deal to her. Carl did not bend, not even to her tears and pleading. More and more, Melissa was simply letting her activities slip; it was easier that way. But it was not a good sign, and Mary Ann worried about the situation each day.

She turned her head and looked the other way. Here was Becca—sweet, lovely Rebecca, all that a mother could hope for. Mary Ann's eyes lifted to her husband now. His head was back proudly, and he was singing with all the fervor of his soul. Her tears overflowed now. She had once nearly given up hope on this man, convinced that he had no spiritual inclinations. She had once cried in despair, because he refused to let her have her own copy of the Book of Mormon. Now he led out with the children each day in the reading of it.

Now let us rejoice! Mary Ann Steed threw back her head and sang, lifting her voice to join with the others in praise to God, unashamed now of the tears that stained her cheeks.

Following the intermission, Joseph stood up and took over the role of conducting the meeting. He gave a short address of exhortation, then led the quorums and the congregation in the sustaining of the various officers and quorums of the Church, beginning with the First Presidency and the Quorum of the Twelve, all of whom were sustained as prophets, seers, and revelators.

As he continued, moving through the quorums, having the people sustain the presidencies of each, Benjamin watched the men who were being named. Here were some of the great men of the kingdom, he thought. In addition to Joseph and Sidney, there was Joseph's father, Joseph Smith, Sr., and the Prophet's brother Hyrum. Oliver Cowdery, David and John Whitmer, William Phelps, Frederick G. Williams, Edward Partridge, Newel K. Whitney.

On one side of the Melchizedek Priesthood pulpits sat the members of the Quorum of the Twelve. Here too there was much that impressed Benjamin. Thomas B. Marsh, David Patten, Brigham Young, Heber C. Kimball, Parley Pratt, Orson Hyde, two of John Johnson's sons. Everywhere he looked, the leaders the Lord had chosen surrounded him.

As Joseph finished and they sang another hymn, Benjamin felt himself overcome by a strange melancholy. The words of the hymn, by Isaac Watts, spoke of Zion being a thrice happy place and of the gospel's "joyful sound," but it did not stir him. The sense of sadness settled in with all the more power.

When Joseph stood to read the prayer of dedication, Benjamin thought that would help. The previous evening, Benjamin had seen Sidney Rigdon and he had told Benjamin that earlier that day Joseph had received the dedicatory prayer by revelation. Benjamin had come specifically anticipating hearing it.

And it was a wonderful prayer, stirring and memorable. Joseph expressed deep gratitude for God's goodness to his people and asked that he would now accept the temple. He noted that the Saints had built it through great tribulation, so that the Savior could have a place where he might manifest himself unto the people. He prayed that the blessings previously promised might be poured out, now that the Saints had fulfilled the Lord's commands. He prayed that Church leaders, members, and the leaders of nations would all be blessed and that the promises about the gathering of scattered Israel might now come to pass. He prayed that, as the people entered this sacred house, all of their incomings and all of their outgoings might be in the name of the Lord, that it might be kept holy.

It was a wonderful, inspired and inspiring prayer, but it did little to lift the cloud that had settled in upon Benjamin Steed.

When Joseph said amen and the congregation echoed it, Benjamin hardly lifted his head.

"My brothers and sisters," Joseph said, "the choir shall now sing a hymn written specifically for this occasion by our own Brother William Phelps. It is found in your hymnals, number ninety, if you wish to follow the words."

Next to Benjamin, Becca opened their hymnal and found the page. Brother Davis, the choir director, stepped forward and raised his arms. The organ began the first strains. Benjamin looked away as the director gave the singers the downbeat and they began to sing.

> The Spirit of God like a fire is burning!
> The latter-day glory begins to come forth.

Benjamin's head came up sharply. When they had entered the temple that morning, Joseph had said it was a day of Pentecost. Benjamin had heard Joseph say something similar earlier; he had referred to the marvelous events of the previous two months as a Pentecostal season. Benjamin had been so struck by the term, he had talked to Mary Ann about it. She reminded him that it came from the Bible, in the book of Acts. That night, while the others in the house slept, he had looked up the story and read it through twice.

Now the images he read about leaped into his mind. It was after the Resurrection. The Savior had ascended to heaven in glory. A few days later, the disciples were gathered to observe the feast of Pentecost, so named because it was the fiftieth day after Passover. Jews from more than a dozen nations had gathered to Jerusalem for the festival season. Suddenly in the place where the Twelve met there was the sound of a mighty rushing wind. Tongues of fire appeared over the head of each Apostle and they began to speak in tongues.

Benjamin's eyebrows lifted suddenly. *Tongues of fire?* His eyes swung down to the hymnal. *The Spirit of God like a fire is burning.*

The room shook with the power of the song as the members

of the choir sang in perfect harmony both of voice and of spirit.

> The visions and blessings of old are returning,
> The angels are coming to visit the earth.

That was it! That was what lay so heavily upon him now. It had been a Pentecostal season of remarkable proportions. For the past two months or more, Kirtland had been ablaze with it. Visions and blessings and angels. The Saints had seen them all.

In the book of Acts, the Apostles had spoken in tongues. Rome, Parthia, Crete, Media—it mattered not from whence the Jewish pilgrims had come; they heard the gospel preached in their own tongues, and they had marveled. In the past two months, Benjamin had seen a similar "feast of Pentecost."

It began in mid-January as Joseph began to administer the ordinances of the "endowment" as far as they had been revealed at that time. As a member of the quorum of elders and also a part of the building committee, Benjamin had been invited to be in attendance in the temple for one of the meetings. After several ordinances were performed, a remarkable thing happened. Joseph suddenly cried out. "The heavens are opened to my view." His face seemed to radiate as Benjamin watched him in awe. Even as he looked on the vision, Joseph told the others what he saw. Gates of encircling fire, streets paved with gold, the blazing throne of God. To his amazement, he also saw his brother Alvin there. Alvin had died before the Church was restored, so it surprised Joseph to see him in God's kingdom. "All who have died without a knowledge of this gospel," the Lord explained, "who would have received it if they had been permitted to tarry, shall be heirs of the celestial kingdom of God."

Following that remarkable experience, the power of the Spirit burst upon the whole group. Some cried out that visions were opened to their view. Others testified that angels ministered to them. Some even said they saw the face of the Savior as they communed with the heavenly hosts.

And now Benjamin understood his own sense of melancholy. That night in the temple, Benjamin had thrilled to it all, believed every man who testified, but he personally saw nothing. And over the following weeks, when men spoke in tongues and others interpreted for them, when they were moved to prophesy or had the visions of eternity opened to their view, he was always an observer, but nothing more.

The choir had come to the chorus of the hymn and, if anything, sang with even greater fervor than before. Benjamin followed the words intently as they sang.

We'll sing and we'll shout with the armies of heaven—
Hosanna, hosanna to God and the Lamb!

It nearly shook the rafters as the Saints in the choir thundered out their hosannas.

Let glory to them in the highest be given,
Henceforth and forever: amen and amen!

Now he understood. His eyes ran from man to man, from leader to leader. These were the stalwarts of the faith. One only had to glance from face to face to know of great sacrifice, great commitment. As a member of the building committee, Benjamin had been in a unique position to know just what this building represented, how many tears had wet the stone walls, how much heart was represented by every course of masonry.

In front of him, directly to one side of the western pulpits, stood Brigham Young. A year ago, Benjamin had been at a neighbor's house and witnessed a scene he would never forget. Brigham Young had come, hat in hand, to ask for a loan of money. He was destitute and his family was starving. The weather had been well below freezing, but Benjamin had watched the sweat roll off Brigham's face as he had to face the humiliation of asking another man for a handout.

Directly behind the Steeds sat Noah Packard and his wife. Baptized by Parley Pratt in 1832, the Packards sold their farm and came to Kirtland. Though it left them impoverished, Noah cheerfully donated more than a thousand dollars to the temple fund. Across the aisle was Oliver B. Huntington. He had been a wealthy farmer back in upstate New York when Joseph had visited there in '35. Joseph asked the Huntingtons to sell their farm and come to Kirtland as quickly as possible. Huntington obeyed, taking a loss of fifteen hundred dollars in order to sell the farm quickly. Further setbacks awaited him in Kirtland. An unscrupulous member of the Church, who later apostatized, cheated Huntington on a mortgage. In a matter of six months Huntington went from comfortable affluence to abject poverty. Just two months ago Benjamin had sent food over to the Huntingtons' house after learning that for the past month they had had nothing but beech leaves, string beans, and an occasional scanty portion of corn bread. Yet day after day Oliver Huntington had been at the temple site, laboring cheerfully in the service of God. Not once had Benjamin ever heard a murmur of complaint from him. Not once had he ever heard him criticize the Prophet for calling him to come to Kirtland.

There were dozens of similar cases. Benjamin shook his head. No wonder they had had a Pentecostal season! And no wonder that he had not. What had he done? Fought Joseph Smith bitterly. Forbidden his family to read the Book of Mormon. True, he had finally come around, he had finally put all that behind him, but it had taken so long. And what had he sacrificed? He was prospering. Everything he seemed to set his hand to blossomed. He and his family had not gone without food. They were in a comfortable home.

> How blessed the day when the lamb and the lion
> Shall lie down together without any ire,
> And Ephraim be crowned with his blessing in Zion,
> As Jesus descends with His chariots of fire!

Benjamin dropped his head, feeling a great shame. Now he understood why on this great day of Pentecost he felt nothing but sorrow.

"Benjamin, my son."

Benjamin's head snapped up.

"Listen to my words, my son. Be still and know that I am God."

Later he would conclude that he didn't hear the voice as much as he felt it. It came inside his mind, but the effect was to permeate every fibre of his being to the point that he felt as if his whole body were on fire.

"Your sacrifice is acceptable unto me. I am well pleased with your desires and with your labors on my house. Murmur not about those things which you have not yet seen. Ye are not able to abide the presence of God now, neither the ministering of angels; wherefore, continue in patience until ye are perfected."

The rest of the dedicatory service was mostly a blur in Benjamin Steed's mind. After the choir finished singing "The Spirit of God Like a Fire Is Burning," the sacrament of the Lord's Supper was administered to all present. Oliver Cowdery spoke. Frederick G. Williams rose and testified that while Sidney Rigdon was offering the invocation earlier, he had seen a being enter through the window and take a seat between him and Father Smith. Joseph later explained that it was the Apostle Peter. David Whitmer testified that he also had seen heavenly beings. President Rigdon arose and led them in the Hosanna Shout, a shout that nearly lifted the roof right off the temple. Brigham Young spoke in tongues, David Patten interpreted.

He was vaguely aware of it all, but for Benjamin Steed one thing burned all the others into insignificance, and that was the words, "My son, your sacrifice is acceptable unto me."

———•———

Lydia stepped back into the kitchen area of her mother-in-law's house.

Mary Ann looked up. "Is he asleep?"

"Yes, thank goodness."

"It's been a long day, but he was so good in the temple."

"I know, it was wonderful." Lydia suddenly stopped, the emotion rising unbidden. "When I think—" She swallowed, then tried again. "When I think about possibly not being there, I can hardly stand it. If we were still in Palmyra . . ." She couldn't finish. Mary Ann patted the chair next to her and Lydia came over, sat beside her, and took her hand.

Jessica sat on a chair in the corner, knitting a shawl for Rachel. She nodded, her own eyes suddenly misty. "And I could have stayed in Missouri," she whispered.

"All right, now," Melissa said, coming in from the parlor where she had been changing little David, "don't make this any harder on me than it already is."

"I'm sorry, Melissa," Lydia said. "I know how badly you wanted to be there."

Mary Ann decided to change the subject. "Do you think the brethren will have anything like that happen tonight?"

They all contemplated that for a minute. Joseph had reconvened priesthood holders for another service. Nathan and Benjamin had left just a few minutes earlier to be in attendance for the evening's meeting.

They all jumped as the front door to the house exploded inward, slamming against the wall. "Mama, Mama!" Little Emily burst into the kitchen with Joshua hard on her heels.

Lydia jumped up in alarm. "What is it?"

"They're meeting on the temple!" Emily blurted. "Come see."

"They're what?" the women all said at once.

"It's true, Mama," Joshua gasped. "Quick, come and see."

In a moment they all rushed through the house and out of the front door. Mary Ann stopped and gaped in amazement. It *was* true. There were people on the top of the temple, walking back and forth. Though it was late afternoon, it was still full daylight, and while they were nearly two blocks away, they could see the people clearly. Then, even as she watched, Mary Ann felt a shiver shoot up her spine. The people on the temple had disappeared. In an instant they were back again, walking and conversing. Then again they disappeared.

"Who are those men?" Melissa asked. "That's dangerous up there."

Lydia was staring, one hand to her mouth. She had seen what Mary Ann had seen. "They're not men," she whispered breathlessly.

Melissa jerked around as though she had been yanked with a rope. It was true. The figures on top of the temple could be seen clearly. They were dressed in white, with robes that came down to the ankles. And they disappeared, then reappeared.

At that moment, Matthew came tearing around from the back of the house, Rachel and young Carl in tow. He pulled up short at the sight of the women. "Listen, Mother!"

Mary Ann looked at him in surprise, but in obedience to the urgency in his voice, cocked her head. The others did the same.

"What is it?" Emily cried in alarm, moving closer to her mother.

"Listen!"

They all heard it together. At first it sounded like the beginnings of a breeze sighing in the trees, but it swelled rapidly in volume. Mary Ann stared upwards at the treetops around them. Nothing there stirred, and the sound was not really coming from above. She turned her head. It was coming from the direction of the temple.

Across the street, their neighbor Sister Carlson came dashing out. She looked up, then when she also saw nothing she ran over to them. "What is it!" She had to shout to make herself heard.

Jessica cupped her hands, instinctively bracing herself against the wind that was not there. "We don't know," she yelled.

All up and down the street now, people were coming out of their houses, staring up into the sky.

Suddenly Mary Ann started. "I know," she cried.

They all swung around to stare at her. "In the book of Acts. Remember? On the day of Pentecost?"

Jessica's eyes widened. Lydia nodded, understanding. Melissa still looked puzzled, so Mary Ann leaned closer toward her. "The Bible says that when the tongues of fire appeared, there was a sound like the sound of a mighty rushing wind which filled the house."

They stood there for a moment in awe, no one moving as the sound finally began to die gradually. Mary Ann turned toward the temple. The roof line was clear now. The figures were gone. She felt a pang of disappointment. But then, just as she was about to turn back, her eyes looked again. The temple seemed to be glowing more brightly.

"Look," Matthew cried out beside her. Then she knew her eyes were not deceiving her.

Melissa unconsciously pulled David closer to her.

"What is it?" little Joshua whispered.

No one answered. A shaft of light, like a mighty pillar of fire, enveloped the entire building now, and the temple glowed as though the very walls were made of light.

"What is it?" Lydia whispered, echoing her son.

Mary Ann slowly turned. "Our sacrifice is accepted," she said slowly. "God has accepted his house."

Approximately four hundred brethren had gathered back in the temple for a special priesthood session called by Brother Joseph. This time Joseph was conducting the meeting. It started out normally enough. After a hymn and prayer, Joseph told those assembled that on the upcoming Wednesday those present would participate in the sacred ordinance of the washing of feet. He cited from the scriptural account of when the Savior performed the ordinance for the eleven Apostles in the Upper Room in Jerusalem, then instructed them as to how the ordinance was to be performed. Nathan was very much sobered by the time Joseph finished. This would be a sacred and holy experience indeed.

But then Joseph's demeanor changed. Now he was speaking to them on the subject of the spirit of prophecy. He indicated that it was one of the gifts of the Spirit, and that as members of the Church and righteous priesthood holders, it was their right and privilege to exercise that gift.

Nathan glanced out of the corner of his eye at his father. Benjamin was leaning forward, totally enraptured with what Joseph was saying. Joseph had paused now. Every eye was on him. No one so much as stirred.

"Brethren," Joseph said quietly, "I now call upon the congregation to speak. The spirit of prophecy belongs to you, so do not fear to prophesy good for the Saints. If you prophesy the falling of these hills and the rising of these valleys, if you prophesy the downfall of the enemies of Zion and the rising of the kingdom of God, it shall come to pass."

His eyes swept over the assembly, seeming to catch each man's eye and to hold it for a moment, though in actuality it was done in one moment. "Brethren, I tell you, the first one who rises to his feet and opens his mouth shall prophesy."

For a moment the group was stunned. They glanced around at each other, and the air was filled with a sudden tension. Then, two rows in front of where Nathan sat, eighteen-year-old George A. Smith, cousin to the Prophet Joseph, stood up. He opened his mouth and began to speak, and Nathan gaped at him. Nathan had traveled for three months with this young man on Zion's Camp. He had seen him wince with pain when his feet were so badly blistered that they left his boots wet with blood. He had stood shoulder-to-shoulder with him on a bluff overlooking the Fishing River and seen him tremble with fear. But now, George A. Smith threw his shoulders back and spoke with the roar of a lion.

Barely had he begun when another sound began to fill the temple. It was a pleasant day outside, and so the windows on both sides of the temple were open to the evening air. At first Nathan thought the wind had started to blow outside, but as he looked out he saw that it was not so. The leaves on the trees outside were limp and still. The sound rose rapidly in volume. It filled the great hall in which they met, like some roaring hurricane that drowned out all sounds but its own.

Without realizing it, Nathan was on his feet. So was every man in the room. Their heads turned this way and that, looking up toward the ceiling to ascertain the source of the mighty roaring. Nathan felt a hand grip his shoulder. He turned. His father was staring at him, eyes wide with amazement and wonder. And then Benjamin began to speak. At least his mouth started to move, and sounds came out, but it took a moment before Nathan realized that it was unintelligible, a babble of sounds and words that made absolutely no sense to him at all.

Then suddenly he jerked forward, his eyes glued on his father's mouth. It was the gift of tongues! His father was speaking in tongues! Nathan felt a jolt shoot through him. It hit him with such force that he groped wildly for the edge of the pew to stop his knees from buckling.

"The temple is filled with angels!"

The cry brought Nathan around to look up at the pulpits. It was Joseph who had shouted out. He was pointing out across the assembly room. Chills and a wild tingling were coursing all up and down the entire length of Nathan's body now. But when he turned to scan the hall, he saw nothing. There was a sharp pang of disappointment. Then suddenly he was aware of another sensation. He felt them! His head came up sharply and he looked around again, focusing inwardly now. It was as if he had suddenly acquired another sense—not seeing, not hearing, but . . . He groped for the right word. *Knowing*! That was it. He knew, as surely as if he saw them, that there were other beings present with them in the room. Tears sprang unbidden to his eyes. He knew! He knew!

The assembly room was now filled with a roar of a different kind. All around him men were talking or calling out excitedly. Some pointed at the air in front of them, crying out that visions were opened to their view. Others evidently were allowed to see the heavenly beings. Some spoke in tongues, many were prophesying.

Nathan whirled back around to his father. Benjamin had stopped speaking now, but his face still glowed with a radiant power, as though inside there was some unseen fire. Nathan reached out and took him by the shoulders and shook him. "Pa," he cried, "you spoke in tongues."

For several moments, Benjamin just stared at him, then suddenly one great racking sob shook his body. "I know," he whispered. "I know."

———————•—•—————

It was eleven P.M. when father and son came out of the east doors of the Kirtland Temple and turned south toward their homes. They were still overwhelmed. And drained! Benjamin could not remember a time when he felt more exhausted. When they came to the gate in front of Benjamin's home, he stopped for a moment. He turned back, and Nathan did the same. For almost a minute they gazed at the great dark silhouette of the building to the north of them.

"*We'll sing and we'll shout with the armies of heaven.*" Earlier that day he had faltered when the choir had begun to sing that chorus from William Phelps's dedicatory hymn. He had felt nothing but sorrow and envy then, and had lowered his eyes, not wanting anyone to see his shame. "The Spirit of God like a fire is burning," the hymn began. This afternoon he had known that to be true, but only for others.

Now all of that was changed. Now he understood.

Benjamin turned to his son. His mouth opened, then shut again—a great lump in his throat suddenly cut him off. It was all right, though. Words could not possibly say what he was feeling. Instead, he held open his arms. Nathan's eyes widened in surprise. Then, in an instant, he stepped into Benjamin's encircling embrace.

For a long time, father and son stood there, not far from the shadow of the temple, holding one another, and silently rejoicing.

Dedication of the Kirtland Temple

Notes

Chapter One

The earliest documented account we have of Joseph Smith performing a marriage for members of the Church is that of 24 November 1835 (see *History of the Church* 2:320; hereafter cited as *HC*). In that account Joseph does not specifically say it was the first marriage he had performed, but that seems to be the implication. Though the form and content of the ceremony as presented in the novel are essentially as described in the 1835 account, having Joseph perform the marriage of Nathan and Lydia in April 1830 is a fictional device, as is the attempt to have the constable arrest Joseph for doing so.

Chapter Three

The depiction of events in Colesville associated with Joseph's visit and the attempts to baptize and confirm converts—principally Emma Smith and members of the Joseph Knight family—is essentially as described in Joseph's history (see *HC* 1:86–88) and noted by Joseph Knight, Jr. (see Larry C. Porter, "The Colesville Branch and the Coming Forth of the Book of Mormon," *BYU Studies* 10 [Spring 1970]: 372–74). The legal harassment Joseph faced at this time, including the change of heart on the part of the constable and his giving Joseph assistance in escaping the hands of the mob, is also recorded in his history (see *HC* 1:88–89).

Chapter Four

The depiction of the trials in South Bainbridge and Colesville, including some of the dialogue and the blasphemous mocking Joseph received at the hands of his enemies, follows the recorded account in Joseph's history (see *HC* 1:89–96). Some of the details are taken from a report made by one of Joseph's defenders, John Reid, which is included in a footnote in that same source.

Chapter Five

Emma was pregnant and in poor health during the time the sisters were sewing clothing for the missionaries to the Lamanites, but refused to use that as an excuse to leave the work to others (see *Church History in the Fulness of Times* [Salt Lake City: The Church of Jesus Christ of Latter-day Saints, 1989], p. 80; hereafter cited as *CHFT*). The Mary Whitmer story is reported by her son David Whitmer (see *CHFT*, pp. 57–58). Emma and Joseph were living with the Whitmers at the time Mary had this experience, and so Emma undoubtedly heard Mary's report. The suggestion that Emma reacted to it with frustration, however, is speculation on the part of the author. Section 25 of the Doctrine and Covenants, wherein Emma is counseled not to murmur, was given in July 1830, about a year after Mary Whitmer had the experience with Moroni.

Chapter Seven

The depiction of Joseph Smith's arrival in Kirtland and his prophetic greeting of Newel K. Whitney is, in general terms, historically accurate (see *CHFT*, pp. 90–91).

Chapter Eight

The giving of the background of the Newel Whitney story (see note for chapter seven) to Carl Rogers is, of course, a fictional device; but the details of that story are accurate (see Andrew Jenson, comp., *Latter-day Saint Biographical Encyclopedia* [1901–36; reprint, Salt Lake City: Western Epics, 1971], 1:223).

Chapter Nine

Lucy Mack Smith makes it clear that she was the one who led the Saints on the canal boat to Buffalo, and then on to Kirtland (see her *History of Joseph Smith by His Mother*, ed. Preston Nibley [Salt Lake City: Bookcraft, 1958], pp. 195–97; hereafter cited as *Mack Hist.*).

Chapter Ten

On the journey to Kirtland, Lucy Mack Smith cared for the needs of her group, settled disputes, and saw to it that the group conducted prayer and worship services while under way. Her speeches of exhortation and encouragement in the novel come largely from her own account. (See *Mack Hist.*, pp. 196–99.)

Chapter Eleven

The group of Saints from the Finger Lakes region was too large for one boat, so a second company, under the direction of Thomas B. Marsh, left at about the same time. They arrived in Buffalo shortly after Lucy Mack Smith's group. The Colesville Branch, under leadership of Newel Knight, had left earlier but were delayed in Buffalo for some time because of the ice. The depiction of the other groups' reluctance to declare their identity is as described by Mother Smith (see *Mack Hist.*, p. 199).

The miraculous parting of the ice that occurs as Mother Smith exhorts the Saints to repent and call upon God for his intervention closely follows her recorded account of this remarkable event (see *Mack Hist.*, pp. 202–5).

Chapter Twelve

Parley's humorous account of his escape from the constable and his dog comes from his autobiography, from which most of the wording in the novel is taken (see *Autobiography of Parley P. Pratt,* ed. Parley P. Pratt, Jr. [1874; reprint, Salt Lake City: Deseret Book Co., 1985], pp. 36–39; hereafter cited as *PPP Auto.*).

Chapter Fourteen

The account of Elsa Johnson and the miraculous healing of her arm is drawn in detail from Joseph's history and from a later report published in the *Millennial Star* (see *CHFT*, pp. 93–94, for more detail and references). Obviously, having her tell it to the Steeds at the June conference is the author's device.

With regard to the blessing of Nathan and Lydia's child, it should be noted that we do not know exactly when the blessing of infants was first instituted in the Church. We know that, in response to Doctrine and Covenants 20:70, children were blessed by priesthood holders (e.g., see *PPP Auto.*, p. 51). The report of an infant being blessed early in Church history comes from George Reynolds, who states that in Kirtland, Reynolds Cahoon asked the Prophet Joseph to bless his newborn son. Joseph did so and gave him the name of Mahonri Moriancumer. The Prophet indicated that this was the name of the brother of Jared in the Book of Mormon. (See *Juvenile Instructor* 27 [1 May 1892]: 282.)

Chapter Seventeen

The details of the laying of the foundation for the first house in Kaw Township and the dedication of the land of Zion on 2 August 1831 come from Joseph's history (see *HC* 1:196) and from John Whitmer's history (cited in a footnote in the same reference).

Chapter Eighteen

Nathan's letter to Lydia reflects a blend of missionary experiences drawn from the journals or personal histories of several missionaries serving on different missions. For example, the "breakfast cursing" comes from Wilford Woodruff (see Richard L. Anderson, "Jackson County in Early Mormon Descriptions," *Missouri Historical Review*, April 1971, p. 279); the "drum and egg" band comes from Parley P. Pratt (see *PPP Auto.*, p. 107); and some of the language and phrasing used by Nathan comes from the missionary journals of Noah Packard (see "The Life and Travels of Noah Packard," in *Voices from the Past*, BYU Campus Education Week, pp. 1–7).

In Jessica's letter, the account of what conditions were like for the Saints in Jackson County during that first winter comes from Parley P. Pratt's autobiography (see *PPP Auto.*, p. 56).

In Joseph's letter, the challenge to the wording of some of the revelations is described pretty much as it happened; the resulting revelation is now section 67 in the Doctrine and Covenants (see *CHFT*, p. 119).

The "vision," as it was called (now section 76 in the Doctrine and Covenants), was given in response to Joseph and Sidney's work on the translation of the New Testament (see *HC* 1:245). The details of Sidney's exhaustion and how the revelation was received are from an account by Philo Dibble, who was present at the time (see J. Christopher Conkling, *A Joseph Smith Chronology* [Salt Lake City: Deseret Book Co., 1979], pp. 30–31; hereafter cited as *JS Chrono.*).

The petty reasons for apostasy listed in Joseph's letter to Nathan are not fictional, though some of the incidents mentioned in this regard occurred elsewhere and not in Hiram (see *CHFT*, p. 113).

The tarring and feathering of Joseph and the mistreatment of Sidney come almost word for word out of Joseph's history (see *HC* 1:261–65).

Chapter Nineteen

Lydia's retelling of the details of the meeting that occurred two days before the beginning of the School of the Prophets is correct. Joseph reported that all present, including some women (who are not named), spoke, sang, and preached in tongues (see HC 1:322–23).

Chapter Twenty

The fact that the First Presidency saw the Kirtland Temple in vision is reported by Truman O. Angell, who was one of the construction supervisors on the project (see CHFT, pp. 162–63).

Joseph's disastrous experience with the store and the Saints who demanded credit is a matter of record (see JS Chrono., p. 36).

The events of July twentieth (and the incidents leading up to them) are recorded in much detail in Joseph's history (see HC 1:372–400) as well as in other places, and the novel generally follows those recorded accounts. Having Joshua Steed present is, of course, a fictional embellishment, as are some of the dialogue segments, but every attempt has been made to keep the subject matter of such dialogue accurate and appropriate to the events of the day. Lilburn W. Boggs, lieutenant governor of Missouri, was present on that day and was supportive of the activities. He later became governor of Missouri and issued the infamous "extermination order" of 1838, when the Saints were driven from the state.

Chapter Twenty-One

The tarring and feathering of Edward Partridge and Charles Allen also comes from Joseph's history, and Bishop Partridge's response comes largely from his own autobiography (see HC 1:390–91).

The experiences of the Rollins sisters recounted in the novel, including Mary Elizabeth's first experience with the Book of Mormon, are historically accurate (see CHFT, pp. 133–34; and "Mary Elizabeth Rollins Lightner," Utah Genealogical and Historical Magazine 17 [July 1926]: 193–97). Having been instrumental in saving several unbound sheets of the Book of Commandments, the two girls were later given bound copies of the book, which they prized for the remainder of their lives. Mary Elizabeth Rollins married Adam Lightner at the age of seventeen. She eventually bore ten children, came to Utah, and lived to the age of ninety-five.

514

Chapter Twenty-Two

Throughout this whole section on the expulsion of the Saints from Jackson County, the author has placed his fictional characters in the midst of actual events. Every attempt has been made to represent the events properly, including the loss of life and the actual names of known persons, both Saints and Missourians. (B. H. Roberts's book *The Missouri Persecutions* [1900; reprint, Salt Lake City: Bookcraft, 1965] brings details from various sources together into one place; the discussion in *CHFT*, pp. 127–39, is also excellent.) To facilitate the flow of the story, in some cases (e.g., the shooting of the man who was ill) an event has been included in the occurrences of a day other than that on which it actually took place.

Chapter Twenty-Three

See general note for chapter twenty-two.

The story of the money being found in the fish's stomach is recorded in the history of Mary Elizabeth Rollins (see "Mary Elizabeth Rollins Lightner," p. 197).

Chapter Twenty-Four

Though fleshed out for the purposes of the novel, the conversation in which Joseph prophesies that Brigham Young and his brother Joseph will return safely is accurate (see *CHFT*, p. 142). The prophecy about the gathering to the Rocky Mountains is reported by Wilford Woodruff (see Ivan J. Barrett, *Joseph Smith and the Restoration* [Provo, Utah: Brigham Young University Press, 1973], p. 278).

Chapter Twenty-Five

The record of Zion's Camp as given in Nathan's diary in this chapter comes largely from Joseph's history (see *HC* 2:63–101). (*CHFT*, pp. 141–51, also contains an excellent summary of Zion's Camp.)

Chapter Twenty-Six

The gathering at the courthouse in Liberty actually took place a day or two earlier than shown in the novel; the time frame has been altered slightly to aid in the flow of the narrative.

The details of the gathering of Zion's Camp on the Fishing River—including the visit of the five Missourians, the terrible swiftness with which the storm strikes and its fury, the hail and the rapid rise of the river—are all from Joseph's history (see HC 2:102–6).

The depiction of the plague of cholera and the resulting deaths is accurate. The reader should be careful, however, not to assume that in all cases those who died were the ones who had been rebellious. Joseph does not make that conclusion in his history. (See HC 2:114–20.)

Chapter Twenty-Eight

The events of this chapter take place in the late summer of 1834. Parley P. Pratt actually did go on a mission to the East, but it took place later than this.

Chapter Twenty-Nine

The description of Kirtland and the events that were taking place between the fall of 1834 and the spring of 1836 comes largely from CHFT, pp. 153–64.

Chapter Thirty

The only liberty the author has taken with the events of the dedication of the Kirtland Temple and the associated Pentecostal season is to place his fictional characters into those scenes. Accounts of the marvelous manifestations that took place during this period in Church history can be found in several excellent sources (see Milton V. Backman, Jr., *The Heavens Resound* [Salt Lake City: Deseret Book Co., 1983], pp. 284–309; CHFT, pp. 164–67; and HC 2:410–28).

Regarding the last illustration, "Dedication of the Kirtland Temple," readers might be interested to know what the letters on the western pulpits stand for. Starting at the top, here are the generally accepted meanings: M.P.C.—Melchizedek Presiding Council; P.M.H.—Presiding Melchizedek High Priesthood; M.H.P.—Melchizedek High Priesthood; P.E.M.—Presiding Elder Melchizedek. (See Backman, *Heavens Resound*, p. 160.) Note also that some of the leaders who were actually present for the dedication services are depicted in the illustration, including Joseph Smith, Jr., Frederick G. Williams, Joseph Smith, Sr., and Hyrum Smith.